Analytical Hypnotherapy

Volume 2
Practical Applications

Jacquelyne Morison

With contributions from Georges Philips

Crown House Publishing
www.crownhouse.co.uk

First published in the UK by

Crown House Publishing Limited
Crown Buildings
Bancyfelin
Carmarthen
Wales
SA33 5ND
UK

www.crownhouse.co.uk

British Library Cataloguing-in-Publication Data
A catalogue entry for this book is available
from the British Library.

ISBN 1899836853

Printed and bound in the UK by
Bell & Bain Limited
Glasgow

Table of Contents

How to Gain Maximum Benefit From Reading This Book

Analytical Hypnotherapy – Practical Applications is essentially a reference book for the practitioner who wishes to gain a comprehensive understanding of the practice of analytical hypnotherapy. A reference book, by its very nature, encourages a dip-and-dive usage. The therapist may, for example, elect to extract from these pages the information and guidance that will be appropriate to his work and then to put the rest on ice for future study. In order to gain maximum benefit from this book, therefore, the practitioner should use it as a servant rather than a master.

The purpose and design of *Analytical Hypnotherapy* will be to enlighten and to inspire the therapist within an eclectic discipline. The message behind the text will be to invite the therapist to partake of the wisdom that is relevant to his practice, to expand his mind in order to embrace a more effective approach and to develop a unique and individual style when working with the client. The practitioner is not being asked to swallow the doctrines contained within these pages as if these were the gospel truth, nor is he being urged to apply techniques that are not in keeping with his individual style or personal belief structure. The therapist may, therefore, read and digest material that is new and exciting for him or may wish to review matter that has previously been studied in order to refresh learning and, perhaps, gain a deeper understanding.

Analytical Hypnotherapy aims to be an invitation and an encouragement for the therapist rather than a prescriptive tenet based on unshakable principles. When reading through the various therapeutic passages, questioning techniques, client profiling and general methodology liberally sprinkled throughout the book and its companion volume, *Analytical Hypnotherapy Volume 1 – Theoretical Principles*, the practitioner will be advised to add his own brand of magic to that which is portrayed here. The therapist will be hereby besought to translate material into his own words rather than use the matter provided in a verbatim and, perhaps, lifeless fashion. Therapy is a creative art and not a rigid set of rules for methodology.

The more creative and flexible the practitioner can be at work, the greater the number of cases he will be able to handle with ease and facility. The secret is to enhance whatever natural style the therapist currently adopts – whether it be highly permissive or somewhat authoritarian. With this premise in view, the hypnoanalytic practitioner – whether a raw fledgling or a seasoned master – can now simply sit back and enjoy *Analytical Hypnotherapy*!

Introduction

Analytical Hypnotherapy in Perspective

The practitioner should have an eclectic vision of analytical hypnotherapy as a powerful, in-depth, therapeutic approach that can
be utilised in order to tackle even the most stubborn of psychological and physiological disorders for which the client may seek
assistance. Analytical hypnotherapy, of course, can be used for a
range of the client's presenting conditions from cases of minor low
self-esteem or minimal anxiety to cases in which she will have suffered the most intolerable traumatic and psychological disturbance. Analytical hypnotherapy, thus, will be versatile and easily
applied by the creative and infinitely-flexible practitioner who is
able to think on his feet.

In the companion volume to this work, *Analytical Hypnotherapy
Volume 1 – Theoretical Principles*, the practitioner would have been
introduced to those disciplines and premises from which the practice of analytical hypnotherapy has been derived. Let us now take
a collective overview of these approaches in order to pinpoint precisely the hallmark of analytical hypnotherapy, its scope and its
philosophy.

The therapeutic premise

> Hypnoanalysis enables the therapist to locate the sources of inner conflicts, and this is the best technique I know for getting at the root causes quickly. It saves months and months of work.
> – *Dave Elman*

Analytical hypnotherapy will, essentially, take a facilitative and noninvasive stance to therapeutic intervention (see Chapter 1 – "The Hypnoanalytic Approach"). The practice will, therefore, be nondirective, noninterventionist and nonjudgmental in order to give the client the maximum chance of finding her true identity beneath the psychological imprinting that she has hitherto accumulated. This therapeutic premise will mean that the client can gently be led towards resolving traumatic, conflicting or distressing aspects of her past experience that have had an inhibiting effect on her self-fulfilment and self-actualisation. During the therapeutic process, the client can be invited to gain insight into her psyche and, in this way, can be freed from having to employ defensive strategies, falsifications and unwarranted reactions. This approach, therefore, will maintain a healthy respect for the client's subjective world. Personal insight and psychic resolution can then, collectively, result in beneficial change at an unconscious level of awareness for the client.

Analytical hypnotherapy will assume that the client has within her all the resources necessary in order to resolve disturbance and to work towards individuation and psychological maturity. The analytical philosophy presupposes that the client will be inherently goal-oriented and capable of self-growth. The practice also endeavours to reintegrate the client into the social world from which she may have strayed in order to establish and maintain her meaningful and purposeful existence in society. The hypnoanalytical therapist will also facilitate the client's search for the meaning of life and will encourage her to take up important life-challenges, to form life-affirming goals, to modify irrational thinking and to rectify unrealistic assumptions. In making such changes, the client can be assured of a more harmonious existence and a richly productive life. The therapeutic premise of analytical hypnotherapy, therefore, will encompass those aspects of humanistic and cognitive practice that will enable the client to grow and to realise her fullest potential.

The therapeutic approach

> Psychoanalysis is concerned with adaptation, with how the subject (or
> ego) deals with stimuli impinging upon him both from without and
> from within.
> *– Anthony Storr*

Analytical hypnotherapy will examine the way in which circumstances and events have had an adverse effect on the client (see Chapter 1 – "The Hypnoanalytic Approach"). The practice of analytical hypnotherapy will invite the client to investigate those memories, dreams, fantasies, thoughts, beliefs, convictions, attitudes and aspirations that relate to her psychic distress. In an endeavour to conclude unfinished business, the client will, thus, be invited to release her pent-up emotive expression, to uncover her innermost thoughts, to heal fragmented aspects of her psyche and to lay bear those psychic impressions that have shaped her entire existence. Once psychic distress has been dealt with by the client's inner mind, her psychological disturbances should diminish and her maladaptive behavioural practices can be eliminated or modified. In resolving aspects of distress within the client's psyche, emphasis can be placed on the influence that childhood relationships will have had on her development by leaving unsatisfied her vital psychological and developmental needs. Any dysfunctional childhood nurturing or unhealthy relationship-attachments will need to be examined with a fine-toothed comb, therefore, in order to allow the client to rid herself of any impediments to forming fruitful and meaningful intimate relationships with others. The therapeutic approach of analytical hypnotherapy, hence, will culminate in the most comprehensive investigative probing that can enable the client to appreciate fully the impact that the past has had on the present.

What is the Key to Hypnoanalytic Practice?

Let us assume that the client wants to divest herself of those presenting symptoms that are causing her discomfiture. In what ways can the hypnoanalytic process be of assistance to the client? By way of introduction, therefore, we shall now outline some of the fundamental premises that obtain in hypnoanalytic methodology.

Facilitating cathartic discharge

> The method was based on the assumption that hysteria was the product
> of a psychical trauma which had been forgotten by the patient; and the
> treatment consisted in inducing her in a hypnotic state to recall the
> forgotten trauma to the accompaniment of appropriate emotions.
> – *James Strachey & Angela Richards*

One of the prime objectives of most forms of therapy – and, in particular, analytical hypnotherapy – will be to empower the client to discharge those pent-up elements that have lain dormant for so long and caused untold damage in their wake. Therapeutic catharsis can be achieved when any thoughts, memories, sensations or emotive expression that have been unconsciously deflected by the client can be invited to surface (see Chapter 2 – "Therapeutic Investigation"). Often the release of an emotive response in the form of an abreaction will, in itself, have a cathartic effect for the client. When the client's thoughts are voiced and her true feelings have been discharged, then she will almost certainly feel a sense of lightness and a relief because the pressure that has built up over time in keeping these elements under wraps can be emitted like steam from a pressure cooker (see Chapter 17, Volume 1 – "The Case for Therapy").

Exploring imaginative imagery

> Dreams, like visions, radiate from a hidden archetypal centre of
> meaning.
> – *Maggie Hyde & Michael McGuinness*

When lifting psychic conflict from within the client, an analysis of dream-imagery and imaginative symbolism can be a valuable asset for the therapist (see Chapter 14, Volume 1 – "Dreams and Symbolic Imagery"). If the client can be encouraged to interpret her own dreams, visual images, thoughts and other symbolic imagery, a source of fruitful and insightful knowledge will often be gained from the experience. Such exploration into the client's mind will frequently be a worthwhile exercise when she is, in any way, distressed or confused. This methodology can be an ongoing process that the client can undertake away from the consulting room in order to ensure a form of continuity of her psychic unfolding.

Imaginative imagery can usually be examined by the client using a variety of therapeutic techniques, most of which will be documented in this work, although numerous techniques can easily be invented and effectively employed by the creative practitioner.

Exploring transference and countertransference

It would seem that successful psychotherapy initiates a process of learning which develops its own momentum. This starts in the relationships between patient and therapist, the crux of all dynamic psychotherapy, whether at the outer levels of support and counselling, or the deeper levels of exploration and analysis.
– Dennis Brown & Jonathon Pedder

A vital tool that the practitioner can employ in the analytic setting will be the exploration of transference and countertransference issues with the client (see Chapter 13, Volume 1 – "Transference and Countertransference"). When manifestations of positive and negative transference can be explored by the client, she may come to realise the way in which significant others have seriously affected her outlook on life, the relationships that she may have formed and the expectations that she may have of others generally. The therapeutic context will be an ideal medium through which the client can project all her emotive responses on to a faceless practitioner who will receive her outpourings with totally impartial equanimity. When the practitioner can receive the child-abuser, the serial rapist and the mass murderer into his practice and accept such a client as he would any other, then he will know that he has actually arrived!

Facilitating cognitive restructuring

Cognitive counselling takes an information-processing approach to clients based on the premise that the way people interpret their experience determines the way that they feel and act.
– Richard Nelson-Jones

The client will soon open the door on the realisation that the past cannot be altered in therapy but that her opinions, reactions and beliefs about previous experiences can be radically changed and that this, in turn, will remedy any negative self-concept or pessimistic outlook (see Chapter 9, Volume 1 – "Cognitive Therapy"). Cognitive restructuring will be an invaluable tool for the analytical hypnotherapist who will seek to resolve inner conflict within the client's mind in order to prepare her for further self-development once she has attained a degree of remedial enlightenment.

Resolving symptomology

> Most people confuse "self-knowledge" with knowledge of their conscious ego-personalities. Anyone who has any ego-consciousness at all takes it for granted that he knows himself. But the ego knows only its own contents, not the unconscious and its contents. People measure their self-knowledge by what the average person in their social environment knows of himself, but not by the real psychic facts which are for the most part hidden from them. In this respect the psyche behaves like the body, of whose physiological and anatomical structure the average person knows very little too.
> – Carl Jung

The client who undergoes cathartic intervention and cognitive restructuring will inevitably be in a position to modify her unwanted behaviour. Any annoying or embarrassing habits that the client may have exhibited in the past, for example, can be relinquished; any unproductive or destructive relationships can be terminated or modified; and any victim-thinking in which the client has previously indulged can be allowed to diminish as she can begin a new journey through life with a somewhat different psyche.

Part I

Therapeutic Guidelines

In Part 1 we shall consider ways in which the practitioner can set about the task of treating the client and accompanying him on his therapeutic journey towards enlightenment and freedom. These chapters will form the preliminary thoughts and highlight the potential obstacles that the practitioner may need to ponder before negotiating her way through the territory. This section deals with the general principles of the preliminary investigative approach to the client as well as offering guidance to the clinician in analytical techniques that may be employed in order to effect beneficial change.

Chapter 1

The Hypnoanalytic Approach

A savage place! As holy and enchanted
As e'er beneath a waning moon was haunted
By woman wailing for her demon-lover!
And from this chasm, with ceaseless turmoil seething,
As if this earth in fast thick pants were breathing,
A mighty fountain momently was forced.

– Samuel Taylor Coleridge

What Is the Hypnoanalytic Approach?

A fundamental concept of all analytically-based therapeutic models is that some especially potent experiences, whether brief and traumatic, repetitive, or continuous and painful, are repressed, blocked from consciousness, and that the repressed "complexes" (the complex constellations of cognition and affect) exert a determining influence on mood, behaviour, apperception and relationships into and through adult life.

– Hellmut Karle & Jennifer Boys

The hypnoanalytic approach is one in which the client's inner world can be investigated with a view to resolving his underlying psychological trauma, conflict, distress, disturbance and faulty misconceptions. This may be achieved by observing a number of unwritten rules in terms of playing the therapy-game and by applying certain techniques that will collectively comprise the practice of analytical hypnotherapy. The therapeutic environment may, therefore, be one that can be partially engineered by the practitioner in order to give the client the maximum chance of success. Let us now consider some of the main elements that constitute the practice of hypnoanalytical therapy.

> Analytical hypnotherapy can be broken down into several stages, each of
> which depends upon an important and logical principle; failure to
> observe each principle is likely to jeopardise the successful outcome
> of therapy.
> – *Edgar Barnett*

The analytic premise

> Psychoanalysts accept Freud's construct of a "mental apparatus" which
> receives stimuli from the external world and which also interacts with
> the internal physiological system of the subject's body.
> – *Anthony Storr*

The analytic practitioner will adhere to the belief that when the client's mind receives incoming stimuli, this information will then have some degree of effect on him mentally, psychologically and physically. Hypnoanalytical therapy, as an insight-oriented therapy, will deal, therefore, with the client's subjective experience of external stimuli and its symptomatic effect. The client can be invited to gain insight into the way in which the past has impacted on the present as if the past were a resonant template or an in-built blueprint that will control his every thought, belief and emotive reaction in the present. The practitioner should, therefore, remember that the analytic approach will attempt to deal with the cause of distress rather than with the client's symptomology. This approach will, naturally, be in contradistinction to those practices that will attempt to rectify the client's unwanted behaviours or to eliminate his symptoms directly. The client's psyche will, moreover, handle his development and adaptation within the social context and, hence, maladaptive processes will also enter into the therapeutic equation. The client's defensive strategies, for instance, may be seen as maladaptive ways of coping with overwhelming pressure from his immediate environment (see Chapter 11, Volume 1 – "Defensive strategies").

The therapeutic relationship

> First, we can observe and describe the experiences of the patient and of
> the analyst; some of these may be more or less typical of the analytic
> encounter. Many statements about psychoanalytic treatment refer to this
> aspect of the problem.
> – *Thomas Szasz*

In analytical hypnotherapy, a therapeutic relationship will develop between the therapist and the client. This will, of course, be an artificial relationship in that, in the main, the client will tell all but the therapist will endeavour to remain obscure and inconspicuous. In forming this unique type of relationship, the client can be encouraged to project all his neurotically-driven thoughts and emotive responses on to the therapist as a means of bringing such realisations out into the open. This projection of thoughts and emotive expression will manifest as transference, that can then allow the client to gain insight into his unique problems so that the work of resolving such disturbances can then begin (see Chapter 13, Volume 1 – "Transference and Countertransference").

There will, of course, be a counterbalance between two irrational factors in any therapeutic relationship. This will mean that the two protagonists are not fixed and determinable quantities but each will bring his or her own well-defined field of conscious experience to the therapeutic encounter as well as an indefinitely-extended sphere of unconscious sagacity. The personality of both the therapist and the client, therefore, will be infinitely more important to the outcome of the therapeutic experience than any other aspect. The practitioner can, for instance, influence the client only if he has a reciprocating influence on the therapist. The therapist who hides behind authority and professionalism will, moreover, deny herself an important organ of communication but will still be unconsciously influenced by the client in consequence. A mutual transformation can be brought about between the therapist and the client in which the stronger and more stable personality can dictate the final outcome – both a powerful and a dangerous tool in the consulting room if it is mishandled. If such a situation *is* mishandled, then serious consequences may manifest for both the client and, perhaps, the therapist as a result of transference and countertransference between the two parties.

> Psychoanalytic treatment is a particular kind of human relationship.
> Only two people are needed for it – analyst and patient.
> – *Thomas Szasz*

The Client

> Hypnoanalysis is not a one-stop therapy; exploration must continue until
> these inner conflicts are resolved, and this sometimes requires extensive
> treatment.
> *– Dave Elman*

The client's decision to enter therapy may often be one beset by
doubts, uncertainties and reservations. The prospective client may
feel certain that he would be taking the right path by seeking therapy as a means to travel further along the road but may then be
bewildered about how to embark upon the journey. The first
assignment for the prospective client will be to find an appropriate
therapeutic medium, a conducive therapeutic environment and,
more importantly, the therapist with whom he can successfully
work.

> The combination of taking charge of your life in specific ways and
> breaking through isolation to reach out for support represents powerful
> and profound growth. It makes a host of other changes possible. Perhaps
> for the first time, you will be able to achieve a perspective on how some
> of your coping methods have served to keep you stuck.
> *– Mike Lew*

Will the time be right for the client?

> The amount of fear you feel about confronting abuse is directly
> proportional to the impact it is having on your life right now. The greater
> the fear, the more the abuse is marring your current life.
> *– Renee Fredrickson*

Initially, the client will need to be in a state of readiness in order to
work in the therapeutic context. Once this essential ingredient has
been put in place, then other factors may have an influence on
whether the client is, in fact, able to address and to resolve his presenting symptoms. When the client first comes into the consulting
room, he may have already started on his therapeutic journey
towards recovery. The client may, for example, have been working
towards this point in his life for some time – perhaps by visiting
other therapists. Alternatively, the client may be merely beginning
the journey, perhaps, immediately following a life-crisis or an
awakening experience.

Often the therapist will ask the client the "Why now?" question, either directly or indirectly. The answer will arrive by carefully noting the client's reactions and what he says in reply during the initial session. Often the therapist will find that a number of questions need to be posed in order to determine whether the client is, in fact, really ready to confront his greatest fears with unswerving determination. Perhaps the therapist could pose a number of questions either by directly addressing the client or by leaving such questions simply hanging in the air.

- Is the client ready to address his past now as an adult because there has been a considerable separation of time and distance from the past?
- Has the client found a safe environment and a supportive listener in the guise of the practitioner to whom he can bear his soul?
- Has the client recently encountered a catalytic event or a traumatic trigger that has initiated his desire to seek therapy?
- Will the client be willing to accept that the past may be a resonant template of the present?
- Does the client feel the need for an emotive discharge and an outpouring of the burdens of his past life?
- Has the client been experiencing an overload of stress in his current life?

When considering this question of readiness to resolve the past, the therapist will need to ask whether the client is at the right time in his life, is in the right place on life's path and has found the appropriate person with whom to share this part of his voyage. If all three preconditions are present, the client may be able to take that initial monumental and terrifying step. Often the client may need to examine, to release and to resolve matters only at a time when he will be really prepared to face the psychic skeletons in the cupboard. The right time will arrive when the client's life has reached a stage in which he is ready to address his deepest misgivings. This occasion may, ironically, be when all else in the client's life is satisfactory enough for him to feel safe and comfortable in a therapeutic context. It may be a time when a great many other forms of psychological baggage have been cleared out of the way or it may be a time when the client is simply sick to the back teeth with his distress and his mind is tired of resisting or denying the past. It may also be a time when the client has nothing else to lose by entering therapy as a last resort. It may, of course, be a time when all the above factors come into play simultaneously and the client generally feels strong enough to cope with the rigours of dumping his psychological baggage.

> It is the consequence of a repression of feelings and memories that renders a person unable to see certain sets of circumstances. This blindness is not irreversible, since everyone can later decide to out an end to his repression. At that moment he needs help from other people, and this he can find if he is genuinely determined to confront the truth.
> *– Alice Miller*

Will the practitioner be right for the client?

> The alliance between patient and therapist develops through shared work. The work of therapy is both a labour of love and a collaborative commitment. Though the therapeutic alliance partakes of the customs of every-day contractual negotiations, it is not a simple business arrangement. And though it evokes all the passions of human attachment, it is not a love affair or a parent–child relationship. It is a relationship of existential engagement, in which both partners commit themselves to the task of recovery.
> *– Judith Lewis Herman*

It will be important for the practitioner to appreciate that the client will need to choose a therapist who will be appropriate for his individual needs. The client will undoubtedly need to select the therapist who will be able to help him to extricate himself from his inner turmoil. Often the choice of therapist will be based on gut-reactions and, when instinct responds, the potential client may possibly disregard or be unconcerned with the methodology to be employed by the would-be therapist. Such a decision can demonstrate that the client will be able to place a degree of trust in the therapist – usually an excellent starting point. When the practitioner has been chosen by the client at an unconscious level, often this choice will draw out of him those underlying responses that will need to surface in order to be psychically excavated. A good deal of transference and projection on the client's part may well go into making a spontaneous choice of therapeutic mentor – another factor that will augur well for the success of the therapeutic encounter (see Chapter 13, Volume 1 – "Transference and Countertransference").

Occasionally, of course, the client may have the best will in the world but will find that the going gets too tough. This may, in fact, be an indication that the therapist has, paradoxically, been an appropriate choice for the client but that he is not yet ready to address painful issues. The therapist, for this reason, should endeavour to gauge the pace at which the client will be able to progress so that the rate of advancement can be accurately aligned in order to match his individual needs and specific developmental abilities.

> Third, we can discuss the analytic game – its aims, rules, limitations, and so forth. We may speak of this, somewhat loosely, as the theory of analytic treatment or, more precisely, as an account of the metagame of analysis (the rules of analysis specifying the object-game). Such a description will be important; without it, our understanding of the analytic game is incomplete and inadequate. But again we must not expect the theory of analytic therapy to do what it cannot do and was never intended to do: provide access to the experiences of the players.
> – *Thomas Szasz*

It would be unwise for the practitioner to give the client any unrealistic expectations about his personal ability to recover in therapy. The therapist cannot, of course, wave a magic wand and instantly rid the client of all his problems and symptoms. A willingness to want to change will be a positive asset for the client but even that element cannot guarantee success. The client's healing can, of course, be possible but may frequently take time, effort, money, determination, energy, patience and a sound belief in success. The client, however, may well not have the requisite qualities and, therefore, may be only partially committed to the success of the venture. Obviously, the client who elects to believe that the therapist will do all the work may well be on a path doomed to failure because he will not be taking responsibility for his own recovery process and will not, consequently, be wholeheartedly involved in it.

> The first principle of recovery is the empowerment of the survivor. She must be the author and arbiter of her own recovery.
> – *Judith Lewis Herman*

Will the place be right for the client?

> The acutely traumatised person needs a safe refuge. Finding and
> securing that refuge is the immediate task of crisis intervention.
> *– Judith Lewis Herman*

The right place should be a congenial therapeutic environment in
which the client can be himself and can feel completely safe,
relaxed and comfortable. This will be an environment in which the
client can be provided with the maximum chance of succeeding in
his mission. When choosing a place in which to work, therefore,
the analytical hypnotherapist may well need to take into consideration the type of client with whom she may be working. Does the
consulting room feel warm and comfortable or austere and clinical? Can the client weep or scream or divulge deadly secrets that
will not be overheard by others? Will the sound of traffic or external disturbance impair the client's concentration? A number of
such factors will need to be carefully considered if the practitioner
wishes to work with the highly agitated or psychologically-
stunned client who, in divesting himself of his inner turmoil, will
need to undergo the most gruelling of ordeals.

What will be the client's role?

> We instruct the patient to put himself into a state of quiet, unreflecting
> self-observation, and to report to us whatever internal perceptions he is
> able to make – feelings, thoughts, memories – in the order in which they
> occur to him. At the same time we warn him expressly against giving
> way to any motive which would lead him to make a selection among
> these associations or to exclude any of them, whether on the ground that
> it is too *disagreeable* or too *indiscreet* to say, or that it is too *unimportant* or
> *irrelevant*, or that it is *nonsensical* and need not be said. We urge him
> always to follow only the surface of his consciousness and to leave aside
> any criticism of what he finds, whatever shape that criticism may take;
> and we assure him that the success of the treatment, and above all its
> duration, depends on the conscientiousness with which he obeys this
> fundamental technical rule of analysis.
> *– Sigmund Freud*

The client will need to be willing to be cooperative and compliant
– with himself, with the therapist and with the therapeutic
medium – even to the extent of suspending his natural disbelief in

the interests of his own recovery. The client should be encouraged, for example, not to intellectually resist the therapeutic process by keeping any items of information back from the therapist – however unpleasant, embarrassing, insignificant, irrelevant or nonsensical he may deem these elements to be. Doing so will inevitably put a block on the analytic process and will be detrimental to the successful outcome of the client's therapeutic resolution. According to Freud, the fundamental technical rule of analysis will be to urge the client to report everything that he experiences in the process of outpouring thoughts and memories. The practitioner, therefore, may beseech the client to be totally frank in revealing every thought, every impression, every sensation and every opinion that crosses his mind during the course of a single session and, often, between sessions. The client, in this way, can be invited to become wholly honest with himself. The client, thus, can then relieve himself of the pressure of inner guilt by sharing the secrets of his past with an attentive yet impartial listener.

Every possible form of barrier to the success of the client's therapeutic journey should be vociferously averted and discouraged by the practitioner. The client's resistance, however, can both impede and aid the therapeutic process when its manifestation is handled skilfully by the practitioner (see Chapter 12, Volume 1 – "Resistance"). When the therapist becomes aware of any form of resistance on the client's part, she will then have identified an area for exploration that, when successfully overcome, will constitute progress for the client. The application of hypnosis will be the therapist's best aid to encouraging the client to reveal all and to surmount any resistance to doing so. The use of hypnosis as the oil for the wheels of therapeutic exploration can, of course, tacitly inveigle the client into complying with this stated or, even, unvoiced request. Hypnosis can put the client in a position whereby he may be disinclined to conceal thoughts often because he cannot be bothered to expend additional effort in order to resist the temptation to hold matter back. The client, in many cases, may not only feel compelled to impart all his thoughts, owing to the powerful access to his unconscious mind that hypnosis can facilitate, but also may become consumed by a pressing urge to activate his resources in order to defeat distress. Because the parasympathetic nervous system will be evoked during the hypnotic process, the client's mind will crave this state, as it can maintain homeostasis for the human organism. The client, therefore, may make life-affirming changes at an unconscious level via hypnosis. The client may, however, be unaware that change has occurred until he notices – as if by accident – that his symptoms have somehow mysteriously vanished.

> Psychoanalysis is a general psychology which applies to normal human beings as well as to neurotics. Since we all have some neurotic symptoms, the difference between neurotic and normal is one of degree, not of kind.
> – *Anthony Storr*

Analytical hypnotherapy can, of course, be applied to treat only those suffering from a neurotically-based disturbance, a stressful condition or a personal malfunction rather than a psychotic condition – although in many cases the distinction may be blurred or arbitrary. A neurotic condition may be defined as a psychological disorder that has been brought about by the events to which the client has been exposed and with which he has hitherto been unable to deal unaided. Analytical therapy, therefore, may be regarded as the ability to treat a so-called normal person who has been subjected to phenomenal distress that has affected him profoundly yet has not completely unhinged his mind. The psychotic suffering from a severe schizoidal and psychopathic personality disorder who has been so badly affected by the past that the balance of his mind has been abnormally deranged will usually not be capable of being retrieved to workable normality by a talking cure. For this type of client, psychiatric treatment – of which drug-treatment may well be an integral part – may be the only option.

> All those who have been severely injured as children have latent psychotic reactions. These are measures taken in self-defence aimed at evading the reality of the abuse they suffered in the past. Had the child been capable of consciously experiencing such abuse, it would have either gone insane or died. Psychoses are generalised, symbolised attempts to interpret and at the same time ward off a murderous past.
> – *Konrad Stettbacher*

The Practitioner

Once you have decided to see a therapist, how do you go about finding
one? How do you know whether the person you've found is competent,
professional, and knowledgeable? And how do you determine whether
this person is the right counsellor for you? These are important
questions. You will be entering into an intimate, trusting relationship
with your therapist, and you want it to be a good one. This isn't
something that can be decided by closing your eyes and picking a name
out of the Yellow Pages.
– Mike Lew

It seems that anyone who dabbles at all in the therapeutic arena
will be exposed to reproach. Certainly every writer and every self-
confessed expert has been bombarded by a torrent of merciless criticism – even from those ostensibly on the same side of the
argument. The counsellor has been criticised for not delving
deeply enough into the client's past. The psychologist has been
criticised for not dealing with the root cause of the client's problems. The hypnotherapist has been criticised for putting thoughts
into the client's mind. The psychotherapist has been criticised for
taking too long to deal with the problem. The social worker has
been criticised for being unqualified to deal with cases of extreme
trauma. The medical practitioner has been criticised for turning a
blind eye and passing the buck. The psychiatrist has been criticised
for dishing out the drugs. Care-workers generally have also been
accused of placing too much emphasis on the damage sustained by
the client in childhood. No-one in the therapeutic caring world, it
seems, can escape the mud-slinging!

So what is the state of play? And where does the truth lie? Every
practitioner will usually be biased in favour of her own discipline
or approach. Every practitioner will have been persuaded – at
some point – by the doctrines of the persuasion in which she has
been trained. Every practitioner will adhere to the principles of the
professional body to which she subscribes. How else could it be?
The healer has to believe in the work she is doing or else cease to
practise. The therapist will need to come to terms with her own
beliefs about what will be fitting and what will be inappropriate in
her own consulting room. Keeping an open mind, however, and
being alert to the possibility of altering approaches and methodology will go some way towards enabling the therapist to cope with

every eventuality when handling the client. Reading this book, of course, will demonstrate, at least, that the reader has been willing, in principle, to keep an open mind on the subject of therapeutic practice and can herself be opening up to the possibility of adopting a range of eclectic methods. Let us now investigate some of the factors that the analytical hypnotherapist will need to consider in connection with her work and the analytic approach.

What are the attributes of an effective practitioner?

To function well as a person, as well as a therapist, your "internal environment" must be both developed and protected. It is very comforting to know that you can use your hypnotic skills to improve not only the lives of your clients, but yours as well.
– Michael Yapko

There are many ways of describing the attributes of the professional practitioner and so perhaps we should document a summary of but a few. Maybe the therapist can reflect on whether the following attributes are those that she would consider to be the most important for the analytical hypnotherapist.

- Does the practitioner have the ability to take an overview of the client's case?
- Does the practitioner have the scope to see the client's problem from all angles and to deliver the goods as promised?
- Does the practitioner have the ability to set clearly-defined goals for the therapeutic encounter?
- Does the practitioner have the wherewithal to remain detached and nonjudgmental and to play naïve when necessary?
- Does the practitioner have any presuppositions about the nature of the client's condition?
- Does the practitioner have any preconceptions about the existence of any repressed material within the client's mind?
- Does the practitioner have the determination not to be deflected or distracted from the purpose of therapy?
- Does the practitioner know when to apply the art of silence – particularly when in doubt about what action to take?
- Does the practitioner have the capacity to be flexible and adaptable?

- Does the practitioner have the potential to be imaginative and creative?
- Does the practitioner have the courage to be daring, cheeky and provocative?
- Does the practitioner possess the ability to be cruel in order to be kind when necessary?
- Is the practitioner able to think and to act quickly, to vary the pace of delivery and to deliver interventions speedily and with an element of surprise when necessary?
- Is the practitioner intuitive and able to step into the client's unconscious mind and modality when necessary?

Personal therapy

> Clearly, to know what it feels like to play chess, one must play chess. One cannot derive or extract the game experience from the game rules, from descriptions of games played by others, or from theories of the game. The same is true of psychoanalysis. Nevertheless, there has been a persistent expectation – by analysts as well as by those who read them – that it ought to be possible to convey the analytic experience in printed form. But this is impossible. To know what it is like to be analysed, one must be a patient; to know what it is like to conduct an analysis, one must be an analyst. It is as simple as that.
> – *Thomas Szasz*

For any newcomers to the therapeutic profession – or anyone else to whom this might apply – it cannot be emphasised too strongly that the analytical hypnotherapist will need to have undergone her own personal investigative therapy prior to conducting any form of analytically-based treatment with the client. This proviso is made without any reservation whatsoever. The work of analytical therapy is arduous and emotionally-taxing at the best of times. Why make it any harder by being in personal denial? When the analytical practitioner can address her own traumatic issues, this process should not only be of inestimable personal benefit but also will be an essential ingredient in terms of her chosen profession. Any practitioner of analytical hypnotherapy, therefore, who has not yet thoroughly addressed the backlog of her own psychic trauma with the help of a competent professional should, without further delay, ensure that this process get under way immediately! The client's psychological health could well be put in jeopardy in the hands of the therapist who is not free of the bulk of her neurotically-endorsed emotive reactions, behaviours, motivations, tendencies, inclinations, beliefs and unconscious drives. There can be no exception to this sacrosanct rule in the field of analytical hypnotherapy.

In what way will the client benefit from the practitioner's personal therapy?

> The greatest mistake an analyst can make is to assume that his patient
> has a psychology similar to his own.
> – *Carl Jung*

Jung originally coined the term "training analysis" in order to describe any form of self-investigation that the therapist or the trainee therapist undergoes as a part of her training programme. Jung stressed the importance of undertaking such personal investigation because of the mutual projection factor – in the form of both transference and countertransference – that will invariably occur between the therapist and the client (see Chapter 13, Volume 1 – "Transference and Countertransference"). This mutual projection will generate unconscious confusion for both parties and could culminate in a situation whereby the practitioner could begin to treat her own psychic disturbances using the client as the vehicle through which to achieve this end.

The neurotically-driven individual will attract into her life people who will fulfil her own psychological needs in an unlimited number of ways. The practitioner who may be suffering from the effects of unresolved rejection, for example, as a result of a dysfunctional childhood, may well reject the client from her practice. The practitioner who harbours guilt and self-blame may well blame the client unduly for resisting treatment. The practitioner who has a need to seek love and attention may be driven to keep the client in therapy for longer than is absolutely necessary. The practitioner who unconsciously requires an index of her own self-worth may measure himself in terms of the success she has with her clientele. These examples, of course, are among the least harmful to the client – the more horrific examples of such manifestations of unresolved psychic trauma might include sexual violation or financial exploitation of the client. For a myriad reasons, it could be claimed that the practitioner will be neglecting, misusing or even abusing the client by not addressing her own personal issues prior to commencing work as a clinical practitioner. The therapist who has unresolved issues connected with childhood sexual abuse, for example, might unconsciously or inadvertently suggest to the client that he has been sexually abused or may feel sexually attracted towards him. The practitioner may also harbour some limiting beliefs that may be severely detrimental to the client who has been subjected to a dysfunctional upbringing. The therapist might believe, for instance, that a parent has the right to violate his or her children by virtue of birthright or that all abusers should be publicly humiliated.

Once the therapeutic journey of self-examination has begun and has unearthed major issues of a disturbing or traumatic nature, the practitioner will then be well placed to recognise and to deal effectively with any distressing residue as necessary. Thus, the practitioner – who, of course, may never become completely disturbance-free – can, by her own therapeutic investigation, render herself in a position to act appropriately when the occasion arises. When psychological danger looms, therefore, it can usually be averted swiftly, effectively and appropriately. Any personal problems, for example, that the practitioner may have that could inhibit the client's advancement can be recognised and then rectified without undue delay. The practitioner's problems, thus, will not impinge on the client or, if they do in any way, they will have only a minimal effect. The therapist's self-investigation, therefore, will be a type of fail-safe insurance policy that will deal, as far as possible, with most, if not all, eventualities.

The practitioner, moreover, will gain a deeper understanding of how the mind works by self-scrutiny. The therapist, of course, will then be ideally placed to appreciate how effectively the client can be treated via analytical hypnotherapy. Undergoing personal therapy will mean that the practitioner will have gained a sound belief in the effectiveness of treatment that will then transmit itself to the client as confidence and enthusiasm. Self-investigation will also assist the clinician when dealing with the client's abreactions – whether psychological or physiological – because she will truly have had first-hand experience of such therapeutic features.

Perhaps the most important and most obvious benefit to the client will, of course, be that the practitioner herself has had the courage to address in depth the backlog of her own psychic trauma. The practitioner, thus, will be of greatest assistance to anyone with whom she comes into contract. The analogy of the wounded healer who has pulled herself out of the mire in no uncertain terms will perpetually obtain in the practice of analytical hypnotherapy. The practitioner will, consequently, emanate the required degree of inner strength necessary for the client to feel safe both with the clinician herself and in the therapeutic environment.

In what way will the therapist benefit from her own personal therapy?

> We are all wounded in some way or another. Our always partial success in healing our own wounds leads us to our calling to explore with others further means of coping and extending the possibilities of our mutually human condition. Patients rightly resent it when they feel they are being manipulated by the "empty technique" employed by an operator who has no personal connection and knowledge of the shared sources of problems and illness within all of us. Such operators attempt to use techniques as a means of power and prestige to control others.
> But of course the patient's unconscious can pick up the shallowness of this empty charade, and nothing really changes; "resistances" only become manifest.
> – *Ernest Rossi, Margaret Ryan & Florence Sharp*

The therapist, too, can benefit from the process of self-discovery and enlightenment by ridding herself of any psychological baggage that could impede her professional success. She can eliminate, or at least reduce to a minimum, any failure-syndrome tendencies that could, initially, limit the client's immediate success and, ultimately, the practitioner's own business prospects and reputation. The therapist, for example, who displays a self-sacrificial attitude will probably deflect attention away from the client's problems. The client, for instance, could well end up feeling sorry for the practitioner and, thus, not get down to the task of solving his own problems. If the practitioner is a poor role-model for the client then such tactics do nothing for her professional reputation and even less for her bank balance! The practitioner, therefore, should strive to meet her own therapeutic demands during personal therapy before she can be assured of having the appropriate influence over the client. This transformational process will require that the therapist can apply to herself – with the same dogged consistency and diligence – that which she will apply to her own clients. The practitioner with the benefit of insight, therefore, can counteract any neurotically-centred desires to succeed in order to feel good about herself. The therapist can, thus, succeed for the client's sake as opposed to having a deep-seated need for victory that may not be realised because of its intensity.

Perhaps most importantly for the hypnoanalytical therapist, the task of dealing with another's traumatic past will, in the vast majority of cases, be an ordeal for even the most experienced clinician. Without the benefit of self-investigation, the practitioner could find, consequently, that the material with which she has to deal can have a traumatising effect on her when witnessing the distress of another (see Chapter 13 – "Post-traumatic Stress Disorder"). After dealing with her own backlog of psychological issues, it will almost certainly be appropriate for the practitioner to maintain regular contact with her own therapist in order to deal with any additional questions that will inevitably arise from time to time – particularly in view of the nature of her work. The clinician can, in this way, maximise her chances of success with the client and minimise her own vulnerability to burn-out or therapeutic fatigue.

> Essentially, if the analytical practitioner has examined his/her own childhood trauma with a microscope and cried and yelled and kicked and screamed over it until the universe resounds, then dealing with another's childhood horror in whatever proportions can be undertaken by the therapist with his/her left hand. Daring to stop supporting others in their illusions allows them the opportunity to grow into a new awareness.
> – Carl Jung

Clinical supervision

> The dialectic of trauma constantly challenges the therapist's emotional balance. The therapist, like the patient, may defend against overwhelming feelings by withdrawal or by impulsive, intrusive action. The most common forms of action are rescue attempts, boundary violations, or attempts to control the patient. The most common constrictive responses are doubting or denial of the patient's reality,

> dissociation or numbing, minimisation or avoidance of the traumatic
> material, professional distancing, or frank abandonment of the patient.
> Some degree of intrusion or numbing is probably inevitable. The
> therapist should expect to lose her balance from time to time with such
> patients. She is not infallible. The guarantee of her integrity is not her
> omnipotence but her capacity to trust others. The work of recovery
> requires a secure and reliable support system for the therapist.
> – *Judith Lewis Herman*

Regular supervision should, of course, be maintained for the duration of the practitioner's working life. This would apply particularly when dealing with the type of client who will be likely to seek analytical assistance. Group supervision may be of benefit to the analytical practitioner if the other members of the group are experienced in similar fields of practice. If this is not the case, then the therapist may find it more beneficial – both personally and professionally – to work on a one-to-one basis with a supervisor who is well versed in analytic methodology.

> Ideally, the therapist's support system should include a safe, structured,
> and regular forum for reviewing her clinical work. This might be a
> supervisory relationship or a peer support group, preferably both. The
> setting must offer permission to express emotional reactions as well as
> technical or intellectual concerns related to the treatment of patients with
> histories of trauma.
> – *Judith Lewis Herman*

The Voyage of Self-Discovery

> Man's main task in life is to give birth to himself.
> – *Erich Fromm*

Early on in the therapeutic process, the therapist may wish to invite the client to enter on a journey of self-discovery (see Chapter 17, Volume 1 – "The Case for Therapy"). This may help to consolidate the client's view of therapeutic intervention and his role in the process. It will also be important for the client to appreciate that he will do as much work as – if not more than – the practitioner in initiating change and in securing a successful outcome to therapy.

The client may be invited to reflect on the way in which his past life has affected his present state of mind. The aim of most therapeutic intervention will be to tempt the client towards finding his true self and often the practitioner can effectively utilise questioning techniques to this end. Let us examine some suggested questions that the therapist might pose to the client in order to stimulate his ability to carry out self-assessment in an honest and fruitful manner.

- Do you feel beset or inhibited by your own lack of enjoyment of life?
- Do you often feel moody and indecisive?
- Do you often despair of ever achieving anything worthwhile in your life?
- Do you regularly suffer from procrastination and intransigence?
- Do you sometimes feel that lethargy will hold you back from achieving certain goals in life?
- Do you often experience a sense or boredom, apathy or restlessness?
- Do you tend to avoid certain situations because you feel awkward or unable to cope?
- Do you find that you continually stagger from one crisis to another?
- Is your life spent worrying about your ill health and fragility?
- Do you often feel a sense of indignation or injustice?
- Do you resent others whom you regard as being happier or more fortunate than you are?
- Do you suffer unaccountably and seemingly uncontrollably from minor fears or phobias?
- Do you take comfort in perpetuating an unwanted habit that is not beneficial to your health, wealth or wellbeing?
- Are you aware of any self-destructive or self-defeating patterns of behaviour in your life?
- Did you find that your so-called friends frequently take advantage of you?
- Do you find that you are hopeless at making satisfactory and mutually-rewarding relationships?

The following suggested metaphorical passage will explain to the client what the rigours of childhood are and how such ostensibly-simple calamities can have a detrimental affect of his wellbeing.

Childhood can be a minefield of disaster ...

Childhood is usually an extremely difficult period of our lives – almost totally bewildering and overwhelming. Our basic instincts dictate our needs and our motivations and yet we have insufficient knowledge and experience of the world to realise what is going on for us beneath the surface of our existence. We, as children, unfortunately do not have the resources of understanding, strength, stature, power, influence and wealth to cope with that which life itself presents. We live in a world of mysterious and omnipotent giants known as adults who hold all the trump cards.

When we may perceive that we are neglected or ignored or unfairly treated or overprotected or overindulged or not given enough freedom of expression or maltreated or misused or, even, abused in any way in our formative years, we are indelibly writing emotional turmoil into our psychological script. These factors will have inevitable repercussions in adult life and there will be nothing we can do to prevent, to halt or to interrupt the process. If we perceive danger in any way – even for a moment in our childhood – we will develop an in-built predisposition to emotional instability in adulthood. When we perceive a threat or a potential threat to our survival – especially in childhood or in early adulthood – this perception will be recorded in our unconscious mind as a psychological conflict or trauma from which we cannot recover unless it is satisfactorily resolved in adulthood. The trauma of the mind will then become locked inside and this process of imprisoning our emotions will be the factor that insidiously does us profound harm. The past will, therefore, return to haunt us!

Because of our desire to please and to keep faith with our parents and carers, any perceived childhood distress will become buried below the surface of our mind simply because it is unpleasant and could threaten our survival. We dare not be critical or unforgiving of our parents because we will be biting the hand that feeds us. And, because we are pleasure seekers and pain avoiders, we endeavour to shelve painful memories, unpleasant experiences or unhappy situations in the hope that they will just melt into thin air. Just as when we accidentally bump our elbow or stub our toe, we wish to distract ourselves from the pain in order to try to forget about it, so it is with our emotions but even more so.

As we approach adulthood, however, this burying or suppression of painful experiences will inevitably emerge as unwanted habits, addictions, obsessions, phobias, psychological turmoil, depressive conditions or psychosomatic disorders. These symptoms of difficulties, thus, are our primitive, yet unsuccessful, attempt to relieve our mind of its relentless anguish as a direct result of our struggle through childhood years. If you cage an animal, it will seek escape because its instinct is for freedom in its natural habitat. And remember: we are only primitive animals with limited intelligence! Nature is raw in tooth and claw because this is how the survival-mechanism works. Unjust and cumbersome, unfortunately, but that's the way it is! Our survival mechanism is primitive and has remained that way unchanged for centuries. But, since it is the only one we have and needs to be able to cope with all emergencies, we have to accommodate it rather than to deny it or to fight against it.

Sometimes our problems remain dormant for a while. Sometimes we can fool the inner mind temporarily into believing that we have resolved all our own troubles. When you are hungry, do you sometimes find that drinking a cup of coffee will assuage your hunger temporarily? You are merely duping the mind for a while. But the respite will only be temporary and the demon will inevitably return with full force when the opportunity presents itself and until a permanent solution can be reached.

Unfortunately, only a very privileged few of us can make the claim that our childhood was 100 per cent happy and that our parents, relatives, teachers and schoolmates were 100 per cent loving and supportive at all times. This is the harsh reality of life! Actually, even a superhuman being cannot really survive childhood emotionally unscathed. At one end of the scale, if you have had a reasonably happy childhood, then you may develop into a reasonably happy adult. If, on the other hand, your childhood was less than somewhat, then you are likely to emerge as an emotionally-unhappy adult. Paradoxically, of course, having a really happy childhood may mean that you do not have the equipment to face the harsh reality of the outside world.

A further problem is that in adult life – and in so-called civilised society – we are inhibited or even debarred from expressing our emotions and so we become reluctant to ask for help or we are ashamed to admit that we are not fully-functioning individuals. A perceived emotional disorder can be regarded as a disgrace and the result of a unique weakness of character – although nothing could be further from the truth. We, therefore, tend to deny or to bury our feelings and to soldier on valiantly at the very times when we should be investing in ourselves and tackling the problem head on with all our energies. When doing this, we pay the added price of suppressing our distress still further and, in doing so, exacerbating or accelerating the condition. In other words, when life is hard, we make it even harder for ourselves by pretending that it is not really that bad at all!

Well you can console yourself with the fact that you have been lucky enough even to have survived childhood at all. However, accept that – through no fault of your own – you still have some work to do on yourself before you can regard yourself as a true, mature and emotionally-healthy adult. The legacy of the past can be successfully resolved and now is the time to change because you owe it to yourself! Remember that you are someone who does possess the necessary strength and determination because you have had the courage to consult me. Quite a feat in itself! The challenge for you now will be to find the real you inside, to discover and to reclaim your inner self – the one locked inside and bursting to break free. Who are you? I wonder. You are the only one who can answer that question, however, and it is certainly worth finding out and making that discovery about yourself. While on your self-discovery journey you may find it exciting or you may find it distressing, but this may have to be the small price you will need to pay for discovering yourself and, in order to find your inner self, you may need to reflect not only on your current circumstances but also on your past life.

Setting the Therapeutic Scene

It is as if a continent has been surveyed by a number of individuals. Each has drawn a map of his own locality and regards the local terrain as archetypal of the whole continent. They therefore regard the others as being substantially in error. But there comes a time when it is possible to unite the maps in such a way that they *add* to each other and help to form a composite map of the entire continent.
– *Dylan Morgan*

For the client who is a newcomer to the therapeutic scene, the practitioner may often need to engage initially in an educative programme. This stance will, thus, introduce the client to the purpose of therapy and to his particular role in the therapeutic encounter. The practitioner may also need to shape the client's expectations in terms of the likely outcome of therapeutic exploration. Sometimes the client may have a realistic expectation of therapy but, on other occasions, the practitioner may need to divest him of any misconceptions and/or misgivings.

By way of setting the therapeutic scene, the following suggested metaphorical passage can be useful for the client who may be bemused about the reasons why he feels so distressed and has so many unpleasant symptoms.

When a baby is born ...

When a baby is born, baby has but one aim in life. One aim that consumes her every thought and to which she directs every attention and expends all her energy. And that is to survive at any cost.

Baby, of course, soon realises that she cannot survive without assistance from others and so baby looks for a helpmate to provide her with the basic needs of life. The basic requirements for survival are food, warmth, clothing, shelter and protection from harm. There is, however, one other vital component that baby requires for her survival and that is love. Love is undoubtedly the most important of all baby's basic needs because love is the key to baby's very survival. When baby is loved by Mum or a Mum-substitute, baby will be able to attain the food, the warmth and the protection that she so instinctively craves.

Baby knows that love is vital to her survival because the carer who loves her will provide for her tenderly and tirelessly. Baby, thus, depends on love and the assurance of continued and unconditional love for her survival from the moment of birth and throughout childhood.

Our baby has a primitive way of communicating her needs. When baby is hungry or in pain or in any discomfort, she will use her lung-capacity to draw attention to her plight. This is because baby will be determined to make some-one aware of her importance, her desire for immediate attention and her intol-erance of delay. If merely crying does not have the desired effect, then baby will increase the volume of the crying and start yelling, go blue in the face, kick, squirm and throw things around until her distress is suitably pacified. This is the way in which baby survives. But what baby is really seeking is love because it will be the essential key to her survival. It will secure all her needs in one go and will be the safest option. And also, when love is constantly forth-coming, baby learns that she can tolerate some temporary distress if the satis-faction of her needs will sooner or later be addressed. Baby, of course, may simultaneously hate Mum when she does not attend quickly and efficiently to her needs and, then, hate herself for feeling that way about her primary carer or for failing to attract Mum's attention effectively. What an enigmatic para-dox of strong and complex emotions, all of which baby transports through childhood into adulthood.

The developing child, too, will contrive to seek the assurance of love continu-ally in her childhood. Our child will constantly ask Mum and Dad to watch her at play, to admire her achievements at school and to take an interest in her daily activities. Furthermore, our child will solicit the approval of all adults in order to secure their affection and she covets the approbation of her contem-poraries in a competitive environment of survival. Our child will be geneti-cally programmed so to do, and yet these motivations are unconscious and instinctive processes. For our child to develop and make a satisfactory transi-tion into early adulthood, that tireless and unconditional love must be unend-ing and constantly forthcoming. Only in this way can our child stand any chance at all of becoming an emotionally-healthy and well-balanced adult.

The Cathartic Approach

Psychoanalysis assumes that some aspects of mental life are inaccessible to consciousness. Although such mental contents may partially betray themselves in dreams, neurotic symptoms, slips of the tongue, and states of mind encountered in mental illness, most can only be brought into consciousness by the special techniques of recovery and interpretation which are an integral part of the psychoanalytic process.
– *Anthony Storr*

The analytical therapist will aim to make it possible for the client to unearth material that will be causing his psychological distress because it will be inaccessible or partially inaccessible to his conscious awareness. In this quest, the practitioner will be concerned with deciphering the client's thoughts, dreams and symbolic imagery (see Chapter 14, Volume 1 – "Dreams and Symbolic Imagery"), interpreting parapraxes (see Chapter 3 – "Unconscious Communication"), exploring transference and countertransference (see Chapter 13, Volume 1 – "Transference and Counter-transference") and working with resistance (see Chapter 12, Volume 1 – "Resistance") as well as analysing his presenting symptoms. For this type of work, the therapist will need to have a belief in the client's ability to be self-determining despite any genetic dictates and environmental influences. The therapist's role will, therefore, be to allow the client to recognise that he is still possessed of a free will and the freedom to make personal choices in his life once traumatic conflicts have been resolved.

Following therapeutic investigation into the root cause of the client's distress, he will then be able to work though the effects of past trauma. This can usually be achieved using a variety of techniques such as ego-strengthening, experience-restructuring, inner-child rescue and cognitive strategies designed to assuage debilitating emotive expression (see Chapter 5 – "Therapeutic Resolution"). Therapeutic resolution will mean that the client can then naturally modify his maladaptive behaviour patterns, can detach from dependencies, can remedy destructive or unproductive relationships, can raise his self-esteem, can relinquish distressing, trauma-related symptoms and can generally discover the ways in which the resonant template of the past has impacted on the present.

Let us now turn our attention to certain key elements in the analytic encounter that have become the hallmark of analytical hypnotherapy.

The cathartic process

> Nature particularly abhors a vacuum in this respect; hence there is
> nothing more unendurable in the long run than a tepid harmony based
> on the withholding of affects.
> – Carl Jung

Therapeutic exploration, confession, abreactive discharge and insight will collectively result in a psychic cleansing process for the client that has come to be known as *catharsis*. In hypnoanalysis, the aim of the cathartic process will be to bring about the gradual or sporadic emergence of the client's unconscious material in the process of self-rediscovery (see Chapter 17, Volume 1 – "The Case for Therapy"). The client's need for personal psychological privacy in the therapeutic encounter may, therefore, prolong his isolation if he elects to keep any opportunities for self-discovery concealed from the practitioner and, if he does so, he will only allow the damage to be partially mended.

Jung advanced the notion that the first beginnings of all analytical treatment of the soul are to be found in the confessional (see Chapter 2, Volume 1 – "Analytical Psychology"). Jung proffered the advice that anything concealed by the client will become a secret and the possession of this secret will act like a psychic poison by alienating the possessor from the rest of the community. Shared secrets are beneficial both for the individual and for the listener, whereas the client's private secrets are self-destructive and may lead him towards carrying a burden of guilt that can result in alienation from others. A secret about which the client will be consciously aware will be far less damaging, of course, than one of which he will be unaware and may be keeping concealed even from himself in the guise of repression (see Chapter 11, Volume 1 – "Defensive Strategies"). The client, of course, will usually be unaware of the fact that he possesses buried psychic material even when he initially enters the therapist's consulting room. Jung considered that a hidden secret could split off from the client's conscious mind and become an independent complex that could then not be consciously rectified. This notion, of course, has been acknowledged clearly in ego-state psychology (see Chapter 4, Volume 1 – "Ego-State Therapy"). This isolated complex would then form a miniature, self-containment within the client's psyche that would then develop a peculiar fantasy-life of its own. Jung defined fantasy as any spontaneous, psychic activity that may well up in the client's mind whenever the inhibitive action of the conscious brain abates or ceases. In sleep, for instance, the fantasy dammed up in this way will have its outlet in the client's dreams. When the client has been under the influence of repressed or unconscious complexes, for instance, he might continue to dream beneath the threshold of his conscious mind. The client's unconscious mind, therefore, will contain its own material consisting of repressions and complexes that may surface into conscious awareness from time to time. All unconscious content, irrespective of source or depth, will, of course, affect the client's conscious mind but, because such material will not surface into awareness, he will be affected by such matter only indirectly. The client's distressing symptoms, therefore, will nearly always be either psychogenic or the effect of shock – the remnants of which will both have lain dormant in his unconscious mind.

Another form of personal secret can manifest when the client withholds his normal emotive expression often because self-restraint will be seen by him as a virtue. This practice, however, may be just as psychologically damaging to the client as a major repression. Jung declared that even a low-grade secret would have attached to it some emotive content that the client had installed in his unconscious mind. Although such a confidence might be hardly worth mentioning to others, the client would still have recorded a degree of distress in his unconscious mind at some critical juncture and this log would then have caused the development of his symptoms. The highly-strung individual who freely indulges in frequent emotive outbursts will be likely to have a hidden secret while the emotionally-resilient individual will suffer from psychological indigestion because of his inability to express his inner emotive reactions. Jung believed that there was a form of conscience within mankind that will punish those who do not, at some time, confess themselves to be fallible and human. Until this happens, Jung claimed, a wall would shut the individual off from his fellow human beings.

> The more complicated and profound process of gaining "insight", which involves affective as well as cognitive recognition of intra-psychic associations, was sought by Freud as a more potent and far-reaching procedure effecting more profound and therefore long-lived changes in intra-psychic organisation.
> – *Hellmut Karle & Jennifer Boys*

The abreactive process

Abreaction is a psychoanalytical term used to describe the weakening or elimination of anxiety by the "reliving" of the original tension-evoking experience. "Reliving" can refer to an imaginal or emotional re-experience as well as to an actual one – **catharsis**.
– Arthur Reber

An abreaction will be a discharge of emotive, cognitive and behavioural expression that will spontaneously occur when the client examines a part of his subjective experience that contains pent-up psychic turmoil. When the client experiences an abreaction, he may cry, wail, tremble, convulse, scream, shake, appear to be restless, perspire or otherwise display a psychological or physiological manifestation of his distress. The client's abreactive process may also propel him out of the trance-state or, even, out of his chair. At such times, the practitioner must remain calm, focused and self-controlled. The abreactive process must be allowed to take its course in order to ensure that a full release of emotive expression has been achieved by the client. The clinician should, therefore, invite the client to cry, to wail and to gesticulate as much as he needs, as this will be the key to his cathartic release. Once the storm has died down, the practitioner might then ask whether the client is able to provide a reason for his outburst. Abreaction may, of course, occur for the client both within the consulting room and away from it as a delayed abreaction.

The client who presents with overt or uncontrollable emotive responses will be likely to experience abreaction in an emotive manner such as crying or screaming. The client who presents with behavioural or psychosomatic symptoms, however, may need to convert these symptomatic manifestations into emotive expression in order to discharge the underlying distress (see Chapter 11 – "Psychosomatic Disorders"). It will be as if the client's emotive expression will be the bottom line and his pent up reaction will manifest on a continuum. The client's inner turmoil, therefore, may be expressed overtly in the form of psychologically-based symptoms of which he will be patently aware, at one end of the spectrum, and, covertly, at the other end of the scale, in the guise of confusing behavioural, cognitive or psychosomatic symptoms (see Figure 1 – "The abreactive process").

Figure 1 – The abreactive process

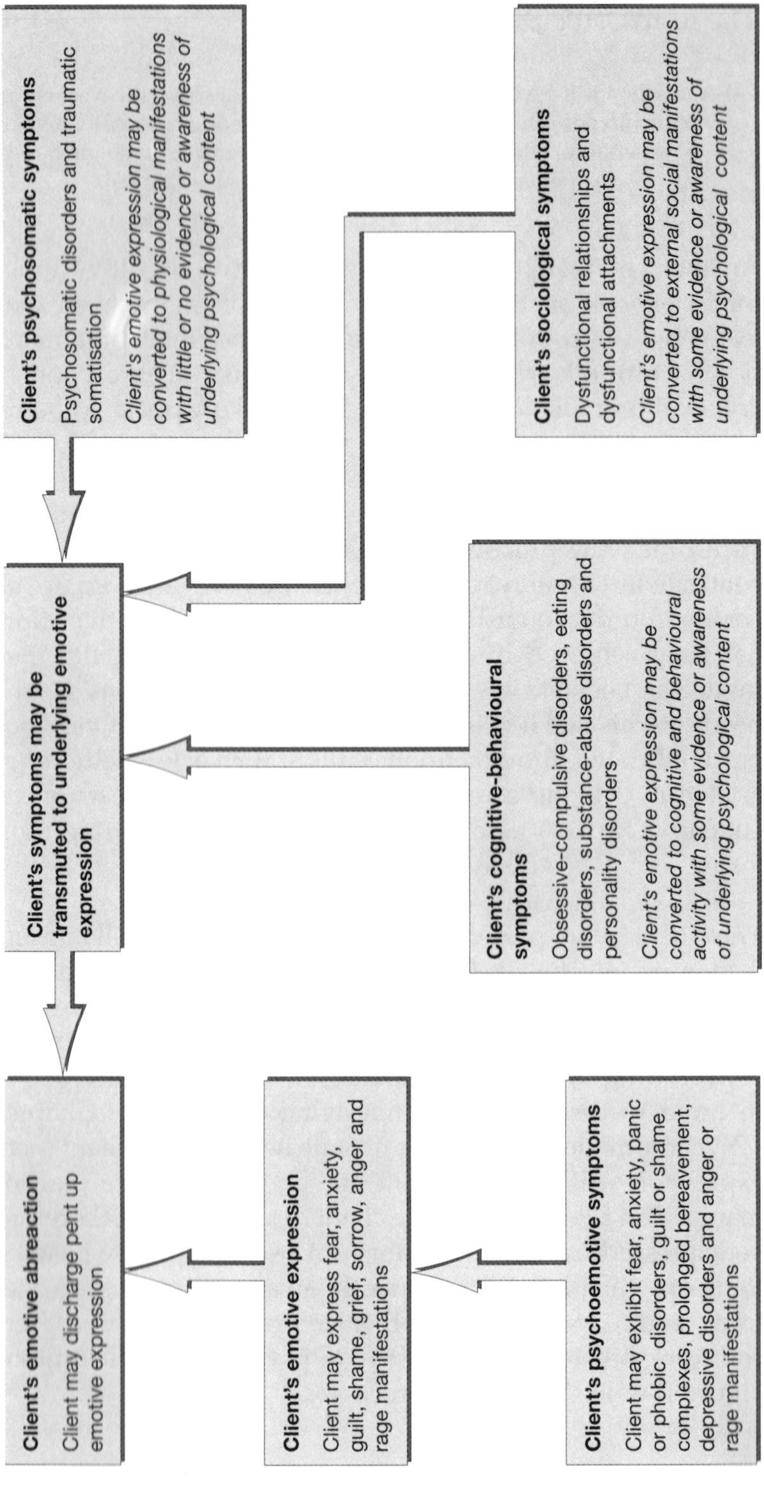

Client's psychosomatic symptoms

Psychosomatic disorders and traumatic somatisation

Client's emotive expression may be converted to physiological manifestations with little or no evidence or awareness of underlying psychological content

Client's sociological symptoms

Dysfunctional relationships and dysfunctional attachments

Client's emotive expression may be converted to external social manifestations with some evidence or awareness of underlying psychological content

Client's symptoms may be transmuted to underlying emotive expression

Client's cognitive-behavioural symptoms

Obsessive-compulsive disorders, eating disorders, substance-abuse disorders and personality disorders

Client's emotive expression may be converted to cognitive and behavioural activity with some evidence or awareness of underlying psychological content

Client's emotive abreaction

Client may discharge pent up emotive expression

Client's emotive expression

Client may express fear, anxiety, guilt, shame, grief, sorrow, anger and rage manifestations

Client's psychoemotive symptoms

Client may exhibit fear, anxiety, panic or phobic disorders, guilt or shame complexes, prolonged bereavement, depressive disorders and anger or rage manifestations

The analytical hypnotherapist will subscribe to the doctrine of cause and effect in that she will endeavour to identify the root cause of the client's trauma rather than merely to treat his symptoms of distress. Because it will have been the psychological effect of circumstances that will have had an impact on the client's psyche, the practitioner will seek to uncover those emotive expressions that will be at the heart of the problem in order to resolve matters. Using hypnosis as the medium through which to undertake analytical investigation will, in addition, allow the client an opportunity to attain a deep state of calmness and, in such a state, it will, naturally, not be uncommon for him to have a sudden abreactive outburst without even knowing the reason. It will take a lot of physiological energy for the client to hold on to repressed or suppressed matter and, as he becomes more relaxed, his mind and body may take the opportunity to free him of some of that confined emotive expression. Sometimes the client's mind may simply be tired of holding on to it. Any restraint will need to find a way out and, while the client is relaxed and his parasympathetic nervous system is engaged, the door of unconsciousness can be gently opened. Once the client has successfully transited the vital abreactive process and released any unresolved tension in the sympathetic nervous system, his parasympathetic nervous system can then engage in order to resolve the original trauma, conflict or distress previously held within both the mind and the body.

> A man who has not passed through the inferno of his passions has never overcome them.
> – *Carl Jung*

The incomplete cathartic process

> Primal therapy is by definition taxing, involving as it does a thorough confrontation with the past. A readiness to go through with that process "come what may" is an essential requirement of any therapy because there is a high probability that in the course of it one will be confronted with terrible, dreadful realities. Despite that, it is a constructive process.
> – *Konrad Stettbacher*

The goal of the cathartic process will be a full and comprehensive confession on the part of the client. This process will be accompanied by confirmation of the client's new-found psychological freedom and the release of pent-up emotive expression combined with his intellectual recognition of the facts. Once catharsis has been achieved, the client will have been successfully treated and often completely cured. There are, however, a few exceptions to this claim that we shall now discuss.

The first is the client with a highly-complex personality who may be very firmly anchored in his conscious thinking and who will not wish to turn to unconscious reflection. This client will be the intel-lectual-resistance merchant personified (see Chapter 12, Volume 1 – "Resistance"). Another problem will occur when the client becomes so attached to the practitioner that, when therapy has been completed, he may relapse because he will mourn the loss of his friend and confidante. The client who becomes dependent on the practitioner – usually as a result of an unconscious need – may be exhibiting the manifestation of a fresh symptom that has been directly unearthed during the therapeutic process. The client, in many cases, will have become unconsciously dependent on the therapist as if he were a parent. This form of transference, there-fore, would need to be thoroughly investigated and carefully han-dled by the practitioner before therapeutic treatment can be successfully concluded (see Chapter 13, Volume 1 – "Transference and Countertransference"). A complete dissolution of transference will, of course, need to be achieved in this case. For those clients who do not develop an attachment to the therapist, the attach-ment-fantasy will remain as fantasy but will not be transferred on to any human object (see Chapter 5, Volume 1 – "Object-Relations Psychology"). This fantasy may still exert the same pull but will result in a dependence on the client's own unconscious mind, wherein his resources are plentiful. A further restriction to cathar-tic resolution will occur when the client becomes so fascinated with his own unconscious mind that he will continue the practice of analysis for himself at the expense of his psychic adaptation and reintegration into society. The client who totally resists any form of catharsis, of course, will be likely to have derived this obstructive trait from the identity and relationship that he once had formed with his parental role-models. This client, for example, will be likely to have subsumed into his psyche parental authority, inde-pendence and critical power. This client will have fallen victim to the unconscious activity of the parental image but will have embraced this trait by unconsciously identifying with his parents.

Jung believed that this client should be told directly and precisely about the substance and meaning of what he was projecting on to the therapist.

Stages of cathartic resolution

> Because it is, in its primal stage, weak and dependent, this system requires the selfless devotion and help of its progenitors and relatives for its survival. To be able to perceive and satisfy its needs, a child's progenitors must establish an affirmative, responsible, and caring relationship to it. If the child's natural, primal needs are satisfied, it will be endowed with a fundamental feeling of security, trust, and vitality. Together these will form the foundation for a positive ability to form human attachments.
> – *Konrad Stettbacher*

According to Jung, the analytical interpretation of fantasy-material will reveal man's shadow-side in all its conceivable filth (see Chapter 14, Volume 1 – "Dreams and Symbolic Imagery"). The elucidation of this substance will make the client's position untenable but he must face up to it and deal with it accordingly during the therapeutic encounter. This operation can, however, occur as a fourfold unravelling process for the client similar to the concepts put forward by gestalt therapy (see Chapter 8, Volume 1 – "Gestalt Therapy").

The cathartic stage
The cathartic stage will occur when the client can devote all his energy to forward-looking and progressive work during therapy.

The elucidation stage
The elucidation stage will occur when the client can learn forbearance with his own shortcomings by turning his back on sentimentality and illusion.

The social education stage
The social education stage will occur when the client can relinquish his childish demands of others and downwardly adjust such

requirements to a more reasonable and socially-acceptable level. The client's stressful disturbance can often give rise to many obstinate habits that will not disappear until replaced by other habits. Appropriate education will be the sole means of replacing childish habits with more appropriate habits because frequently the client will need to employ some determination in order steadfastly to adopt a mature trait in adulthood. Insight into the self will often be sufficient to drive forward the client who is more morally sensitive. The client's self-knowledge, however, without the spur of external necessity can frequently be ineffective. This may be where Adler's work with its goal-seeking approach will come into play in the therapeutic context (see Chapter 3, Volume 1 – "Individual Psychology").

The transformational stage
The final stage of cathartic resolution for the client will be the transformational stage. The practitioner should, however, remember that the aspirations of the average client may simply be to become a normal member of society. The client, of course, who is of an above-average ability may, conversely, consider that to be normal would mean boredom, sterility and hopelessness. There may be the client, therefore, who will be distressed because he will believe that he is normal as well as the client who will become discontent because he feels abnormal. It will, of course, not be appropriate for the practitioner to impose her view either to adapt the client to being normal or to inspire him to reach for the stars. The client will be unique and individual with unique and individual needs. The client may find satisfaction and fulfilment only with what he does not have and not with that of which he already has a surfeit.

During the closing, transformational stage of the therapeutic process, the same problems from the client's past will often come into view again but, this time, taking on a different importance. The emphasis may not now be placed on examining the development of patterns that have led to the present situation but rather on re-educating the client. Frustration, resentment, loneliness and grief associated with the client's personal problems, for example, will still be present but will lose their strength and significance. Events in the client's life can now become seen in terms of their intentionality as if all experiences were manifestations of some purposive function that has been appropriately called goal-directedness of psychic energy. Jung purported that this energy can provide the thrust for individuation and maturity as if the client were being drawn inwardly towards a central resplendence. Jung stated that to dive straight in rather than take time to consolidate psychic change would be rather like a moth flying straight into a flame or the earth diving into the sun. Jung claimed that mankind will encircle this luminosity and will maintain an orbital tension in a relationship between the small finite being of the ego towards an energy that has no limit. Jung advanced that this luminosity is the self or the mysterious non-ego that will be the centre of the client's being and will be that which the ego resolves.

Client Profiling

The analytical-hypnotherapy practitioner may wish to ponder the following points when formulating a profile for the client.

- What beliefs does the client have about the therapeutic process?
- Is the client able to grasp the significance of what undergoing therapy involves?
- Does the client have a clear idea of what therapy entails?
- Is the client ready to undertake the therapeutic process?
- Is the client prepared to undergo any emotive pain that may be involved in the unravelling of his psychic trauma?
- Can the therapist and the client form an effective and appropriate working relationship?
- Can the client feel safe and supported in the therapeutic context?
- Does the client understand what his role is in the therapeutic process?
- Does the practitioner appreciate what the attributes of an analytical therapist are?
- Is the practitioner in any need of therapeutic intervention or supervisory support?
- In what ways can the practitioner contribute to group supervision meetings?

- Does the client understand the way in which the analytical process could unfold?
- Is the client prepared to express his painful emotions during the therapeutic encounter?
- Is the client able to achieve a catharsis during the therapeutic process?
- Does the client fully experience the abreactive process when this naturally arises during the therapeutic process?
- Is the client in any way unable to complete the cathartic process?
- Can the practitioner identify the ways in which cathartic resolution has unfolded for the client?
- Will the client be able to move on from the therapeutic setting once the therapeutic process has been completed or has come to a natural conclusion?

Chapter 2

Therapeutic Investigation

An angry man opens his mouth and shuts his eyes

– Marcus Porcius Cato

What Does Therapeutic Investigation Achieve?

It is the aim of psychoanalysis to arrive at an insight into the unconscious processes which the patient has right now. Psychoanalysis is not historical research per se.
– Erich Fromm

One of the main premises of analytical therapy will be that the client will be asked to probe her own mind in order to explore its contents with a fine-toothed comb (see Chapter 17, Volume 1 – "The Case for Therapy"). The aim of this approach will be to excavate from the client's mind those limitations that she has to psychic freedom and psychological contentment. Analytical investigation, in many ways, will involve frequently looking in the fridge until the mould has been identified and then setting about finding the disinfectant in order to eradicate it. Opponents of the analytical paradigm frequently claim that this will be a morbid waste of time that simply retraumatises the client and exacerbates her symptoms. This simplistic and short-sighted view of therapy could, however, rob the truly dedicated practitioner of the reward of effecting permanent change within the client who has suffered from the rigours of life and from traumatic past experience. Critics – almost invariably – are those people who would rather emigrate or starve than even open the fridge door!

In order to effect the client's recovery and her freedom from distress, she will need to accept aspects of her past. Once these elements have been accepted and understood by the client, then change can take place. The client cannot change or accept that which she does not know or understand – consciously or otherwise. Sometimes a conscious understanding of the client's life-events will suffice but, in most cases, it will be her unconscious enlightenment that will bring about permanent and beneficial change. Investigative probing, therefore, will be a necessary tool in the practitioner's therapeutic toolkit in order to render the ground fertile for the client's personal growth and expansion. Let us now consider some of these forms of investigative and explorative methodology.

Free Association

> Free association is the central technique in psychoanalytic therapy. In essence, clients flow with any feelings or thoughts by reporting them immediately without censorship.
> – *Gerald Corey*

In collaboration with Josef Breuer (1842–1925), Freud discovered that the client could identify the birthplace of a given symptom and, if this recollection were accompanied by the abreactive process, the client's presenting symptoms would then be alleviated or abated (see Chapter 1 – "The Hypnoanalytic Approach"). From this discovery, Freud formulated the therapeutic technique known as free association, that has become of fundamental importance not only to the analytical hypnotherapist but also to virtually every other clinical-psychology discipline. The use of free association, therefore, will be one of the principal ways in which the client can investigate the driving forces within her own mind.

> Nothing takes place in psychoanalytic treatment but an interchange of words between the patient and the analyst. The patient talks, tells of his past experiences and present impressions, complains, confesses to his wishes and his emotional impulses. The doctor listens, tries to direct the patient's processes of thought, exhorts, forces his attention in certain directions, gives him explanations and observes the reactions of understanding or rejection which he in this way provokes in him.
> – *Sigmund Freud*

What is free association?

> Instead of urging the patient to say something upon some particular subject, I now asked him to abandon himself to a process of free association – that is, to say whatever came into his head, while ceasing to give any conscious direction to his thoughts. It was essential, however, that he should bind himself to report literally everything that occurred to his self-perception and not to give way to critical objections which sought to put certain associations on one side on the ground that they were not sufficiently important or that they were irreverent or that they were altogether meaningless.
> *– Sigmund Freud*

Free association permits the client to move freely within her own mind from one idea to another in order to connect thoughts, ideas, physical sensations and emotive responses that have a common thread at an unconscious level. Free association will be a memory-recovery and insight-oriented process whereby the client can link one memory or sensation with the next in sequence in a seemingly random manner because one thought or sensation will prompt the formation of the next. Often the practitioner will encourage the client to undertake this process with minimal intervention – interjecting, for example, only a limited number of reflective comments when absolutely necessary.

As a treatment method, the technique of free association can be used for locating, uncovering and resolving memories of experiences that have played a key role in the development and manifestation of the client's presenting symptoms. By this means, the client's new-found knowledge and insight will, in itself, generate self-respect and this form of self-enhancement will, in turn, have the effect of bolstering her self-esteem. Free association will provide access to the client's unconscious wishes, fantasies, conflicts and motivations that will evacuate the restrained substance of her memories as well as clarify incomplete or partial memories of experiences. The free-association process can be utilised in order to gain effective access into the root cause of the client's distress by locating the memory-trace and, hence, the source of the conflict in this seemingly haphazard way (see Chapter 10, Volume 1 – "Memory"). Because the client's memories will be encoded in her unconscious mind according to emotive content, the practitioner can be sure that free association will lead towards unearthing anxiety-provoking and stressful components. The common thread that will weave the client's psychic tapestry may be either a recollection of a single event or a series of events together with the accompanying emotive force. It will, of course, usually be the client's abreaction to an event-memory that will provide the lock-opener to her psychic distress and will give an indication to the practitioner that repair-work will be required at this juncture. Simultaneously, the client may have a somatic memory or a cell memory that may provide the required access to her distress perhaps in connection with a psychosomatic symptom (see Chapter 11 – "Psychosomatic Disorders").

In order to ensure that the client will be able to associate thoughts and ideas freely, she should be instructed by the practitioner to reveal whatever comes to mind regardless of how painful, silly, trivial, illogical or irrelevant the matter may seem. In the process of investigating the past, the client should be invited to explore thoughts, images, impressions, perceptions and sensations without any editing of her psychic script. The client should, therefore, be urged to report thoughts without censorship in order to ensure a successful analytic process. The free-association process can then be used in order to unearth traumatic chapters in the client's life and to resolve conflicts that have been set up in order to support presenting symptoms. The client's symptoms can be regarded as a surface-level manifestation of suppressed or repressed traumatic material that has been converted into psychological distress or physiological malfunctioning. Any resistance to this instruction to reveal all should, of course, be noted by the practitioner as being significant because the client's resistance can often be the gateway into her deeply-rooted problems in that what is not actually said will usually be of particular relevance to therapeutic investigation (see Chapter 12, Volume 1– "Resistance").

What is not free association?

> But it is not only in the saving of labour that the method of free association has an advantage over the earlier method. It exposes the patient to the least possible amount of compulsion, it never allows of contact being lost with the actual current situation, it guarantees to a great extent that no factor in the structure of the neurosis will be overlooked and that nothing will be introduced into it by the expectations of the analyst.
> – *Sigmund Freud*

A distinction should be made between free association and the other memory-retrieval processes. Cognitive recollection and comparative recall of memories, for example, are linked to the mind's logical and deductive reasoning and not to unconscious processing. The cognitive-recollection process will enable the client to recognise information such as names, faces and locations. Cognitive memory will be used by the human organism in order to recall facts that have usually been acquired by conscious learning. Comparative-memory processing will be undertaken by the client using a matching principle whereby she will scan her memory for an existing match. Comparative memory will be used by the client in order to recall information that has been previously stored as part of the process of general conscious awareness.

Because the human mind can readily switch from one memory process to another, the practitioner should ensure that free association will be undertaken as far as possible during analytical investigation and that the client does not switch into either rational cognitive or comparative processing. The client's cognitive and comparative information processing will be handled by the language skills and learning areas of the cerebral cortex in the human cerebrum, that will control mental activity. Free association, on the other hand, will seek to engage the client's illogical and irrational faculties, that are governed by the thalamus and the hypothalamus in the limbic system. The thalamus will relay sensory information and the hypothalamus will control the client's autonomic nervous system, emotive expression, sexual behaviour and her body's biological clock. If these mechanisms are engaged by the human system, free association will, thus, be going some way towards effectively accessing the client's instinctive and primitive being.

> Free association can be seen as a "controlled" therapeutic form of regression useful in the working out of neurosis.
> – *Richard Appignanesi & Oscar Zarate*

Utilising the free-association process

> We can specify the rules of the analytic game: for example, the requirement that the patient lie on the couch or that the analyst interpret the transference neurosis. If successful, such an account would specify what analysis is (and, by inference, what it is not).
> – *Thomas Szasz*

The main benefit of utilising free association will be the speed and the accuracy with which the client can access unconscious distress and conflict held just below the surface of her mind. When this process can be aided by a trance-state, the results may be startling for both the client and the practitioner. The client can be encouraged to employ free association by gentle prompts from the practitioner, if necessary, that can successfully nudge her forward at an appropriate and beneficial pace. Some suggestions are given below for the therapist to consider as a means of generating beneficial shift for the client.

- Can you tell me the very next thought that enters your head?
- And what is the next thing that comes to mind here?
- And what is the very next thing that occurs to you now?
- What are you thinking about now?
- What is that thought right there?
- What is going on for you now?
- What are you experiencing now?
- What is the emotional content of your recollection?
- What are you thinking and feeling here?
- What are those thoughts there buzzing around in your head?
- How do you truly feel about this situation?
- Can you search your soul and honestly feel the way it was right now?
- Can you bring the past right here into the present?
- What is your body telling your mind?
- And what happens then a moment later?
- Now where has your mind taken you?
- What thoughts or feelings have drifted into your mind now?
- Can you share those thoughts with me?
- What messages are you receiving here from your unconscious mind?

When employing free association, it may be important for the practitioner to ensure that the client can fully explore every opportunity that may arise whereby unconscious matter can be unearthed. Every effort should be made by the therapist to identify and to examine carefully any gaps in the fence because it may be likely that this will be the place in which the nuggets of the client's disorder will reside. If necessary, the practitioner may need to cajole the client into probing a past recollection second by second –

especially if the client has a tendency to cycle around a set of memories or she returns repeatedly to a long-forgotten incident from childhood. It may be necessary, for example, to interrupt somewhat or to slow down the client's flow in order to keep her in the moment. This will ensure that she does not speedily skim over those aspects of her inner world that she would rather not address. For this purpose, it would be preferable for the practitioner to use the present tense when addressing the client in order to ensure that she stay with her current thoughts. The practitioner should aim to encourage the client to experience the past as if it were happening in the immediate present – a process that can, of course, be significantly aided by the trance-state – because this will ensure a direct access to underlying irrational memory-elements. It should be appreciated by the clinician that memories of the past are, in fact, manifestations in the client's present. Some subtle questions or remarks as given below can often be judicially used by the practitioner in order to tease out the essence of the client's distress.

- So what is happening now in your mind?
- What have we got here?
- Can you stay in that place and extract the essence from it?
- Can you just stay in that scene and discover what else you can extract?
- Can you investigate this element further?
- What else can you learn from what you are experiencing right now?
- I am confused over this, can you explain this to me?
- What else happens here?
- What do you think the other people in this scene are thinking about the situation?
- Can you imaginatively read the minds of those about you?
- Can you just allow your mind to show you what it needs to show you here?
- Could you pause a moment and see if you can investigate this further?
- Could you pause a while in this scene, take your time and see if there is anything else you can learn from this situation?
- Can you review this event, second by second, to discover if there is anything else you can extract from it?

Often the client can be introduced to the free-association process in just one or two sessions. Once the skill of free association has been acquired by the client, she will be able to employ it with ease in order to explore her own psyche. By this means, the client will have been given a tool that she can utilise in subsequent sessions or, indeed, on other occasions when she needs, for example, to find an object that she has lost or to retrieve a forgotten memory.

If the client is in full flight when the session-time is drawing to an end, however, the practitioner will need to negotiate carefully with her in order to ensure that she does not lose the benefit derived from the session yet, at the same time, she does not leave the consulting room having opened up Pandora's box. The therapist, in such circumstances, might tactfully ask the client to take a snapshot of her recollections or imagery and to put this precious material in a safe place such as an envelop or a casket. The client may then be given the post-hypnotic suggestion to return to this place for further work unaided or on the next occasion when she meets the practitioner. The client may now be invited to continue to process and/or to resolve this issue but will also have been given licence to return to the matter in future sessions should the need be pressing.

When the client stubbornly refuses to submit to the process of free association, this form of underlying resistance can often be overcome by directly addressing her unconscious mind in a manner that can indicate that it has failed her. In this way, the client will not take on the blame for any resistance because she will, in any case, be at the mercy of her own unconscious processes. The following passage will have the effect of mounting an assault on the client's unconscious mind for failing in its duty of care and protection.

Waging war on the unconscious mind ...

Even though you can hear me, I shall now be addressing only your unconscious mind. You can, therefore, relax now and let your mind listen quietly to what I have to say.

Unconscious, I need to have a serious word with you because you are failing in your duty of care and protection of my client. I was relying on you to deliver the goods and, in fact, I now realise that you are neglecting your duties and taking time out for a holiday. This is not your role in life because your role is the care and protection of my client. I have asked my client to relate her thoughts to me as a therapist charged with the assistance of one who is in much distress and now I find that you are letting my client down. My client needs to resolve her distress and, in order to do this, I need to be able to communicate with her. It is, therefore, your job to get on with the task of recalling, examining, investigating, exploring and considering her thoughts, sensations, imagery, impressions and recollections. It is your role to spill out your contents together with your reactions, opinions, attitudes and feelings. This is the way in which my client can recover from her distress and live a full and fruitful life free from emotional baggage.

My client, therefore, desperately needs your help. My client is begging and crying out for your help and I am relying on you now to assist her in this important process. So, I would ask you now please to reveal to me and my client those aspects of her past that are of vital importance to her healing process. Thank you, unconscious.

Age-Regression

> Fundamental to all uncovering of forgotten memories is the notion that,
> in order to reach them, one must regress in time to the experience that
> has to be recalled.
> *– Edgar Barnett*

Often the analytical hypnotherapist will need to utilise techniques of age-regression combined with free association in order to assist the client in accessing those experiences that have caused her distress and that reside in the past and, especially, in childhood. The practitioner, however, should bear in mind that, when the client appears to be accessing aspects of the past, these experiences are, in fact, held in her mind as if they were constituting the present. The client can be encouraged to investigate her own psyche using a range of regressive techniques under the therapist's guidance. Let us now consider a number of techniques that can be used by the therapist in order to assist the client to access disturbing or traumatic experiences.

> Age regression as a category of techniques provides the opportunity to
> go back in time, whether it be into the recent or distant past, in order to
> recover forgotten or repressed memories of significant events or to "work
> through" old memories in order to reach new conclusions.
> *– Michael Yapko*

Age-regression will almost always be a major part of therapeutic practice because past trauma will need to be unearthed by an investigation of the client's past experience – both her recent history and the far distant past. Although the human organism will live in the present moment, the client will be an undeniable product of her past experience and will combine the past with the present as if it were one single unit. It has been said that thoughts in the client's mind that constitute so-called memories of the past are really only a manifestation in the present and symptoms will remain when the past/present matter cannot be successfully accessed and resolved. The traumatised client, for instance, may well have only a very vague memory of events in the past and most, if not all, of her recollection of any traumatic experiences may have been either totally or partially repressed by her unconscious mind. Often when the client reports total memory-loss for childhood, this can be an indicator than trauma, neglect or abuse, in some form, may have occurred in her life. The practitioner, however, should be careful not to pounce on this information and make a definitive pronouncement to the client. It will be the practitioner's professional duty to keep any such suspicions or theories firmly imprisoned within his own mind. Failure to carry out this inviolable golden rule will constitute therapeutic malpractice on the practitioner's part.

If the client truly has difficulty in accessing her childhood recollections and this obstacle cannot be overcome, then it may, perhaps, be more appropriate for her to describe the present. The client, for example, who may talk about a disgruntled manager at work, an uncaring friend or an unreasonable partner may well be describing a relationship with a significant other in which negative transference has developed (see Chapter 13, Volume 1 – "Transference and Countertransference"). The client, in such circumstances, should be encouraged to relate all her thoughts and feelings about the present-day problem-person as a means of realising the significance of her outpourings. Often this course of action will lead the client to gain the appropriate insight as a natural process whereby the long-forgotten horrors of the past have manifested in the readily-recalled present. It matters not, therefore, where the client cuts the washing-line because any point along the line will inevitably bring it down, although some clothes will hit the ground first. The practitioner should, of course, be aware that while age-regression can be purposely induced in hypnosis, the likelihood will be that the client may spontaneously regress into the past – usually because her psyche will take the opportunity in the therapeutic setting of gaining access to stress-related matter that remains unresolved.

In undertaking age-regression with the client, the therapist may wish to focus on experiential memory, emotive memory or somatic memory (see Chapter 10, Volume 1 – "Memory"). Let us consider the nature of these differing forms of recollection in the context of regressive therapeutic techniques.

> There are three phases of regression therapy. The first phase is client preparation, normally done during the pre-induction interview and/or the previous sessions. The second phase is to guide the client back into time in his/her mind – like imaginary time travel – and getting and keeping the client in the regression. The third is the handling of abreactions – the actual emotional clearing itself, and the re-learning that follows.
> – Roy Hunter

Exploring experiential memory

> When does memory begin? What is the youngest age from which an adult may have a clear and direct recollection of an event? What is *your* earliest memory, and how old were you when the event occurred? Your earliest memory is most probably very much like a snapshot – an image without continuity.
> – Michael Yapko

Experiential memory will be that part of the client's experience that will relate to her recollection of the events in her life. The client, for example, might recall being told off at school or sitting alone in her bedroom at home as a child.

Regressive techniques may be employed in order to access the client's experiential memory in general or, alternatively, the practitioner may use this methodology as a means of event-pinpointing. The client, for example, who had a number of presenting symptoms and a number of pockets of anxiety-provoking episodes to consider might be advised to take an overview approach using free association. Alternatively, the client who presents with one specific symptom – such as examination nerves or nail-biting – could be guided towards the event that she might, perhaps, consider to be the seeding event. This course of action could be taken when the practitioner believes that the client should be directed towards a given period of her experience as a starting point for investigative therapy.

The practitioner may use a variety of strategies in order to encourage the client to examine the past. The client could, for example, be invited to visualise a photograph album or a picture-book in which snapshots of her early life are portrayed. Similarly, the client may be asked to visualise and then to open a precious casket or a fascinating book. The client could also be asked to recall key events in her life such as a birthday or a Christmas celebration in early childhood. The client could be asked to describe what it would be like to be a child as if she were taking someone on a journey through her own childhood. The client, moreover, could be invited to imagine what life was like on the day on which she was born. There will be no limit to the variety and plethora of imaginative ways in which age-regression can be engendered for the client. The practitioner, however, would be advised to induce hypnosis using some relaxation techniques or some safe-place imagery before embarking on regressive methodology.

> A regression is much more powerful if re-lived in the imagination rather
> than simply remembered with the logical mind.
> *– Roy Hunter*

The following passage can be used by the practitioner in order to encourage age-regression in the client who appears to be susceptible to a fairly straightforward and direct approach. The piece could, for example, be suitable for the first occasion when the client is invited under hypnosis to reflect on the past.

Reflecting on the past …

And maybe now that your work for the day is done, you can reflect on your life. Perhaps you can reflect on your current life. Consider your home and family and the way things are at home. Consider your work and the colleagues, customers or other people whom you meet daily. What are these people like and how do you react to them? Do you feel intimidated by work colleagues or superiors? Do you feel that you are the only one with dedication to the job? Do people make impossible demands on your time or your patience? Perhaps you can consider all these factors now as if you were actually at work or at home.

Perhaps you can also remember that time when you first went out to work. That time when you were launching yourself on the world. That time when you left the safety of home or school and were obliged to earn your own keep. That time when you were trying to assert your independence, aiming to launch yourself into adult life and planning to carve out a career for yourself. Maybe you can now consider all the uncertainties of that enterprise. Consider how you felt and how you were accepted by others.

Maybe you can also think of your school-days. What was it like then? Perhaps you can remember your last day at school or your first day at school. How different those two occasions were. When you left school you were stepping out into the big wide world and trying to make your mark – perhaps overshadowed by others who had trodden that path before. Maybe you can think about school. Who was there? Who loved you and who hated you? Were there many bullies or did you do most of the bullying yourself? Were there teachers who were helpful and kind or were they unjust and bad-tempered? When you first started school, did you dread leaving home? Just have a close look now at your first day at school – see it as it really was. Remember the fears or uncertainties, the confusion and the sadness at having to leave home.

Now maybe you can think of those days long ago before you ever went to school. When there was just you and your siblings, or just you and Mum or just you on your own – perhaps alone in your room lost in your own thoughts. How did you feel back then? Just let your emotions gently guide you. You know, the mind has a magic way of simply taking you where you need to go. A magic way of looking at and examining that which you may need to look at today – right now. Just let your mind drift and relax. Just let your thoughts and feelings take you where you need to go. Be guided by those innermost feelings that can now come to the surface. Let your feelings guide you because, in a moment, I am going to ask you where your mind has taken you. And, you know, you can easily speak to me and still remain very relaxed and lost in your own thoughts. Speaking to me and, yet, really just talking to yourself. So let your mind take you where it needs to go and, perhaps, you can very slowly and gently share some of your thoughts with me now – whenever you are ready. Where has your mind taken you?

The passage below also demonstrates the way in which the practitioner can stir up the client's imaginative processes or appeal to her childish instincts when undertaking regressive techniques. This passage may also serve to break down any logical resistance that the client may have to therapeutic investigation.

Fairies at the bottom of the garden ...

You know, when we are very young, we are often told that there are fairies at the bottom of the garden. And, when we are very small, we believe everything that those giants, known as adults, tell us. In fact, we might one day look out of our bedroom window and believe that we actually see the fairies dancing at the bottom of the garden. We watch with excitement as they play. Perhaps we see a fairy curling up in the centre of a flower or hanging from the branch of a tree. Perhaps we see the fairies dancing in a magic fairy-ring or casting enchanting magic spells. Perhaps we can watch a fairy fly or turn into a pumpkin – just for our own entertainment. One day perhaps a fairy may hop up on to our windowsill and beckon us to join the fairy-ring so that we too can dance and play in the sunshine or in the moonlight. You can follow the fairy down to the bottom of the garden. You can follow the fairy-footsteps or a trail of sparkling fairy-dust in order to reach the fairy-dell.

When we get older, however, we soon learn, sadly, that there are no fairies at the bottom of the garden. We may unhappily miss their enchantment or we may never give it a second's thought. When we really grow up, however, we learn that there are, indeed, fairies at the bottom of every garden and we have simply to look in order to find them again.

Perhaps you can remember that time when you first met the fairies at the bottom of the garden – perhaps a time when you were looking out of your bedroom window and thought you caught a glimpse of them. Can you remember that time? Can you tell me about that time in your life when you may have been sitting quietly in your room or looking out of your bedroom window?

Exploring emotive memory

> Watkins gave the name affect bridge to a technique in which regression is accomplished by means of establishing a direct connection between the present, in which an uncomfortable emotion exists, and the earlier situation in which this same emotion was first experienced. In practice the hypnotherapist draws the patient's attention to the emotion that he is feeling or to the symptom that is present; such emotion is enhanced by increasing the focus of attention, and when sufficiently strong, the therapist is able to lead the patient back to its origin and effectively bridge him from the present to the past causative experience.
> – *Edgar Barnett*

When accessing emotive memory, the client can be guided back into the past by being asked to focus on current emotive responses that can provide a link to past experiences. This technique has also become known as the *affects bridge* or the *emotive link* because the client's emotive manifestations can form a bridge between her current experiences and the negative aspects of her past that have resulted in current-day psychological distress. When the client has difficulty in accessing emotive reactions from the past or when she claims that her mind has gone blank, for instance, then the practitioner may decide to approach her past distresses using an emotive bridging technique. The passage below will provide a basis for age-regression utilising emotive-bridging methodology.

Let your feelings speak …

Just allow yourself now to focus on those feelings inside. Perhaps you can even amplify those feelings. Perhaps look more intently at the quality of those feelings. Are they confusing or well defined? Are they strong or vague? Do they give you a sinking feeling? Do they make you feel despair or hope for the future? Maybe those feelings have a story to tell. Maybe there is a message which that part of you deep inside has to convey. Listen quietly and intently to those inner messages.

Feel those feelings and amplify them still further. The more you can feel those feelings, the more you will be able to release them. Perhaps you can imagine those feelings draining away from you. Making their way down through your limbs and out through the palms of your hand or the soles of your feet or, even, out through the top of your head. And, as these emotions begin to release, maybe you can also let them tell their own story. How long have they been around? When have they appeared in the past? When was the very first time you might have noticed those unpleasant sensations? Just let your emotions talk to your mind. Just let your feelings guide your thoughts to the place where they need to go.

Maybe count up to three in your mind and then let your mind reveal the place way back in time where those feelings were born. The mind has a magic way of taking you to that place that will have been the birthplace of those feelings. Just let it happen and when you are ready perhaps you can share with me the first thought – whatever it may be – that comes to mind.

The "affects bridge" is the technique by which the patient is guided to discover the relevant point in his life, the source of trauma and its consequences. The underlying hypothesis for this method is that the affect the patient currently experiences inappropriately, in the context of any symptom he may manifest, reflects the affect related or bound to the causal or archetypal experience.
– *Hellmut Karle & Jennifer Boys*

Exploring somatic memory

> Body work involves the use of therapeutic massage or touch to aid in the
> release of feeling blockages centered in the body. When areas of your
> body that contain a body memory are subject to pressure, there is
> increased sensitivity in that area. Often imagistic, feeling or acting-out
> memories are also stimulated. By sorting through the reactions your
> body has to the massage or touch, you can reconstruct a memory or a
> fragment of a memory.
> – Renee Fredrickson

When accessing somatic memory or cell memory, the client can be
guided back into the past by being requested to observe those bodily sensations that can provide a link to past experiences. This technique has also become known as the *somatic bridge* or *bodily link*
because the client's physical sensations can form a bridge between
her current experiences and the negative aspects of her past that
have caused physiological discomfort or tissue-damage. The following passage could be used by the practitioner in order to access
the client's somatic memory.

Let your body speak …

Sometimes when we have a cold or a headache, these symptoms are trying to
tell us something of importance that affects our wellbeing. It is as if the body
is trying to communicate with the mind. It can be almost as if there were a
wire or a silver thread that gives a direct link to your mind and attaches those
sensations directly to your thoughts. See what your body has to say to your
mind?

When we are frightened, we tend to withdraw and our whole body will adopt
a shrinking or cowering posture. When we are angry, we tend to wave our
arms about or punch the air. When we feel unwell, we tend to hide under the
bedcovers and retreat from the world in the hope of soothing our pains. Just
ponder for a moment on the way in which your body may have reacted in the
past. That pain in your neck or that ache in your back may be trying to tell you
something. That touch of flu may have a reason for being there. That nagging
headache can be examined in order to decipher its meaning and its reason for
existence.

Perhaps you can consider and reflect on your thoughts and slowly pick up the
messages that your body is desperate to convey. Take time out now and allow
your body to speak to your mind. Often the body can allow the mind to settle
in that place way back in the past that has significance for you. Sometimes,
when the body speaks loud and clear, your mind can take you to that exact
spot back in your past. Sometimes we can relive the past right here in this

moment as if it were happening right now. Just let that process slowly and gently occur for you. I shall count to three, and then maybe you can share those thoughts with me – whatever they may be, however, nonsensical or mysterious your thoughts may be. Perhaps you can tell me now in as much detail as possible what it is that you are thinking about.

> A human being – in other words our biological system – is composed of memories – memories born of experiences compiled in the organism by numerous biological systems. These may even reach back beyond the origins of mankind. These biological memories form the basis of our physical being.
> – *Konrad Stettbacher*

Past-Life Regression

> The topic of past life regression is still very hotly debated both inside and outside the hypnotherapy profession. It is a proven fact that clients in hypnosis may be intentionally guided into what seems to be memories of a former lifetime. Stranger yet is the fact that some clients who do not believe in former lives may, on rare occasions, trip out spontaneously into real or imagined memory of a "past" life during what was intended to be a present life regression. Regardless of whether one chooses to facilitate past life regressions, they will occur – and therefore simply cannot be ignored.
> – *Roy Hunter*

Past-life regression can be a means of enabling the client to access a reality for which she cannot account in terms of her current life. Often, this form of regression can be undertaken when standard age-regression methodology seems to have only a limited efficacy for the client. A number of explanations – mostly of a controversial nature – have been put forward in order to account for this phenomenon. The nature of beliefs in this area will, of course, be a matter of personal preference for the practitioner. The therapist who is not committed to any given steadfast belief, however, may simply wish to consider this approach without too much enquiry or scepticism as a means of assisting the client.

Past-life regression, when the phenomenon is taken literally, is believed to be a manifestation of a previous life that the client has led as part of the theory of reincarnation. The hypnotherapist who actively and successfully practises psychospiritual forms of therapy will fall into this category. Possibly the most famous advocate of this principle was Jung himself, who acknowledged the power of the collective unconscious mind and who delved committedly and unequivocally into mysticism. Alternatively, the phenomenon of past-life regression has been accounted for in terms of metaphorical imagery (see Chapter 14, Volume 1 – "Dreams and Symbolic Imagery"). This school of thought will explain past-life regression as a means whereby the client can elect to distance herself from unacceptable or psychologically-painful experiences while, simultaneously, finding within herself a viable means of tapping into such information. The client, therefore, can explore her own psyche, can discharge unpleasant emotive reactions and can reconcile her conflicts by dissociating herself from the distressing knowledge that trauma has previously afflicted her in her early life.

Although past-life regression will be a subject that can be hotly debated in therapeutic circles, the value of it as an imaginative technique can be utilised in hypnoanalytic practice – particularly if the practitioner enjoys working in this way regardless of his personal beliefs. In general, however, it would be arrogant of the practitioner to attempt to impose his personal views on the client or to persuade her either of the validity or the falsehood of what she imagines in the therapeutic setting. The practitioner should, naturally, respect the fact that the client has a mind of her own. The client's mind will, after all, be her own personal property and she should be entitled to her own steadfast beliefs or her unshakable scepticism as part of the process of independence, maturity and self-discovery that she seeks. Often, however, the client who will be inclined to follow a spiritual path will be attracted to the practitioner who may practise techniques appropriate to a spiritually-oriented discipline. The analytical therapist of whatever persuasion, therefore, may be advised to keep an open mind on the use of past-life regression.

> Overloads of pain, feelings of torture and being left alone before, during, and after birth will permanently impair our ability to lead a fulfilled life and detract from our pleasures at being alive.
> – *Konrad Stettbacher*

Let us now consider a case-study example in which the client explored the reasons why she had a guilt-complex by entering what could have been an alternative existence. Neither the therapist nor the client had a belief in reincarnation but the imaginative process served to give the client an appreciation of her residual guilt and to understand that there are certain things in life over which one does not have control. Although past-life regression is a controversial subject, this case-study example illustrates the way in which such methodology had a positive benefit for a client who was a confirmed sceptic.

Case-study example – suicidal tendencies

A female client was suffering from suicidal depression and had, for some time, been unsuccessfully searching for some meaning in her life.

The client found herself imagining a scene – without any prompting from the therapist – in which she was dying from consumption in a previous century. The scene was clearly not depicting a realistic event from the client's current life but she claimed that she felt as if the scene were a part of a previous existence. The client described herself in the scene with her son and her sister at her bedside. The client, incidentally, was an only child and had no children. At the doorway of the room was also a shadowy figure whom the client described as her sister's husband. Both her son and her sister were distraught because the client was dying while the man regarded her impending death as an inconvenience. The client expressed extreme agitation because she was leaving her young son without a mother to take care of him. The client realised, however, that she could not prevent her own death and that she was not dying out of choice. The client kept repeating the words "I am not to blame" and this theme was echoed in many ways throughout her therapy.

Finally, the client realised that her son was a manifestation of the aggressive and guilt-ridden part of her own psyche and that her sister and brother-in-law were representations of her own parents. The client's brother-in-law, who had appeared as the sinister figure in her imagination, was to become her neglectful father in her current life. This imaginative trip into a supposed previous life was the client's way of telling herself that she was not the guilty party when her father had physically deserted her in childhood. Furthermore, the client's son was a personification of the deep sorrow that the client had experienced throughout her life.

Guided Imagery

> It is important to remember that retrieving repressed memories is never
> an orderly, logical process. When you access your imagistic memory,
> other kinds of memory are stimulated also. Images are interspersed with
> feelings, body memories, and urges to say or act out what happened
> to you.
> – *Renee Fredrickson*

Guided imagery (or *guided-affect imagery*) can be utilised by the
practitioner as a means of enabling the client to express herself in
imaginative terms in order to provide her with access to her unconscious processes. The client may be encouraged by the practitioner
to describe her semiconscious thoughts or daydreams as a
reflection of the contents of her psyche (see Chapter 14, Volume 1
– "Dreams and Symbolic Imagery"). Usually, the practitioner can
kick-start a guided-imagery process but, in doing so, can then
encourage the client to take the lead in telling her story – making
full use of her creative and imaginative faculties. Guided-imagery
methodology can take many forms, so let us consider some examples.

> GAI [Guided Affective Imagery] works with symbolic representations of
> subconscious problems. The client is asked to imagine part of a
> landscape. This can be, for example, a meadow, a stream, a forest or a
> mountain. The therapist suggests one of these pictures, say the meadow,
> and asks the client to describe in great detail what sort of meadow he can
> see in his imagination. The client will come up with a spontaneous image
> that will allow insight into his attitudes and background.
> – *Vera Peiffer*

The case-study example below neatly illustrates the way in which
symbolic imagery can reveal aspects of the client's unconscious
material.

Case-study example – lack of control
This male client sought therapy because he felt that other people
were continually manipulating him and taking advantage of him.

During hypnotic investigation, the client visualised a boat with its
sail up. At the front of the boat was a young man looking ahead
while, at the rear of the boat, was an older man who was steering.
Judicious enquiry on the practitioner's part allowed the client to
make an instant interpretation of his imagery. The client recognised

that he had never been allowed to direct his own life and that his father (an officer in the navy) had always decided where and what he should do in life. The client, therefore, had spent most of his life trying to rebel against his father's dictates. This realisation served to release the client from this former tyranny that had manifested in terms of his current relationships with others.

Creative visualisation

> Emotional problems are revealed in the symbolism of the landscape and any animals or objects in it. Other people can be perceived as far-away houses, indicating the detachment the client experiences from others.
> – *Vera Peiffer*

Creative visualisation can often be a useful means of allowing the client to explore aspects of her psychic conflict. Creative visualisation will be particularly useful when amalgamated with hypnotic techniques because the client will naturally be employing imaginative processes and, therefore, will be in a suitable frame of mind be to gently nudged forward by the practitioner. By employing her imaginative processes, the client may be invited to envision a scene or a landscape – preferably one in which she can view herself. From this initial image, a story can then evolve that will purely be the product of the client's imagination and this experience can then tell a significant tale that can reveal aspects of her psychic distress.

> Creative visualisation is the technique of using your imagination to create what you want in your life. There is nothing at all new, strange, or unusual about creative visualisation. You are already using it every day, every minute in fact. It is your natural power of imagination, the basic creative energy of the universe which you use constantly, whether or not you are aware of it.
> – *Shakti Gawain*

The following case-study example illustrates the way in which creative visualisation can be effectively utilised by the analytical practitioner.

Case-study example – anxiety states
A client who was suffering from a series of high-anxiety states was invited by the practitioner to explore an image that came into his mind when he entered the hypnotic state during analytical therapy.

The client described an outdoor scene in which he was looking down a hillside towards a country cottage. The sun was shining in this scene and the client was content to observe it. The client was then invited by the therapist to go down the hillside and to explore the cottage. The client found that the cottage was well furnished, clean and tidy, but that the back garden was very unkempt. The client was then asked whether he was happy with the way in which the garden appeared in his imaginative scene. The client replied that he was very anxious about the way in which the garden had been treated and then, of his own volition, set about tidying it up. The client removed weeds, laid a lawn and a path and generally landscaped the garden to his own design. The client also discovered some rusty farm machinery in his garden that he was able to restore and then return to the local farmer.

At the next session, this client was able to report that the excavation of this garden had lifted a great load from his mind and had relieved him of a great deal of anxiety over the state of his own property. It was as if the imagery contained within his own creative imagination was reminiscent not only of the client's current life but also of his therapeutic journey.

Hidden-observer techniques

> GAI [Guided Affective Imagery] not only allows the therapist insight into the client's emotional condition, it also gives her a tool to bring about positive change and to combat long-standing fears by helping the client confront them in his images.
> – *Vera Peiffer*

Hidden-observer techniques (or *dissociative techniques*) can assist the client to arrive step by step at the primary incident in which traumatic stress was originally seeded. By using these back-door techniques, the client can often allow the accompanying pent-up emotive expression to be fully released when more direct methods have proved ineffective. The client may be asked, for example, to view herself from a distant vantage-point in order to review an episode in her life that has previously caused overwhelming distress or about which she may feel disinclined to deal directly.

In my view, the process of encouraging clients is often one of guiding
them into a position where they can acknowledge personal strengths and
resources previously overlooked in themselves.
– *Michael Yapko*

In the case-study example below, hidden-observer techniques were
employed virtually spontaneously by the client when dealing with
a consignment of guilt and fear about the fact that she had been
physically abused by her mother.

Case-study example – childhood violence
This female client reported a childhood of violent abuse that had
left her with a guilt-complex about the fact that she had probably
been a naughty child and, therefore, had warranted the
punishment.

The client regressed to some of her earlier experiences but kept
coming up with the belief that she had been a naughty child and a
nuisance to her mother. The client considered herself to have been
inherently a problem-child and deemed that she deserved some
form of punishment. When asked to explore this erroneous belief,
the client visualised a scene in which her mother was standing in
her bedroom looking sternly at her. The client also saw another
person in this scene whom she could not easily identify. The client
was then asked to imagine who this unknown person was, what
she was thinking about and what she was feeling. After a long
silence, the client replied that this unknown person was feeling
guilty and yet she was afraid of the stern looks from the mother-
figure. The client was then invited to see if this unknown person
had a name. Again after a long silence, the client replied that the
person's name was Justice. Justice was then invited to judge the situation that she was beholding.

The client observed that Justice was afraid that the young child
would be severely beaten by her mother, who was angry and frustrated at that time. Justice was also invited to view things realistically and to decide whether the child had, in fact, committed any
heinous crimes for which such punishment should be exacted.
Justice considered that there would be no justification for such a
degree of violence but felt that the young child had needed a way
of explaining her mother's actions because she had been unable to
stand up for herself when she had been physically abused.

This client, therefore, came to an important realisation by dissociating herself from the reality of her childhood. Simultaneously, of course, the client learned to appreciate that her mother's conduct was utterly unacceptable and that she herself was in no way to blame for actioning this violent behaviour.

Revivification

> I have known doctors who, for practice, will take the time to regress a
> patient to an early age to see reactions that are not of a startling nature;
> they like the idea that they can take a patient back to the time when he
> was two or three years old and let him see again how the toys under the
> Christmas tree looked.
> *– Dave Elman*

Revivification implies that the client will relive an aspect of her past experience in the therapeutic setting rather than merely recall an event from memory. With this method of enquiry, therefore, the client might be invited to relive a specific aspect of the past as if it were occurring in actuality. Alternatively, the client might be requested to describe imaginatively and hypothetically the way in which she might have been teased at school or might have been reprimanded by an aggressive teacher rather than struggle to recall a specific incident from childhood. Revivification techniques, therefore, echo the sentiments of gestalt therapy and can also be combined with other forms of regressive methodology (see Chapter 8, Volume 1 – "Gestalt Therapy").

Great caution, of course, will need to be exercised by the practitioner when using this method of enquiry with the client who might confidently believe that certain events actually took place. The practitioner should be aware that the mind is readily capable of confabulation, especially in hypnosis, and that information envisioned in this way could present the client with additional difficulties if she elects to act on the product of such revivification. If the client "relives" an abusive incident, for example, that did not, in fact, occur – even though it may, indeed, have a symbolic significance – then this may lead her to level a false accusation against an innocent party.

Age regression is an intense experiential utilisation of memory. Age
regression techniques involve either taking the client back in time to
some experience in order to re-experience it (called "revivification") as if
it were happening in the here-and-now, or simply having the person
remember the experience as intensely as possible (called "hypermnesia").
In revivification, the client is immersed in the experience, reliving it
exactly as the memory was incorporated at the time it actually happened.
In hypermnesia, the person is in the present while simultaneously
recalling vividly the details of the memory.
– Michael Yapko

The following case-study example relates to a client who was beset
by a low sense of self-esteem and illustrates the way in which
revivification methodology can be used in order to access the truth
of a situation.

Case-study example – low self-esteem
This male client had been the victim of bullying at school and had,
consequently, suffered from a low sense of self-worth and a
debased self-esteem.

The client reported that he had been the subject of intensive bullying at boarding school because he was timid and shy as a child. As
a developing child, the client had been terrified by this victimisation but had been unable to tell anyone in his family of his plight. The
client also mentioned that he had been picked on by teachers and, on
a few occasions, had been sent to the headmaster for punishment.

The client was invited to relive his schooldays under hypnosis and
encouraged to imagine himself back at school. The client clearly
remembered standing outside the headmaster's room awaiting the
dreaded caning. When he was able to relive this episode, the client
was able to describe his feelings in detail, his physical sensations
and his thought processes. The client was, therefore, able to relate
what actually happened to him in the headmaster's office step by
step. The client shook in the chair, perspired and recaptured the
intense form of anxiety that he had, no doubt, experienced at the
time. In this way, the client was able to explore in minute detail his
thoughts and feelings about his punishment. The fact that the client
could relive this aspect of his traumatic past experience paved the
way for him to initiate abreactive discharge and to resolve his feelings of lack of self-worth once a cognitive appreciation of his ordeal
had been explored.

Rebirthing

> Each birth has different consequences. It can become a lifelong support,
> the foundation of our primal trust – or it can disfigure every day of
> our lives.
> – *Konrad Stettbacher*

Rebirthing will be a means of dealing with an unresolved birth trauma from which the client may be suffering. If the client can be asked to imagine her birth process and to link her current psychological problems to this event, then a resolution of current trauma can occur. The client who had a difficult birth might, for example, wish to express fear and uncertainty about her arrival in the world. Sometimes the client may well be expressing her feelings about the family or the situation into which she was born during rebirthing and such suppressed emotion can, therefore, be naturally discharged in this way. No-one has ever been able to prove or to disprove whether the mind is capable of recalling the birth-experience but, when using this methodology, the client can often find a means of expressing her negative or distressing feelings about her initiation into family life (see Chapter 10, Volume 1 – "Memory").

> Birth experience information was obtained from 876 patients, generally
> those seeking therapy during the latter stages of the period surveyed.
> Of these, 245 or 28% reported negative feelings attached to the occasion
> of their own birth.
> – *Edgar Barnett*

The following case-study example is indicative of the way in which the client can benefit from exploration of the birth-experience.

Case-study example – agoraphobia
This female client suffered severely from agoraphobia, that had confined her to her home on a number of occasions.

The client, under hypnosis, found herself feeling as if she were in her mother's womb. The client was then invited to stay with this sensation and simply to observe her impressions, feelings and imagery. The client reported initially that she felt safe and warm but later remarked that she felt anxious because she could hear noises that she could not identify. It transpired that these noises were the sound of raised voices but the client could not understand what was being said. The client was, in fact, remembering that her parents had been in constant conflict and their arguments had been a major feature of her childhood for as long as she could remember.

This prebirth experience – whether real or imagined – was the client's way of facing up to the fact that her fears and terror of the outside world were attributed to the unhappy climate into which she had been plunged at birth.

Therapeutic Writing and Drawing

Another means of helping the client to access her unconscious conflict can be achieved by asking her to represent her thoughts either in written or in pictorial form. This medium can often be very useful for the client who may need to find an alternative means of expressing herself other than via the spoken word. This form of therapeutic unravelling can take place either in the consulting room or away from it. The client may, for example, be invited to engage in automatic writing or drawing under the influence of formal hypnosis or self-hypnosis. Moreover, the client may wish to continue the outpouring process away from the consulting room and these techniques can provide a convenient means of satisfying this need. Let us now consider the various ways in which the client may benefit from utilising writing and drawing techniques.

Journal-writing

> Writing, especially spontaneous, free-association writing, can often tap into buried memories.
> – Renee Fredrickson

The client may be asked to keep a journal that can be written between therapeutic sessions as a means of enabling her to keep up a continual dialogue with her own unconscious mind. Such writing can involve the client not only in the outpouring process but also as a means of resolving conflicts and disturbance on an ongoing basis. A therapeutic journal may be used to record the client's daily events, dreams, thoughts, ideas, attitudes and insightful experiences. When the content of such a journal is left to the client's discretion, a full and fruitful cathartic process can often be enhanced by this means.

Letter-writing

> A therapy based on writing and reflection cannot, however, be a complete substitute – at least not a reliable one – for the speaking/feeling part of the therapy that completes the therapeutic interaction.
> – *Konrad Stettbacher*

When the client has a number of issues with a third party, she could be asked to write an imaginary letter to that person without any intention of sending it to its recipient. Letter-writing as a therapeutic technique may also be combined with self-hypnosis as a means of aiding the client's thought processes and free expression of opinions, feelings and convictions. The advantage of employing this methodology will be to give the client carte blanche to state her case safe in the knowledge that the intended recipient cannot retaliate or use persuasive argument in order to counteract any claims. The client may wish to write just a single letter or, perhaps, a series of letters to the problem-person. A series of letters written over an extended period of time can usually render some positive results for the client because she will be given an opportunity, at leisure, to divest herself of damaging emotive reactions and disturbing thoughts. The client will usually be asked to write such a letter away from the consulting room at a time when she feels fully inclined to express herself without let or hindrance. This method, of course, can also be employed by the client long after she has fled the therapeutic nest.

Automatic writing

> Age regression testing demonstrates the tendency for some hypnotic subjects to experience the events of the past and the present at the same time while producing convincing performances of successful age regression response in other ways. An example of this is the age-regressed subject who writes in childlike fashion when asked to indicate his or her name, but who describes the scene unfolding as one that is enjoyed while the subject knows at the same time that he or she is really somewhere else.
> – *Peter Sheehan*

Automatic writing is yet another device for unearthing the client's unconscious conflict or trauma. With this technique, the client can be put into trance and then asked to write a message directly from her unconscious mind. The process of accessing the client's unconscious mind via symbolic imagery in this way can be awesome and profound. By this means, a seemingly nonsensical word or a phrase written in hypnosis may later reveal to the client its unconscious meaning. In many cases, what appears ostensibly to be meaningless to the practitioner will frequently have a special significance for the client when her writing can be leisurely studied and deciphered. Automatic-writing methodology can often be utilised by the practitioner when the client experiences difficulty in consciously communicating with her unconscious material. If the client, for example, were to experience difficulty with the free-association process or were finding difficulty in interpreting the information that her unconscious mind had delivered, then this indirect approach can often be employed to great effect.

The following passage could be employed by the practitioner in order to facilitate the hypnotic-writing process and should provide some inspiration for formulating a suitable technique for the client. In employing such an approach, the practitioner's objective will be continually to encourage the client to reproduce something on the writing-paper for later analysis and interpretation.

Automatic writing …

Make yourself still more comfortable and allow yourself to find a level of hypnosis that will encourage a still deeper relaxation and calmness. Accept that for a while there will be nothing whatsoever for you to do. Just continue to listen to the sound of my voice and allow yourself to be guided down to a still calmness – a kind of serene stillness. Perhaps you can find for yourself a place of peace where no-one wants anything from you, where no-one needs anything from you. A place where there is simply nothing for you to think about or to do – only to be.

Now for a while I want you just to allow that feeling to continue and allow it to guide you down with every out breath. And just relax while I speak to your unconscious mind. Just for a short while, I want your unconscious mind just to do nothing because, in a moment, I shall pass to you a pad of paper and a pen and I want your unconscious mind to take control of your writing hand. I would like your unconscious mind to write, draw or doodle something that is directly related to the question you have come here to resolve. That's right, to write, draw or doodle something that will help you to understand the nature and the cause of your discomfort. Now it does not matter how this is done. Your unconscious mind will automatically select for you the most appropriate way of showing you – by writing, drawing or doodling – something that will shed sufficient light on the matter to enable you to understand clearly the nature of your problem.

Now that you have the pad and pen right there in your hands, I want your unconscious mind to write, draw or doodle something that will help you to gain the necessary understanding in order to free yourself from the problem you came here to resolve. And when you have finished – and not before – you can then place the pad and pen together and hand it back to me – that's right.

Now, in a moment, I shall hold the pad in front of you so that you can see what your unconscious mind needs to communicate to you. Take some time and allow your sight to adjust as you open your eyes – still remaining relaxed and allowing your mind to absorb the information. Soon the reason for your disturbance may become very apparent to you.

> Automatic writing clearly requires significant conscious/unconscious dissociation and the writing hand must be beyond conscious control or awareness. In the use of this technique, unconscious information is communicated to the therapist without conscious knowledge.
> – *Edgar Barnett*

Below is a case-study example that shows the way in which the impact of written symbolism can have a profound effect on the client.

Case-study example – depressive disorder

This female client sought therapy because she felt emotionally oversensitive and would burst into tears far too frequently.

When hypnotic drawing was used with this client, she reproduced the word "dead" in a childlike scrawl. The client then immediately started to cry and claimed that she thought she had dealt with this issue previously in therapy. The client was then encouraged to revisit the scene to which her mind had guided her. The client recalled that her mother had died when she was four and that no-one had told her anything about this loss. The client could see several people crying around her but no-one had spoken to her. The client had previously intellectualised her recollection by simply understanding her reactions logically. Now the client gave herself permission to mourn this tragic loss via the hypnoanalytic route. Automatic hypnotic writing, thus, had facilitated the grieving process that the client had never hitherto been able to do. The client's depression lifted within weeks of this abreactive release.

Automatic drawing

> Art therapy involves the use of the creative process to surface feelings
> and memories. Either the survivor re-creates a portion of the memory in
> the artwork, or the completed work acts as a trigger for the recovery of a
> repressed memory. Art therapy can be used as the major source of
> memory recovery or as an adjunct to other forms of recall.
> – *Renee Fredrickson*

Automatic drawing, similarly, can be undertaken while the client is in trance. The aim here will be to invite the client to reveal unconscious substance when she puts an image on paper. The client's ability to draw accurately will not be necessary and, in some cases, may be an impediment to therapeutic resolution. The idea behind this technique will be that the client will undoubtedly produce a meaningless scrawl that she can then analyse and interpret. Again, a series of drawings on a number of subjects over an extended period of time will usually have beneficial effects because the client can be given licence to express herself freely in a comprehensive medium.

Frequently, the drawing or the doodle that the client will produce may not make sense to the practitioner and, of course, may not be readily apparent to the artist herself initially. The important factor, however, will be that the client can eventually gain insight from the material that will have been dredged up from the depths of her unconscious mind. It will only be a matter of time before she will attain the necessary realisation about the meaning of her supposedly meaningless scrawl. Sometimes, of course, no really profound understanding will be gained by the client but, in fact, her symptoms will just simply vanish as a result of this form of mind-exploration. Perhaps the client's mind will merely release its distress at an unconscious level and her inner awareness will then appreciate that her symptoms are no longer valid. Frequently, the client will experience confusion when interpreting a drawing reproduced under hypnosis and may protest that the imaginary was merely a figment of her imaginative processes rather than an actual event or a tangible product. In such cases, the client may either have recalled a repressed memory that she feels disinclined to believe or simply be utilising symbolic imagery in order to solve a difficulty.

The case-study example below provides a specimen of a typical instance in which automatic hypnotic drawing can be utilised effectively in order to assist the client. In this example, the client made full use of his imaginative powers – or, perhaps, even entered a previous incarnation – in order to resolve the problems of today that were distressing him greatly.

Case-study example – panic attacks
This young male was experiencing panic attacks that led him to believe that he was going to die from a heart attack because the pains in his chest were so severe.

In hypnosis, the client drew a picture of a man in a suit of armour. When the client was asked what the significance of his drawing was, he went quiet for a while and then closed his eyes again. The practitioner then asked the client to state where he had gone to in his thoughts. The client claimed that he was on a battlefield and that he was on a horse and charging at the enemy with his troops to the side and behind him. The client reported that he was now charging faster and another horseman was charging at him with his lance. The client continued to charge at his opponent faster and faster. Suddenly the client screamed and jumped out of the therapeutic chair – clutching his chest with both hands. The client then exclaimed, "I've been stabbed with the lance – it's gone through to my heart." The client's narrative continued to relate the fact that he had fallen off his horse and was just lying on the ground. The other troops had gone on while the client still lay there.

The practitioner then asked the client, "And if you were not there where else would you be?" The client's narrative continued. The client stated that he was in his classroom as a child during a history lesson. The client was listening to the teacher talk about a historic period when men wore suited armour. The client continued to listen to the teacher but, at the same time, he was gazing out of the window and looking at the open field, where he began to imagine the battle in progress. The client, of course, had a gift of being able to imagine so vividly that he could, in essence, experience the very thing that he was imagining. The client's pain and fear then disappeared completely from his life because he was able to access his imaginative processes without feelings of guilt.

Therapeutic Re-enactment

Hypnodrama involves the hypnotised patient being encouraged to play a role in a drama which parallels his own conflict. In such a manner, he is able to re-enact his own inner conflicts and discover solutions to them.
– *Edgar Barnett*

Therapeutic re-enactment has the advantage of enabling the client to become wholeheartedly involved in her own therapeutic progress. The client may be asked to re-enact a portion of her past experience and, in doing so, to reveal the underlying unconscious processes that are related to a given event. Hypnotic re-enactment (or *hypnodrama*) may take several forms whereby the client will be, to a greater or lesser extent, physically involved in the process. Therapeutic re-enactment can allow the client to become immersed in her past experiences and can bring a true flavour to the reality of an event in which she has previously participated – even merely as an observer. This methodology, of course, borrows heavily from gestaltian methodology (see Chapter 8, Volume 1 – "Gestalt Therapy").

The case-study example below shows the way in which therapeutic re-enactment can be beneficially utilised by the practitioner.

Case-study example – relationship difficulties
This female client found herself constantly at the mercy of a dictatorial husband. Once transference had been explored in therapy, the client had realised that her husband was a direct personification of her dictatorial father. Having dealt with many issues in connection with her relationship with her parents, the client was now faced with the task of standing up to her husband in her current life.

The client was, therefore, invited to summon her deceased father and her husband into the consulting room in her imagination. The client was now encouraged to draw the parallels between these two major figures in her life and to reprimand both parties for misusing her. Once the re-enactment was in full swing, the client was able to give full vent to her bottled-up rage at the injustice of her treatment at the hands of these two ostensibly more powerful figures. The client had, thus, during the session, been overtaken by her emotive reactions and had used the session to re-enact aspects of both her past and her current life. This licence that the client granted to herself then became the catalyst for her to make significant changes to her relationship with her husband.

Ideomotor Investigation

Most of the recent advances in analytical hypnotherapy can be directly attributed to the increased use of the ideomotor questioning techniques.
– *Edgar Barnett*

Ideomotor investigation has been based on the assumption that an idea in the client's mind can automatically be translated into muscular activity under the control of the body's motor neurons. Ideomotor methodology, therefore, will endeavour to elicit a response to a question directly from the client's unconscious mind that can completely bypass her conscious faculty. This procedure will endeavour to engage the client's motor areas and memory areas of the cerebral cortex. Let us now consider ideomotor investigation both from the point of view of interrogation and negotiation with the client's unconscious mind.

Interrogating the unconscious mind

Ideomotor methodology can be employed by the practitioner in order to draw out from the client something that may stubbornly refuse to reveal itself by other means. When the practitioner elects to utilise ideomotor methodology, therefore, he will usually need to have a clear or, at least, reasonable idea of what to pinpoint during the session.

When interrogating the client's unconscious mind, it will be necessary for the practitioner to set up a simple YES/NO hand-signalling communication system. The therapist, however, would usually suggest to the client that her more dominant hand could be utilised for YES replies. The client, of course, could be asked to speak to the practitioner during an ideomotor conversation but it will usually be preferable for her to remain silent. Usually an ideomotor response can be readily detected by the astute therapist while, ironically, the client may be unaware of the process. Sometimes, however, the client's ideomotor response can be so minute that the practitioner will, on certain occasions, need to place his own hand on the back of the client's in order to feel the response. This type of minute physical movement will usually feel like a tremor when the client makes an effort to raise her finger and the therapist should feel the muscle tightening when this response is made. The practitioner, of course, will need to gain the client's consent to being touched in this way. The therapist could explain the need to touch the client's hand by telling her that the response will be very minute and, therefore, contact with her responding hand will remove any possibility of misinterpretation. This means of receiving the message will, of course, be extremely effective because the average practitioner's sense of touch will often be very much more sensitive than his sight alone.

Sometimes the client will obviously be controlling her finger-movements consciously but the practitioner should endeavour to circumvent this form of resistance (see Chapter 12, Volume 1 – "Resistance"). Conscious resistance to this investigative process can usually be detected when the client shows a decisively rapid and strong movement during her finger-signalling. When this occurs, the practitioner could then ask the client's finger to allow her unconscious mind to communicate. The client can be instructed simply to do nothing and merely to allow her unconscious mind alone to move the finger. Normally, when the ideomotor resource is unconsciously moving the client's finger, her movement will display a hesitancy, a jerkiness, a quivering or a somewhat less powerful movement than voluntarily-controlled motor coordination.

The following suggested passage could be used by the practitioner in order to initiate direct communication with the client's unconscious mind by setting up the hand-signalling communication system.

Now unconscious …

But now, for the next few minutes, I am talking directly to the unconscious part of your mind. The fact that your conscious mind can hear me is of absolutely no importance whatsoever. Everything I say, everything I ask, will be directed at your unconscious mind only. At this time now I am speaking only to the unconscious part of your mind. It's OK that you can hear me on a conscious, everyday level, at the same time, but, for a while, I am speaking only to your unconscious mind and your conscious brain does not need to take any decisions at all.

Unconscious, I would like to set up a communication system with you whereby you can let me know the things my client needs to know. If you are agreeable, the communication system I would like to put in place will make use of my client's fingers. If this is OK with you, let us use the index finger of the right hand to mean YES and the index finger of the left hand to mean NO. So would you please show me the YES signal by raising the index finger of my client's right hand? Thank you, unconscious mind. And now, just to test this communication system and to make sure we all know exactly what each signal means, would you please now show me the NO signal and raise the index finger of my client's left hand. Also, unconscious, if you wish to answer I DON'T KNOW, then please use the thumb of my client's right hand and please now show me this signal. Thank you.

It will be important for the practitioner to define clearly the difference between talking solely to the client's unconscious mind and communicating with both her conscious mind and unconscious mind simultaneously. When the ideomotor session has been initiated, the practitioner may, therefore, wish to make some form of physical contact with the client in order to establish an initial rapport with her unconscious mind. The practitioner could, for example, lightly touch one of the client's hands, apply a light fingertip pressure to her forehead or rest a hand on her forearm while communicating directly with her unconscious mind. Alternatively, when the ideomotor enquiry has been completed, holding both the client's wrists could indicate to her that it is time to resume normal communication with both her intellect and her unconscious processes. When making physical contact with the client for any reason, it will, of course, be crucially important for the practitioner to ensure that the contact with her can, in no way, be misconstrued. For this reason, it may be better to touch a wrist, a forearm or the client's forehead, because these will be neutral areas of her body.

It will frequently be advisable for the practitioner to take time to thank the client's unconscious mind at the conclusion of the ideo-motor session – particularly if he plans to employ ideomotor techniques regularly. The following passage will demonstrate the way in which the client's unconscious mind can be thanked and praised for its valuable contribution to the therapeutic process. This passage also prepares the client's unconscious mind to lower its guard when defensive strategies have manifested (see Chapter 11, Volume 1 – "Defensive Strategies").

Thanking the unconscious mind …

Unconscious, I would like to thank you from the bottom of my heart for being there for my client twenty-four hours a day – guarding, guiding, loving and protecting. Back in those days even before my client was born, before her conscious awareness really existed, you were there twenty-four hours a day – guarding, guiding, loving and protecting. Helping that little body to form normally, naturally, keeping her blood circulating and keeping my client nourished and safe. And even when her conscious awareness gradually took on more and more of a role, you still took full responsibility. You were there for her from the moment of her birth twenty-four hours a day – guarding, guiding, loving and protecting. Getting my client's attention when she needed it in the only way you knew, by screaming or crying when she needed food or warmth or dryness. Keeping that little heart beating and those small lungs breathing.

And as my client grew, you were still there for her twenty-four hours a day – guarding, guiding, loving and protecting. Healing those cuts and bruises and scrapes as she started moving around. Learning to walk with those inevitable falls and bumps. Fighting off infections and childhood illnesses. Protecting her in the best way you knew. And you are still there now, all these years later, still there twenty-four hours a day – guarding, guiding, loving and protecting.

But you know, unconscious, sometimes those ways of protecting and guiding that were wonderful for the child are no longer appropriate for my client as an adult. Sometimes those defensive mechanisms can cause her more harm than good, you know. Sometimes the need to protect in a certain way will no longer be necessary. Or protection from a specific thing will no longer be needed because that danger is no longer with my client. And, when this happens, you are actually failing in your primary duty – your primary responsibility of giving my client a long, healthy, happy and fulfilling life.

An alternative means of using the ideomotor system would be to use the client's eyes in order to indicate unconscious activity within her mind. The following suggested metaphorical passage could be used to initiate eye-movement with ideomotor-response methodology.

Eyes right ...

Unconscious, I wish to talk only to you and not directly to my client, who may not wish to listen. If you are in agreement, the communication system I would like to put in place will involve the use of my client's eyes. If this is OK with you, please let us use a response in the right eye to mean YES and a response in the left eye to mean NO. And I really don't know what your response will be, but I do know that it will be something that my client's conscious awareness could not possibly do – something that only you can achieve.

So, whatever your response is, maybe a twitch in the eyelid or a feeling of a flashing of light in that particular eye, maybe a feeling of pressure on the eyeball, maybe something completely different. I really don't know what you will choose. But would you please show me the YES signal, whatever that may be, in my client's right eye. Thank you, right eye. And now – just to test this communication system and to make sure we all know exactly what each signal means – would you please now show me the NO signal by making that response in my client's left eye. Similarly, if you wish to respond I DON'T KNOW, then perhaps, unconscious, you could indicate that signal to me now. Thank you, unconscious, for your cooperation.

When using ideomotor-response techniques in this way, the clinician should take due note of whatever the client presents. If the client claims that she does not receive a response yet the practitioner has detected a twitch or a movement in the client's eyes, it may be that she was unaware of this movement. In the following case-study example, the client was unaware of any eye-movement at all.

Case-study example – eye-movement ideomotor response
A female client was encountering difficulty with extracting information from her unconscious mind.

When the ideomotor response was sought from her right eye, the client made a fascinating movement in which the eyelid and the lashes began to invert in the middle. The client, however, was totally unaware of this movement and claimed that she had made no response. The practitioner merely informed the client that a response had been received and then continued nonchalantly with the procedure while carefully watching the client's eyes throughout the session.

Negotiating with the unconscious mind

Sometimes the client's unconscious mind will still refuse to cooperate when ideomotor techniques are applied – particularly when
the problem involves deeply-rooted psychological trauma.
Ideomotor methodology may, then, fail totally for the client or may
simply refuse to shift matters with certain conditions. It may be
wise, in such cases, for the practitioner to talk gently to the client's
unconscious mind about her problems and, finally, to give her
mind permission to change when appropriate. Perhaps the client's
unconscious mind can be asked whether it has had a change of
heart and, if the therapist has been persuasive enough, it will.
Perhaps the client's mind could also be requested to approve of
allowing her to be free of her symptoms. If the client's mind will
still not comply, then the practitioner could, perhaps, negotiate in
order to secure agreement to a reduction of her symptoms or habitual behaviour to a more bearable level.

It will normally be to the practitioner's advantage to have an
understanding of the use of ideomotor-response methodology as a
means of negotiating beneficial change or symptomatic resolution
for the client. Ideomotor responses can then enable the client to
indicate a reply to a question posed by the therapist without
employing speech. After a hypnotic session using ideomotor negotiation, the client may even report that the response was unexpected and was, in fact, opposed to the way in which she was
thinking. The case-study example below illustrates the way in
which one client responded to ideomotor negotiation.

> **Case-study example – weight loss**
> A female client wished to lose weight and, although she con-
> sciously had every intention of doing so, some underlying force
> was holding her back. The client had thoroughly examined the root
> cause of her disorder at length but she still seemed to be unable to
> shed her excess weight. Negotiation with the client's unconscious
> mind took the following form.
>
> THERAPIST: Unconscious, are you clear about how to answer
>   questions using your fingers?
> CLIENT: Yes.
> THERAPIST: Has my client seen what is necessary for her to see
>   in order to enable her to lose weight?

CLIENT:	Yes.
THERAPIST:	And can you now bring my client's weight to a balance that will be just right for her?
CLIENT:	Yes.
THERAPIST:	Will this happen at a rate of eight pounds per month, do you think?
CLIENT:	No.
THERAPIST:	Seven pounds?
CLIENT:	No.
THERAPIST:	Six pounds?
CLIENT:	Yes.
THERAPIST:	So are we to understand and confirm that my client will let go of six pounds per month?
CLIENT:	Yes.
THERAPIST:	So my client will reach her target weight in two months and one week? Is that right, unconscious?
CLIENT:	Yes.
THERAPIST:	Thank you for taking the time to explain to my client all she needed to know in order to allow her to be more the person she wishes to be and has a right to be.

Once the ideomotor response had been set up for this client, a process of elimination was followed in order to arrive at a conclusion. This could have been a very lengthy process and could have run the risk of suggesting to the client's unconscious mind that it could take its time. In this case, the client was so ready to comply with the request to lose weight because, previously, the root cause of the problem had been identified and worked through. The purpose of this form of negotiation with the client's unconscious mind, therefore, was to allow her to reintegrate and adapt to more normative behaviour that had previously been unconsciously driven.

Gold Psychotherapeutic Counselling

During our early development childhood years we are in a very precarious position. On the one hand we will give total and unconditional love to our key role models (usually our mother and father) and will do what we can to keep them happy. Whereas, on the other hand, we haven't as yet learned whether that which they want us to be, say or do is fair or right or appropriate.
– *Georges Philips & Lyn Buncher*

Gold psychotherapeutic counselling is a means of identifying and restructuring limiting or destructive beliefs that can cause the client distress and psychological upheaval. This methodology can be an effective analytical tool because the client can specifically identify an originating belief and from that vantage point can be encouraged to resolve it.

The gold psychotherapeutic method is a three-stage process whereby the client will be asked to make a list of her thoughts and impressions and then to map these elements in a pictorial form in order to identify the essence of her negative or destructive beliefs. The client can then be invited by the practitioner to regress to the seeding event that helped her to form her unwanted belief so that it may be resolved successfully. Let us now examine a brief description of this form of analytical investigation.

> In order to understand which thoughts your client holds as primary beliefs, he must first create a list detailing all his thoughts about the chosen topic. This topic list should contain ALL of the beliefs, memories, and comments that come into his conscious mind when he considers the chosen topic. Some may be positive and others negative. Some may be clearly related and others, apparently unconnected.
> – *Georges Philips & Lyn Buncher*

Initially, the client will be asked to make a list of the beliefs that she has on a given topic. The client could, for example, make a list of her thoughts about a topic such as low self-esteem, depression, blushing or fear of failure. The client can be asked for such a list during hypnosis or may be instructed to make the list at some time between sessions. The client will next be asked to link each of the thoughts in her list to one other belief so that she can then see the way in which her beliefs on the chosen topic are related.

> The linking of the list will reveal both the **primary** and **secondary** beliefs in the client's belief system. The primary beliefs are in effect the foundations and the secondary beliefs the building blocks.
> – *Georges Philips & Lyn Buncher*

An example of a typical gold psychotherapeutic counselling case has been given below on the theme of despair as the client's principal presenting symptom. The case-study example below shows the list of beliefs that the client had compiled and the way in which her beliefs could be mapped out. Using regressive techniques, the client was, finally, permitted to resolve certain aspects of her unconscious conflict.

Case-study example – despair

A female client was asked to list her beliefs on the topic of despair as her main presenting symptom during analytical therapy.

A – I utterly despair of ever feeling happy
B – Unhappy and miserable
C – There is no point in life
D – I feel unloved
E – I cannot get my life together
F – I am hated by everyone
G – I have no friends
H – I want my partner to love me but he doesn't
I – I feel utterly isolated and lonely

The client then linked her list of beliefs in the following manner:

A – I utterly despair of ever feeling happy: C
B – Unhappy and miserable: D
C – There is no point in life: E
D – I feel unloved: I
E – I cannot get my life together: D
F – I am hated by everyone: D
G – I have no friends: I
H – I want my partner to love me but he doesn't: D
I – I feel utterly isolated and lonely: D

When depicted pictorially, the client's belief structure on the topic of despair could then be represented in the form of a map as shown opposite.

This map identified the fact that the client's primary belief structure was the D–I combination. The client's beliefs about despair, therefore, centred on "I feel unloved" and "I feel utterly isolated and lonely". Age-regression techniques were then employed by the practitioner in order to identify the fact that the client had, as a child, felt unloved by her dictatorial father. This feeling of rejection had, subsequently, led the client into a loveless relationship as a

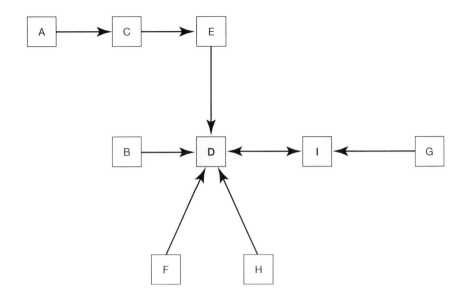

means of mirroring the past. By this means, the root cause of the client's problem was identified and from here resolution work could then be undertaken.

Client Profiling

The analytical-hypnotherapy practitioner may wish to ponder the following points when formulating a profile for the client.

- In what ways can the client benefit from therapeutic investigation?
- Is the client able to accomplish fruitful free association?
- Does the client in any way avoid her natural flow of thoughts?
- Has the client adopted the habit of reporting all her thoughts in an uninterrupted manner during free association?
- Does the client ever stray into purely cognitive processes during free association?
- Can the client contact her true emotive expression and undertake full abreactive discharge during free association?
- In what ways can age-regression be effectively employed by the practitioner?

- Has the client been given an opportunity to explore her experiential memory, her emotive memory and her somatic memory during the age-regression process?
- In what ways can past-life regression be judicially employed with the client?
- Is the client able to utilise creative visualisation during the therapeutic process?
- Can the client contact certain problematic aspects of her past through hidden-observer or revivification techniques?
- Could the client benefit from a review of her birth experience?
- Does the client keep a therapeutic journal or have a need to express herself in any way via the written word?
- Is there any element of the client's past that could possibly be unearthed via automatic writing or automatic drawing?
- Could the client in some way re-enact her traumatic issues or distresses?
- In what ways could the client's mind be interrogated using ideomotor techniques?
- Does the practitioner need to negotiate in any way with the client's unconscious mind?
- Would an appreciation of the originating cause of the client's belief structures be of benefit to her?

Chapter 3

Unconscious Communication

Why, then 'tis none to you; for there is nothing either good or
bad, but thinking makes it so; to me it is a prison.

– William Shakespeare

Verbal and Nonverbal Communication

So do not let us underestimate small indications; by their help we may
succeed in getting on the track of something bigger.
– Sigmund Freud

The client will be able to communicate with the astute practitioner
in a myriad of different ways. The practitioner will simply need to
maintain an alert and open mind in order to be observant without
drawing overt attention to this process. The practitioner, in fact,
can become highly accomplished at absorbing information conveyed from the client by fully exploiting her own intuitive faculties. Usually the hypnotherapist will be adept at this practice
because of the nature of her training. The client may communicate
underlying disturbance in speech patterns, vocal inference, tonal
inflexion, body posture and coordinated movement as well as conveying distress in terms of dress and physical appearance. Let us
now consider some of these verbal and nonverbal modes of communication that can be of interest to the analytical practitioner.

Verbal statements

Most people in our culture have become cut off from their awareness of
who they really are. They have temporarily lost their conscious
connection with their higher selves and thus they have lost their own
sense of power and responsibility for their lives. In some inner way, they
have a sense of helplessness; they feel basically powerless to make real

> change in their lives or in the world. This inner feeling of powerlessness
> causes them to overcompensate by striving and struggling very hard to
> have some degree of or control in their world.
> – *Shakti Gawain*

Often the client will use language patterns and speech modes that will reflect his negative outlook on life and his opinion of his symptoms. Such linguistic modalities may often provide the ever-vigilant therapist with a clue to the client's psychic conflict or distress. Here are some of examples of phrases and statements that the client may use and, in doing so, can inadvertently reveal the true nature of his psychological distress.

- I cannot see the point of life all.
- I think that life is one long uphill struggle.
- I sometimes feel as if I could die of despair.
- I feel as if I am a victim of my own emotions.
- I feel powerless to dig myself out of the rut.
- I cannot face another sleepless night.
- I am constantly tormented by nightmares.
- I am afraid of things that go bump in the night.
- The weather is endlessly dreary.
- I cannot bear waiting in queues.
- There are not enough hours in the day.
- I never feel satisfied with my own efforts.
- I am always rushing about.
- I am tired and yet I cannot rest.
- I just do not know how to sort myself out.
- I cannot seem to get it together.
- I am always getting myself in a stew.
- I am beset by too many worries.
- I am overwhelmed by stress and confusion.
- I never look forward to coming home from work.
- The rush-hour is a time that I dread.
- My colleagues at work are driving me crazy.

The practitioner could also judiciously enquire about the client's underlying messages with regard to his preferences for books, songs, films and sporting activity. Does the client, for example, relish violent films or salacious television programmes? The client who loves the film *Gone with the Wind* or *Titanic* may well have grief and sorrow issues with which to deal (see Chapter 9 –

"Sorrow and Grief Disorders"). The client whose favourite song is "Shout", "Tears of a Clown" or "I Will Survive" may be unconsciously conveying to the therapist his innermost disposition. The practitioner may wish to make direct enquiries about the client's preferences but, sometimes, a more subtle approach to asking about the ways in which he has spent his leisure time will be just as effective.

Nonverbal statements

> Many people believe that Freud discovered the unconscious, while the
> more cynical would even claim that he invented it.
> – Mick Power

The practitioner should be observant of the client's general demeanour because here may lie many clues to his inner world. The way in which the client presents himself will usually reveal a storehouse of information. Does the client dress in a manner that conveys a flamboyance or a disguise behind which he can hide? Does the client adorn his body with make-up or jewellery that will be designed to give a false impression? Does the client parade an expensive car that he wishes all to admire? Does the client appear ill at ease in his body as if he were not truly inhabiting it?

The client may well have a degree of unconscious conflict if he had been forced as a child to use his right hand when he was naturally left-handed or had been obliged to stand up straight and, in doing so, placed too much strain on his physique at an early age. A means of detecting unconscious conflict may be to ask the client whether he is naturally right-handed or left-handed. The client may then be asked to clasp his hands together and the practitioner can note whether the position of the dominant thumb is in accord with his hand-usage preference. If the client's right thumb is placed above his left thumb when his hands are clasped, then he is likely to be a naturally right-handed person. Although this is not a foolproof test, the practitioner could utilise it as a means of identifying any potential conflict. Frequently, when the left-handed child, of course, has been forced to use his right hand, this can cause distress and may well be an indication that he has been consistently misunderstood or ill-considered during school years. Similarly, the child may elect to adopt a right-hand or a left-hand dominance in order to please a parent or studiously to avoid being different from his schoolmates.

> Consider the position of a car mechanic. He might well be able to put quite a few things right by following a few tried and tested procedures that he has found to be effective in some instances. But unless he understands the principles governing the function of the various parts of the machine, his ability is going to be strictly limited: he will have no real idea of why the changes he makes are effective, and so his work will remain rather hit and miss. He has to know how and why the parts move or operate in order to understand things properly.
> – *Dylan Morgan*

Often the client's outward statements can be fodder ripe for analytical investigation. The client, for example, who wears excessive jewellery, who is heavily tattooed or who has indulged in body-piercing may be indicating a self-punishing mechanism and a low sense of self-esteem. Body piercing – despite being a fashion statement – could perhaps reveal an unconscious programme that the client has been running. Perhaps the client with a ring through his nose will be expecting to be led by another controlling person. Perhaps the client with a navel ring may be attempting to reconstruct the umbilical cord. Perhaps the client with pierced genitalia has learned to associate sex with pain. Perhaps the client who may be susceptible to every fashionable trend will be unable to think independently or will rely heavily on the approbation of others for his self-respect. A primary candidate for investigative analysis will often be the client with bizarre or unusual tattoos. In the case-study example below, for instance, the client's tattoos told his entire life story.

Case-study example – alcoholism

This male client had come into therapy for an alcohol problem. The client also possessed several tattoos, most of which had been purchased while he had been intoxicated. On one occasion, for example, he woke to discover a tattoo that he had no recollection of ever having had done the night before.

The client had one tattoo on his chest that read "Made in England" and another that read "I love my Mum". It transpired that the client's father had been a racist and the tattoo had been an attempt to gain his father's approval and acceptance. Having had one tattoo done for his father, the client now felt guilt about not having one in favour of his mother and so the second appeared shortly afterwards.

Once these facts had been established, the practitioner began to enquire about the client's relationship with his parents. Issues of neglect, abandonment and rejection were high on this client's agenda. This discovery led the client to realise that he felt unloved and that this factor had affected his self-esteem and contributed to his alcohol problems.

Parapraxes

> Slips of the tongue do really occur with particular frequency when one is tired, has a headache or is threatened with migraine. In the same circumstances proper names are easily forgotten.
> – *Sigmund Freud*

A parapraxis is an unconsciously-motivated faulty act or unwitting mistake that the client will make. From Freud's observations of the mind's tendency to conflict and compromise, he identified the concept of parapraxes – the famous "Freudian slips" – as being manifestations of hidden messages from the client's unconscious mind. In one sense, a parapraxis will be a form of suppression or concealment of the client's psychic life that he does not wish to acknowledge. If the practitioner, however, can be alert to such clues, she can then gain an understanding of some of the client's unconscious processes, emotive disturbance and psychic distress. Freud claimed that such phenomena can give the therapist a glimpse of that part of the client's mind that will be chaotic, instinctive, uncontrollable, full of contradiction and often juxtaposed with his conscious awareness and intention. The important point for the practitioner to bear in mind with regard to parapraxes is that the client will normally be oblivious of his mistake and may frequently be surprised when it has been pointed out to him. It will be as if a parapraxis is beyond the conscious control of the client. Parapraxes will occur for everyone in everyday life. It does not, of course, signify that the individual is abnormal but simply that his unconscious activity is unwittingly and momentarily breaking through to the surface of his conscious mind. The client, of course, may be more inclined to divulge inadvertently his secrets in the therapeutic environment because, in this setting, he can be encouraged to be himself and, hopefully, to relax. Of course, hypnosis can be an ideal vehicle within which to aid the surfacing of such hidden material from the client's mind.

> It is in general true that only a certain proportion of the errors which occur in ordinary life can be looked at from our point of view. You should bear these limitations in mind when henceforward we start from the assumption that parapraxes are psychical acts and arise from mutual interference between two intentions.
> – *Sigmund Freud*

Parapraxes manifestation

> So, was Freud right about Freudian slips? Rightness, particularly in our business, is not an all-or-nothing thing. He was probably not right in asserting that all (or nearly all) slips are in some way intended. But if we ask whether Freud was correct in his view that slips represent minor eruptions of unconscious processing, then the answer would be an emphatic "yes".
> – *James Reason*

The client's parapraxis can manifest in a number of forms when he unknowingly makes an error or is prone to forgetfulness. The client may make a slip of the tongue or, similarly, a slip of the pen – hopefully not when writing out a cheque in payment of the practitioner's fee! The client may also misread the written word or misuse a spoken word in the course of an everyday conversation. The client, for example, say or write a word or a phrase that has the opposite meaning to that which he intended to impart. The client may also transpose, replace or substitute a word or a phrase in place of what was originally intended. Freud also drew attention to the fact that the client may have a tendency to utilise puns and verbal jokes in speech patterns in order to create an impression. The client, furthermore, may temporarily forget a person's name, an important event, a crucial date or time that he ostensibly maintains was vitally important to him. The client may, moreover, forget an impression or an experience of something that would normally leave a mark. The client may temporarily mislay an object that he claims is of significance to him. Finally, the client may simply become clumsy and perform what Freud described as bungled actions. The client may, for instance, trip on the carpet as he enters the consulting room or drop his wallet on the floor. Is the client, therefore, anxious to enter the therapeutic environment or is part of him still wishing to remain outside?

The mildest forms of neurotic distress are temporary memory loss, inadvertent clumsiness and simple misunderstandings. Jung maintained that a thorough investigation of all such psychic material would invariably reveal the existence of unconscious content that would then distort the performance of the client's conscious awareness in some indirect manner. Jung documented his opinion that even inherently-reasonable people, when afflicted with conditions that might lead a weaker person to suicide, could develop an unconscious suicide-complex (see Chapter 9 – "Sorrow and Grief Disorders"). This would be displayed in symptoms such as a sudden liking for dangerous sports, attacks of dizziness in exposed places, inadvertently administering the wrong medication and hesitation in front of a moving vehicle. Once this complex has been brought to the client's conscious awareness, he could then recognise such tendencies and may subsequently avoid corresponding situations that might further tempt him to self-destruction.

> Contraries have a strong conceptual kinship with each other and stand in a particularly close psychological association with each other.
> – *Sigmund Freud*

Parapraxes utilisation

> Parapraxes are the product of mutual interference between two different intentions, of which one may be called the disturbed intention and the other the disturbing one.
> — *Sigmund Freud*

The importance of the client's parapraxes to the therapist will, of course, be that such errors can contain a wealth of information and can form the basis of enquiry into his unconscious life. The perceptive practitioner can become adept at detecting parapraxes and then discovering what purpose or intention lies beneath the shallow surface. This analysis can often be achieved without necessarily letting the client know of such detection unless, of course, it will be in his interest to have his attention drawn to a mistake of this nature. Freud claimed that the therapist's strength could often lie in attaching importance to detail and, even, triviality in terms of what the client presents in the consulting room. Freud proffered the advice that within minor parapraxes were the gems and nuggets of information that could be the key to momentous discovery. The practitioner, therefore, should seek to identify the purpose behind the client's mistake and to act accordingly. Occasionally, a mistake may reveal something that the client would want to do. The client, for example, might have a desire to change to a new job or to leave an intimate partner and the practitioner might feel inclined to discuss this issue with him. Alternatively, a parapraxis might reveal a form of resistance that the client has to the therapeutic process that often the therapist can surreptitiously help him to overcome (see Chapter 12, Volume 1 – "Resistance").

A parapraxis occasionally may be readily recognised by the client himself and its significance will then be abundantly apparent to him. Conversely, the client may note his slip but be unaware of its significance. The client, moreover, may totally reject any inference that his error has any underlying significance other than its superficial quality. In such cases of blatant suppression, the client may not currently wish to address or be equipped to face this aspect of his unconscious essence. When this factor has been detected by the practitioner, it might be prudent to change the focus of therapeutic enquiry in order to address the issue of avoidance or resistance. A parapraxis, of course, may also indicate to the therapist that repression can still be lurking in the client's mind and further work may need to be undertaken in order to unearth it (see Chapter 10, Volume 1 – "Memory").

> Intentions are forgotten and a quantity of other undersigned actions
> become noticeable if we are absent-minded – that is, properly speaking, if
> we are concentrating on something else.
> – *Sigmund Freud*

The following case-study example shows the way in which the practitioner can skilfully utilise the client's unconscious communication.

Case-study example – guilt-complex
This male client attended therapy in order to resolve an impasse that he experienced in terms of his relationship with his father. The

client felt totally ruled by and overshadowed by his manipulative father and believed that this element was cramping his style.

The client was in the habit of recording his dreams and making a list of his thoughts during the previous week. Some way through therapeutic investigation, the client wrote out the contents of a dream that he wished to relate to the practitioner. In order to write out this dream before he forgot it, the client tore a scrap from a newspaper that had been lying by his bed. The one word of the headline that featured prominently on this scrap of newspaper was the word "secrets". The session, thus, began by investigating the inherent secrets that the client held within his mind. This revealing investigative session on the theme of secrets allowed the client to realise that he felt overwhelmingly guilty about his desire to break free of his father's unhealthy dominance over him.

Word-Association Testing

Jung's next group of studies was based upon the word-association test. A list of a hundred words is read out, and the subject is asked to respond to each with the first word that occurs to him. By timing the interval between stimulus and response, it becomes possible to show that, unknown to themselves, subjects are influenced by words which arouse emotion and slow down their responses.
– *Anthony Storr*

A word-association test will be a means of asking the client to respond verbally to a number of words in a random list that are presented by the practitioner. The aim of this methodology will be to invite the client to state the first word that comes instantly to mind when the stimulus-word has been spoken. This technique will be another means of identifying the client's unconscious processes that can usually be carried out with the aid of hypnosis. Word-association testing was originally devised by Jung, who has given the therapeutic community yet another method of accessing material from the client's unconscious mind. Word-association testing was Jung's reply to Freud's free-association technique and, even though it has been little used in clinical circles, the methodology can still have a value in given therapeutic circumstances.

Below is a typical example of a word-association test that the therapist can use when employing this technique. The client should be instructed to say the first word that comes into his mind when the therapist reads the words from the list. The practitioner can also use a copy of this list to note any of the client's unusual reactions to a given word-stimulus while in hypnosis.

Home	Brother	Happy
Uncle	Holiday	Sleep
Sister	Aunt	Field
Mother	Dreams	Cat
Failure	Gamble	Baby
Trousers	Chocolate	Sex
Night	Food	Ideal
River	Lost	Birth
Evening	Alcohol	Drink
Car	Dog	Tree
Chair	Memories	Father
Innocence	Caring	Shop
Church	Mouth	Penis
Mad	Water	Fire
Husband	Bright	Sick
Hate	Shame	Day
Complete	Parents	Love
Wife	Guilt	Success
Family	Morning	Death
Cloud	Breast	Son
Desire	Sad	Control
Table	Grief	Head
Urge	Body	School
Shock	Marriage	Child
Toilet	Jealous	Touch
Adolescent	Tail	Break
Virgin	Teacher	Talk
Crisis	Real	Violence
Daughter	Wedding	Hidden
Clean	Pain	Private
Dull	Heaven	Past
Fertile	Taste	Embarrassed
Road	House	Panic
Fun	Relationship	Dark
Help	Work	Money

When employing this methodology, the practitioner should observe any occasions when the client stumbles or hesitates. The therapist should also be on the lookout for any indications of conscious censoring or unconscious resistance that the client may exhibit (see Chapter 12, Volume 1 – "Resistance"). Any emotive significance, furthermore, that the client attaches to a given word-association should also be noted by the practitioner. The therapist may also wish to consider a number of factors when employing the word-association method.

- Does the client's repetition of the stimulus-word indicate a blockage to responding?
- Does the client deliberately misunderstand the presented word?
- Does the client pause or are there long delays in his reaction-time when responding?
- Does the client give idiosyncratic or anomalous responses?
- Does the client make unrequested comments about the stimulus-word?
- Does the client make auditory associations (known as clang-associations) whereby he responds with a word having the same sound as the presented word?
- Does the client exhibit detectable nonverbal behaviour such as unusual body movements, mannerisms and facial expressions when responding to the stimulus-word?
- Is the client's overall response to the stimulus-word unusual in any way when it accompanies his response?

It will not, of course, be necessary for the practitioner to time the client's responses with a stopwatch, as Jung did, but when he is under hypnosis often any irregularities of response will provide a basis for further analytical investigation.

> The prolongation of the reaction time is of the greatest practical importance. You decide whether the reaction time is too long by taking the average mean of the reaction times of the test person. Other characteristic disturbances are: reaction with more than one word, against the instructions; mistakes in reproduction of the word; reaction expressed by facial expression, laughing, movement of the hands or feet or body, coughing, stammering, and such things; insufficient reaction like "yes" or "no"; not reacting to the real meaning of the stimulus word; habitual use of the same words; use of foreign languages – of which there is not a great danger in England, though with us it is a great nuisance;

> defective reproduction, when memory begins to fail in the reproduction
> experiment; total lack of reaction. All these reactions are beyond the
> control of the will.
> – *Carl Jung*

Natural Laws of the Mind

> The scientific world is beginning to discover what metaphysical and
> spiritual teachers have known for centuries. Our physical universe is not
> really composed of any "matter" at all; its basic component is a kind of
> force or essence which we call *energy*.
> – *Shakti Gawain*

There are a number of natural laws or universal laws that can affect
human thinking, behaviour and motivation and these can merit
our attention. A knowledge of such observations of mankind will
aid the practitioner in understanding the client in terms of the way
in which his unconscious mind may drive him. When the practitioner examines the natural laws of the mind, this study can assist
her to appreciate the underlying cognitive processes and belief
structures to which the client may subscribe. Let us now consider
some of these natural inclinations that have been documented by
many philosophical thinkers, including Freud and Jung.

> If you are wondering what your premise is, just look at your experiences
> in life.
> – *Burt Hotchkiss*

The law of cause and effect

> Psychoanalysts, when considering mental activity, follow Freud in
> subscribing to determinism. That is, they consider that mental events are
> subject to the laws of cause and effect.
> – *Anthony Storr*

The natural law of cause and effect is considered to be the universal law and, simply stated, implies that for every effect, there will
inevitably be a specific cause. Every event that occurs in the client's
life can, therefore, be attributed to a given cause – even though he
may not know the precise nature of that cause. For beneficial
change to take place, therefore, the client must first discover the
cause of his problems or difficulties. The law of cause and effect

will be the principle that profoundly underlies analytical hypnotherapy. Thoughts will play a significant role in the law of cause and effect because, in the realms of the client's unconscious mind, thoughts and emotive responses are the causes and the effects of his thinking are the symptoms that will be superficially evident in the way in which he has conducted his life.

> Every action generates a force of energy that returns to us in like kind …
> what we sow is what we reap. And when we choose actions that bring
> happiness and success to others, the fruit of our karma is happiness and
> success.
> – *Deepak Chopra*

The law of accident

> It's interesting and mysterious that we humans have little instinct-
> motivated behaviour.
> – *Margaret Reinhold*

The law of accident, in contrast to the law of cause and effect, forms the notion that every event that occurs in the client's life will happen by coincidence or by accident. This school of thought, therefore, purports that all events occur by haphazard chance. This will mean that matters are deemed to be out of the client's control and that he himself will be controlled by external events. The client with this philosophy will believe that there will be no point in planning because one never knows what will happen next. The client who subscribes to a belief in the law of accident will generally fail to plan and, thereby, plan to fail. In analytical hypnotherapy, the client might be encouraged to explore the possibility that he can be the author of his own destiny and that self-determination can be placed within his grasp.

The law of control

> Good luck occurs when preparation grasps opportunity.
> – *Burt Hotchkiss*

The law of control states that the client will be able to determine the course of his own existence. It has now been generally accepted

– at least by most therapists and healers – that the degree of control that the client perceives he has in his life will be in direct proportion to his degree of psychological and physiological health. The client's self-regard will, thus, equal the degree of self-control that he perceives he is capable of attaining. If the client, however, feels that he is not in control of circumstances or concludes that other people control his life, he will then be likely to take a proportionately pessimistic view of the future. The practitioner would, therefore, be advised to discover at the outset of therapeutic enquiry what the client actually believes with regard to who will be in control of his therapeutic process.

> Every achievement has started with an idea.
> – *Vera Peiffer*

The law of belief

> It all comes down to expectation and belief. The child was brain-washed to the point where she does not realise that there is anything amiss with her thought processes.
> – *Georges Philips & Terence Watts*

The law of belief states that, whatever the client believes, his mind will always achieve (see Chapter 2 – "Therapeutic Investigation"). What the client believes will, consequently, become his personal reality. The client's belief structure, therefore, will be the sum total of what he is and what he has become. Most of the client's beliefs will have been installed without question, usually in his formative years. The client may also assume that he is consciously aware of most of his beliefs. Part of the therapeutic process, therefore, may be engaged in allowing the client to disrobe unconscious understanding and to explore those beliefs that have become invisible and obscure.

> A certain amount of pain is inevitable, but suffering is optional.
> – *Burt Hotchkiss*

The law of expectation

> Everyone has a purpose in life … a unique gift or special talent to give to others. And when we blend this unique talent with service to others, we experience the ecstasy and exultation of our own spirit, which is the ultimate goal of all goals.
> – *Deepak Chopra*

The law of expectation states that whatever the client expects to happen with certainty will be likely to occur. When an end-result has been suggested consciously to the client, therefore, he will then frequently adopt this suggestion because his unconscious mind will subsequently find a way of achieving this idea. The practitioner, hence, might regard the law of expectation as the self-fulfilling prophesy. The client, for example, who steadfastly believes in his ability to recover from an unpleasant past will almost certainly be able to do so successfully because this notion will match his inner reality.

> Perhaps the shaman is uniquely qualified among the practitioners of the healing arts to give "the doctor inside a chance to go to work".
> – *Michael Harner*

The law of attraction

> Our law of energy is this: energy of a certain quality or vibration tends to attract energy of a similar quality and vibration.
> – *Shakti Gawain*

The law of attraction states that the client will assume the role of a psychic magnet. The client may, for instance, attract into his life people who harmonise with his most prominent thoughts. The client may, alternatively, find himself in circumstances that, similarly, have a mysterious pull. The adage "as a man reaps, so shall he sow" aptly summarises this concept of the law of attraction. The client, for example, who monotonously repeats patterns of engaging in a dysfunctional relationship or who continually will be dismissed from his employment may unconsciously be attracting these situations into his life (see Chapter 12 – "Dysfunctional Relationships").

Whatever you send out to others will come back like a boomerang.
– Vera Peiffer

The law of intention

Inherent in every intention and desire is the mechanics for its fulfilment
... intention and desire in the field of pure potentiality have infinite
organising power. And when we introduce an intention in the fertile
ground of pure potentiality, we put infinite organising power to work
for us.
– Deepak Chopra

The law of intention states that whatever the client thinks about on
a continuing basis will become a part of his experience. The law of
intention will, thus, mean that the client can dwell on thoughts that
will then become the product of his ideas. It will be as if the more
the client concentrates on a thought, the more he will become the
thought on which he dwells. The client, for instance, who can
become immersed in his therapeutic endeavours will be more
likely to succeed than one who regards therapy as a part-time
interest.

When you have total intention to create something – that is you deeply
desire it, you completely believe that you can do it, and you are totally
willing to have it – it simply cannot fail to manifest, and usually within a
very short time.
– Shakti Gawain

The law of dominant effect

When your willpower conflicts with your imagination, your imagination
will always win out.
– Vera Peiffer

The law of dominant effect states that whatever idea the client
most dwells upon will become realised by his unconscious mind.
Because his unconscious mind has limited resources and could not
actualise every one of his thoughts, he will, therefore, display a
tendency to focus on specific ideas. This phenomenon will occur
because he can expend energy on only a limited number of
thoughts, ideas or feelings at any time. The human organism has
only limited energy resources and this scarcity will strenuously

need to be conserved for survivalist reasons. The client, therefore, needs to put his therapeutic journey at the top of his list of priorities.

> A wish is a declaration of the mouth that the mind knows is a lie.
> – *Burt Hotchkiss*

The law of reversed effort

> The symptoms can also be reversed. The fat child/adult eats for comfort
> because she is fat and therefore unlovable.
> – *Deepak Chopra*

According to the law of reversed effort, any idea that gives rise to a suggestion in the client's mind will take hold. It will be as if the client's mind will go into rebellion-mode and steadfastly refuse to budge. If a suggestion, for example, has been consciously counter-acted, it may gain greater force and take deeper root in the client's mind. The client who tries to deny a negative suggestion consciously will, in fact, actually reinforce that idea. The more resistance the client puts up to the suggestion, the more power it may be given. The client's unconscious mind, therefore, will take a negative thought and make it happen. The more effort the client uses to deny the suggestion, the more powerful the suggestion will become. In this sense, the client's own resistance to therapeutic enquiry may be the very mechanism by which he can come to terms with his dilemmas (see Chapter 12, Volume 1 – "Resistance"). In practice, if the practitioner incites the client not to think about a given topic, the likelihood will be that he will strongly focus his mind on it. This concept, of course, has been the basis of therapeutic paradoxical intervention.

> Often we achieve things which we have been desiring and visualising,
> and we forget to even notice that we have succeeded!
> – *Shakti Gawain*

The law of least effort

> Nature's intelligence functions with effortless ease … with carefreeness,
> harmony, and love. And when we harness the forces of harmony, joy, and
> love, we create success and good fortune with effortless ease.
> – *Deepak Chopra*

The law of least effort states that the client's unconscious mind will be minimalistic and will do the bare minimum amount of work in order to achieve the desired outcome. The client will, consequently, use the smallest amount of effort in order to achieve the maximum result. This concept will be analogous to a flow of water seeking the path of least resistance to its natural flow. For this reason, hypnotic intervention can assist the client to overcome any resistance he may have to investigating his fears and uncertainties.

> The more will-power you employ to reach your target the less you can
> do it.
> – *Vera Peiffer*

The law of generalisation

> When your mind must choose between what is or what should be, if
> there is a conflict, it will always report what should be.
> – *Burt Hotchkiss*

The law of generalisation states that the client has an unfortunate tendency to label one experience in such a way as to make him believe that this label will apply to all experiences. The client may, therefore, presuppose that all outcomes are based on one experience. If, for example, the client fails an interview for a job, he may be likely to believe that he will fail on subsequent occasions. The practitioner, of course, should endeavour to divest the client of any limiting beliefs he may have about his ability to succeed in the therapeutic context.

> Unfortunately, most of us are unable to identify what it is that is actually
> limiting us.
> – *Georges Philips & Lyn Buncher*

Client Profiling

The analytical-hypnotherapy practitioner may wish to ponder the following points when formulating a profile for the client.

- What is the essence of the verbal statements that the client makes?
- In what ways does the client communicate nonverbally and what messages are being conveyed by him?
- Does the client attempt to portray a given image to the world?
- In what ways have any parapraxes been manifested by the client?
- Would the client benefit from a conscious awareness of his parapraxes?
- Would it be appropriate to employ word-association testing with the client?
- In what ways might the client resist a word-association testing process?
- Does the client believe that he is the author of his own destiny or does he tend to take a fatalistic view of life?
- Does the client feel that he is in control of his life-circumstances?
- Does the client feel that he is in control of the outcome of his therapeutic process?
- What does the client believe about himself?
- What does the client believe about and expect of the therapeutic process?
- Has the client formed a pattern of being attracted to unfavourable circumstances or unpleasant persons in the past?
- What does the client mostly focus on in his thoughts, notions and ideas?
- In what way could paradoxical intervention be employed with the client?
- In what ways does the client's mind appear to be minimalistic?
- In what ways does the client make unhelpful sweeping statements or generalisations?

Chapter 4

Therapeutic Enquiry

A mind not to be changed by place or time.
The mind is its own place, and in itself
Can make a Heaven of Hell, a Hell of Heaven.

– John Milton

What Does the Client Hope to Achieve in Therapy?

Most people most of the time make decisions with little awareness of
what they are doing. They take action with little understanding of their
own motives and without beginning to know the ramifications of
their choices. Do we really know what we are doing when we accept or
reject a potential client?
– Scott Peck

It can be tempting for the practitioner to lose track of what the
client wants from therapy. It will be as if the therapist can become
so absorbed with getting the client back to psychological good
health that he cannot see the wood for the trees. In such circumstances, the practitioner may begin to apply techniques in the hope
of initiating change in the client rather than being guided by what
she has requested. It will be essential for the practitioner, therefore,
to establish precisely what the client seeks to achieve in analytical
therapy. By this means, an outcome can be agreed between both
parties in the therapeutic transaction. If the client, for example,
seeks therapy initially in order to assuage panic attacks, the practitioner should not undertake to rid her of her smoking habit unless
this has been specifically requested. In analytical terms, of course,
the goalposts may well shift during the course of the client's therapeutic encounter but, if the final goal were to change, this would
need to happen with the full knowledge and consent of both parties in the exchange. The analytical practitioner should remember

101

that it must be the client who should set the agenda in terms of therapeutic outcome. If the practitioner takes it upon himself to dictate the path of therapy, then it may well be incompatible with the client's requirements and, as a result, beneficial change may not take place or she will leave as a dissatisfied customer (see Chapter 6 – "Therapeutic Planning"). When this I'm-in-charge notion has been taken to extremes by the practitioner, he can easily lose sight of the client's initial presenting symptoms and may need to consult his case-study records in order to be reminded. The analytical hypnotherapist will provide a service for which the client pays. The practitioner, therefore, will be duty-bound to provide that service once a fee has been agreed. This contract – whether oral or written – will then have a binding effect on both parties. For this reason, it will be essential that the clinician be in no doubt whatsoever about what the client wants before making such a contract. If necessary some kind of well-formed outcome enquiry may need to be initiated in order to keep the practitioner on track.

So how does the therapist establish precisely what the client wants? Ideally, the prospective client will telephone or meet the practitioner in order to discuss matters openly prior to making an appointment. At such time, an initial screening process can be undertaken by the practitioner while the client, simultaneously, will have an opportunity to assess what therapeutic intervention would involve prior to committing herself to a series of sessions. The client may have been attracted by the practitioner's advertising or, preferably, will seek therapy with a given therapist as a result of a recommendation. In both cases, it may be wise for the practitioner to ensure that the prospective client will be given an opportunity to read any promotional literature that has been prepared. The prospective client, in this way, may be able to gain a basic understanding of what the practitioner has to offer, what analytical therapy can entail and what her role in the process will be (see Chapter 1 – "The Hypnoanalytic Approach").

How Does the Client Approach Therapy?

Just as the pleasure-ego can do nothing but wish, work for a yield of pleasure, and avoid displeasure, so the reality-ego need do nothing but strive for what is useful and guard itself against damage.
– *Sigmund Freud*

It will be important for the practitioner to note the manner in which the client approaches the prospect of therapy. Does the client welcome the relief of speaking to another in confidence? Does the client appreciate the depths into which psychic exploration may need to delve? Does the client have a useful attitude towards undertaking therapy? Does the client positively view the encounter as a means of transporting herself further along the road of life or does she regard therapy as a necessary evil to which she must unwillingly submit? However difficult the process, it will be enormously helpful if the client has a positive attitude towards her own self-investigative process. There are, in general, two categories of client with whom the analytical hypnotherapist will be dealing: the one who genuinely seeks self-knowledge and the one who merely wishes to eliminate her tiresome symptoms. Often the seeker and the avoider can be easily identified but the practitioner cannot always bank on the fact that the client's disposition will be overtly recognisable.

> Are you a "victim" or are you taking responsibility for your life? So many of us *think* we are taking responsibility for our own lives when we simply are not. The "victim" mentality is very subtle and takes many forms.
> – *Susan Jeffers*

The seeker

> The seeker regards the analytic enterprise as a means of achieving a particular goal, for example, better self-control, increased ability to work, a happier marriage or divorce. He has a commitment to certain values, formed before he undertakes analysis, and he seeks ways to realise his aspirations.
> – *Thomas Szasz*

The client who is a seeker will obviously be the easier type with whom to work. The seeker will be someone who has a problem but will be looking for a definitive solution. The seeker will also know exactly what she wishes to achieve during her therapeutic journey. Here will be the client who – having felt the rapport developing between herself and the practitioner – will do everything in her power to help herself. This client will fully cooperate with the practitioner because she will consider that this course of action will be in her own interests. It will be as if the seeker will be willing to face the horrors of her past and will regard resistance merely as an obstacle to be speedily surmounted. The seeker, therefore, will be the client who craves self-knowledge in order to alleviate suffering and will be prepared to put in the necessary work in order to achieve this aim. The seeking client, therefore, will be likely to be compliant with the therapist's requests and will be as prepared as she can be to face the ordeals of exposing the hidden skeletons in her psychic cupboard.

The avoider

> The seeker is like the businessman or entrepreneur whose aim is maximal profits; the avoider, like the employee or labourer whose aim is minimal effort. Because of the nature of so-called psychiatric symptoms, many patients receiving psychotherapy – and most of those who do not want it for themselves but are coerced into it – are motivated largely by the desire to avoid, rather than overcome, problems.
> – *Thomas Szasz*

The client who is an avoider may be a very different creature indeed. The avoider will generally desire to avoid the pain of life but may not want to do anything very much in order to help herself achieve this goal. This client, furthermore, may not have a clear idea of what her symptoms are and may show little obvious desire to discover the place from which her problems might originate. The avoider, for example, may state her symptoms in negative terms or be vague about her difficulties. Often the avoider will protest with "Yes, but ..." phraseology. Working with the avoider, therefore, can sometimes be an uphill struggle for the practitioner. With this client, it may be better for the therapist to minimise conscious verbal communication in order to reduce any opportunity she may have for overt and determined resistance (see Chapter 12, Volume 1 – "Resistance").

> When a psychiatrist makes the diagnosis of a character disorder, it is because the pattern of avoidance of responsibility is relatively gross in the diagnosed individual. Yet almost all of us from time to time seek to avoid – in ways that can be quite subtle – the pain of assuming responsibility for our own problems.
> – *Scott Peck*

We shall now look at a case-study example that aptly illustrates the way in which the client can utilise avoidance tactics when being questioned by the practitioner. This client might be typical of one exhibiting the avoider syndrome that can usually be identified at the outset of the therapeutic encounter.

Case-study example – avoidance tactics
A male client wished to improve his golfing strategy but he was uncertain of his motivations for change and had little appreciation of his underlying anger. The client was, therefore, questioned by the therapist during the initial session in the following manner.

CLIENT: I don't want to keep losing my temper when I'm playing golf.
THERAPIST: So what would you like when you are playing golf?
CLIENT: I just want to enjoy playing the game.
THERAPIST: And what ability do you need to be able to enjoy playing golf?
CLIENT: I suppose to be more patient.
THERAPIST: You don't seem sure whether, if you have patience, you will enjoy playing golf.
CLIENT: Yes, I am … I'm sure.
THERAPIST: That's good.

The practitioner was then able to assist the client to investigate both his underlying anger and his lack of self-satisfaction. In this way, the client's confusion was shifted from a vague notions of his problems to a more specific identification of his needs. Therapeutic enquiry was then able to focus on the client's anger and impatience manifestations.

Taking the Client's Case-History

Charles Tebbetts believed strongly that the client was far more able to disclose the real cause of his/her problem than an outside person simply diagnosing (if the cause is not organic). He believed that even when the client could not identify the cause at a cognitive level, the answer was still inside the mind of that very same client – buried deep inside the subconscious.
– Roy Hunter

Initially, the analytical therapist will usually need to take a case-history of the client. Often case-history notes will be written during the first session, although occasionally the practitioner may wish to conduct a purely oral questioning session when the client begins her therapeutic journey. Ideally, a combination of these two approaches will best serve the client. The practitioner may, for example, pose a number of client-assessment questions either formally or informally in order to encourage her to reflect on herself and her past. The client should, of course, be entreated to answer all questions in an honest manner and, for this purpose, the practitioner could explain that her answers would be designed to allow her to gain personal insight rather than purely to edify the clinician. The aim of client-assessment questioning will be to stir up her psychic system and case-history questions will, thus, be as much for the client's benefit as for the therapist's enlightenment – if not more so.

The practitioner would be advised to pose questions relatively speedily and with a degree of nonchalance in order to avoid unduly influencing or deterring the client. At all times, however, the client should be encouraged to speak from the heart and should, in every way, be assured that her replies to questions will be met with caring impartiality by the practitioner. If the client were to gain the impression that the practitioner might require a certain answer, then she could unwittingly comply with this tacit request rather than answer honestly from the depths of her innermost being. The practitioner, of course, should remember that the client who is an avoider may have several ready-made answers in order to explain her problems. The avoider, therefore, may simply expect the therapist to concur with these glittering pearls of wisdom. This client may, however, have fundamentally failed to appreciate that therapeutic intervention will not be a logical process and may need to be convinced on this front.

Let us now contemplate the general aspects of the client's life and her psyche that the practitioner may wish to enquire about when taking her case-history notes. No specific examples of questions have been given here but a comprehensive case-history questionnaire can be obtained from the International College of Eclectic Therapies that may provide a starting point for the practitioner (see Appendix 1 – "Professional Training and Development Resources").

Personal details

The practitioner will, of course, need to make a note of the client's personal details such as name, age, address and other contact information. The practitioner should also endeavour to address the client by the name by which she prefers to be known. This may be a nickname or a shortened version of her full name and may well not be the name that her parents assigned to the child. In this way, the client will be given her own identity and rapport can be better established with the practitioner.

Occupational details

The practitioner may wish to ask about the client's current and previous occupation. Often this enquiry will reveal to the clinician obvious pockets of stress in the client's life. If the client states, for example, that she has left a previous job in favour of a less stressful one, then the therapist will have an indication of the way in which she will be progressing in life. This change of employment may be the client's means of initiating beneficial change by recognising harmful stressors. Often such a line of questioning will convey whether the client has been stagnating in a given occupation and this, in turn, may indicate an area from which positive movement could emanate. If the client, for example, has been undergoing a definite period of change, then this will be a good omen in terms of the prognosis of the therapeutic outcome.

Educational details

The practitioner may wish to ask about the client's schooling. Perhaps the client excelled at school or perhaps she was a dismal failure and this imprint may have affected her life subsequently. Perhaps the client was bullied at school and has subsequently felt downtrodden as a result. Conversely, the client may have been the bully herself in former days and will harbour guilt about this knowledge. Perhaps the client had to attend boarding school and was forced to live away from her parents who could not understand her loneliness or were not there for her to consult when necessary.

Medical history

The practitioner may wish to make detailed enquiries about the client's medical history and physiological state. Recent visits to other healthcare practitioners can often indicate whether the client has been seriously ill recently and has been taking her wellbeing seriously. It may sometimes be appropriate for the therapist to ask the client for details of any medical practitioners who are treating her but, of course, discretion will be required at this juncture because she should not, in any way, feel that a breach of confidentiality might occur.

The practitioner will obviously need to enquire about the client's psychological health. The therapist will need to know, for example, of any family history of psychiatric disorders or any treatment that the client has received with regard to a possible psychotic condition that could not be addressed via hypnotic intervention. The clinician may also be advised to ask whether the client has ever suffered from epilepsy as hypnosis may not be indicated in such a case. If at all in doubt, of course, the practitioner should consult his supervisor or should decline to treat the client. Another safeguard would be to ask the client whether she had ever had any open-heart surgery and to discover whether a pacemaker had been fitted.

Perhaps the most important question of all will be for the practitioner to ask the client about any medication that she is currently taking. The professional practitioner will, of course, require a reliable reference book that will give him comprehensive information about proprietary drugs. The client taking psychotropic drugs, for example, may need to be declined for treatment or, alternatively, a written confirmation from her general medical practitioner would need to be obtained before treatment could commence. Occasionally, the analytical practitioner may be asked to work with the client in conjunction with medical or psychiatric intervention, but this would normally be the exception rather than the rule. If the practitioner were at all in doubt, at any time, then the best course of action would be to refer the client back to her own general medical practitioner for treatment. It would, of course, be a great disservice to the client to build up her hopes of cure or recovery if this were not possible or, even, if her symptoms might be exacerbated by hypnotic investigation (see Chapter 1 – "The Hypnoanalytic Approach"). It will, of course, be generally unwise for the client to be taking chemical medication that will suppress her emotive expression such as antidepressant, sedative or soporific drugs. If the client is taking this form of medication, this practice may either halt or put a significant blockage on proceedings in analytical therapy. The client, in this case, should be warned of the restrictions that such suppressive drugs may have on her progress in therapy and, perhaps, referred back to her medical practitioner. The therapist should also remind the client that any additions or changes to her medication routine should be reported to him. The case-study example below illustrates the way in which the client's treatment was significantly impeded because he did not report a change in his drug regime. In this case, the client began to administer a propriety drug regime midway through therapy that presented an obstruction to effective progress and an appropriate outcome. This alteration to his drug regime was identified during a session in which automatic writing was employed by the therapist (see Chapter 2 – "Therapeutic Investigation").

Case-study example – inappropriate medication
This male client suffered from anxiety and worry, for which he sought analytical hypnotherapy.

The client made good progress and had received eight or nine sessions. The client, however, then reported that he had started to feel constantly dizzy and had feelings of disorientation. Initially, the practitioner assumed that these feelings were related to the client's anxieties, but was puzzled about the mysterious reason why progress had been somewhat halted. The client's dizzy spells, moreover, appeared to be getting uncontrollably worse. Because of this increasingly-apparent impasse, the therapist finally decided to employ the automatic-writing technique while the client was in hypnosis. The practitioner then asked the client's unconscious mind the question, "Unconscious, is there any other reason why my client should continue to experience anxiety and dizziness?" The client was then invited to write a word, a sign or a symbol that would help him to understand the cause of his dizziness. The client then spontaneously reproduced the word "medicine" on the paper in front of him. When the therapist consulted his preliminary case-notes, however, there was no mention of the fact that the client was on any proprietary drugs or any other form of medication. The client, in this case, had unconsciously revealed the source of his mysterious symptoms while having no conscious appreciation of what was causing them. Here then was a classic example of the way in which automatic writing could reveal the root cause of the client's disorder with accuracy and clarity.

It transpired, subsequently, that the client has omitted to mention that some way into therapy his physician had prescribed a dosage of antianxiety drugs that were being steadily increased as part of the regime. The therapist, therefore, brought this factor to the client's attention and he was referred back to his doctor. Once the dosage had been adjusted, the client's disorientation and dizziness began to subside. In fact, the client subsequently elected to tail off the drugs and made a full recovery in therapy.

Health matters

A client may be invited to reveal other information in connection with her health. The clinician might, for example, enquire whether the client wears contact lenses, as hard lenses might cause a distraction when her eyes are closed during hypnosis. The client may also be dissatisfied with her weight – even though she may have sought therapy for an entirely different reason. The client could also be asked whether she smokes heavily, drinks excessively or takes recreational drugs. If the client reports overindulgence in harmful substances and obsessional tendencies are indicated, then this would render her a prime candidate for analytical investigation because the root cause of the problem will need to be unearthed. Certainly an intake of more than 25 to 30 cigarettes per day will be bordering on an obsessive-compulsive disorder rather than simply being a futile habit (see Chapter 7 – "Fear and Anxiety Disorders"). If the client reports that she is a habitual drug-user, then the therapist may be advised to enquire whether she has experienced any side-effects. If the client, for example, reports any "bad trips" while in a drug-induced state, it may well be that a traumatic memory has seeped into her conscious mind during such a trip. The nature of the trip manifestations, therefore, may need to be explored in therapy.

All such enquiry will give the practitioner a complete picture of the client and help him to appreciate the ways in which her inner distress may have affected her. Any improvement in weight or drug-intake, moreover, during the course of therapy will indicate to the practitioner that progress is being made by the client. Similarly, positive progress can be indicated when potential self-harming habits are naturally relinquished by the client.

Intimate relationships

The client may be asked whether she has a current partner and about the nature of this relationship. If the client has a nurturing and loving partner, then her passage through therapy can be assisted by this means of support. If, conversely, the client reports any unhappiness or a degree of discontentment in an intimate relationship, then the practitioner may wish to consider the reasons why this situation has arisen (see Chapter 12 – "Dysfunctional Relationships"). Does the client feel trapped by an unsatisfactory or an abusive relationship? Does the client consider that she has a duty to remain with her partner through thick and thin, even though the relationship may have gone stale or sour long ago? Does the client have such a low sense of self-esteem that she will accept only second best in a relationship? The practitioner may also wish to enquire the age and occupation of the client's partner. Perhaps the client has been associated with a parent-figure. Perhaps the client's partner has been a good provider and she may be reluctant to leave an unhappy relationship in consequence.

The practitioner may also wish to investigate the client's reaction to any relationship breakdowns. If the client has been left distraught or devastated, for example, when an intimate partner has been unfaithful or has left her after a lengthy relationship, then issues of rejection, deception, hurt, abandonment and resentment may need to be worked through during therapeutic intervention. Enquiries about previous relationships of an intimate nature will also reveal valuable information and may show repeating patterns as well as any progression that the client has made. Often making such enquiries will reveal that the client has made a degree of progress in recent years and has reached a point whereby she will not tolerate unsatisfactory relationships any longer.

If the client speaks of any form of sexual dysfunction, the practitioner may wish to make enquiries about the state of the client's sexual health. Does the client have any difficulty with showing affection in a sexual context? Does the client fear or avoid sexual intimacy? Does the client have an obsession for sexual activity? Does the client indulge in perverted sexual encounters? Does the client have any highly unusual or repeating sexual fantasies or inclinations? If the client reports some impairment to her performance abilities or displays tendencies for unusual practice, the practitioner may wish to enquire discreetly about any occasion when the client may have been the subject of sexual abuse (see Chapter 15 – "The Effects of Childhood Sexual Abuse").

Children

The client may be asked about her progeny – both natural children and stepchildren. As she may often reveal aspects of herself in her attitude towards her children, the astute practitioner should make a mental note of all the client's statements and reactions with regard to those in her care. Does the client, for example, take an overcaring and highly solicitous attitude to her children? Does the client interfere too much in the lives of her offspring? Does the client treat her children in a dictatorial or guilt-engendering manner? Does the client fear excessively for the welfare of her children? In many respects, the client may be projecting or introjecting feelings on to her children as a means of attempting to cope with her own inner distress (see Chapter 11, Volume 1 – "Defensive Strategies").

The client, furthermore, who has, in any way, maltreated a child will almost certainly need to face the guilt that such action may have provoked in the therapeutic setting (see Chapter 8 – "Guilt and Shame Disorders"). It may also be politic for the practitioner to ask the age of the client's children. It may well be that the client will personally identify with a child or a close relative. The client, for instance, may relate to a child who may have reached the age at which she herself experienced most of her childhood distress.

Obviously, the client should be asked about any children who are deceased or who have been lost through abortion or miscarriage. It may be that the client did not receive counselling at the time of the loss and, therefore, some bereavement issues may surface during therapy (see Chapter 9 – "Sorrow and Grief Disorders"). The client, in this case, may exhibit a tendency towards self-punishment and may harbour deep regret if she feels that she was instrumental in terminating a pregnancy. This manifestation of regret, of course, can apply equally to the male client as well as to the female client. The effects of this scenario can be ably illustrated in the case-study example given below.

> **Case-study example – effect of abortion**
> This female client sought therapy because she had an inability to conceive a child.
>
> Analytical investigation took the client to a time when she had elected to have an abortion because she had become pregnant as a teenager. When exploring this issue, the client discovered that she was harbouring intense feelings of guilt over killing her unborn child. The client was now left with a feeling of being unworthy to conceive any other children. Knowledge of this fact and the resolution of the accompanying guilt-complex enabled the client to let go of her blockage to conception. The power of the unconscious mind was starkly illustrated in this client's case.

Professional recommendation

The practitioner may also wish to enquire who recommended the client to his practice. This can have the effect of instilling confidence in the client in that she can gain some assurance that the therapist has treated other cases successfully. It may also give the client the impression that all clients come to the therapist by recommendation. These factors will help to build rapport with the client and can instil in her a trust in the practitioner – both elements of which will be vitally important for analytical hypnotherapy.

Contractual arrangements

It will be wise for the practitioner to leave the client in no doubt at all at the outset that the path towards better health via analytical therapy may not be a soft option. Analytical work will involve a degree of commitment, hard work, dedication and a willingness to face those aspects of the client's psyche that have caused her the greatest pain and distress. This confrontation may be no mean task and, therefore, it will be the responsibility of the practitioner to outline the pitfalls and the drawbacks in order to ensure that the client has been fully apprised of her responsibilities and requirements (see Chapter 1 – "The Hypnoanalytic Approach").

Whether or not a written contract has been drawn up for signature by both parties, the ground rules should be spelled out for the client as to what will be required of her. The client should, therefore, be informed of the need to attend regularly, to arrive on time and to pay fees promptly. If the client elects to have her fees paid by a third party, then the dynamics of the relationship with the fee-payer may need to be established in order to ensure therapeutic success. If a third party has agreed to pay for therapy, for example, the practitioner may wish to consider the reason why in order to identify whether this will, in fact, be in the client's best interests. Is the client, for example, wishing to pass the buck and merely to survive the therapeutic encounter? Is the client relinquishing any responsibility for her own part in the process? Is the client unable to stand on her own feet financially? Does the client rely too heavily on others for assistance? Is the client using revenge tactics by making a parent or a loved one pay the cost? Is the client surreptitiously getting a covert secondary gain by making a third party support her financially? Is the client genuinely financially destitute but has found a means, in some way, of grasping an opportunity and going all out to divest herself of psychological trauma with a dogged determination to succeed? Is the client's parent, lover or friend who pays for therapy, however, expecting to exercise any control over her or the therapeutic process? Is the third party somehow attempting to relieve any residual guilt or exercising a manipulative hold over the client? Is the third party being an overcaring rescuer or basking in the glory of being a bountiful benefactor? The practitioner will need to be alert to the pitfalls of such a situation inasmuch as these factors may affect the health of the client and may impinge upon the successful outcome of therapy.

What Causes the Client's Psychological Distress?

Apart from providing a setting which is as far as possible neutral enough to ensure the true freedom of a client's associations, what contributions can the counsellor make to assist clients in "telling their story", and developing their own associations?
– *Michael Jacobs*

In analytical hypnotherapy, the practitioner's role will be gently to tease out of the client her underlying psychological distress. The therapist can investigate the extent to which the client may have been at risk from an inadequate or unsatisfactory upbringing with regard to the way in which her parents or primary carers behaved towards her in childhood. Often this information may be gleaned from taking a detailed case-history but sometimes this data will simply reveal itself during the therapeutic process. The practitioner could, for example, utilise questioning techniques in order to discover any possible scenarios whereby the client may have been at risk in childhood from being psychologically upset by people, events or situations.

Let us now consider some of the questions that the practitioner may wish to pose – particularly in the preliminary sessions with the client – that can help to identify the source of her anxieties, distress and psychological disturbance. It will be imperative for the practitioner to appreciate that the example questions given in this section should be used merely as a guide. The precise wording of questions should, of course, be posed in the practitioner's own words in order to ensure that they appear to trip off the tongue naturally and in a nonchalant, throwaway fashion. Any suspicion that the client may have that the practitioner has rehearsed a given question or is reciting from a book may give her a feeling that she is being grilled by an automaton.

What happened in the client's childhood?

If the counsellor is to attend carefully to what is said and not said, then to make sense of the material, it is essential that he or she hold back from saying too much, because the more he or she gets drawn into the to-and-fro conversation, the harder it is to concentrate upon the client.
– *Michael Jacobs*

In general terms, too much responsibility forced upon the client too early in life will rob her of her childhood and will impair her natural development. If the client answers affirmatively to the majority of the questions cited below, then the practitioner will have an indication of what may need to be dealt with in therapy. At best, affirmative answers to these questions can highlight occasions when the client may have been catapulted into the adult world without adequate resources to deal with the situation. At worst, the client would have been plunged into a state whereby she feared for her life or physical integrity. The practitioner can explain to the client who admits to a number of unpleasant occurrences in childhood, however, that most adults when faced with life-threatening danger could not cope adequately. How then can a mere child be expected to cope with untoward danger or uncertainty? The solution will be that the child does survive to adulthood but then the adult will have to pay an extremely heavy price.

The soul-searching questions listed below can be posed by the therapist in order to elicit information about the client's childhood background and can highlight areas where conflict or trauma may have manifested. These questions, if answered honestly, will encourage the client to assess her own level of exposure to childhood psychological damage. This knowledge will be the first step towards healing the client's distress and may even identify a suitable method for tackling her problems. This list below will obviously not be exhaustive but may serve, in general, to indicate the reasons why the client may consider herself to be in need of help. The practitioner, of course, may not wish to pose such questions during a single session but, perhaps, may elect to intersperse these questions within ostensibly-casual conversation with the client over a number of sessions.

- Do you regard your childhood as having been a happy one?
- Do you consider that your parents sincerely loved you when you were young?
- Did your parents show you genuine and heartfelt affection when you were a child?
- Did your parents spend time with you when you wanted them to during childhood years?
- Did your parents genuinely praise and encourage you as a child?

- Were you supported by your family when at school and during leisure-time activities?
- Did you find that your parents or teachers negated the efforts you put into schoolwork and/or leisure-time activities?
- Did your parents frequently criticise you or humiliate you?
- Did you ever detect an unpleasant atmosphere at home or at school?
- Did you often have fights or disputes with siblings or schoolmates?
- Did you ever feel that your brother/sister was the favourite child of your parents?
- Did you ever feel in any way inadequate when you compared yourself with other children?
- Did you ever find that you tended to be bullied at school?
- Did you feel that you were singled out for punishment or humiliation by teachers?
- Did you have a dictatorial parent, relative, carer or teacher when you were growing up?
- Were you the victim of excessive strictness at home or at school?
- Were your parents inflexible and unforgiving in their attitudes towards you when you were a child?
- Did you ever feel that you had a lack of personal freedom either at home or at school?
- Were you ever physically or emotionally neglected as a child?
- Did you ever experience any overt physical or sexual abuse in your childhood?
- Were you ever aware of any sexual innuendo in your dealings with adults when you were a child?
- Did your parents show affection towards one another when you were a child?
- Were your parents living together throughout your childhood?
- Did you ever hear or see your parents rowing or fighting?
- Did your parents get divorced or separate during your formative years?
- Did you constantly live under the threat of parental separation?
- Were you ever aware that your parents were emotionally unstable?
- Did your parents ever act irrationally or unpredictably?
- Did your parents have irrational or unpredictable mood swings?

- Was one of your parents ill for a long period of time when you were growing up?
- Did one of your parents have any obsessions or phobias?
- Were you ever forced to be away from your home and your family for a prolonged period of time when you were growing up?
- Did one of your parents die when you were very young?
- Did one of your parents commit or attempt suicide?
- Did you ever have to assume responsibility for your parents or your siblings?
- Did your family ever suffer from financial instability or severe hardship?
- Did you ever have to assume responsibility for the family home?

How did the client perceive childhood?

> The fundamental datum of endowed temperament is therefore developed and modified in its expression by the earliest experiences of the infant, especially by those which have major affective impact through the fulfilment of basic needs and the experience of pleasure or pain. This is necessarily an interactive process, in which the child is as much actor as recipient. This latter point is important, since the experience of producing responses from others is central to be developing self-image of the client.
> – Hellmut Karle & Jennifer Boys

When assessing the client, the practitioner will also need to encourage her to consider what the effect of any childhood distress may have had on her. The client will, of course, need to ponder the way in which she personally perceived any traumatic events or conflicting situations. The client may, perhaps, need to be reminded that she is a unique individual and will, therefore, have experienced life in a manner different from the way in which others, such as a sibling, beheld the world. One client's dream will be another's nightmare. A relatively insignificant, single episode in the client's childhood, in some cases, can do infinite damage because of the way in which she perceived that event. If the client, for example, were living in a reasonably happy and cosseted childhood environment, sometimes she will then not have developed the necessary resources to cope with unexpected danger in the external world because of its rarity. The average rough and tumble of school, for instance, could have a devastating impact on the mollycoddled child. Obviously, an ongoing situation of hardship, neglect or abuse will be likely to have a lasting and detrimental effect on the client until it is resolved. If the client knows that she was ever in a significantly life-threatening situation or was ever in physical danger at any point in her life, then this may well be her reason – consciously or otherwise – for seeking professional therapeutic help.

The client, of course, will be equipped with a more-or-less efficient coping-mechanism that will permit her to get through the rigours of life. The client will then adopt her strategy in order to secure her passage during childhood and, subsequently, throughout adult life. If the client has a high coping-ability, then she may be more likely to be able to withstand a substantial amount of buffeting prior to reaching breaking-point. If the client has not been so fortunate, however, she may quite apparently display, for all to observe, the signs of psychological distress in daily life. In both cases, however, attention will need to be paid to the client's psychological difficulties without delay. The following statements are those that the client may make and, in so doing, indicate to the therapist areas for investigation because in such statements she may be revealing the source of her disturbance.

- My parents always had rows after I had gone to bed.
- My parents separated when I was young.
- My father died when I was young.
- My stepfather never showed me any affection.
- I was bullied mercilessly by my older sister.
- My mother ignored my anguish when my pet rabbit died.
- My mother used to drink a lot.
- I think my mother was jealous of me.
- I was sent to boarding-school when I was young and it was awful.
- I never seemed to make friends at school.
- I hated my grandmother because she was so cold and distant.
- I never really knew the members of my family.
- We only saw my aunt and uncle at Christmas.
- There was only one teacher at school who seemed to like me.

When a statement of this nature has been proffered by the client, the practitioner would be wise to enquire how she felt about that event or situation. Did the client, for example, feel confused, scared, lonely, embarrassed, ashamed, ungrateful, cross, resentful, sad, upset, rejected, bewildered or strange? Perhaps, the client can be asked to gauge her emotive reactions with a high, medium or low rating or, alternatively, on a 1-to-10 rising scale.

Let us now consider a number of case-study examples in which the client's rating of childhood experiences led to the discovery of the root of distress, the knowledge of which, subsequently, facilitated its resolution. The case-study example given below shows the way in which the client can rate a number of childhood experiences.

Case-study example – lack of confidence

A male client who had suffered from a low self-confidence was asked by the therapist about his childhood experiences. The client reported that, when he was a young child, his parents often had rows after he had gone to bed and this had made him feel lonely and isolated. This loneliness was given a high rating by the client because he felt that he had no-one to whom he could turn. Later, the client's parents had separated while he was still young and this had made him feel sad. The client, however, gave this a medium rating because – by the time his parents had split up – he was more or less resigned to the inevitable.

On further investigation, the client was able to trace his lack of confidence back to those times when his parents had been constantly rowing and he had felt powerless to control events. The client's profound feeling of loneliness that developed from this unhappy situation had led him to become withdrawn and to lack the assertiveness necessary to interact successfully with others.

In the following case, the client had suffered from a depressive disorder that was crippling her ability to function.

Case-study example – depressive disorder

A female client who had suffered for some years from depression was asked by the practitioner about her childhood experiences. The client mentioned that her father had died when she was a young child and that she could not really remember him when he was alive. The client stated that she felt sad and confused when reporting that she could not even remember her father. The client gave these feelings a medium rating. After her father had died, the client's mother had remarried but her stepfather had never shown her any real affection. The client reported feeling cross that this was so but gave this emotion only a low rating.

To add to her problems, the client's older sister had bullied her but her mother did not seem to come to her defence. The client stated that she felt bitter about the fact that her mother had let her down and gave this emotion a high rating. It transpired that the client felt most keenly the fact that her mother had let her down and this then became the root of her distress. The client also felt the loss of not having really had a father-figure in her life. The client's childish logic, furthermore, had reasoned that her father must have died because her mother was such an uncaring person.

In the next case-study example, the client suffered from bouts of uncontrollable anger and this was threatening a current relationship.

Case-study example – temper tantrums

A female client who had suffered from bouts of uncontrollable anger had, on several occasions, physically attacked her partner. The client was asked by the practitioner about her childhood experiences and, when questioned, she reported that her mother had been an alcoholic throughout her childhood. The client felt confused when reporting this fact and gave this reaction a low rating.

The client also stated that she felt that her mother had always been jealous of her. Even though she felt curiously angry and ashamed at mentioning these facts to the practitioner, the client gave both these feelings a high rating. Subsequently, the client realised that because she had felt guilty when her mother had been jealous of her, she had endeavoured to suppress her anger about such treatment. In therapy, however, the client began to realise that her anger towards her mother was justifiable and that she no longer needed to displace her anger on to her partner.

In the case-study example given below, the client had suffered from anxiety attacks and the discovery of the originating cause took a circuitous route.

Case-study example – panic attacks

A female client who had suffered from panic attacks was asked by the therapist about her childhood experiences. The client reported that she had been sent to boarding school at an early age but had never seemed to make friends at school. The client reported that she felt resentful about being sent away from home and gave this a medium rating. The client, moreover, had also felt lonely at school and gave this emotive response a high rating.

Next, the client mentioned that her grandmother, whom she had often stayed with in the school holidays, had been cold and distant towards her and her brother. The client also expressed a feeling of indifference, on the one hand, but a feeling of being cross, on the other. The client gave a low rating to her indifference but a high rating to her anger. On further investigation, the client discovered that the combination of her loneliness at school, her grandmother's coldness and her parents' general rejection of her had led her to feel that she had been abandoned by all. This feeling of abandonment then gave rise to her panic attacks and bouts of anxiety.

How does the client express emotion?

> Problems, depending upon their nature, evoke in us frustration or grief or sadness or loneliness or guilt or regret or anger or fear or anxiety or anguish or despair. These are uncomfortable feelings, often very uncomfortable, often as painful as any kind of physical pain, sometimes equalling the very worst kind of physical pain.
> – Scott Peck

The client may have difficulty in expressing her emotions – principally because the release and realisation of the impact of negative emotive expression will not normally be a pleasant experience. For this reason, therefore, the client may need to be introduced slowly to the fact that emotive discharge can have a cathartic effect (see Chapter 1 – "The Hypnoanalytic Approach"). Disturbing incidents that have occurred in the client's life will affect her not merely because of the event or because of her perception of it but because of the way in which she reacted to it psychologically and physiologically at the time. When the client's emotive responses are involved, she will be affected profoundly and at the deepest levels of her being. The client's emotive expression, moreover, will come into play in terms of everything that she experiences. The more deeply she has been affected by an event or circumstance, the greater will be the power of the effect on the client. The client's emotive expression, therefore, will be at the very core of her existence. The human organism cannot experience any event in life without its having a unique emotive effect, to a greater or lesser degree, that will impinge upon her psychology. The snag, however, will occur when the client, for any reason, experiences an inability to discharge emotive expression and, consequently, may need some gentle persuasion from the practitioner. Often the blockage of emotive responses will be an unconscious defensive strategy on the part of the client (see Chapter 11, Volume 1 – "Defensive Strategies").

Once the client's emotive processes have been contacted, it may, of course, be possible for her to bounce off from any positive recollections towards more disturbing material (see Chapter 5 – "Therapeutic Resolution"). The following list of questions can be utilised by the practitioner in order to help the client to make contact with any happy events in which a personal expression of deep emotion has been shown by her.

- Do you feel joyously moved when you watch a romantic play or a film?
- Do you derive pleasure from communication with children?
- Do you enjoy observing and interacting with nature?
- Do you feel stimulated if you rise to a challenge and then achieve success?
- Do you feel pleasantly excited when you watch a competitive game or sport?
- Do you feel enthusiasm for other people's achievements?
- Do you look forward with eager anticipation to weekends and holidays?
- Do you find yourself daydreaming about pleasurable things?
- Do you feel a warmth of love surrounding you?

Again, such questions do not need to be posed by the practitioner in a formal context but may be left simply to hang in the air for the client to ponder and can, of course, be interspersed during general conversation. The client can also be questioned about those times in her life when happiness manifested itself. For the client in dire distress, of course, the search for happy occasions may prove to be entirely fruitless, but this form of enquiry can serve to demonstrate to her that her therapeutic investigation will need to deal with negative emotive reactions.

The suggested passage below can serve to imbue the client with the courage to face up to her painful emotive expression by focusing initially on positive experience as the key to more distressing matter.

From happy to sad ...

When we experience positive events, we experience positive emotions as well and, then, all is well. Positive emotions bring us joy and happiness, peace and tranquillity. Positive emotions bring harmony and balance into our lives. These are the emotions that make our existence worthwhile and from which we will derive the greatest pleasure. We are inherently and instinctively pleasure-seekers and our existence craves such positive emotions. Perhaps you can think of some occasions when you felt joyously happy, contented or, even, elated?

If, however, we experience a surfeit of negative emotions, our life can be severely hampered or restricted. We are instinctively pain-avoiders and our aim in life will be continually to overcome and resolve negative feelings. The principal negative emotions are those of fear, guilt, anger and sadness and their by-products. These are the emotions that can overwhelm or even obliterate our positive emotions and, in doing so, can have a detrimental affect of our wellbeing. We suffer to a greater or lesser extent from a combination of negative emotions but you may find that you will suffer principally from perhaps one or two. Also, one emotion will often lead to the next in a sort of viscous-cycle action. If you feel fear or guilt, this could lead to your feeling angry or sad. If you feel angry, then, this may engender sadness. If you feel sad then this may, in turn, give rise to anger or fear. In other words, our emotions are frequently on a continual merry-go-round. We can also suffer from a roller-coaster syndrome whereby a feeling of sadness may be followed by a feeling of joy. Or a period of joy can be followed by a sense of despair. Or a period of feeling guilty could precede an angry outburst. Sometimes we find that the root cause of our problem resides in fear or guilt and that anger and sadness are the knock-on effects.

Once the client has been able to express some form of positive emotive response, she may then be ready to explore the negative side of her psyche. In order to investigate the client's negative thoughts and feelings, the following questions may be posed by the practitioner.

- Do you frequently think that life has no purpose for you?
- Do you feel uncertain or indecisive about where you are going in this world?
- Do you sometimes consider that the weather has an effect on your mood?
- Do you feel despondent if you have a row or a disagreement with a family-member?
- Do you ever feel frustrated when waiting in a traffic jam or in a bus queue?
- Do you regard work as a drudgery or a necessary evil?
- Do you despair when your partner arrives home from work or comes into the room?
- Do you frequently feel alone in the crowd?
- Do you consider that you are the slave of your negative emotions?
- Do you feel that you are in a hole from which you cannot dig yourself out?
- Do you believe that you are constantly rushing around and yet getting nowhere fast?
- Are you sometimes beset by an overwhelming sense of confusion?
- Does despair sometimes utterly overtake you for no apparent reason?

The practitioner might also wish to make a careful mental note of the client's language patterns when these denote positive emotive expression (see Chapter 3 – "Unconscious Communication"). Often when the client focuses on the positive aspects of her life, she may be expressing optimism at her personal ability to recover from the distresses of the past. Positive phraseology may also indicate that the depressed or suicidal client, for instance, has not yet given up hope. The client's pleasant thoughts, furthermore, can also indicate a desire on her part to get on with her current life and to move forward. In the following case-study example, the client had suffered from suicidal depression for a number of years, owing to the fact that she had been severely deprived and neglected as a child. This example, however, illustrates the way in which therapeutic progress can be made for the client who was able to turn profound unhappiness into positive joy via investigative enquiry.

Case-study example – depression and anxiety
This female client suffered from severe depression and anxiety because of the way in which she had been neglected in childhood.

The client was asked to consider extensively the toll that her neglectful childhood had exacted. Towards the latter end of therapy, however, she made a number of unprompted statements that indicated to the practitioner than she did have a positive purpose in life and had found a truly supportive partner who could see her through her distress. Some examples of this client's statements were:

- I love playing with my children
- I cherish the moments I spend with my partner
- I really do love making love
- I love stroking and caressing my cat
- I am fond of sitting by the fireside and reading
- I often cry tears of joy when I see a beautiful landscape
- I love sitting by a lake and watching the birds
- I adore watching the sunset
- I love watching the rain and snow from my window
- I love pottering about the garden on a Sunday afternoon
- I adore cooking and entertaining and home-making generally
- I enjoy listening to good music and have a large collection

Because there was genuine hope in this client's life, she became a seeker rather than an avoider in therapy. The client had, therefore, found a means to pull herself through even the most gruelling aspects of therapy. The practitioner, moreover, was able to capitalise on the client's underlying optimism and to utilise her love of nature when inducing hypnosis.

Motivating the Client

Time doesn't really exist, except as an abstract concept in your head.
The present moment is the only time you have.
Make something of this moment!
– *Andrew Matthews*

When dealing with the client who utterly despairs of success in therapy and cannot possibly see the proverbial light at the end of the tunnel, the practitioner may be able to make judicious use of rhetorical questioning techniques in order to resolve the impasse. Here are some examples of suggestions and questions that again can merely float in the air in the consulting room rather than be formally posed by the practitioner. They can be delivered in a throwaway manner but can institute an inner search in the client's unconscious mind and may, of course, initiate a chain of much-needed further reflection.

- Perhaps caution could persuade you to stock up for the winter?
- Perhaps you could feel a tinge of excitement when planning your new life?
- Maybe you could see yourself as a wise old owl?
- Could you prevent yourself from wondering what others are thinking of you?
- Could you dump your guilt and just be yourself when delivering your next speech?
- Maybe you could consider your opponent's feelings when playing your next game of tennis?
- Perhaps you could wash the kitchen floor for your own satisfaction rather than for the benefit of the family or the neighbours?
- Perhaps you could decline that invitation to go to the pub at lunchtime?
- Could you permit yourself to relax occasionally and find creative ways of achieving this for yourself?
- Could you believe in yourself more when planning new projects?
- Could you invest in a labour-saving device in order to streamline your work?
- Could you allow yourself to be fired up once a week instead of every day?

- Could you count your achievements in life rather than your failures?
- Could you make hay while the sun shines and rest when it sets?

The following suggested passage could also be used in order to motivate and inspire the client towards self-actualisation by addressing the question of motivation.

What motivates you?

We are motivated by our own unconscious processes that dictate our behaviour patterns. Let us consider, first of all, the negative aspects of motivation in terms of our negative emotions.

Sometimes we are motivated by fear. If a man-eating tiger were to approach you in the street, what do you think you would do? Stand there and let him devour you? Or, perhaps, run away and hide? Sometimes we are motivated by guilt. How many times do you visit your old Auntie Betty or Uncle Bob because you feel you ought to? How frequently do you put a coin in a charity collector's box because you feel it might do someone some good? Sometimes we are motivated by anger. How often do you feel like killing someone but go and clean the car instead? How often do you feel like having a good scream but refrain from doing so because you might upset the neighbours? How often do you kick the cat or bark at the kids when you are feeling wretched? Sometimes we are motivated by sadness. How often do you take yourself to the cinema or go out for a meal because you feel depressed? How often do you have a good cry because you feel alone and lost? How often do you withdraw from social interaction because you simply do not feel up to it?

Well, we can turn these negative motivations around and get them to work in our favour. Turn fear into excitement, adventure and anticipation. Turn guilt into reliability, fair play and honesty. Turn anger into enthusiasm, strength and determination. Turn sadness into caring, nurturing and loving. Can you think of any creative ways in which you could utilise your negative emotions in order to motivate yourself in a positive manner?

Similarly, the client can be stimulated towards setting life-goals. The following suggested passage could, perhaps, be employed in the later stages of therapy when the client will be endeavouring to reintegrate herself into society.

Where are you going?

In setting your goals in life, you will need to bear in mind where you are going and how you are going to get there. Essentially, goal-setting and goal-attainment will require that you become realistic and thorough and that you do not collapse in a welter of hopelessness if the going gets tough. Learn to be realistic, therefore, when setting your goals. Don't draw the chalk line too high or too far away so that you cannot possibly jump over it. Sometimes we punish ourselves in this way. We set ourselves impossible tasks and then beat our bosom when we obviously cannot attain our ideals or maintain our ridiculously-high personal standards. Often we do not know that it is best to quit when we are winning rather than to continue and to push our luck too far towards failure. Set goals with realistic time-frames, therefore, when planning operations. Do not expect instant or overnight success. Give yourself the maximum chance. Make a realistic estimate of how long you will need to spend on a given project and then plan accordingly. Again avoid bringing the self-sabotage mechanism into play by expecting too much of yourself in too short a time.

Remember to do your homework thoroughly when preparing to accomplish a project or undertake a given task. When you go on holiday, you will, of course, need to pack a suitcase, order the travellers' cheques, take a map and plan your route. It will be the same when you are planning to achieve a goal. If you are taking a driving test, learn the highway code. If you are giving a speech, prepare your material well and rehearse in advanced. If you are going to tackle the boss about a pay-rise, then find out what is a reasonable salary for the job you are expected to do.

Also, take things one step at a time when working towards your objective. Aim for little bit-size pieces rather than trying to swallow a big chunk in one go. Perhaps you could do a little each day or do things gradually. In this way you will then see steady progress. Reward yourself regularly, of course, for the progress you make at every stage. Make a mental note of the progress you have made in therapy perhaps by reflecting back on the past and considering what you have achieved. You have made tremendous progress with me. Always give yourself a pat on the back when a job has been well done. Do not spend time dwelling with regret on abortive attempts or abandoned projects – this will be a waste of your precious mental energy that could undoubtedly be put to better use. Value yourself by appreciating and rewarding your own efforts.

Client Profiling

The analytical-hypnotherapy practitioner may wish to ponder the following points when formulating a profile for the client.

- Is the practitioner clear about what the client hopes to achieve from therapeutic intervention?

- Has the practitioner allowed the client to position the goal-posts in terms of the therapeutic outcome?
- Does the client appreciate what her role will be in therapy in order to achieve her specified outcome?
- Is the client a seeker or an avoider in terms of her attitude to the therapeutic process?
- Has the practitioner gained an overall picture of the client's psychological and physiological health?
- Does the client have an appreciation of the stresses that her occupation or other work-activity may be imposing on her?
- Does the client understand the way in which her schooling and educational experiences have effected her?
- Can the client learn to appreciate the way in which her relationships with others are dictating her existence?
- What type of relationship has the client formed with her children?
- Does the client exhibit any unresolved grief due to the loss of a child or a near relative?
- Has the practitioner gained an impression of those aspects in the client's past for which investigative exploration could be beneficial?
- What has most affected the client in terms of her familial upbringing?
- What perceptions does the client have of her childhood experiences?
- How does the client express her positive and negative emotions?
- Does the client in any way hold back her emotive expression?
- Does the client need to be motivated in order to address the past?
- In what ways can the client become motivated in order to uncover her most distressing experiences?
- Does the client know where she is going in life and does she believe that she has a purpose?

Chapter 5

Therapeutic Resolution

I disapprove of what you say, but I will defend to the death
your right to say it.

– François Marie Arouet Voltaire

What Does Therapeutic Resolution Achieve?

Transforming trauma isn't a mechanical ritual that traumatised people
can perform and then sit back and complacently expect results. There is
no magic pill. Transformation requires a willingness to challenge your
basic beliefs about who you are. We must have the faith to trust
responses and sensations that we can't fully understanding, and a
willingness to experience ourselves flowing in harmony with the
primitive, natural laws that will take over and balance our seemingly
incongruous perceptions.
– Peter Levine

When undertaking investigative analysis, the therapist may be
tempted occasionally to forget that therapeutic exploration alone
will not be the key to the client's recovery. When the client
unearths distressing material from his psyche, this will be but a
starting-point for the work of resolving the distress that has put
disturbing material in place initially. Therapeutic resolution can be
regarded, therefore, as the cement that will seal the cracks and prevent leakage even in stormy weather. In this chapter, therefore, we
shall discuss those aspects of therapeutic intervention that deal
specifically with resolving the psychic material that the client has
brought to the surface through the investigative and enquiry
process.

Although a great deal of analytical hypnotherapy may involve
shaking the cage continually until the bird falls out, the practitioner should not overlook the fact the client must make

realisations and gain insight in order finally to become free of his symptoms. Acceptance of the past as a life experience that the client has surmounted and can now look upon with equanimity will be of paramount importance to the successful outcome of analytical therapy. Therapeutic resolution, therefore, will be the process of consigning the past to insignificance but not, of course, denying its existence. The client can now come to realise that there can be a distinction between event, effect and consequences. The event could be, for example, that the client was beaten as a child. The effect then might be the physical injury that the client sustained, the psychological damage that transpired and the coping strategies that he has adopted. The consequences of the occurrence of the event and its effect would, moreover, have had repercussions throughout the client's life – affecting his behavioural tendencies, emotive inclinations, self-concept and social interaction. Therapeutic resolution, therefore, should equip the client to come to terms with these factors and to iron out the consequences long after he has left the consulting room.

Therapeutic resolution will usually take the form of encouraging the client to relinquish manifestations of guilt and shame, feelings of low self-worth and any erroneous beliefs about his personal inadequacy or incompetence. From this vantage-point, the client can then desist from actions, behaviours and motivations that have reflected his formerly low self-esteem. The client, for example, can be guided towards breaking self-destructive habits or modifying unproductive relationships (see Chapter 12 – "Dysfunctional Relationships"). This winning combination of identifying the originating cause of the client's conflict and then working through this disturbance will inevitably transport him to a stage whereby he can become virtually symptom-free, can be reintegrated into society and can resume a harmonious daily life. Usually the client will progress from identifying the root cause of his trauma, to discharging accompanying emotive expression, to realising the irrelevance of such negative expression and, finally, to relinquishing the need to express such emotive responses before he can begin the process of rehabilitation. This transition may, of course, occur in a number of stages that are blended seamlessly into one integrated whole rather than separated into discrete phases. Suffice it to say, however, that the therapeutic process will not be concluded until the client has journeyed through each of these distinct phases.

Much time and effort have been expended in devising increasingly
effective methods of uncovering critical experiences; all too frequently,
the successful location and identification of these experiences have been
equated with successful therapy. In truth, therapy has only commenced
when this stage has been reached.
– *Edgar Barnett*

The client should also learn to find his true personality throughout
the therapeutic process and develop faith and trust in the dictates
of his unconscious mind (see Chapter 2 – "Therapeutic
Investigation"). The client can be invited to realise that he has an
inner voice and can be taught to listen to it. The inner voice will be
the client's instinct and intuition, that will constantly need to be
consulted. The client's inner voice can tell him when he needs comforting. The client's inner voice can tell him when his body is ail-
ing, when his spirits are flagging and when he might be in need of
therapeutic support. This inner wisdom can help the client to take
decisions by telling him what would be right or wrong for him.
Inner wisdom can inform the client whom to trust and whom to
avoid. Inner wisdom can also discover which path would be
appropriate for him to take in life. The client may, in the past, have
learned not to trust his inner guide because he previously felt that
it had let him down far too often. Once the truth about the past has
emerged, however, it will be time for the client to begin to rely on
himself. The process of guilt-stripping will also mean that the
client can come to terms with what his emotive needs really are
and then pursue them earnestly. It will be as if the client who may
have been a victim of neglect, trauma, misuse or abuse will be getting to know the person he really is and can become acquainted
with this new friend.

When children are abused, their perceptions become threatening to them.
To acknowledge that the neighbor who pushed you on the swings and
gave you birthday presents was also the man who made you suck his
penis was unbearable. To admit that your father, who went to work to
support you and stayed up late to make you a dollhouse, had a scary
smile on his face when he touched your genitals was too terrifying. So
you pretended they weren't doing these things or that these things were
really all right. The lengths to which children go to distort their
perceptions are striking.
– *Ellen Bass & Laura Davis*

Inner-Child Methodology

> Many survivors have a difficult time with the concept of the child within,
> even though forgiving that child is an essential part of healing. Too often
> women blame her, hate her, or ignore her completely. Survivors hate
> themselves for having been small, for having needed affection, for
> having "let themselves" be abused.
> *– Ellen Bass & Laura Davis*

Inner-child work can be a method of utilising the client's imaginative and intellectual faculties in order to resolve unconscious childish logic. This methodology can dovetail admirably into the
practice of analytical therapy because it can assist the client who
has been left vulnerable to unconscious psychological distress by
the rigours of his past. The client may, for instance, be beset by
emotive or childish logic that will ensure that he remains wedded
to his traumatic past. The adult client, therefore, may cry like a
baby, may shudder with childlike terror, may mourn the loss of
love in his childhood and may feel indignant at the negligence of
his parents or primary carers. Expressing and releasing such childish emotive responses – perhaps even adopting the foetal position
or cowering with infantile shame – will, naturally, relieve the client
of the bulk of his psychic distress because it will be a means of discharging crippling psychological manifestations.

Inner-child work will often form the missing piece in the client's
psychic jigsaw puzzle. The client will frequently need to appreciate unconsciously how he actually felt as a child. Why did the child
adversely react when his wrathful teacher approached? Why was
the child so naïve and vulnerable when being required to look after
a drunken parent? Why was the child so afraid of his dictatorial
babysitter? Why was the child so willing to believe that he had
committed a heinous crime by not tidying his room? Why was the
child so susceptible to being deceived when his parents insisted
that they were not rowing? Why was the child so in awe of parents
who had supposedly caused him no harm? The inner child will be
the one who suffered mercilessly at the hands of neglectful or abusive adults. The inner child felt the pain and torture. The inner
child repressed his thoughts, memories, emotive reactions and
physical pain in the interests of his own survival. The inner child
could not escape the agony. The inner child was incarcerated by
circumstances, parental shock-reactions and society's shortcomings.

In therapy, it will be the inner child – as a metaphor for the client's unconscious mind – whose turn it will be to speak freely and to release all. The practitioner's endeavour should be to get into the mind of the child within the client in order to invite him to see life from an immature and illogical viewpoint because this will then bring about much-needed insight into a problem at its root. The basic premise of inner-child methodology will be to encourage the client to imagine himself as a young child in need of help and then to summon the assistance of his adult self in order to balance the scales. The adult self, thus, will become a close ally and tenacious being who befriends, protects, guards and loves the childish nature of the client. Let us now enumerate and explore some of the con-figurations that inner-child therapy can take.

> We can learn so much from children. And most of us have the good fortune to get closely reacquainted with the magic of childhood twenty or thirty years after we were children. If our children then have children, we get another lesson some years further down the track.
> – *Andrew Matthews*

Rescuing the inner child

> Victims often find themselves, as adults, displaying childish behaviour. For instance, they may be very fearful of putting petrol in their car at the petrol station, worrying that they may do it wrong and make a fool of themselves. When angry about something, perhaps they throw a childish tantrum. Others may have problems during conversations, by butting-in in an attempt to direct the attention to themselves or by trying to "top" other people's stories with "Yes, but listen to what happened to me ..." or "You think that's bad – I ..."
> – *Penny Parks*

When rescuing the inner child, the client may be asked to recall himself in a hazardous situation in which he felt defenceless and needed to be promptly rescued from the impending danger. Often, of course, he will see himself as the victim of circumstances in which he was at the mercy of another. When rescuing the inner child, the client's adult self will need to arrive on the scene, to take immediate charge of the situation and then to effect a dramatic and powerful rescue-operation. The client, in this respect, will be taken from a position of helplessness into a status of triumph and bravery.

The following case-study example will provide an illustration of the inner-child rescue technique whereby the client was able to extract himself from an unhappy home-life.

Case-study example – childhood neglect

This male client had been severely neglected as a child by his foster parents. The client's own parents had been killed in a plane-crash when he was a small child and he had been placed in the care of foster parents who had then neglected him badly.

The client pictured himself in a scene whereby he was alone in the house late at night. The client felt cold because there was no heating in the house and his foster parents had gone out for the evening. In this scene, the client had not been fed that day and his hunger pangs, therefore, were keeping him awake. The client began to panic and to cry at this recollection.

The practitioner invited the client to verbalise his feelings and to express them in an appropriate manner. The client reported that he felt utterly alone, helpless and vulnerable as a young child in such circumstances. The practitioner then encouraged the client to see himself as a suitable rescuer. The client imagined himself as a fire-fighter who was as tall as a house and as strong as an ox. The client was able to visualise a rescue-operation in which his home was broken into and the firefighter then stormed in and swept the child up in his arms. The child was then taken away to safety by the fire-fighter, who spoke gently to him, lovingly wrapped him in a blanket and fed him. In this case, the client was able to effect his own rescue from appalling home conditions and an impossible situation while, at the same time, dislodging his negative emotive reactions.

Empowering the inner child

> The best guide for healing is your own inner voice. Learning to trust your own perceptions, feelings, and intuitions forms a new basis for action in the world.
> – *Ellen Bass & Laura Davis*

When empowering the inner child, the client may be invited to recall himself as a powerless or a helpless victim. The client's adult self can then enter the scene, befriend the child and imbue him with sufficient power and strength to weather even the most violent storm. The client, thus, will be recognising his own inner strengths and engendering the necessary courage to face what he has perceived to be a fearsome ordeal.

> Psychologically deprived and damaged children will find themselves very much less able to withstand even the normal wear and tear of adult emotional life.
> – *Gael Lindenfield*

In the case-study example given below, the client contacted and derived great personal strength from employing inner-child methodology in order to empower herself.

Case-study example – interview nerves
A female client who had recently lost her job sought therapeutic assistance because she was terrified of going to interviews.

The client had not done particularly well academically at school and, when she had been chosen to play the lead in a school play, her parents had not even bothered to watch her perform. The client was asked to return to the time when she was performing in the school play. The client remembered the arduous rehearsals that she had to attend and how it took her many weeks to learn her lines. The client also remembered her first night nerves as well as the way in which she had been praised for her performance both by staff members and classmates.

The client was then asked to visualise that time when she felt disappointed that her parents had been too busy to watch her performance. The client keenly felt the disappointment at their absence on the one occasion when she had excelled. The client was then invited to summon a recording angel to visit her parents and to reprimand them for their neglect of the schoolchild. The child then listened to her parents being sternly reprimanded and begging her forgiveness, that she grudgingly granted out of the kindness of her heart. The recording angel was also sent to visit the young child, who was then empowered with strength and determination to go to her next interview. The client's younger self was then invited to merge with her adult self – safe in the knowledge that the angel would guard over her while she attended her forth-coming interviews.

Protecting the inner child

> Many survivors have lost touch with their own vulnerability. Getting in
> touch with the child within can help you feel compassion for yourself,
> more anger at your abuser, and greater intimacy with others.
> – *Ellen Bass & Laura Davis*

When protecting the inner child, the client may find himself in a situation in which he will earnestly require protection from a foe or an external hazard. The adult self can then be invited into the scene in order to provide care and protection for the child. In this scenario, the client will be acknowledging the fact that he has within him the power of self-protection and the means by which to pull himself out of the mire in any difficult circumstances.

> During childhood, most children don't consciously recognise that they
> are being abused or ill-treated, unless the parents' behaviour is very
> overt and flagrant. The developing child, from infancy to the end of
> adolescence, is at the mercy of its parents or those adults surrounding it.
> The child attempts to survive. If survival becomes threatened by the
> behaviour or feelings of parents, the child is able to switch off its
> attention, or lessen its awareness of specific events and behaviour.
> – *Margaret Reinhold*

The following case-study example provides an illustration of the inner-child technique whereby the client was able to afford herself protection from an abusive schoolteacher.

Case-study example – timidity in relationships
This female client had become the subject of severe punishment at school at the behest of her form teacher and, in consequence, she had developed a profound fear of any social interaction.

When the client had been in senior school, she had been the victim of a great deal of humiliation because she felt hated by her teacher. The teacher had constantly reprimanded the client for her late attendance at classes, the poor quality of her homework assignments and her general appearance. The client had, on several occasions, been unfairly sent to the head teacher and been given detention or extra work as a form of punishment. It was as if the teacher had a personal vendetta against the client.

When the client was recalling a given incident in which the teacher was loudly shouting at her in front of the whole class, the practitioner suggested that the child might find a way of protecting herself from the teacher's wrath. The client was then guided through a scene in which her adult self entered the classroom and lashed the teacher with a cat-of-nine-tails whip. The client put all her force into thrashing this teacher and humiliating her in front of the entire class. The young child was also invited to cheer while this process was happening. The client was urged to dole out an even worse punishment to the teacher than she had herself received. The client was able to achieve this anger expulsion with acclaim – showing the teacher no mercy and sparing her in no way at all.

Finally, the client decided to kill the teacher and to bury her beneath the school building along with the head teacher, who had also been instrumental in contributing to her timidity in adulthood. The client also elected to kill and bury some of her classmates, who had bullied her at school. This session was the turning point in the client's therapeutic recovery process.

Loving the inner child

> A "block" is a place where energy is constricted – not moving, not flowing. Usually blocks are caused initially by repressed emotions of fear, guilt, and/or resentment (anger) which cause a person to tighten up and close down spiritually, emotionally, mentally and even physically.
> – *Shakti Gawain*

When the client can engage in loving the inner child, his whole concept of self can begin to improve. Initially the client may be asked to imagine himself as an unhappy and lonely being in childhood. The adult self can then be requested to show the child love as if he were his own progeny. This technique, of course, can be particularly powerful when the client has young children or is anticipating starting a family. The client may be invited to show love for his inner child as a means of acknowledging that he was unloved in childhood but that he can now provide himself with the love that had previously eluded him.

> We all unconsciously strive to reach that more mysterious, perhaps more
> wonderful world were animals live, where feelings are paramount and
> conceptual thinking takes second place.
> – *Margaret Reinhold*

The case-study example below illustrates the way in which the inner child can be lovingly nurtured by the adult client.

Case-study example – bereavement

This female client had recently lost her mother but had been unable to grieve over this significant loss at the time of her mother's death.

The client had spoken at length about her association with her mother. The client had reported how her mother had read to her when she was a young child, how she had helped her with her studies when she was at school and how she had taken a great interest in her career advancement. The client remembered one time, however, when her mother had forgotten to send her a birthday card when she had first gone to boarding school and acknowledged the disappointment that this oversight had caused.

The client was then asked to visualise herself as a young schoolchild who was feeling lonely and neglected. The client was asked to imagine the way in which she would treat such a lonely and neglected child. The client responded by stating that the child, at that time, had needed a lot of love and affection. The practitioner, therefore, encouraged the adult client to nurture and to pamper the young child, to hug her, to kiss her on the cheek and to stroke her brow as if she were her own daughter. The client then took her child-self away from the boarding school to a place of peace and rest. In this place, the adult client was able to explain to the child-self the reasons why she had been neglected by mother on this occasion and gave her permission to express her regret about the past. Following this session, the client was able steadily to unload her grief reactions, that, consequently, included feelings of resentment and guilt.

Self-Advisory Methodology

> Less direct methods of uncovering have also been developed by analysts who have evolved special skills in their interpretation. Every analytical hypnotherapist should acquire these skills because they occasionally offer an alternative avenue of therapy when the direct methods have been rejected by the patient.
> – *Edgar Barnett*

A number of techniques can be utilised in analytical hypnotherapy that make a direct contact with the client's unconscious mind, even though such contact will be made in an indirect manner. Let us now consider some of the ways in which the client's unconscious mind can be accessed in a self-advisory capacity.

> Proper use of this technique requires an interactive trance in which you periodically question patients about who their adviser is and what their adviser says or does.
> – *David Bresler*

Discovering the inner adviser

> This is primarily an insight-oriented hypnotherapy technique for uncovering information related to physical or psychological symptoms. Essentially, this method gives form and voice to the "unconscious" mind or inner wisdom of the patient.
> – *David Bresler*

A number of techniques can be devised that place the client in a self-advisory role whereby he can become his own counsellor. By this means, the client would be consulting an aspect of himself and, in the process, would gain an insight into his true inclinations. The client's inner adviser, in many cases, may initially appear to be reticent and so the practitioner will need to tease out this particular manifestation of inner wisdom.

> Shamans have long believed their powers were the powers of the animals, of the plants, of the sun, of the basic energies of the universe. In the garden Earth they have drawn upon their assumed powers to help save other humans from illness and death, to provide strength in daily life, to commune with their fellow creatures, and to live a joyful existence in harmony with the totality of Nature.
> – *Michael Harner*

The following suggested metaphorical passage can be used to inveigle the client into becoming his own counsellor and tapping into his own internal sagacity.

Your inner adviser ...

I am going to ask you to meet a very special person who resides in your own mind. This person will speak only to you. This person will be your inner adviser. Take yourself to a place of beauty and safety and afford yourself a degree of rest and relaxation in readiness for this encounter with your inner self. Just wait a moment and he or she will appear. This person is now coming to meet you, so discover him or her for yourself. This person may, of course, be a bit shy at first but give him or her time to materialise.

I don't know whether your inner mentor is a man or a woman but I do know that you will know when you see him or her. Alternatively, you may see a very special creature – perhaps an animal or a mythical being. This will be your inner adviser. Perhaps you can describe your inner adviser to me now.

Now get to know your chosen counsellor and let him or her communicate with you. Allow him or her to communicate with you perhaps in words or maybe telepathically. Your inner mentor will find a way of communicating with you that will be right for you. Let him or her speak to you now and, maybe, you can share with me the message that your counsellor is giving you? And is there anything else that your adviser wishes to tell you? Give him or her a chance to impart all that he or she needs to convey. Perhaps you can consult your inner adviser on a regular basis because, you know, he or she will always be there for you.

Consulting the inner adviser

> In my view, the process of encouraging clients is often one of guiding them into a position where they can acknowledge personal strengths and resources previously overlooked in themselves.
> – Michael Yapko

Once the client's inner adviser has been discovered, it should then be a reasonably straightforward job to be able to consult him or her for a myriad of reasons. When consulting the inner counsellor, the client can be given free reign to decide on the shape, the form and the gender of his inner adviser and to enter the realms of fantasy, mysticism or spiritualism if he so desires. The client should also be encouraged to develop a rapport with his adviser so that information can be readily elicited from his unconscious mind. Perhaps the inner adviser can help either to explain a problem or to advise the client about the way in which a difficulty could be resolved. The practitioner should, of course, ensure that the client's inner adviser has communicated fully with him during the session and that further consultation can take place when required. The client can also be encouraged to arrange regular meetings with his adviser in the future, either within or outside the therapeutic context.

While the client may usually find this consultation an easy procedure, he may initially find it difficult because of the imaginative and fantasy-related aspects of this methodology. If the client, for example, displays a tendency to feel foolish about working in this way, then, perhaps, an alternative methodology could be utilised. The client, however, can be informed that it is perfectly natural to feel this way and that the aim of all therapeutic intervention should be to function within his comfort-zone.

There may, of course, be times when the client will give no response to any form of direct communication or unconscious consultation with his inner adviser. When this occurs, the practitioner could ask the reason why the client's unconscious mind has declined to respond. If the client still fails to respond, then ideo-motor-response techniques could perhaps be employed and the unconscious mind could then be asked some further questions. The practitioner may also wish to ponder the reasons for this impasse as suggested below.

- Does the client's condition require medical attention?
- Does the client's plight have a practical purpose?
- Could the client's unconscious mind rectify this situation if it were appropriate?
- Does the client's predicament serve any beneficial purpose?
- Does the client hesitate because of a surfeit of embarrassment?
- Is the client resisting the process because he has not yet learned to trust himself?
- Does the client feel that he should be dependent only on others for guidance and not on himself?
- Could the client be persuaded that this self-advisory process is a perfectly natural and beneficial agency?

The therapist should remember that sometimes the client will have a tendency never to complete any project that he begins because circumstances will always occur that prevent completion of such tasks. This factor may well arise for the client because he will fear being judged by his completed products. This tactic can, therefore, be a means of opting out of taking responsibility and a way of evading criticism largely due to the client's unconscious fear of failure. This deflective device, thus, can be classified as a secondary gain (see Chapter 12, Volume 1 – "Resistance"). When the client opts out of healing, the practitioner should, of course, bear this factor in mind rather than indulge in self-blame. The problem might then be surmounted by further investigative methodology before attempting therapeutic resolution.

Parts Methodology

> In hypnoanalytic ego-state therapy we are constantly moving back and
> forth between activating regressed states, lifting repressed material,
> analyzing means, then contacting and integrating with the normal,
> egotized executive state of the patient.
> – *John Watkins & Helen Watkins*

Parts therapy deals with elements of the client's psyche that may contain problem-areas, be in perpetual conflict or have been disowned because of negative associations. The client, for example, may be torn between wanting to relinquish a habit or electing to remain with his source of supposed comfort. The client, alternatively, may feel anxiety but yet not be able to realise that this emotive expression may be underpinned by guilt. Sometimes it may be beneficial for the client to symbolically envisage aspects of himself who may wish to negotiate or to resolve some form of conflicting impasse. Parts methodology has, of course, been based on the theories put forward by ego-state psychology (see Chapter 4, Volume 1 – "Ego-State Therapy"). The following case-study example illustrates the way in which a client came to terms with her internal conflict using this creative methodology.

Case-study example – boarding school blues
This female client was beset by feelings on indecision and confusion and the main thrust of her therapeutic enquiry centred on unfolding this inner conflict.

The client recalled a time when she was at boarding school and felt terribly alone and miserable – a state that she described as "boarding-school blues". The client found that she was confused by her circumstances but could not easily verbalise the feelings she harboured about this situation. The client was invited to consider the people at her boarding school and to note her personal reactions to her tutors and her classmates by way of manifesting her concealed emotive responses. The client spoke of one girl who was aggressive and domineering to whom she reacted by being cowering and afraid. This part of the client was imaginatively personified as a girl called Help. Next the client recalled another girl who was cold and dismissive and her reaction to this classmate was one of hurt. This feeling gave birth to the symbolic representation of a small child whom the client named Baby Girl.

The client now imagined Help and Baby Girl together in the dormitory of her boarding school. Help stated that she had nowhere to turn and was thoroughly misunderstood while Baby Girl felt utterly immobilised and alone because she had suffered under the tyranny of several inmates. Finally, the client was asked to bring a stronger version of herself into the scene. After some reluctance, the client manufactured a being known as Rescuer who was able to negotiate with Help and Baby Girl by telling them that boarding school days are now over. The client was able to appreciate that Help and Baby Girl were able to keep each other company in times of need but that they now no longer needed to fulfil this important function.

By this means the client was able to identify and to express her feelings of fear and loneliness but then to consign these immature states to the past and to move on in her life having cleared up her former confusion and distress.

Cognitive Methodology

> Balancing is the discipline that gives us flexibility. Extraordinary flexibility is required for successful living in all spheres of activity.
> – Scott Peck

When the client has uncovered his innermost secrets and has abre-acted about the effects of his recollections, the practitioner may still need to ensure that he can become reconciled to his past trauma-seeding experiences. The use of cognitive strategies, at such times, can, therefore, be effectively employed in order to assist the client with the resolution of his difficulties (see Chapter 9, Volume 1 – "Cognitive Therapy"). The client's aim should be to reintegrate his past experiences into his newly-structured psyche. Cognitive restructuring and reframing strategies could be employed, for example, in order to help the client to eliminate guilt or to recon-textualise a pressing problem. The client's low opinion of himself, moreover, may need to be changed. The client may need, for exam-ple, to adopt a different view of his body-image or attractiveness to others. The client may also wish to adopt a more optimistic view of the future or to consider that he can have the courage to face any forthcoming confrontation or similar ordeal.

The case-study example below illustrates the way in which the client can be induced to come to terms with a traumatic past once detailed investigative therapy has been administered.

Case-study example – dysfunctional childhood
This female client had undergone an extensive amount of therapy in order to deal with the fact that she had been unable to form con-genial relationships with others.

The client's dysfunctional childhood patterns of relating to others had been explored in depth in therapy. The client was now left with a feeling of hopelessness about the fact that she had been damaged for life as a result of her childhood experiences, at which time she was given no blueprint by which to interact successfully with oth-ers. The client had left a trail of unsuccessful relationships behind her and had never been able to find the life-partner whom she so desperately sought.

From this position of despair, the client was asked to review her thoughts about her life. The client concluded that she could not possibly find the right partner because she had been so used to forming unproductive relationships. The client was invited to express her opinions about this situation with a view to coming to terms with her difficulties and, perhaps, changing her standpoint.

The client was invited, for example, to consider the possibility of remaining single or gathering about her a number of platonic relationships with others. The client conceded that she might well be content not to entertain any further relationships with sexual partners for a while. The practitioner also invited the client to consider that she might require a rest from the ordeal of finding a partner. The client accepted that she was still young enough to find a partner and that a brief period of abstinence from the chase might be in order for her right now – particularly in view of the fact that she had only recently shifted the major bulk of her distress. The client also appreciated that if she did not earnestly try to find a lover, she might, in fact, then find one by accident.

Facilitating Therapeutic Resolution

> As you move through these stages again and again, you will reach a
> point of integration. Your feelings and perspectives will stabilize. You
> will come to terms with your abuser and other family members. While
> you won't erase your history, you will make deep and lasting changes in
> your life. Having gained awareness, compassion, and power through
> healing, you will have the opportunity to work toward a better world.
> – *Ellen Bass & Laura Davis*

The time will eventually arrive for the client when he can begin to let the past go and can leave the safe haven of the therapeutic setting. Distressing or traumatic events will not hold the same significance in the client's mind as they did when he first intrepidly entered the consulting room. The client's psychic trauma or conflict and its surrounding circumstances cannot be forgotten but the heat within his memories can begin to subside. This stage can arrive only after the client has exorcised the pain of the past and has put the whole of his life into context.

At the end of a period in therapy, sometimes the client may be reluctant to face the external world because he may have learned to appreciate that reality may not be all a garden of roses. It has been claimed that the most difficult thing that the client will have to do in life will be to free himself from the bondage and tyranny of childhood dependency on his parentage. This will be what the analytical client will have to do when he leaves the therapist but, perhaps, the prospect may be even more daunting. It will be as if the client will need to rip off the identity-label that was placed on his forehead long ago. The client will now need to rely solely on his own personal resources in order to rescue himself rather than be supposedly rescued by the practitioner. The client will now need to count on himself as a fully-functioning member of society without the impediments that the past may have placed upon him. The client may, however, come to realise that, in a bizarre way, the past will have imbued him with considerably more strength and endurance-capacity than the average person. During this reclamation process, the client will recover his true self-identity and can then choose a path in life that will currently be appropriate for him.

> Recovery can take place only within the context of relationships; it cannot occur in isolation. In her renewed connections with other people, the survivor re-creates the psychological faculties that were damaged or deformed by the traumatic experience. These faculties include the basic capacities for trust, autonomy, initiative, competence, identity, and intimacy.
> – *Judith Lewis Herman*

When moving on from the past, the client can start to live a normal existence. The bulk of his psychological baggage will have been dumped, disturbing memories will have surfaced, perceptions will have been thoroughly examined and related symptoms can now begin to subside. Old habits and destructive relationships can dissolve and the client can begin to lead his life in his own way. The client may now become untrammelled by overbearing influences and psychological drives but he will still need time to adjust to his newly-found mindset.

> Authentic moving on is a natural result of going through each step of the healing process. It comes slowly and sometimes takes you by surprise.
> – *Ellen Bass & Laura Davis*

The client may decide to pursue a vocation that will be more in keeping with his true self and, perhaps, will reflect his valuable life-experiences. The fledgling can, thus, set out to achieve those things that he has always wanted to do but has never dared to seek. Sometimes pursuing spiritual activities – such as becoming a carer or a healer or becoming interested in the progress of the universe – can be of benefit to the client. The client may also find that taking an interest in artistic or creative hobbies may fulfil a need. A greater involvement in and enjoyment of nature can similarly be a pursuit to which the client may direct his energies.

Success in a chosen career may simply become a natural progression. An important career move, for instance, can ensure that the client will be able to excel in an area for which he has natural talent. Forging ahead in life will not be uncommon for the client who has undergone analytical therapy. As long as the client's interest in such matters does not become obsessive and, therefore, will have the effect of perpetuating his psychological disturbance, then such activities and pursuits can be regarded as healthy and healing.

> There's a part of everything living that wants to become itself – the tadpole into the frog, the chrysalis into the butterfly, a damaged human being into a whole one. And that's spirituality: staying in touch with the part of you that is choosing to heal, that wants to be healthy, integrated, fully alive. The little part of you that is already whole can lead the rest of you through the healing process. It's the inner voice that you learn to trust again.
> – *Ellen Bass & Laura Davis*

The following suggested passage can enable the client to appreciate the benefits of the ongoing process of gaining personal independence.

Attaining emotional freedom ...

So what does emotional freedom mean and how will you know when you have finally secured it?

Emotional freedom means the freedom to be yourself and to satisfy your own needs untrammelled by the expectations of others. Emotional freedom means not allowing yourself to be downtrodden or exploited by others. Emotional freedom means demanding that others respect you as much as you respect yourself. Emotional freedom means living in the here and now – not in the murky past or in the dreams of the future. Emotional freedom means loving yourself – warts and all. Emotional freedom means taking responsibility for all your thoughts, feelings and actions. Emotional freedom means praising yourself for your efforts whether you win or lose. Emotional freedom means accepting that your failures cannot destroy you. Emotional freedom means having a high degree of unshakable self-respect. Emotional freedom means that you are free to express your emotions. Emotional freedom means the ability to empower yourself to get what you want out of life and, occasionally, to accept that you may never be able to attain it.

> Everything you need or want is here for the asking; you only need to
> believe that it is so, to truly desire it, and to be willing to accept it, in
> order to have whatever you wish. One of the most common causes of
> failure to get what you want is "scarcity programming".
> – *Shakti Gawain*

The practitioner may often need to plant seeds in the client's mind
that will expose him to the concept of change. After investigative
work has been undertaken, therefore, the client may require an
invitation to forge his own path and to shake off the shackles of the
past. The metaphoric imagery contained within the suggested passage below has been designed to implant in the client's mind the
notion that he can be the author of his own destiny.

The changing seasons ...

Winter is the time of the year for conservation. All nature conserves industriously those things that she needs for the coming months. The swan finds her
nest in the reeds. The fox keeps to his lair. The fireside becomes our sanctuary
and our comfort. We look inwardly at ourselves. We contemplate our existence – perhaps by the fireside watching the flames licking the coals or logs.
We reflect on and consider the past, the present and the future. We look out of
our window at the snow and icicles and are glad that we kept to the hearth.
Winter brings rest and much-needed peace. But winter is a time of expectancy.
We wish to put the past behind us and we long for the longer days and the
shorter nights. Winter, therefore, is a forward-looking time, filled with hopes
and aspirations.

The daffodil heralds in the spring. It trumpets in new beginnings, freshness
and excitement. The snowdrop ventures forth expectantly, taking courage in
its tiny enterprising way. The snowdrop is the smallest of all flowers and yet
it pushes its way triumphantly and unaided through the hard earth. Warmth
comes to the earth, to the flowers, the shrubs and the trees in spring. Our furry
friends scurry about busily. Our feathered friends build their nests industriously, making ready for those all-important forthcomings. Spring personifies
the regeneration of life.

When life is recreated, summer begins. The river is in full flood. The sky is
pure blue and cloudless. The sun's rays can be felt on our skin. We can shed
our outer garments, drift out of our routine, take that well-earned rest. We can
go away to far-off lands and places, taking the train or the plane, exploring,
investigating and absorbing the atmosphere of all we behold anew. Returning
refreshed, invigorated and exhilarated – ready to settle, to regenerate and to
recharge our batteries anew.

Autumn is the season in which we make ready. A settling period when we can
watch the leaves fall and make preserves from the produce of summer. The

farmer reaps and stores his harvest. Our furry friends burrow in readiness for the frosts. We gather about us those things that we need to get us through those coming restful days. Those days that inevitably lead us onward.

And, just as sure as day follows night, summer follows spring and autumn follows summer and autumn precedes winter. So the round of the seasons continues, year after year and with an inevitability about the cycle of the seasons. As every age has its grace, so each season has its own unique importance and offering. Each season brings its own special qualities. Each plays its part. A cycle of change, each season having its own pattern and place in the scheme of things. The changing seasons regenerate life. So rest now and regenerate.

Validating Therapeutic Success

> A critical experience, and the Parent/Child conflict resulting from it,
> cannot be regarded as having been satisfactorily dealt with until it is
> certain that the conflict is indeed at an end and all of the associated,
> outdated, uncomfortable and unnecessary tensions responsible for the
> symptoms have been relinquished.
> *– Edgar Barnett*

During the final stages of therapy, the client can be encouraged to confirm the results of his success in therapy so that he can be assured that his problems are truly at an end by putting himself to the test. This validation may, of course, happen naturally or the client may need to venture forth in order to be able to see the light at the end of the tunnel. The phobic client, for instance, could approach the source of his fears (see Chapter 7 – "Fear and Anxiety Disorders"). The obsessive or compulsive client could gain evidence that he no longer needs to carry out the ritual. The depressive or reclusive client could begin to take an active part in life (see Chapter 9 – "Sorrow and Grief Disorders"). This phase of the client's therapeutic voyage may be a critical time of testing and verification of progress and can, of course, be met with both the joy of success or the disappointment of failure. Can the alcoholic remain dry? Can the drug-addict stay squeaky clean? Can the compulsive eater continue not to binge? Can the anorectic maintain a healthy diet?

The practitioner's job at this final juncture will be to reassure the client that positive success can be within reach despite any human lapses. The practitioner should also endeavour to instil confidence in the client by explaining that progress can take time before it can be soundly maintained. If necessary, further therapeutic work on the originating cause may still need to be undertaken. Perhaps the client will still need to go through the process of putting the past in context by tying up some of those loose ends. By this means, the client will be able to gain concrete evidence of the release of his distress and, indeed, can watch his symptoms diminish in time. Continued freedom from symptoms will, in itself, be reassuring for the client. Often the client will notice that his symptoms have abated by their absence rather than by a conscious awareness of not succumbing to temptation. The client's confidence can, furthermore, be rebuilt by his remaining symptom-free and knowing that he has mustered the strength to conquer his problems.

> Rehabilitation indicates that this is the final but certainly not the least important stage of therapy. It is the phase necessary to ensure that the patient makes the essential post therapy adjustments in order to remain free from the symptoms.
> – *Edgar Barnett*

Client Profiling

The analytical-hypnotherapy practitioner may wish to ponder the following points when formulating a profile for the client.

- In what ways will the client need to resolve his past distressing experiences?
- What forms can therapeutic resolution take for the client?
- In what ways can inner-child methodology assist the client?
- Does the client feel in need of protection as a result of his childhood experiences?
- Does the client lack the capacity to love himself?
- What might transpire if the client were to consult his inner wisdom?
- In what ways could the client visualise an inner adviser?
- Could the client benefit from the use of cognitive reframing or cognitive restructuring methodology following investigative therapy?
- What will the client need to achieve in order to move on from his past?
- In what ways could change be facilitated in the client?

- In what ways can the client attain emotional freedom?
- In what ways can the client validate his success in therapy?
- Does the client experience any difficulty in moving away from the practitioner?

Chapter 6

Therapeutic Planning

Skill without imagination is craftsmanship and gives us many useful objects such as wickerwork picnic baskets. Imagination without skill gives us modern art.

– Tom Stoppard

Why Plan Analytical Hypnotherapy?

What the hypnotist is interested in is a certain class of changes in the functioning of the mind and body brought about in a non-physical and naturalistic way.
– Dylan Morgan

The practitioner may wish to undertake a certain amount of strategic planning, particularly when dealing with a potentially problematic case. An overall concept of what will be required of the client in therapy, an appreciation of where her path may be going and an understanding of the therapeutic purpose can greatly assist the practitioner. Preplanning – especially for the fledging practitioner – will give a degree of confidence and a general direction to the client's therapeutic work. The clinician should, of course, remember that an inappropriate or obsolete plan should be instantly abandoned if it proves to be unworkable. The plan should, therefore, be the practitioner's guide and not his master. The plan should give an appreciation of what will be required but should not force the client into a rigid structure that can engender self-blame if she does not happen to comply totally with the practitioner's wishes. Let us now consider with an open mind the basis for analytical hypnotherapy and the shape a series of sessions may be likely to take for the client.

> The purpose of training in psychotherapy is to facilitate the exercise of
> natural abilities and acquired skills to best effect.
> – *Mark Aveline*

Fundamental Principles of Analytic Practice

> What characterises good psychotherapy of any sort is a sustained,
> affirmative stance on the part of an imaginative, seasoned therapist who
> respects and does not exploit. I hope that my relationship with the
> patient is both passionate and ethical, for both these elements are
> necessary if personal change is to occur. In the interplay of therapy, I
> influence and am influenced by what passes between us. It is the other
> person's journey in life, but it is a journey for us both and one in which I
> may expect to change as well as the patient. It is a journey and not an
> aimless ramble: though the ultimate destination may be unknown, the
> way-stations are known by the therapist and aimed for; the therapist has
> expertise in guiding the other through terrain which is new to them.
> – *Mark Aveline*

The fundamental principles of analytical therapy are wide and varied in that the methodology will embrace a climate of exchange in
which the client can unload the intolerable burden of her psychological baggage in the most effective way and in the shortest time
possible. Let us now examine in broad outline these fundamental
principles in terms of the practitioner's facilitative interaction with
the client.

> The pressure toward health makes therapy possible. It is an absolute *sine
> qua non*. If there were no such trend, therapy would be inexplicable to the
> extent that it goes beyond the building of defenses against pain and anxiety.
> – *Abraham Maslow*

Providing direction

> How do we learn to play games of skill and strategy? It is important that
> we be clear about the answer to this question, for what is true of games
> of this sort is also true of psychoanalysis. There are some things about
> games that can be taught and learned through the printed word and
> through didactic instruction; there are other things, however, that cannot
> and that must be acquired through practice.
> – *Thomas Szasz*

Essentially, the practitioner should be instrumental in dictating the
overall direction of analytical therapy and the way in which it can

unfold while, simultaneously, handing back control to the client for the direction of her life. It will, therefore, be the ultimate responsibility of the practitioner to engineer all therapeutic strategies in the interests of the client's personal growth. Ultimately, it will be the practitioner who will be responsible for what occurs in the therapeutic environment. Even when the client appears to be taking control in terms of therapeutic direction, this act should still be at the behest of the practitioner.

The therapist may adopt this strategy because he may deem it to be of benefit to the client's recovery. The practitioner, in this case, will be, so to speak, giving the client permission to do precisely what she needs to do in order to bring about her own therapeutic progress. The analytical practitioner, thus, can empower the client by directing the therapeutic process. The client may, of course, expect the therapist to orchestrate her therapeutic sessions and, if the practitioner deems that this would be appropriate, then the lead may need to come from him. The practitioner, however, may wish to relinquish the leading role if the client seems to be unable to take any decisions unaided, owing to overdependence on others (see Chapter 13, Volume 1 – "Transference and Countertransference"). Similarly, the practitioner may need to take absolute control if the client appears compulsively to assume control as a means of resisting the therapeutic process (see Chapter 12, Volume 1 – "Resistance"). At the final reckoning, the choice of direction and strategy, therefore, must be the practitioner's responsibility. If therapeutic assistance will be ultimately directed by the client, in some way, then there may be ample opportunity for her to resist strenuously the process and merely survive analytical investigation rather than benefit unequivocally from it.

Even within this premise, the role of the practitioner should, fundamentally, be to follow the client in respect of her therapeutic needs. The practitioner will, of course, need to make an informed assessment of the client's requirements and then to adapt the therapeutic strategy accordingly. Giving direction and guidance does not, however, mean that the therapist should lead the client, make suggestions or deliver dogmatic pronouncements on the basis of assumption. If the practitioner feels at all uncomfortable or indecisive either about assuming control of the therapeutic process or about relinquishing it in the best interests of the client, then, of course, it would be appropriate for him to consult a supervisor in order to resolve this impasse.

Adopting a neutral stance

> Another great challenge of our times to the psychologist is to develop an approach that is focused on constructing the new, not repairing the old; that is, designing a society in which problems will be less frequent, rather than putting poultices on those who have been crippled by social factors.
> – *Carl Rogers*

The practitioner should, on all occasions, remain in a neutral position when providing therapeutic assistance (see Chapter 6, Volume 1 – "Client-Centred Therapy"). By taking a neutral stance, the therapist can, hence, become the client's supportive lifeline. The practitioner should, therefore, remain impartial, nonjudgmental, unbiased, unimpressionable and dispassionate in his dealings with the client and with whatever she brings into the consulting room. From a neutral position, the client can then divest herself of psychological pain without fear of criticism or judgment. If the practitioner, moreover, keeps a respectful distance from the client, a climate will be created in which transference manifestations can freely develop (see Chapter 13, Volume 1 – "Transference and Countertransference"). The therapist's professional boundaries should, it goes without saying, be maintained at all times both in the interests of the client and, of course, in order to ensure his own continued psychological health. Analytical therapy can take a most exacting toll on the practitioner and, consequently, the importance of personal therapy and regular supervision cannot be overemphasised (see Chapter 1 – "The Hypnoanalytic Approach"). When the practitioner maintains personal psychological health, he can then be of greater service to the client.

Planning Therapeutic Strategy

> The starting point of all hypnotherapy is a client saying, "I have a problem". And the goal of therapy is that same client being able to say honestly and happily, "I no longer have that problem". (It is to be understood that this is not achieved by means of brushing the problem under the carpet and that it is not achieved at the expense of introducing a new and perhaps worse problem.)
> – *Dylan Morgan*

As a rule-of-thumb approach to undertaking analytical therapy, the practitioner may wish to consider a means of guiding the client to that place where she needs to go in accordance with her therapeutic requirements. For this reason, a typical skeletal outline of the unfolding process of the client's therapeutic journey has been set out below.

The introductory session(s)

> The counsellor encourages free expression of feelings in regard to the problem. To some extent this is brought about by the counsellor's friendly, interested, receptive attitude. To some extent it is due to improved skill in treatment interviewing. Little by little we have learned to keep from blocking the flow of hostility and anxiety, the feelings of concern and the feelings of guilt, the ambivalences and the indecisions which come out freely if we have succeeded in making the client feel that the hour is truly his, to use as he wishes.
> – *Carl Rogers*

The introductory session(s) should have the function of setting the scene and acclimatising the client to the therapeutic process. This will also be the occasion when the client can be introduced to the way in which the practitioner conducts therapy. The initial session(s), therefore, will prepare both the client and the practitioner for the work to be undertaken in the fullness of time.

During the initial session, the practitioner may wish to devote the entire session to case-history-taking and similar therapeutic enquiry (see Chapter 4 – "Therapeutic Enquiry"). This preliminary investigation may include a number of assessment techniques or psychometric testing. The practitioner, for example, may favour the application of the Luscher colour test as a means of personality-assessment or use of the galvanic-response meter in order to monitor stress-levels in the client. Essentially, such enquiry will not only familiarise the practitioner with the client's case but also will direct the client towards the unconscious work that she may need to accomplish. The client should, of course, be given an initial opportunity to state her case, to outline her symptoms and, generally, to furnish the practitioner with as complete a picture as may be necessary during the preliminary stages. This introduction will also provide an opportunity for the practitioner to establish rapport with the client and to allow the transference-relationship to develop (see Chapter 13, Volume 1 – "Transference and Countertransference").

The hypnotherapeutic practitioner may also wish to give the client an opportunity to get used to his voice and may accelerate this process by providing her with a relaxation tape if this has been deemed appropriate. If the client's case is complex, it may be unlikely that there will be time for hypnosis during the introductory session. It may be politic, of course, for the practitioner to perform some suggestibility testing with the client prior to the application of hypnosis as a means of introducing this therapeutic vehicle. The practitioner may, in some cases, for example, require a degree of assurance that the client has the ability to plummet the depths of her unconscious mind when analytical investigation needs to be undertaken as indicated by the multitude or the extent of her symptoms.

The ground rules of therapy should, of course, be established during the introductory session(s) with regard to the client's regular attendance, payment for sessions, cancellation fees and any other logistical requirements. The client can, hence, be provided with an upfront framework within which she can operate for her personal benefit with no room for any backtracking manoeuvres. In the process of creating the secure therapeutic environment, the client may, of course, come to the realisation that analytical investigation can be a painful process and, therefore, the practitioner may need to be very careful when setting the scene. The practitioner may need to juggle finely those factors that will contribute to success in therapy – namely, a thorough investigation of the client's painfully-emotive issues in a conducive climate aimed at abreactive release, personal insight and psychological freedom. Getting this delicate balance accurately right will, of course, mean the difference between success and failure because the client must commit heart and soul to the therapeutic encounter and then stay the course in order to overcome any seemingly insurmountable obstacles. At the end of the preliminary session, for example, the practitioner should feel entirely happy about working with the client and could, perhaps, ask her whether she would be willing to undergo the form of therapy that has been has outlined. With the client's consent and agreement, the practitioner may now wish to book a series of sessions in advance if this is at all possible in order to secure the client's further commitment to the process.

The introductory session(s) will also provide the practitioner with the opportunity to make an assessment of the client and perhaps to ponder on the proceedings for future reference. Is the client, for example, confused or disoriented in any way? Is the client understandably fearful at the prospect of therapy and likely to present a plethora of resistance tactics (see Chapter 12, Volume 1 – "Resistance")? Is the client perhaps over-enthusiastic or too optimistic about the outcome of therapy? Is the client overemotional and likely to burst the banks of her own dam at any moment? Is the client ice-cold and intellectual? Does she display any inclining at all about the real cause of her symptoms?

The follow-up introductory session(s)

> The modern concept of freedom is a complex one. It stems from various sources and reflects the aspirations of men who lived under varying conditions; its aims differ accordingly.
> *– Thomas Szasz*

The secondary phase of the therapeutic process will be the time to put the train on the track and to negotiate any junctions that may be encountered on the client's therapeutic journey. During the follow-up introductory session(s), the client may now capitalise on the foundations that have been laid after the initial introductory session(s). Any matters arising from the initial enquiry can be ironed out for her and rapport and transference can continue to develop at this stage. Sometimes this process of opening up the client's mind may be assisted by the judicial use of posthypnotic suggestion in order to speed up the unfurling of her psychic distress. Should the practitioner also wish to teach the client self-hypnosis as an aid to therapeutic investigation, then this period may be an appropriate time to employ this methodology by way of providing her with a portable lifeline for everyday use or for use in emergency.

This follow-up phase may well be the time when the client will be introduced to hypnotic intervention. Even when the client has experienced hypnotherapy previously, she will still need to be

introduced to the methodology used by the practitioner. These follow-up sessions will be likely to provide the requisite opportunity
for the client's mind to open up like a flower, to explore her imaginative processes and to be introduced to investigative methodology such as free association (see Chapter 2 – "Therapeutic
Investigation"). The client's sensory world can also be probed
using imaginative and sensory imagery in order to provide a
sound means of accessing her recollections, impressions and bodily sensations. The client could also be introduced to the concept
that her dreams may be of significance (see Chapter 14, Volume 1
– "Dreams and Symbolic Imagery"). Perhaps she can be encouraged to relate a recent or recurrent dream and to appreciate the significance of such representations in terms of both emotive
expression and symbolism.

Let us now consider a case-study example that illustrates the
impact that a follow-up introductory session can have on the client.
The client, in this case, took flight at the prospect of investigative
probing but returned to complete therapy after the shock of her initial realisations.

Case-study example – relationship difficulties

This client sought therapy because she was having trouble with
forming a long-term relationship with her intimate partner. The
client reported a series of disastrous relationship break-ups, all of
which had left her distraught and devastated.

In the second therapy session, the client, under hypnosis, instantly
recalled a time when her father had sexually abused her at a very
young age. This recollection, however, was met with total disbelief
by the client. The practitioner wisely made no comment about the
form or the content of the client's supposed recollection.

The client refused to attend any further sessions and therapeutic
assistance was, therefore, terminated at this point but the door was
tentatively left open by the practitioner. The client, however, rang
out of the blue some three years later and requested a further session. At this prearranged session, the client then asked the practitioner to remove the memory of incestuous abuse from her mind.
The practitioner willingly agreed to the client's request. The client
was given hypnosis using a quick induction method, after which

the practitioner, using a cunning tactic, merely said, "It didn't happen", and then brought her instantly out of trance. The client, after a moment, replied nostalgically with the words "But it did!" It had taken the client about three years to come to this realisation and requesting this session was her way of finally seeking therapeutic help at a time when she was able to deal with matters. Therapy was completed successfully with the client and it transpired that her initial resistance was due to the fact that she had herself contemplated touching a child's genitals.

One particularly significant breakthrough during this therapeutic encounter was the way in which the client's mother had received the news of her husband's abuse of her daughter. When the client confronted her mother about her father's abuse, her mother then continued to live with the abusive father. The client, thus, found her mother's intrinsic condoning of the incestuous abuse to be a major turning point in her realisation of what the situation had actually represented. This compliance on her mother's part, furthermore, had been reminiscent of the way in which the client herself had refused initially to accept the veracity of her initial recollections.

The subsequent sessions

> In our transactions with experience we are again the locus or source of
> valuing, we prefer those experiences which in the long run are
> enhancing, we utilise all the richness of our cognitive learning and
> functioning, but at the same time we trust the wisdom of our organism.
> – *Carl Rogers*

Once the client has well and truly decided to embark on the therapeutic journey and has not been frightened off by realising what may be to follow, subsequent therapeutic sessions may proceed in a manner that will accommodate her requirements. Techniques such as free association, age-regression, ideomotor investigation and judicious questioning, for example, may be employed in order to unearth buried or underlying material (see Chapter 2 – "Therapeutic Investigation"). Similarly, methodology aimed at cementing a resolution can assist the client's enlightenment process (see Chapter 5 – "Therapeutic Resolution").

This middle phase will be the time for peeling off the layers of negative programming that the client has built up over many years and for demolishing outmoded defensive strategies (see Chapter 11, Volume 1 – "Defensive Strategies"). In a sense, the practitioner will be working from the general factors to the specific elements of the client's underlying problems. It should be during this phase that the client can begin to reveal to the practitioner those darkest secrets that have been locked tightly within her breast for many years. These subsequent sessions, therefore, will provide her with the opportunity to investigate her psyche at the deepest levels and to expose those things that may never have been revealed to another living soul. This act of bearing the soul will be the client's passport to success and the magnitude of its empowering value should not be underestimated. During this investigative phase, of course, the practitioner should be constantly vigilant when handling the client in order to ensure that those innermost skeletons do not stay in the cupboard. The practitioner should, therefore, be alert for hesitations, breaks in the memory-chain and general reluctance that may constitute unconscious resistance to the unravelling process (see Chapter 12, Volume 1 – "Resistance").

The number of sessions required for this phase of therapy may be anything from three to thirty-three, as a general rule of thumb, depending of the extent of the client's distress, the amount of material that surfaces during therapy and the degree of compliance with the process that the client will be willing to undergo. For this reason, it may well be impractical and, if not, slightly arrogant of the practitioner to give the client any definitive prescription in terms of the number of sessions that she will require. Perhaps the practitioner could give guidance in the light of experience following the introductory session(s), but certainly should not provide any guarantee or definitive prognostication with regard to the client's therapeutic outcome. The situation really amounts to asking "How long is a piece of string?"

The concluding session(s)

Detecting illnesses in persons you have never seen is astonishing enough,
but we never let go at that. Into the bodies where we project our
awareness we also project healing.
– José Silva

When psychological freedom has been attained by the client, it will, of course, be the time for her to move on and this factor should be recognised by the practitioner (see Chapter 17, Volume 1 – "The Case for Therapy"). The practitioner, therefore, should not lose sight of the fact that the ultimate aim of all therapeutic intervention will be for the client to break free of her therapeutic dependence and to start that important new life. Sometimes the client may know when it will be time to leave and will voluntarily wish to terminate sessions. The practitioner should, of course, be able to assess whether the time is, in fact, right from the point of view of the client's wellbeing. A desire to leave therapy, in some cases, of course, may be a resistance ploy on the client's part and it may be appropriate to apprise her of this fact.

Alternatively, the client may regard therapeutic assistance as the comfort-zone in which she has nicely settled and a reluctance to leave the therapeutic environment may indicate an unwillingness to move forward. In such a case, it may be that the client's transference manifestation will need to be resolved by a gentle push from the practitioner. It may well be that being supposedly cruel will also be a kindness to the client. The practitioner could, for example, give the client notice that sessions will shortly be terminated as a gentle inducement to start considering the breakaway process. As a rule of thumb, about twelve to sixteen sessions should be sufficient for the average client undertaking short-term analytical hypnotherapy for relatively major problems. If the practitioner, therefore, detects in the client a wish to remain in her safe seat, then a gentle nudge will have the effect of allowing her to break away and, perhaps, to sever any transference manifestations. Perhaps the client may feel disloyal about leaving the practitioner as she might neglect to pay attention to a parent and then start to feel guilty about it. If the client still feels a degree of rejection or a fear at the prospect of the future at this point, then this transference manifestation should be therapeutically considered. Should the practitioner feel a pressing reluctance to part with the client, on the other hand, then some personal investigation may need to be undertaken in order to discover whether any unhelpful countertransference has been in evidence within the therapeutic relationship.

Because all therapeutic work will be a lifetime's journey, all the practitioner can undertake to do will be to move the client further along the road. It will be unlikely that the client with ever be totally free of a psychological disturbance, whatever method of therapy has been employed. There can be no such thing as a total cure because of the constantly fluctuating dynamics of the client's mind and the fact that she will, on a daily basis, be faced with the testing rigours of social interaction. In principle, at least, therapeutic assistance could continue for the rest of the client's life but, in practice, this would be an unwise course of action. The client may be relieved of certain symptoms and come to accept the past with equanimity as a result of undergoing analytical therapy, but this will not be to say that further progress cannot still be achieved.

The point must surely arrive, however, when the fledging must flee the nest and must fly independently with her own wings. On the positive side, a total absence of any therapeutic intervention at all will not be in the best interests of the client and so her therapeutic journey should have been worthwhile even if only a limited degree of change has occurred. The client should, of course, be given hope and inspiration but, perhaps, not a blinkered view of an idealistic utopia attainable via therapeutic intervention. After all, one of the aims of therapy will be to put the client in touch with stark reality and enable her to accept that reality as concrete fact. As a safeguard for the therapist, he might inform the client that she could, if all goes according to plan, expect a symptomatic improvement in the region of 30 to 40 per cent after a series of sessions. This somewhat arbitrary percentage figure would usually, in reality, be considerably higher for the average client who undertakes comprehensive analytical hypnotherapy, but if this quotation can be placed on the conservative side then neither the client nor the practitioner will be disappointed.

The practitioner will usually know intuitively when it will be time for the client to leave the therapeutic enclave or when she has achieved all that of which she is capable at this juncture of her life. Other indications may be that the client may tend to go over familiar ground that has previously been excavated. Similarly, the client may deviate significantly from her usual routine. The client may, for example, sit in a different chair, sit in the therapist's chair, arrive late or cancel a session. The astute practitioner will be able to read the signs easily. If additional work is indicated and the client appears to be just about to swoop on a fresh consignment of enlightenment, then all will be well and the therapeutic encounter can fruitfully continue. If, however, the clinician gains the impression that the client is merely attempting to cling to the therapeutic setting, then kindly untying the apron strings may well be what will be required in the best interests of therapeutic progress. In such cases, the transference that will have manifested here will complete when the client finds herself out on a limb and forced to fend for herself without the substitute-parent lifeline (see Chapter 13, Volume 1 – "Transference and Countertransference"). The practitioner, in this situation, may content himself with leaving the door wide open for the client to return and/or indicating that help may again need to be sought elsewhere in a variety of forms in order to further her therapeutic journey.

We shall now consider some case-study examples that will serve to track the client's progress as well as to illustrate the way in which the hypnoanalytic process can be put into practice. In the case-study example below, the practitioner decided to take things slowly initially with his male client and to acknowledge that he had suffered from his problem for many years. Because the client, moreover, was able to regard the therapist as a father-figure – evident because he treated the practitioner with deference – this manifestation of transference significantly assisted him.

Case-study example – believed insanity
A young man sought therapeutic assistance because he feared that he was going insane. The client felt that he was reaching the point where he could not sleep and that something unaccountable was keeping him awake at nights.

During the first session, the client revealed a great deal about his childhood and he was taught self-hypnosis. The client, however, experienced difficulty when learning self-hypnosis, owing to his hypervigilance, and he became incapable even of closing his eyes. The client's fear, however, was well concealed with a nervous laugh. Towards the end of the session, the client confessed, however, that there was a voice in his head that had kept him awake at nights and this statement appeared to be highly significant.

Most of the following session was spent teaching the client self-hypnosis and his relaxation technique began to improve. No

attempt was made, however, by the practitioner to employ investigative methodology with the client until he had perfected this
ability to achieve hypnosis. The client's transference, fortunately,
was beginning to be established in that he began to treat the practitioner with a degree of deference as he might a parental figure.

The third session with this client was perhaps the most revealing.
When the client entered hypnosis, the practitioner asked him about
the voice that had kept him awake. The client stated that the voice
was always there – thus slightly evading the original question. The
client was then invited to welcome the voice and asked if it would
be appropriate for Voice to join the session. The client agreed that
Voice could join the session, even though surprise at this unortho-
dox request had been shown on his face. The client was then asked
to thank Voice for doing such an amazing job at keeping him awake
at night. The client was next encouraged to relay as much detail as
possible about Voice, so that it could be recognised and understood. The client mentioned that Voice was young and that it was
sitting on a three-legged stool in the back of his mind. The client
was next invited to ask Voice how long it had been given the
responsibility of preventing him from falling asleep at night. The
client stated that Voice had manifested when he was three years old
and the practitioner remarked, therefore, that Voice had been doing
its job for many years.

Voice was then asked to guide the client through the events that
had led him to require assistance in keeping awake. It transpired
that the client's father had been very aggressive and that his rage
had not been limited to merely shouting at the young self. Voice
reported that his father's anger had also turned to extreme violence
that was unleashed particularly at the client as a young child. The
client, for example, was whipped by his father on more than one
occasion for wetting the bed and was then ordered to wash his
sheets. The beating had been so severe, therefore, that the client
had done his best to stay awake at night in order to avoid being
punished any further.

The next six sessions worked through the client's repressed fear
and associated feelings of guilt about being beaten by his father.
Finally, the client agreed that Voice no longer had to stay up at
night in order to protect him. It was, therefore, agreed between the

client and his Voice that it could join him and rest at night with him.

In the next case-study example, the client was able to deal with her relationship problems effectively using hypnoanalytic methodology in order to unearth repressed material.

Case-study example – relationship difficulties

A female client entered therapy because she was experiencing difficulty in her relationship with her partner.

In the first session, it transpired that the client had been in a relationship for several years with a man who, in many ways, had been a good companion and a good provider. The client's symptoms, however, were particularly damaging to her relationship with her partner. The client revealed that she could not abide the smell of smoke on her partner's breath and could not stay in bed with him if she smelled the slightest hint of alcohol on his breath. The client also reported that she would lie on the edge of the bed as far away from her partner as possible and then try to stay awake. If her partner moved, however, the client would bolt out of the bed.

The idea of lovemaking, moreover, was abhorrent to the client. When the client felt that the pressure from her partner to indulge in sexual intercourse was too great, however, she would submit reluctantly but would want the act to be over as quickly as possible. The client also reported the fact that sexual intercourse was extremely painful but that several medical examinations had shed no light on the problem at all. Indeed, the client had baffled her examiners because even when she was being medically examined she complained of pain.

Once the practitioner had taken a full case-history of the client, the therapeutic process was clearly explained to her during the second session. The client was then encouraged to learn to relax sufficiently in order to allow her mind to begin gently to reveal the driving force behind her sense of extreme fear. The client, however, had been unable to close her eyes during hypnosis and so the practitioner proceeded to ask her to fix her attention on one spot in the room while still leaving her eyes open.

When investigative therapy began, the client, however, had no rec-ollection of any critical incidents in her life. What occurred over the next six sessions, therefore, was quite a revelation for the client. Each session revealed approximately five minutes of a real-time event in the client's life. The client began the investigative process, virtually immediately, by recalling going to a funfair when she was a teenager, where a young man was making eyes at her. The client kept saying that this recollection amounted to nothing and that she could not see the point of recalling this event. The more the client investigated the recollection, however, the more she became highly disturbed. The client was then told to slow down her mental activ-ity during hypnosis and to allow herself to see just as much as she was able to cope with at any point along the way. No pressure at all was put on the client from the practitioner but, of course, pressure had been coming from her partner, who had started to suggest that he would leave her because he felt that her refusal to have sexual intercourse was unfair on both of them.

The third session began more or less where the second session had ended. The client again recalled being with her friend at the funfair. The client felt very grown up because of the young man's overtures and, after a while, he approached her and encouraged her to go off with him. Throughout this session, a disturbing amount of under-lying dread and fear had been evident in the client. The client, how-ever, had been informed by the practitioner that she would discover moments during the week that could enable her to ques-tion whether or not to continue her treatment. This advice had been given deliberately by the practitioner as the level of fear that the client had been experiencing may well have prevented her from completing therapy and so, by pre-empting her thinking, she would be able to overcome her own resistance.

The fourth session covered much the same ground and revisited the same event. The client became even more disturbed as she began to untangle the source of her deep-seated fear.

By the fifth session, the client was ready to recollect a completely repressed memory of the past that was of an intensely traumatic nature. The client, having left the amusement-park with the afore-mentioned young man, was taken by him to an isolated area. This young man then sexually attacked her at knifepoint and raped her while, simultaneously, verbally abusing her by calling her some atrocious names. The rapist also proceeded to insert a piece of wood into her vagina and, of course, the client virtually fainted with the pain. The rapist then continued to make threats such as suggesting that he was going to burn her vagina. The client pleaded and pleaded with her attacker, but to no avail. Finally, the rapist spat on her and then left her lying on the ground. The client, however, managed to collect herself sufficiently to return to the friend who had accompanied her to the funfair and together they walked back home.

On the way home, however, the client fainted. The client's friend then helped her up but she said nothing about the incident, either to her friend or to anyone else. The client simply returned home, told her mother that she was not feeling well and that she would have a bath and go to bed. The client, thus, had no conscious rec-ollection of the event whatsoever. Great doubt occurred in the client's mind about the validity of the information that her mind had revealed during this session. It then took the client approxi-mately six further sessions merely to recall her thirty-minute rape ordeal. At the time of the rape-incident, the client's mind had made a split-second decision that had caused her to repress the memory of this event.

Later, it also came as no surprise to the client that there were numerous similarities between her former attacker and her current partner. Both had several characteristics in common. Both men had straight hair and were approximately the same height, both smelled of tobacco and alcohol and both had grubby hands. The client's partner had an engineering job that meant that his hands were often stained, giving the appearance of dirt.

The repair work, however, was completed only after the entire scene had been revealed by the client's mind. Therapeutic investi-gation continued for a further four sessions – this time being spent in tying up loose ends and in ensuring that the client's fear and guilt over this rape-incident had completely subsided. The client came to realise, finally, that she had not, in any way, been respon-sible for what had happened to her and she also came to under-stand the reason why her mind had obliterated the memory. Following her therapy, the client then completely changed her life and she elected not to remain with her partner.

Client Profiling

The analytical-hypnotherapy practitioner may wish to ponder the following points when formulating a profile for the client.

- In what ways can a therapeutic strategy for the client be planned in advance?
- Is there any way in which the practitioner's strategy for the client could be varied or, even, abandoned in favour of a new scheme?
- In what ways could the client be given therapeutic direction?
- Does the client need to be led or, alternatively, invited to take the reins?
- Does the client desire to assume control of her therapeutic intervention?
- Why does the practitioner need to adopt a neutral position in his dealings with the client?
- In what ways could the practitioner organise the client's introductory session(s)?
- In what ways could the practitioner introduce the client to the therapeutic process?
- In what ways could the client's transference be engendered in the initial stages of therapeutic interaction?
- What therapeutic methodology could be beneficially employed by the practitioner in order to investigate the client's past experience?
- Why might it be folly to prescribe a definitive number of sessions for the client who wishes to undertake analytical hypnotherapy?
- In what ways can the client's therapy be brought to a close?
- Might there be occasions when the client's therapy could beneficially be prolonged?
- In what ways might the practitioner analyse the client's progress in therapy?

Part II

Therapeutic Strategies

In Part II we shall examine in more detail the specifics of treating given symptoms and conditions that the client may present. The analytical practitioner will, thus, be introduced to the ways in which psychological distress and conflict may manifest in the client's symptomology. The aim of this part of the work will be to bring together the practitioner's learning by focusing on specific areas that may require specialised handling and by providing ideas and suggestions for specific treatment applications.

Chapter 7

Fear and Anxiety Disorders

Let me assert my firm belief that the only thing we have to
fear is fear itself.

– Franklin D Roosevelt

What is Fear and Anxiety?

Breaking down emotional impact into specific reactions, the most
common initial effect noted in empirical studies, similar to reports in the
clinical literature, is that of fear.
– David Finkelhor & Angela Browne

Fear and anxiety are the human organism's natural responses to
danger, threat and confusion. Such instinctive emotive reactions
are likely to underpin most of what the client will be feeling about
himself, about his symptoms and about resolving issues under
therapeutic guidance. The client's presenting fear-based or anxiety-based symptomology may, therefore, be extreme in nature and
wide-ranging (see Figure 2 – "Symptomology"). Most fear and
anxiety symptoms will manifest because the client will be attempting to deal with distress that has resulted from a disturbing experience. Fear will usually transpire when the client – perhaps as a
child – finds himself in a situation that he cannot comprehend and
with which he does not have the resources to deal. Although the
child may not necessarily fear for his life, the emotive effect of an
overwhelming experience may give him the impression that he is
in grave danger. The presenting symptom of fear in the client will,
thus, be likely to emanate from some form of perceived psychological or physiological abandonment, exploitation, neglect or
abuse.

This aspect of fear will, in a way, be the child's naïve means of expressing helplessness, powerlessness and a feeling rejection. The client will, of course, need to appreciate that his perception of the original fear-provoking experience had a protective component at the time that then became submerged and, in turn, gave vent to his symptoms. As a child, the client may also have suffered from anxiety disorders such as distress conditions, phobias, sleeplessness, enuresis or eating disorders that occurred as a direct result of the fear that he experienced in childhood. In adulthood, such fear may arise in the form of nightmares, flashbacks, panic attacks and major phobic conditions, as well as generalised anxiety and obsessive-compulsive disorders.

> Anxiety is another common emotional reaction. It is often expressed in increased fearfulness, somatic complaints, changes in sleep patterns, and nightmares. Victims often also experience a sense of personal powerlessness.
> – *Jeffrey Haugaard & Dickon Reppucci*

Fear Manifestations

When fear becomes installed and locked into the client's mind, it may surface in a number of supposedly mysterious ways. We shall now consider some of the most common forms of irrational fear manifestation – namely, fears of rejection, abandonment and failure.

Fear of rejection

> Loneliness is often the result of a closed heart. Our fear of being hurt, rejected or judged keeps us frozen in our loneliness. We are not able to open our hearts enough to allow in the warmth of others which would melt the pain we feel inside.
> – *Susan Jeffers*

The client's fear manifestation may result principally in a fear of being rejected by others. A fear of rejection can, of course, cause the client to become withdrawn and, indeed, to fend off any possible approaches from others. The caustic client, for example, who delights in offending others or who alienates people by being patronising may well be concealing an underlying fear of rejection.

A mother who suffers from chronic depression may find it especially
difficult to be celebrational at the birth of her child. A new-born child will
sense a mother's rejection at such a time, and will probably feel that he is
somehow the cause, and that he is not really wanted.
– *Joel Covitz*

If the client fears rejection, it may well be that the practitioner will
need to tread delicately when handling him. The client, for example, may project these fears on to the therapist and so may fear disapproval or may be overanxious to please. The client, moreover,
may be reluctant to leave therapy or may request additional
sessions.

Often the practitioner can make discreet enquiries in order to allow
the client to reveal his strategies for avoiding rejection or initiating
rebuff. Perhaps the therapist may wish deliberately to provoke the
client in order to reveal any strategies that he may employ for getting others to reject him. The therapist may wish, therefore, to
utilise some questioning techniques with the client who exhibits a
fear of being rejected (see Chapter 4 – "Therapeutic Enquiry").
Perhaps some surreptitious questioning can run along the lines of
the questions given below. Not only will such probing techniques
uncover the client's fear of rejection but also may reveal his unconsciously-motivated strategy in order to court rejection.

- Do you frequently get butterflies in the stomach or a lump in
  the throat when your partner comes home a few minutes late?
- Do you sometimes suffer from bodily coldness or shaking
  when you are asked a testing question?
- Do you sometimes feel reluctant to express your feelings or
  your opinions to others?
- Do you believe that asking for help means that you are a
  failure?
- Do you ever feel self-conscious when dealing with people?
- Do you feel reluctant to approach people?
- Do you have a fear of being put on the spot by others?
- Would you suffer badly if you failed to get a job for which you
  had been short-listed?
- Do you generally avoid parties or social gatherings?
- How do you get people to reject you?
- If you wanted me to reject you, how would you go about
  achieving that?

- How might you get your partner or a friend to leave you alone?

The passage below can be used by the therapist in order to encourage the client to relinquish fears of rebuff from others, especially when such fears have stemmed from childhood conflicts and will be affecting his current interactions with others. The practitioner should, of course, remember that it would be wise to investigate the root basis of the client's problem before inviting him to consign the past to insignificance and to resolve past distresses with regard to issues of rejection.

Why feel fear?

Begin to accept that you no longer need to feel afraid of life. Once, you may have found the world a confusing or mysterious place. Once, you may have tried to make sense of what was nonsensical. Once, you may have tried to please another, but felt that you had manifestly failed. Once, you may have considered yourself to be too small or too insignificant to count for anything. Once, you may have felt unloved or neglected badly.

These things are all in the past now. Now is the time to let go of such fears. They are now all insignificant. The past is an illusion. The past matters not at all in terms of the present. The present is what matters. Do not tolerate anyone who takes advantage of you or capitalises on a situation in which you are exposed or vulnerable. Do not allow any injustice to continue to your own detriment. Do not allow yourself to be put upon in order to accommodate someone else's needs. Strive for a workable solution to your problems. Now is the time to get on with today. Have confidence in yourself, expand your horizons, increase your circle of friends, attract success and amass love and affection. Be happy in seeking your goals. Be happy in dispelling fears. Be happy in taking yourself on this exciting journey. Bon voyage!

Fear of abandonment

Overloads of pain, feelings of torture and being left alone before, during, and after birth will permanently impair our ability to lead a fulfilled life and detract from our pleasure at being alive.
– *Konrad Stettbacher*

The client's fear manifestation may be characterised by a fear of being abandoned by others. Often the child will feel that circumstances have conspired to leave him alone, helpless and unable to care for himself when a parent has displayed an air of coldness, has been abusive or has been neglectful in any way. The fear of abandonment will, of course, be the ultimate fear that the child will dread because it would constitute certain death in terms of the way in which his unconscious mind may view the situation.

> Children abandoned by a parent who has gone to live elsewhere and seems not to want to see the children ever again, have a special problem. Not only is there an intense sense of being "not good enough" to hold the parent's interest and love, there's an additional tantalising rationalisation that "there must be some mistake …". Abandoned children have always in their mind – usually buried in unconscious mind – that somewhere in the world there lives a person who is their parent.
> – *Margaret Reinhold*

The practitioner may wish to utilise some surreptitious questioning techniques in order to tease out the basis of the client's fears of abandonment and some examples are given below.

- Do you regularly have unpleasant nightmares or recurring dreams about being left alone?
- Do you ever get a sense of impending doom for virtually no reason?
- Do you ever fear the daunting power of a person in authority?
- Are you ever afraid of going out alone especially after dark?
- Are you ever afraid of any natural elements or natural phenomena?
- Do you fear taking responsibility for yourself or for others?
- Do you often find yourself grovelling to others who appear to be elusive?
- Do you generally feel unloved and uncared for?
- Would you dread living on your own in isolation from others?

Fear of failure

> Within the boundaries of normal, understandable human error, the child should be given support and love regardless of his choices, styles, and tastes. Unconditional acceptance implies that a child has the right to be a nurse, or a fireman, or a poet – even though there might seemingly be "better" options.
> – *Joel Covitz*

The client's fear manifestation may mean that he will suffer from fearing his own failure. This fear, of course, will be likely to prevent him from doing anything out of the ordinary. The client may, for example, lack initiative, may not see projects through to a logical conclusion and may appear unduly reticent. The client may also sit back and allow others to take the reigns of power and responsibility and, when this occurs, he can then become overly dependent on his assumed benefactor.

For the client who suffers from a fear of failure or a failure-syndrome, the practitioner may wish to utilise some judicious questioning techniques – some examples of which are given below – in order to bring to light this manifestation of fear.

- Do you feel that you are somehow inferior to others?
- Do you ever doubt your own abilities or your inherent potential?
- Do you feel uncomfortable if you are not in control of yourself or in command of a situation?
- Do you often feel disinclined to take even reasonable risks?
- Do you dread any change in life's pattern or circumstances?
- Do you regard anything new as a potential source of worry?
- Do you feel anxious or afraid most of the time when you are at work?
- Do you loathe meetings or interviews when you consider that you are under scrutiny?
- Do you believe that your work colleagues are always judging you?
- Do you tremble at the thought of speaking in public?
- Do you recoil on occasions when you feel that all eyes are on you?
- Do you ever have the courage to speak up or to answer back?
- Are you ever despondent if you miss a train or are late for an appointment?
- Are you quite happy to sit back and let others take the initiative?
- Are you fond of getting others to take all the decisions?

The following case-study example highlights the client's fear of failure – a fear of which she was ostensibly unaware when she first sought therapy.

Case-study example – fear of failure

This female client exhibited a fear of failure that took her some time to identify in therapy. The client wanted very much to change her career but she felt fearful at the prospect. After judicious questioning, the client confessed to having a fear of failure that prevented her from taking that initial step.

In hypnosis, the client spontaneously regressed to the time when she was a child learning to play the flute and was taking a number of musical examinations. The client reported that her mother had been encouraging but, unfortunately, there had been some uncertainty in her mother's manner. After passing one particular examination, her mother had exclaimed with relief, "I knew you could do it!" This apparently-innocent statement conveyed to the young child the fact that her mother had not really been fully confident of her ability to pass the flute examination. This incident, therefore, had instilled doubt in the client's mind and a belief that change might bring about failure and, consequently, her mother's displeasure.

Anxiety Manifestations

> Also essential to the psychoanalytic approach is its concept of anxiety.
> Anxiety is a state of tension that motivates us to do something. It
> develops out of a conflict among the id, ego and superego over control of
> the available psychic energy. Its function is to warn of impending danger.
> – *Gerald Corey*

In classical psychoanalytic theory, the state of anxiety is regarded as being the root of all evil and the point from which the client's psychological disturbance or personality disorder may stem (see Chapter 1, Volume 1 – "Psychoanalysis"). This theme has, of course, permeated many other therapeutic disciplines both within and outside the hypnoanalytic bracket. In psychoanalytic terms, anxiety will be the state that renders the ego desperate to regain control of the self (see Chapter 15, Volume 1 – "Personality Structure"). The client's state of equilibrium can become unbalanced by troublesome experiences when his mind cannot overcome the anxiety state. When the client cannot deal with life rationally and pragmatically, however, his mind will go into overdrive and will generate an anxiety state. Such states may result from the client's perception of reality, from his belief about what will be expected of him and from his own conscience. We shall now consider this conventional wisdom with regard to anxiety that can manifest within the client's psyche.

> Symptoms had a meaning and were residues or reminiscences of those
> emotional situations.
> – *Sigmund Freud*

Realistic anxiety

> Realistic anxiety strikes us as something very rational and intelligible. We
> may say of it that it is a reaction to the perception of an external danger –
> that is, of an injury which is expected and foreseen. It is connected with
> the flight reflex and it may be regarded as a manifestation of the self-
> preservation instinct.
> – *Sigmund Freud*

The client may experience realistic anxiety when he perceives that quantifiable danger is nigh. Any form of danger that could be classified as a threat to the human organism's existence or that could harm the client's physical being will be experienced as realistic anxiety. Here the client will literally be facing the reality of danger to life or limb. The victim of a violent attack, for example, will be likely to face realistic anxiety when the perpetrator physically assaults his person. Milder forms of realistic anxiety will be exhibited when practical difficulties are encountered that upset the even tenor of the client's life, such as financial difficulties, homelessness and the loss of a loved one.

> Reality anxiety is the fear of danger from the external world, and the
> level of such anxiety is proportionate to the degree of real threat.
> – *Gerald Corey*

Neurotic anxiety

> If we now pass over to consider neurotic anxiety, what fresh forms and
> situations are manifested by anxiety in neurotics? There is much to be
> described here. In the first place we find a general apprehensiveness, a
> kind of freely floating anxiety which is ready to attach itself to any idea
> that is in any way suitable, which influences judgement, selects what is
> to be expected, and lies in wait for any opportunity that will allow it to
> justify itself. We call this state "expectant anxiety" or "anxious expectation".
> – *Sigmund Freud*

The client may experience neurotic anxiety when he believes that his actions or behaviours are antisocial. The client could, for instance, consider that his tendencies may lead him towards something for which he will attract punishment and, consequently, social isolation. In this bracket, the practitioner will also find guilt-complexes and irrational fears and phobias. The client who has been the victim of childhood abuse or neglect, for example, may consider that he has been labelled as weak, cowardly or contaminated as a result of the abusive attacks and, therefore, will be shunned by society (see Chapter 15 – "The Effects of Childhood Abuse"). The client may also fear that he has personally sinned for his participation in events or not been strong enough to resist the abuser's advances. It will be as if, in such cases, realistic anxiety will feed neurotic anxiety because of the client's subjective perception of his experiences.

> Neurotic anxiety is the fear that the instincts will get out of hand and cause one to do something for which one will be punished.
> – *Gerald Corey*

Moral anxiety

> We know the self-observing agency as the ego-censor, the conscience; it is this that exercises the dream-censorship, during the night, from which the repressions of inadmissible wishful impulses proceed. When in delusions of observation it becomes split up, it reveals to us its origin from the influences of parents, educators and social environment – from an identification with some of these model figures.
> – *Sigmund Freud*

The client may experience moral anxiety when he feels the pangs of conscience. The client may devise a moral code to which he may attempt to adhere, but, when he judges himself to be a failure in this respect, anxiety as well as feelings of guilt may be the result. The conscious-stricken client may then indulge in self-punishing mechanisms such as self-mutilation, substance-abuse or self-denial.

> Moral anxiety is the fear of one's own conscience. People with a well-developed conscience tend to feel guilty when they do something contrary to their moral code.
> – *Gerald Corey*

Panic Disorders

> Intense, acute episodes of anxiety can be labelled panic or acute anxiety
> attacks, in which all of the physical symptoms of anxiety (e.g. sweating,
> hyper-ventilation, nausea, diarrhoea, shortness of breath, choking etc.)
> are frequently accompanied by a strong feeling of helplessness. Bellack
> and Small, in their therapeutic approach to panic states, sought to link
> features of the current precipitating event with significant events of the
> past and believed that this correlation enabled them to discover the
> actual cause of the panic.
> *– Edgar Barnett*

A panic attack (or an *anxiety attack*) will frequently be an indication
that the client has experienced past trauma. The panic disorder will
usually be evidence of the fact that the client's physiological system has remained overstimulated in response to the former threat
(see Chapter 13 – "Post-traumatic Stress Disorder"). Panic-disorder
attacks may be triggered by social confrontation, by fear-provoking situations or by objects associated with terror in the client's
mind. When experiencing a panic attack, the client may relive an
originating experience both psychologically and physiologically
when the fear-source has been encountered. Similarly, fearful
nightmares and hallucinations may dominate or intrude on the
client's thought processes. It will be as if these tactics are the
human organism's primitive way of attempting in vain to discharge pent-up emotive expression and to rectify inner strife.

The anxiety-disorder sufferer may report a number of symptoms to
which the practitioner should be sensitive. The client's symptoms
may include apprehension, feelings of impending doom, helplessness, vulnerability, irritability, trembling, tension aches, muscular
pains, sweating, coldness, dizziness, fatigue and a dry mouth.
When the client experiences a more severe attack, his symptoms
may also include feelings intense horror, feelings of overwhelming
terror, heart palpitations, hot or cold flushes, choking or smother-
ing sensations and a sense of unreality.

Phobic Disorders

> Phobias, for example, are an obvious result of inappropriately expressed fear, but most of the power of the phobias emanates from the underlying guilt that is always a prime factor. Much of the fear that the phobic patient experiences is, in reality, a fear of the punishment that he unconsciously awaits as a consequence of his transgressions. The phobic sufferer has always had experiences which in themselves have been extremely fearful and that have given him a yardstick by which he can gauge the terror he is certain awaits him. By attributing these fears to certain fearful situations, he endeavours to isolate them and control them. By avoiding the phobic situations he can cope with life in a somewhat limited fashion.
> – *Edgar Barnett*

A phobic disorder will be a condition in which the client will react violently when he encounters a given situation or a specific object. A phobic reaction will usually provoke an extreme reaction from the client, who may suffer from feelings of anxiety when confronted with his fear-source. The phobic-attack sufferer may report a number of symptoms that can include overwhelming terror, dread and panic when faced with the triggering object, situation or activity. The client may, for example, have a phobic reaction to a given object such as an extreme fear of spiders or knives. The client may, alternatively, fear a situation into which he could be plunged, such as a fear of public speaking, a fear of social gatherings or a fear of enclosed spaces. The client may also fear certain types of experience such as receiving an injection or climbing a high mountain. The client's phobic reaction will undoubtedly be irrational, inappropriate, uncontrollable, excessive and out of all proportion. The phobic attack, furthermore, will occur for the client with absolute certainty when the trigger-mechanism has been initiated.

During a phobic attack, the client's reaction will be likely to mirror the fear that he experienced when he first encountered the source of his fear at the time when the phobia was manifested. The client, for example, who has a fear of dogs may have previously been bitten by a dog. The client, in this case, could find that, by accessing the originating cause of his fears, he may well have gone much of the way towards resolving the problem. With a more complex form of phobic reaction, conversely, such as a social phobia, the client's condition may have been manifested due to a number of contributing factors. The client who, for example, suffers from a fear of eating in a restaurant may discover that the originating cause of his terror would be a feeling of shame resulting from a childhood misdemeanour. The client's phobic reaction, in this instance, and the root cause may have little or no apparent resemblance.

An object of fear may have, of course, a symbolic significance for the client. The client with a fear of snakes, for example, could have been a victim of childhood sexual abuse, or a hydrophobic sufferer could have feared being drowned at sea because his parents were psychologically far away when he was a child. Similarly, the client suffering from agoraphobia may harbour a fear of self-exposure and, with claustrophobia, the sufferer may conceal a fear of being confined or trapped. In these cases, the trigger for the phobia may be related only nebulously to the original experience or series of events that have seeded it. The therapist will need to be wary if the client complains of a fear of sex or an avoidance of sexual intimacy. This may, in many cases, indicate the presence of some form of trauma associated with sexual activity to which the client has been subjected. On the other hand, of course, the client may merely feel a reluctance to enter the adult world or may manifest a timidity in connection with adult intimacy. In all cases, of course, the practitioner should endeavour to show the client the significance of his symbolic representations of fear and reserve judgment on any personal theories.

The following client narrative will illustrate the way in which a client viewed his fears of social interaction that manifested in numerous ways.

Client narrative – my social phobia …

If I went to a social gathering of any kind, I would often feel desperately alone and I dreaded this feeling. I might be animatedly talking to several people at once but, in fact, I felt alone in the crowd. Because the feeling frequently troubled me at such events, I tended to dread all social occasions as a result.

This no-win situation also operated when I went out to a party or a similar function in order to seek company. If I felt lonely and went out to a party, it would nearly always aggravate the feeling and, therefore, I often left in a more miserable state than I had arrived. I also had the added embarrassment of having somehow to provide my host with a reason for an early departure. Not easy!

Obsessive-Compulsive Disorders

> The role of anxiety in these symptom complexes can more clearly be
> recognised when any attempt is made to impede the compulsive
> behaviour. For example, if the heavy smoker is deprived of his cigarettes,
> be becomes intensely anxious. The anxiety that he feels is only an
> increase of a constant anxiety that is persistent below the level of
> conscious awareness, but is apparent even to the casual observer.
> – *Edgar Barnett*

An obsessive-compulsive disorder (OCD) will manifest when the
client's anxiety-state has become trapped in a repetitive or ritualistic pattern of obsessional thoughts or compulsive behaviours (see
Figure 2 – "Symptomology"). It will be as if the client's anguish has
settled in his mental faculties rather than having an emotive outlet
and will then make him act and think irrationally without his
being able to control these processes (see Figure 1 – "The abreactive
process"). The client's psychic disturbance could, for example,
have reached an emotive overload when his cognitive and behavioural mechanisms were targeted by traumatic or anxiety-provoking distress. In some ways, the client's ideomotor mechanism may
also have become distorted by an overwhelming experience when
an idea has become associated with a physical movement or a bodily posture (see Chapter 2 – "Therapeutic Investigation"). Similarly,
the client may feel an unconscious need to repeat constantly a
given statement or a question aloud when cognitive processes
have been affected by trauma or distress (see Chapter 9, Volume 1
– "Cognitive Therapy").

The obsessive-compulsive disorder sufferer will often be unconsciously making an attempt to take control of a former life-threatening situation. The client may be trying endlessly to recapture
control and to render himself safe from real or perceived harm. For
the OCD sufferer, the compulsion to act or the obsessive thought
processes that he will experience may be a way of coping with psychological anxieties. The repeated and ritualistic nature of the disorder, therefore, may be the client's way of attempting to gain
control of a situation in which he was once absolutely powerless. A
ritualistic compulsion, moreover, will frequently be a way of trying
to eliminate obsessive thoughts. Anxiety-oriented behaviours
might include checking and rechecking, exercising extreme caution
or being overcautious, counting, saving or collecting objects and

Figure 2 – Symptomology

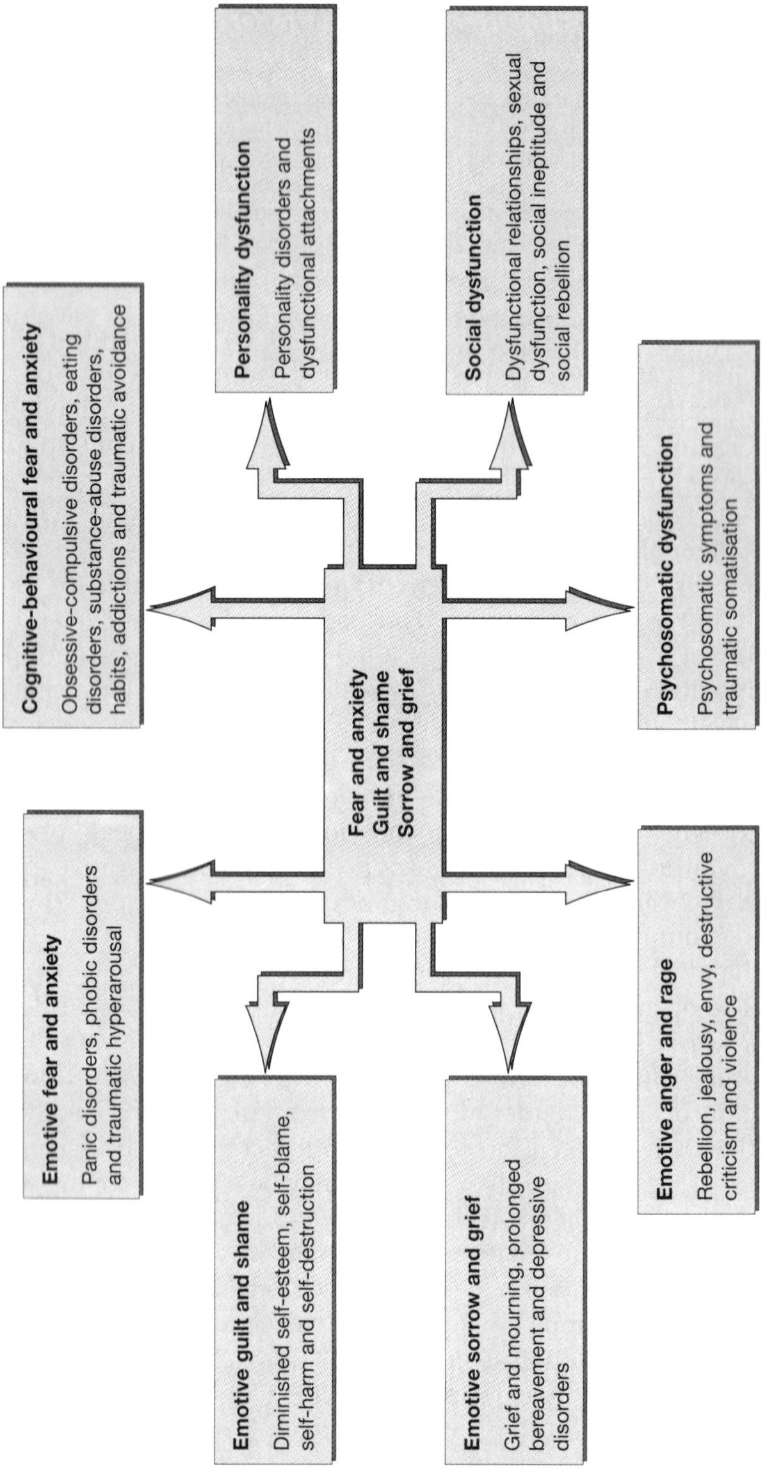

Cognitive-behavioural fear and anxiety
Obsessive-compulsive disorders, eating disorders, substance-abuse disorders, habits, addictions and traumatic avoidance

Personality dysfunction
Personality disorders and dysfunctional attachments

Social dysfunction
Dysfunctional relationships, sexual dysfunction, social ineptitude and social rebellion

Emotive fear and anxiety
Panic disorders, phobic disorders and traumatic hyperarousal

**Fear and anxiety
Guilt and shame
Sorrow and grief**

Psychosomatic dysfunction
Psychosomatic symptoms and traumatic somatisation

Emotive guilt and shame
Diminished self-esteem, self-blame, self-harm and self-destruction

Emotive sorrow and grief
Grief and mourning, prolonged bereavement and depressive disorders

Emotive anger and rage
Rebellion, jealousy, envy, destructive criticism and violence

keeping objects in order, perfectly aligned or in precise symmetry. The client might also fear the possibility of harming others, fear that he will become unwell or dread becoming disabled. It will be as if, because the client has learned unconsciously that he can get out of control, he will then develop a secondary means of losing that control when he most needs it. It will not be uncommon, thus, for the client who has been a childhood victim of neglect or abuse to suffer from this disorder.

> The functions (such as eating, sleeping, sex, and general activity)
> regulated by the reptilian brain make a broad and fertile place for
> symptoms to take root. Anorexia, insomnia, promiscuity, and manic
> hyperactivity are only a few of the symptoms that can ensue when the
> organism's natural functions become maladaptive.
> – *Peter Levine*

Often the sufferer will be aware of the senseless nature of his disorder but may be incapable of exercising personal control despite many endeavours. The rituals of the OCD sufferer will nearly always engender shame in the client, who may desperately attempt to hide his embarrassing malfunction (see Chapter 8 – "Guilt and Shame Disorders"). The client with a compulsive need for cleanliness of himself and his environment, for example, will be a typical manifestation of this phenomenon. Compulsive rituals in which the client may be concealing guilt-provoking thoughts, for example, might include washing the body or scrupulously cleansing his living environment because he has an underlying fear of contamination. Similarly, if the client has a compulsion to wash his hands, he may be symbolically washing away obsessive thoughts of a deep-seated desire to indulge in a socially-unacceptable sexual practice such as masturbation or sexual sadomasochism. An obsession with sex or sexual deviation may also be a typical manifestation of a desire to be loved or cared for even though this might seem a bizarre way of expressing such a need.

The analytical practitioner's role in treating the OCD sufferer will be to assist him to identify the seeding event of his symptoms and then to allow him to feel the safety that was once totally illusive. Often, this can be a long, drawn-out process for the client because of the high degree of anxiety-manifestation that will have occurred when the condition was set up in his psyche.

> Every form of addiction is bad, no matter whether the narcotic be alcohol
> or morphine or idealism.
> – Carl Jung

In the following case-study example, the client reported obsessive thoughts and beliefs that stemmed from the ill-treatment she received as a child at the hands of her parents.

Case-study example – obsessive thoughts

This elderly client entered therapy in order to overcome obsessive thoughts that included thinking that anybody whom she touched would die and, especially, any babies. The client reported that she felt as if she wished to harm others and yet, paradoxically, did not want anything to happen to them. This client also undertook compulsive behaviours that included hand-washing up to sixty times per day, constantly cleaning and constantly checking to see whether her pants had been soiled.

Analytical investigation revealed the fact that the client's mother had exhibited a phobia of germs and had, consequently, resisted cleaning the child's bottom. Further investigation revealed that the client's father had sexually abused her between the ages of four and fourteen years. One image the client recalled was of her father having full penetrative sex with her while her mother was standing at the door observing the act. The client also believed that she needed to submit to this abuse in order to prevent her father from hurting her younger sister. The client's father claimed that he had abused her because she was a naughty child and was responsible for the death of her twin brother while he was still in the womb. The client's twin brother had been stillborn.

A clear memory that seemed significant for the client was the fact that she recalled an event of killing a baby, feeling guilty and then telling her mother. The client remembered seeing a baby lying face down on the gravel path of her home and believing that she had been responsible for its death. The baby was, in fact, a porcelain doll that she took back indoors, only to be told by her mother that she had killed the baby.

In this case, the client had developed obsessive thoughts because lies had been installed in her mind by her parents. The client had unconsciously believed her parents and had taken on the guilt for her supposed actions. Exploration of these aspects of the client's childhood had then led her to feel safe enough to relinquish her unwelcomed habits naturally.

In the case-study example below, the client suffered from innumerable obsessive and ritualistic behaviours that controlled his existence.

Case-study example – compulsive behaviours
This male client found it difficult to leave his home without the need to check whether light switches and electrical equipment had been switched off. Such rituals were escalating into agoraphobia for the client and so, in desperation, he sought therapeutic assistance.

Under hypnosis, the client reported that as a child he had feared many things such as demons and monsters under the bed and that these fears had prevented him from sleeping. The client also experienced constant anxiety as a child and would often have to be more or less dragged to school by his mother.

The client also mentioned that his father had been a shift-worker and, therefore, he was frequently uncertain about when he would return home from work. This confusion set up such anxiety in the client's mind that he began to fear that his parents would one day die or somehow be taken away from him completely. In order to resolve the client's excessive fear, the practitioner asked the young child to speak. The child expressed his fears in the form of the demons and monsters that resided under his bed. The client was invited to speak to the monsters in order to discover whether they were friendly or unfriendly beings. The client replied that the monsters had been unfriendly when he was a child but that now they were quite harmless. The client, thus, in facing his demons had transformed his fears via this form of inner-child work. The session concluded by asking the client to show affection and protection towards his child-self. The client also assured the child of his continued faith in his ability to love, care and protect him.

Eating Disorders

> Another somatic outcome connected with sexual abuse in the literature is
> the development of eating disorders. In a British clinical program aimed
> at the treatment of women with eating disorders, 34% had been sexually
> abused before the age of 15 (about one-third with anorexia and two-
> thirds with bulimia). These researchers speculated that eating disorders
> may be a more common long-term effect of childhood sexual
> molestations than is currently recognized, even in non-clinical
> populations, as a reaction to coping with stress in adolescent and adult
> sexual life.
> – *David Finkelhor & Angela Browne*

An eating disorder has been frequently cited as a symptom of traumatic experience and such psychic disturbance can encompass
compulsive overeating, obesity, anorexia nervosa and bulimia nervosa. The client's eating disorders will undoubtedly have an
unconscious purpose or benefit that will serve as a defensive strategy (see Chapter 11, Volume 1 – "Defensive Strategies"). It will,
therefore, be valuable for the client to realise what his unconscious
motivation has been in retaining the abnormal-eating tendency.
When the client's unconscious mechanism has been brought to the
surface of his mind, he may then naturally be inclined to drop the
habit. The analytical hypnotherapist can intercept such conditions
by identifying the root cause and by assisting the client to resolve
his childish need for comfort, security, protection and self-blame.

> Some of the common secondary dependencies are eating disorders,
> overworking, compulsive shopping, gambling and smoking, all of which
> have their own recovery programs and resources.
> – *Ken Graber*

Compulsive overeating

> Whether or not it is the raised blood sugar that acts as a tranquilliser, the
> compulsive overeater has discovered that food makes him feel more
> comfortable and is a means of dealing with feelings that he will not allow
> himself to express more appropriately. Many obese patients are aware of
> the compulsive nature of their eating. It seldom has anything to do with
> actual hunger, but rather is a ritualistic means of dealing with
> uncomfortable feelings which they feel bound to suppress. Some have a
> fear of being thin and feel helpless to deal with situations that they
> unconsciously believe would overwhelm them. In such cases their
> motivation is clearly to remain fat and safe.
> – *Edgar Barnett*

Compulsive overeating may occur for a number of reasons of which the client may not be so blissfully unaware. Perhaps the client's habit has a perceived comfort-factor attached to it, although the consequences for him may be to engender guilt and shame (see Chapter 8 – "Guilt and Shame Disorders"). The term "comfort-eating" will so aptly describe the client's way of commiserating with himself for painful psychic manifestations. Overindulgence in food may also provide the client with a means of supposedly stifling painful emotions. The client may, for example, turn to food in times of extreme stress, at which point he will have lost the behavioural control he so desperately desires.

> Eating disorders have also been investigated in relation to childhood trauma, but with conflicting results. Most of the work has been carried out on clinical populations. In the main, it appears that bulimic behaviour may be more highly associated with a history of CSA [Childhood Sexual Abuse] than anorexia. More representative studies are needed, although those that exist show CSA to be a risk factor for eating disorders.
> – *John Morton*

Obesity

> Stress can make us fat as people often eat for comfort, and obesity can increase our stress because slimness is equated with beauty while obesity is equated with gluttony, sloth and ugliness. The guilt associated with such feelings can turn us to food for comfort and the viscous circle is perpetuated.
> – *Chandra Patel*

Obesity and compulsive overeating often go hand in hand. The propensity to retain body-weight can often be the client's unconscious mechanism that will be designed to protect him from the pain of rejection. The therapist should bear in mind that excessive weight may also be the means by which the client's unconscious mind can render him unattractive. Thus, the victim of childhood abuse, for example, may unconsciously feel that if he is unattractive, then he will dispel the approaches of an attacker. For the victim of childhood sexual abuse, an unsightly body-image could turn his abuser's attentions elsewhere – or, at least, this may be the childish logic behind such irrationality (see Chapter 15 – "The Effects of Childhood Abuse").

Anorexia nervosa

> Conversely, the anorectic keeps thin and safe. Many anorectics are also
> compulsive eaters and express their anger not only in compulsive eating
> but also in the ritualistic vomiting which must take place
> immediately afterwards.
> – *Edgar Barnett*

Anorexia nervosa will be a form of psychological punishment and self-destruction that the client may have an unconscious need to perpetrate against himself. The anorectic will usually, therefore, be unconsciously attempting to control that which is uncontrollable – namely, his emotive expression. The anorectic client will suffer from an extreme loss of appetite and often an unconscious suppression of the desire for food – despite sometimes experiencing chronic hunger pangs. The client may fear gaining weight even though he may be less than 85 per cent of his ideal body-weight. The client may often exhibit a distorted view of his own body-image and may sometimes believe that he is fat when, in reality, he is emaciated. The disorder will tend mostly to affect a female during her adolescent years and may, subsequently, develop into bulimia nervosa. Food-deprivation, however, will often result in a cessation of menstrual periods in women and impotence in men.

Fasting, dieting or starvation may be seen unconsciously by the client as a means of suppressing those emotive reactions that he would rather not express. Starving the body may be envisaged by the client as a means of stifling his feelings of guilt while, simultaneously, depriving himself as a means of self-punishment. The anorectic client may also consider, therefore, that he can take control of his life and can rebel against any maltreatment or domination from others. The fear of normal body-weight can also be the client's expression of avoiding entry into the adult world. Untreated anorexia can, of course, lead the client to serious consequences of malnutrition, heart disease and suicide. Symptoms of depression may also be the lot of the anorectic client.

> Anorexia nervosa occurs when someone deliberately resists their food
> intake beyond the point where the body is able to sustain itself.
> Technically someone is defined as anorexic at the point at which they
> have lost 25% of their body-weight; although, of course, in order to get to
> that point the person must have had the problem for quite a long time.
> – *Nicky Hayes*

Bulimia nervosa

> Despite popular belief, empirical evidence linking childhood sexual
> abuse with bulimia nervosa is sparse. A recent paper by Wonderlich et al
> provides some evidence of an association between the two but does not
> support a causal link.
> – *Sydney Brandon*

The bulimia-nervosa sufferer will indulge in uncontrollable binge-eating – particularly of junk-food – followed, sometimes, by purging of what has been consumed, owing to feelings of guilt. Frequently, such practices are carried out in secret and this will, of course, further increase the client's feelings of shame (see Chapter 8 – "Guilt and Shame Disorders"). The client with a need to purge food-consumption may regularly indulge in self-induced vomiting and may use laxatives, diuretics or enemas in order to assist with the expulsion of food. Alternatively, the bulimic client may adopt a policy of compulsive overexercising or enforced starvation as his compensatory means of purging food-intake. With bulimia, the issue with the client may also be that of gaining control of his generally-unbridled emotive expression. The bulimic client, therefore, may also be prone to mood swings, depression and substance-abuse disorders.

> Bulimia nervosa is an eating disorder which is closely related to anorexia,
> and which also mainly affects teenage girls. Like anorexia, though, it can
> affect older people too. In this syndrome, the person is still extremely
> concerned about their weight, but they also become obsessed by food.
> For this reason, bulimia is sometimes considered to be an example of an
> obsessional neurosis.
> – *Nicky Hayes*

Substance-Abuse Disorders

> An association between child sexual abuse and later substance abuse has
> also received empirical support. Peters, in a carefully controlled
> community study, found that 17% of the victimised women had
> symptoms of alcohol abuse (versus 4% of non-victimised women), and
> 27% abused at least one type of drug (compared to 12% of
> non-victimised women).
> – *David Finkelhor & Angela Browne*

Substance-abuse disorders will embrace excessive usage and overdependence on drugs such as alcohol, stimulants, opiates, hallucinogens, marijuana, nicotine, sedatives and tranquillisers. Alcohol, nicotine, hard and soft drugs, over-the-counter and prescribed drugs are all a means of attempting to deaden the client's painful memories, thoughts and emotive reactions. When the clinician refers to substance-abuse, she may be tempted automatically to bring to mind the so-called recreational or illicit drugs. Substance-abuse, however, will encompass the client's over-indulgence of food, caffeine, alcohol, tobacco, over-the-counter drugs and prescribed medication. The habit of substance-abuse, of course, will often become a crutch without which the client will feel bereft, and this form of indulgence may often be his attempt at gaining oral satisfaction. The addict who may be given to reflection will know that he should stop but yet somehow cannot.

> Drug addictions are the cause of much human misery and distress, but
> the reason for them lies in the effectiveness of certain drugs to suppress
> emotions which the addict cannot allow normal expression.
> – *Edgar Barnett*

Substance-abuse disorders can, of course, lead to significant impairment and distress in the user and will often arise in dependent personalities. Any form of substance-abuse will be damaging to the client's body. The client will, of course, consciously know this fact yet may be unable to prevent his indulgence – perhaps further damaging his self-esteem as a result. When the client's self-esteem is reasonably high, for instance, he may not desire to abuse his body.

Substance-abuse disorders can also initiate a vicious-circle mechanism within the client. Anger directed at the self for an inability to stop can develop into a deep self-loathing that will further increase the client's dependency on whatever has been the source of his addiction in order to relieve this tension. This particular cycle has often been reported across all forms of substance-abuse.

> Primary dependency includes alcoholism and other drug addictions.
> These addictions are characterised by an uncontrollable urge to
> experience the effects of the alcohol or drugs. They are considered
> primary due to the extensive nature of the associated mental and
> behavioural distortions. Left untreated, they progress rapidly toward
> institutionalized and death.
> – *Ken Graber*

Certain correlations have been found between the substance being abused by the client and the nature of the root cause of his habit. A strong correlation, for example, between alcoholism and the fact that the client may be hiding from psychic pain has been suggested. An equally strong kinship between food-abuse and the client's feelings of rejection has also received notice. Smoking, too, can indicate the client's need to belong or to imitate others. Some parity also seems to exist between the client's abuse of medicinal drugs and his irrational fear. Similarly, recreational drugs have been linked to a wide variety of the client's emotive reactions, including anger, pain and fear.

There also seems to be an element of attracting attention in many of these practices in which the client may unwisely indulge. A theory has been put forward that supports the fact that substance-abuse is a symptom of severe childhood trauma (see Chapter 15 – "The Effects of Childhood Abuse"). Here it seems as if the client's abuse of himself may be a form of self-punishment for his own perceived guilt with regard to past abusive incidents. Alternatively, an unmanageable substance-abuse disorder may be the client's method of suppressing his sorrows and may be a way of anaesthetising himself against the painful recollections of the past. A number of addictive habits can develop when the client is transiting teenage years, where a strong element of rebellion will also be present. It is almost as if the teenager would be trying to say "I am me, I will do as I please, it is my life, it is my body" while at the same time saying "See me, stop me, please help".

The underlying causes of substance-abuse will vary, of course, from client to client, and the practitioner should not assume that the client's substance-abuse will solely be the direct result of psychological pain. The therapist may need to consider that there could be a strong element of psychological pain involved but that there might also be other factors that may contribute to the client's current lifestyle predicament and trigger the habit. Such factors can, of course, be revealed by analytical investigation (see Chapter 2 – "Therapeutic Investigation").

Held within the symptoms of trauma are the very energies, potentials, and resources for their constructive transformation. The creative healing process can be blocked in a number of ways – by using drugs to suppress symptoms, by over-emphasising adjustment or control, or by denial or invalidation of feelings and sensations.
– Peter Levine

Drug-dependence

The transition from use to abuse in drinking and drugging often begins when the substance is used as a solution for other problems: anxiety in social situations, stress at work, insomnia, disappointments, physical pain.
– David Conroy

The analytical hypnotherapist may be required to deal with the client who has become dependent on illicit or recreational drugs. Where drug-abuse has been a problem, the client may also have additional presenting symptoms that may include panic attacks, a surfeit of free-floating anxiety and a degree of paranoia – symptoms that are known to result directly from drug-usage. The practitioner can, therefore, usually expect resistance to be apparent with many users or ex-users of drugs because of these underlying anxiety-factors. It may, thus, be necessary for the practitioner to spell out to the client that he would not have become a drug-abuser in the first place unless he had an underlying psychological condition that created this habit. It may also be necessary for the therapist to explain to the client that the effect of drug-taking will usually take a very long time – in some cases years – to be fully flushed out of his physiological system. The reason for this will be that the substance itself will latch on to receptor-sites in the client's brain and will block the production of the feel-good chemical serotonin. The client, thus, will be rendered prone to those unpleasant symptoms of drug-withdrawal.

The practitioner should, of course, take great care when dealing with the client who has a problem with overusing antidepressants or soporific drugs. The client should be urged to consult his general medical practitioner and the therapist should then work in conjunction with this medically-qualified person, if necessary. Of course, if the clinician does elect to work with the client who takes antipsychotic drugs and who may have a history of suicide-attempts, she should, without fail, ensure that the appropriate medical supervisor knows about the hypnoanalytical work that she will be undertaking. A failure to report to a member of the medical profession the fact that the therapist is working with the client using this form of methodology could be construed as professional negligence.

Once investigative work has identified and partially resolved the client's need to be dependent on proprietary drugs, then his brain can be invited to resume the work of manufacturing its own calming chemicals. The following case-study example illustrates the way in which a client was helped to understand his drug-induced condition. Similar metaphorical methodology can, of course, be used with the drug-addicted client who will be in the final stages of recovery.

Case-study example – drug-abuse

This male client had been a heavy drug-user but through investigative therapy he had come to appreciate the way in which his abusive childhood had caused him to turn to drugs. The client's mother had been prone to bashing his head against the wall and, at one stage, she had thrown him across the room. Therapeutic resolution mostly entailed allowing the client to come to terms with the fact that these actions were totally inappropriate because he had utterly failed to realise that his mother's abuse of him was in any way wrong.

Although, the client had kicked his habit, his body still needed help in order to eliminate the damage that had been sustained. The client was, therefore, asked to visualise his brain as a printed circuit-board because he had been a computer programmer. The client was asked to compare the circuits on the board to pathways in his brain and to compare the solder-nodes to chemoreceptors. The client was then asked to examined the circuit-board in order to discover any breaks or blockages in the pathways, to look for accumulations of dirt or anything else that was not exactly as it should be.

When some malfunction was discovered by the client, he was then invited to initiate whatever repair work was necessary and also to give the circuit-board a good clean. The client was then requested to scan his whole body to see if there was a build-up of the drug anywhere else. When the client discovered an accumulation of gunge, he was then able to flush it away efficiently. This procedure was repeated as often as was necessary for this client. Furthermore, the client was taught to carry out this procedure for use at home on a regular basis.

Alcohol-dependence

> Over time psychological dependence develops into physical dependence. As drugs and alcohol become a bigger part of the person's life, everything else shrinks. Relations with family and friends usually change for the worse. Many substance abusers eventually find themselves with lifestyles or behaviour that they regarded with disapproval at earlier points in their lives. As their pool of personal and social pain-coping resources diminishes, they become increasingly dependent upon the substance.
> – *David Conroy*

Alcoholism will also be a form of coping-strategy that will have got out of hand for the client. Often the client will turn to drink in order to obliterate his psychological disturbance but will then find that he has become reliant on this form of psychic anaesthetisation. Let us now consider a number of case-study examples that can enable the practitioner to gain an understanding of the ways in which the client's alcohol problems could be tackled.

The case-study example below shows the way in which a client was able to realise the negative effects of his drinking habit and illustrates ways in which such a situation could be rectified. A similar technique can, of course, be used for other addictions such as excessive caffeine consumption. The practitioner, for example, could talk to the client about the effects of overstimulating the body with caffeine and causing dependency.

Case-study example – excessive drinking
A male client had virtually become an alcoholic and his problem had started to affect his family life.

Initially, the client spent some time in identifying and resolving the originating cause of his drinking disorder. The client next entered an adjustment period whereby he was slowly learning to relinquish his habit. The client's wife had been very upset by his drinking and this had placed a great deal of strain on their relationship. The client also believed that his drinking was spoiling the quality of his time with his children. The client was, therefore, asked to think about the way in which his habit had been poisoning his relationship with his wife, poisoning the atmosphere in his home and poisoning his time with his children. The word "poison" had been repeated many times by the therapist in order to submerge the thought in the client's mind. The client's unconscious mind was then asked whether or not he was willing to relinquish his habit. When the client, at last, conceded that he no longer wished to be a poisoner, the practitioner then asked when the habit could be relinquished and invited him to begin the process immediately.

The client was, subsequently, asked to begin the process of de-alcoholising his body from the poison that had accumulated over the years. The client was also told of the likely damaged that could occur if the habit continued but that any current damage could be rectified over a somewhat shorter period of time. Finally, the client was reminded that his unconscious mind was capable of eliminating 100 per cent of any poison that his body was currently carrying and that this was an unstoppable process in itself.

The case-study example below illustrates the way in which a recovery technique could be used for a client with a drinking habit once the root cause of the disorder had been isolated.

Case-study example – alcohol-abuse
A female client had a serious alcohol problem that she was desperately endeavouring to overcome.

During therapeutic investigation, the client had identified the fact that her drinking problem was fundamentally due to her mother's misuse of her at an early age and that she had blamed herself for this ill-treatment.

Initially, the client was asked to keep a daily record of how much she was drinking and to bring it with her to the next therapeutic session. The daily listing allowed the client to keep an eye on the incidence of her drinking as well as being able to record the total amount she had consumed. It transpired that the client was going on a binge about once a week rather than spreading out her drinking pattern. The client also discovered that, when stress arose at work, she turned to drink. The client was, most importantly, somewhat relieved to discover that her drinking was not a daily occurrence and that it actually served a purpose in attempting to alleviate work-stress. The client was brought to realise, however, that drinking was not, in fact, a way of relieving stress in any situation.

The client's realisation of this work-stress trigger then enabled her to make progress. Within two weeks after the client had started to record her drinking habit, there was a sudden change in the pattern. Not only had the client reduced its consumption but she had also learned how to manage stress at work successfully.

Personality Disorders

> The old and somewhat black joke runs: the neurotic builds castles in the air, the psychotic lives in them, while the psychiatrist collects the rent!
> – *Michael Jacobs*

A personality disorder can develop when the client experiences a serious difficulty in interacting with others in the social world. A personality disorder will often leave its victim with an inflexible pattern of responding to others and a narrow view of life that will impair his normal psychological functioning. To the observer, the personality-disorder sufferer may display eccentric, erratic or anxious behaviour. The practitioner can usually detect the presence of an underlying disturbance when the client's symptoms are pervasive, persistent and enduring in terms of his relationship with himself and with his immediate environment.

When considering categories of a personality disorder, it should, of course, be strongly emphasised that these categories originated with conventional psychiatric practice where diagnostic procedures are an integral part of treatment. The analytical hypnotherapist would, therefore, be ill-advised to label the client in any way whatsoever according to these guidelines. While a full-blown personality disorder will usually be the province of the psychiatrist, however, it can be useful for the analytical hypnotherapist, at least, to have an appreciation of such disorders because this knowledge can help her to recognise a tendency that the client may exhibit. The practitioner should remember, of course, that often such states will be engendered by the client's underlying fears and anxieties. The adoption of behavioural traits at an unconscious level will usually be the client's primitive means of masking his true feelings, creating a distraction from such feelings, attempting to put matters right and grasping at the illusion of self-respect. We shall now consider some of the most common personality types and associated disorders from which the client may be suffering, to a greater or lesser extent, when he visits the analytical hypnotherapist.

> Judith Herman and Bessel van der Kolk have recently reviewed the existing literature and suggested that the distorted survival strategies that result from inescapable stress in humans include, predictably, depression and anxiety; somatic symptoms; dissociative symptoms; compulsive re-enactment; susceptibility to revictimisation; intimacy and relationship disorders; and some personality adaptation in the borderline, narcissistic, antisocial, or schizoid realm.
> – *Mark Schwartz, Lori Galperin & William Masters*

The avoidant personality

> At the core of the avoidant personality disorder is a turning away: from people, from new experiences, and even from old ones. The disorder often combines a fear of appearing foolish with an equally strong desire for acceptance and affection.
> – *David Rosenhan & Martin Seligman*

The avoidant personality can develop when the client feels that he has been severely hurt and could not, at any price, tolerate a recurrence of this experience. Because such treatment has rendered the client hypersensitive to being rejected or abandoned, he will strenuously endeavour to avoid intimacy and interpersonal relationships. The client will also fear criticism, will shun social interaction and will avoid committing himself to any activities that may warrant personal involvement. The avoidant personality, furthermore, may often be excessively shy and fearful of appearing foolish in company. This client may appear reticent to reveal personal facts about himself to the practitioner and, thus, this form of avoidance may impact on the therapeutic encounter.

The dependent personality

> The central characteristic of the dependent personality disorder involves
> allowing others to make the major decisions, to initiate the important
> actions, and to assume responsibility for significant areas of one's life.
> People with this disorder often refer to spouse, parent, or friend
> regarding where they should live, the kind of job they should have, and
> who their friends should be.
> – *David Rosenhan & Martin Seligman*

The dependent personality can develop when the client exhibits dependent or submissive behaviour in the presence of others. The dependent personality will, thus, cling to others as his only life-raft to existence. The client will often keenly fear loneliness, disapproval and rejection, and will lack self-reliance. The client may fear that the practitioner will disapprove of his conduct and may appear to be a typical people-pleaser when in the consulting room.

The obsessive-compulsive personality

> The obsessive-compulsive personality disorder is characterised by a
> pervasive pattern of striving for perfection. Those with the disorder
> demand perfection in themselves as well as others. Nothing they do
> seems to please them, however excellent the outcome.
> – *David Rosenhan & Martin Seligman*

The obsessive-compulsive personality will usually develop when the client has become overconscientious or overambitious and displays perfectionist traits. The client will also be reliable, orderly and methodical, and will give great attention to detail. The result of these traits may also mean that the client can become stubborn, inflexible and somewhat indecisive. Often the compulsive client will be striving to gain control of uncontrollable emotive reactions, unpredictable events and intense feelings of isolation and inadequacy. The self-punishing elements of this personality disorder may often stem from unconscious feelings of guilt (see Chapter 8 – "Guilt and Shame Disorders"). This client may, therefore, resist the therapeutic process by insisting on keeping control during therapeutic intervention. The obsessive-compulsive personality has been linked to Freud's oral-schizoidal personality classification (see Chapter 15, Volume 1 – "Personality Structure").

The hypermanic personality

> The mood of an individual in a manic state is euphoric, expansive and elevated.
> – *David Rosenhan & Martin Seligman*

The hypermanic personality will be characterised by traits of compulsive and feverish activity on the client's part. The client may be constantly alert and working overtime, his mind may be racing and he will appear to be overly energetic. The client will often, of course, be unable to sleep as a result of both psychological and physiological overexertion. The client may experience difficulty in relaxing during hypnotic intervention. The hypermanic personality disorder has been linked to the manic-depressive disorder (see Chapter 9 – "Sorrow and Grief Disorders").

The depressive personality

> Psychodynamic theorists since Freud have emphasised a personality style that may make individuals especially vulnerable to depression: the depressive depends excessively on others for his self-esteem. The depressive desperately needs to be showered with love and admiration. He goes through the world in a state of perpetual greediness for love, and when his need for love is not satisfied, his self-esteem plummets.
> – *David Rosenhan & Martin Seligman*

The depressive personality will be exhibited when the client has considered that life is not worth living because he feels unworthy and unloved. The client will essentially feel that he has been so severely rejected or discarded by others that love has become an utterly illusive quality. The client will then conclude that a world without love cannot be one in which he will wish to participate. Withdrawal, isolation and a low feeling of self-worth will, therefore, characterise this personality classification. The depressive personality disorder has been linked to the depressive disorder (see Chapter 9 – "Sorrow and Grief Disorders").

The dissociative-identity personality

Three clinical studies of Multiple Personality Disordered [MPD] patients
in particular have shown rates of between 75 per cent and 90 per cent for
CSA [Childhood Sexual Abuse] and 50 per cent and 82 per cent for
CPA [Childhood Physical Abuse].
– John Morton

The dissociative-identity personality will be one in which a part of the client's personality will have split off from the rest of his central core of personality. It will be as if the client's psyche wished to dissociate itself from unacceptable elements of his personality and this will, therefore, be his way of denying that part of himself. Dissociation or ego-splitting will be a coping-strategy used by the client's mind when he has perceived that unpleasant aspects of the self – in terms of emotive expression, characteristics and unacceptable recollection – are in evidence. This notion, of course, underpins the philosophy and concepts of ego-state psychology (see Chapter 4, Volume 1 – "Ego-State Therapy").

The dissociative-identity victim may suffer from an extreme form of dissociative disorder known as *dissociative-identity disorder* (DID) or *multiple-personality disorder* (MPD) whereby the client has created for himself a series of alternative personalities. It has been theorised that the client will cope with excessive trauma by splitting his mind into separate compartments or fragments. The client with such fragmentation may often be fantasy-prone and highly suggestible. Often a DID client will be overwhelmed by his feelings and harbour a variety of fears and phobias frequently in keeping with the nature of his past experiences. With severe DID, the client may be unaware of what happens in the highly-disturbed states into which he can enter. The client who outwardly appears reasonably emotionally stable, therefore, can suddenly switch into a violent rage and then can later have little or no conscious recollection of the acts committed or the behaviours exhibited while in the rage-state.

Multiple personality disorder (MPD), which is called dissociative identity
disorder by DSM-IV [*Diagnostic and Statistical Manual of Mental Disorders,
Volume IV*], is defined as the occurrence of two or more personalities in
the same individual, each of which is sufficiently integrated to have a
relatively stable life of its own and recurrently to take full control of the
person's behaviour.
– David Rosenhan & Martin Seligman

The narcissistic personality

The narcissistic personality is characterized by a grandiose and
exaggerated sense of self-importance and an explosive attitude toward
others, which serve the function of masking a frail self-concept. Such
individuals seek attention and admiration from others. They
unrealistically exaggerate their accomplishments, and they have a
tendency toward extreme self-absorption.
– Gerald Corey

The narcissistic personality can be developed by the client as a
means of hiding or masking his anxiety. The client, essentially, will
feel a degree of inferiority, loneliness and emptiness and his narcissistic disorder will develop as a means of coping with such feelings. The sufferer may also feel underlying guilt and shame and
have a self-destructive nature beneath the bravado (see Chapter 8
– "Guilt and Shame Disorders"). The narcissistic tendency will
develop because the client needs to feel safe with a perception of
invincibility. Such insensitive grandiosity will, however, be a precarious commodity that can shatter the client if his image of self-
importance cannot be sustained. The client, therefore, may exhibit
traits of self-importance and grandiosity as a means of denying his
fears. The narcissistic personality, moreover, will display a range of
symptoms that can include a grandiose sense of self-importance,
exhibitionist tendencies, a need for excessive admiration and an
expectation of favourable treatment from others. The client may
also harbour fantasies of success, power and brilliance and, as a
result, may automatically expect that others will comply with his
wishes. The client may also be prone to exploit others and have a
lack of empathy with those about him. A narcissistic tendency,
moreover, will lead the client to display a contemptuous indifference to criticism from others. The client may also exhibit a need to
devalue and to discredit low-profile people because he will have a
need to associate with and to idealise high-profile people.

A narcissistic disorder will be said to develop when the child has
been given a poor sense of self by his parents. A parent's words or
deeds will reflect back to the child a validation of his own self-
worth as if his parent were holding up a mirror in which he can
view himself. This mirroring should constitute an empathetic res-
onance because the parent should be sensitively showing the child
what his true value is as a human being in his own right as well as

being a beloved child (see Chapter 6, Volume 1 – "Client-Centred Therapy"). A distorted or inadequate mirroring by a parent, however, will mean that the child will develop an unhealthy or mangled self-image. The client's distorted self-image will then need to be compensated for and, thus, a narcissistic disorder may surface. The practitioner, of course, can go some way towards counteracting narcissistic feelings within the client by showing genuine empathy and by reflecting his true worth in a judgment-free environment (see Chapter 13, Volume 1 – "Transference and Countertransference").

> The central feature of the narcissistic personality disorder is an outlandish sense of self-importance. It is characterised by continuous self-absorption, by fantasies of unlimited success, power and/or beauty, by exhibitionist needs for constant admiration, and by the use of a substantially more benign stand for evaluating self than for judging others.
> – *David Rosenhan & Martin Seligman*

The histrionic personality

> People who have long histories of drawing attention to themselves and of engaging in excited emotional displays that are caused by insignificant events are captured in the diagnosis of histrionic personality disorder. Such people are apt to be superficially charming, warm, and gregarious, but they are often viewed by others as insincere and shallow.
> – *David Rosenhan & Martin Seligman*

The histrionic personality will be the client's childish way of capturing the attention of others in a dramatic and theatrical fashion. The client may go overboard when turning on the charm in the vain hope that he will be admired. The client may also be flirtatious yet superficial and insincere. The client may, thus, appear to be overemotional and may be prone to resorting to emotional blackmail. Such tactics will, of course, be designed to bolster the client's low self-opinion and to vanquish deep-seated fears of inadequacy. The practitioner can assist the client by clearly demonstrating that attention-seeking behaviour is unnecessary in the nonjudgmental therapeutic context.

The antisocial personality

The suffering in an individual with the antisocial personality disorder is
muted. The hallmark of the disorder is a rapacious attitude toward
others, a chronic insensitivity and indifference to the rights of other
people that is marked by lying, stealing, cheating and worse.
– David Rosenhan & Martin Seligman

The antisocial personality will be exhibited by the client who displays a tendency towards breaking the moral code of social behaviour that will generally be laid down by society. The client may behave irresponsibly with little or no remorse and may sometimes have had a brush with the law. This type of behaviour will be the client's way of relieving tension and frustration by acting out his fantasies in the form of rebellion. Perhaps this client will not wish to cooperate fully with the practitioner.

The borderline personality

Studies of clinical populations show raised rates of trauma of between
90 per cent and 50 per cent of patients reporting a major physical or
sexual assault at some time in their lives. Furthermore, a number of
studies have shown that patients with such histories have more severe
symptoms, borderline diagnoses and more suicidal symptoms than
other patients.
– John Morton

The borderline personality will be exhibited when the client becomes unstable in terms of social interaction, mood and self-image. The client will often display dramatic mood fluctuations, indecisiveness and erratic behaviour. Sometimes this disorder will stem from a sense of rejection and the client's symptoms of instability will simply be a reaction to this perception. The borderline personality will display a range of symptoms that can include frantic efforts to avoid real or imagined rejection and abandonment, feelings of emptiness, a lack of stability particularly in interpersonal relationships and a degree of intensity in interpersonal communication. This client, furthermore, may have an unstable self-identity, may display a frail self-image, may be impulsive or reckless, may have a tendency towards substance-abuse and may have self-mutilation or suicidal tendencies.

A borderline personality can develop when the young infant perceives that his mother-figure has rejected him. This usually occurs when the child begins to attain a degree of independence and mother then ceases to be as attentive as she was when he was totally helpless and required round-the-clock nurturing. Often the mother-figure will withdraw emotional support from the child when she perceives that he is not quite as demanding as he was immediately following birth. The borderline personality category reflects the thinking of object-relations psychologists (see Chapter 5, Volume 1 – "Object-Relations Psychology"). The borderline personality has been linked to the borderline personality disorder (BPD).

> Borderline people are characterised by instability, irritability, self-destructive acts, impulsive anger, and extreme mood shifts. They typically experience extended periods of disillusionment, punctuated by occasional euphoria.
> – *Gerald Corey*

The paranoidal personality

> The prominent characteristics of the paranoid personality disorder are a pervasive and longstanding distrust and suspiciousness of others; hypersensitivity to slight; and a tendency to scan the environment for, and to perceive selectively, cues that validate prejudicial ideas and attitudes.
> – *David Rosenhan & Martin Seligman*

The paranoidal personality will be one in which the client will be ever-watchful and suspicious of others and situations. The client may be easily offended by what others say and will take even slight criticism personally. This client will be acutely aware of his self-image and will be likely to overreact at the slightest provocation. The client will, generally, display a tendency to high-anxiety states and states of becoming overanxious.

The schizoidal personality

> The central feature of the schizoid personality disorder is a defect in the capacity to form social relationships, as reflected in the absence of desire for social involvements, indifference to both praise and criticism, insensitivity to the feelings of others, and/or lack of social skills. Such people have few, if any, close friends. They are withdrawn, reserved, and seclusive.
> – *David Rosenhan & Martin Seligman*

The schizoidal personality will be characterised by the client's tendency to shun the company of others. The client will, therefore, be earnestly disinclined to want to mix with others socially. It will be as if the client wishes to remain aloof and indifferent to the opinions of others whom, in any case, he will seek to dismiss from his presence. As a result, this client may display extremely socially-disruptive and rebellious tendencies. It is unlikely that the schizoidal client could be treated using hypnotic intervention.

Attachment Theory

> We now know (and the dissolution of family life in contemporary society
> proves the point) that if the normal processes of separation are disrupted
> in any way, if fantasy becomes reality and the love objects die, leave,
> reject, batter, disparage, react too possessively or obsessionally, lose face,
> become depressed, unemployed, redundant, are forced to move home,
> these disruptions of a normal interaction are likely to take a pathological
> course later in life.
> – *Cassie Cooper*

Attachment theory was first muted by John Bowlby (1907–1990) in order to account for the way in which the child develops a relationship with people and objects in his immediate world. Attachment theory considers the nature of the child's attachment to love-objects based on the degree of separation-anxiety to which he has been exposed. The child, therefore, may form either a *secure attachment* or an *insecure attachment* to his love-objects. The child will, for instance, form a secure attachment to his carers if his needs are generally catered for adequately and he can develop without the manifestation of any undue anxiety. The child who has been neglected or haphazardly cared for by irresponsible parentage may become wary, unstable and unable to trust others because he will have formed an insecure attachment to those about him in developmental years. This theory forms part of object-relations psychology (see Chapter 5, Volume 1 – "Object-Relations Psychology").

Bowlby categorised types of insecure attachment according to the effects on the client. An insecure attachment might, for instance, provoke anxiety, self-reliance or compulsive-nurturing behaviours in the client. Bowlby also put forward the notion that an insecure attachment would generate a separation-response from the child, who would begin to express concern as a form of protest by showing signs of distress. The child would, perhaps, enter a stage of despair in which misery, grief and apathy would be displayed and, then, eventually move towards detaching from his care-givers by becoming indifferent to any further advances.

> When the parent or other attachment figure is reunited with the child after a period of separation, the child's response may be quite complex. It often includes a period of anger and rejection, as the child goes through an emotional readjustment at the return, and expresses its feelings of anger at having been abandoned. This may also be followed by a period in which the child is more "clingy" than usual, as it expresses its need for reassurance that the parent is still available.
> – Nicky Hayes

The anxious attachment

The client who displays an anxious attachment will be beset by excessive anxiety that can cause him to become overdependent on his parents until the attachment has been resolved. The client may still cling to his parents, may earnestly seek their approval and may constantly elicit their opinions. Sometimes the client will be disinclined to move from the family home and may refrain from taking an intimate life-partner. For the client who does manage to enter into an intimate relationship in adulthood, it will usually be inevitable that overdependency and co-dependency will be the result in such a union.

The compulsive self-reliant attachment

The client who displays a compulsive self-reliant attachment will find it difficult to form any kind of adult intimate relationship. With this type of insecure attachment, the client will experience difficulty in accepting love and affection from others. This client will usually be fiercely independent and almost unable to accept any help from others because of his inability to trust people. This client may, of course, experience difficulty with trusting the therapist and may appear to be suspicious of her competence.

The compulsive care-giver attachment

The client who displays a compulsive care-giver attachment will discover a means of allowing himself to receive the illusion of love and affection of which he has been deprived in infancy. With this type of attachment, the client will find a way of forming relationships that go some way towards compensating for anxiety-related distresses. The client here will be attempting to reconstruct the caring environment that he himself lacked in infancy.

Those in caring professions can sometimes become obsessively preoccupied with the need to care for others often to their own detriment. This may mean long hours, gruelling work and emotional distress for the carer. Although it has been said that the human organism has a natural need to be a carer, the excessive carer often attends to others at great cost to himself. In extreme cases, the compulsive carer may indulge in prostrating himself as a severe form of self-denigration. If the practitioner were to become a compulsive care-giver, she may find that she will be symbolically providing the client with the love that was blatantly absent in her own childhood. Similarly, the excessive carer may be attempting to put right the perceived injustices in society. If the therapist finds herself performing in this role, then it would be advisable for her to seek further personal therapy and supervisory support.

The anxious-resistant attachment

The client who displays an anxious-resistant attachment may fear and fiercely resist parental separation. With this form of attachment, the child will often have been the victim of inconsistent care whereby the parent will have shown love one minute and hatred or neglect the next. The child will, then, become so confused by these haphazard emotive expressions that he will find it difficult ever to be consoled or comforted as a result of the anxiety and confusion that has been generated. This client may, therefore, feel insecure with any form of separation, betrayal or rejection from another.

The anxious-avoidant attachment

The client who displays an anxious-avoidant attachment may elect to withdraw from the love-object that he perceives has withheld love or support. In this case, the child will tend to avoid or ignore his carers and, indeed, may reject any attempts by the parental guardian to show any affection. This client may be likely to reject any form of affection, help or care in later life on the basis that he will believe that relationships will inevitably result in rejection or abandonment.

The disorganised-disoriented attachment

The client who displays a disorganised-disoriented attachment may react to inconsistent care by becoming dazed, confused and disoriented by such experiences. This form of attachment will be likely to develop in cases when the care-giver threatens the child, makes love a conditional component of care or, alternately, proffers and then withholds love. This client may, therefore, find relationships in adult life confusing and can become indecisive with regard to commitment to any form of intimate partnership.

Exploring the Client's Fear and Anxiety Disorders

> If children believe that they are in mortal danger and that the threat is embodied by the people on whom they are most reliant, the result is a feeling of profound powerlessness that any will to continue is totally eradicated. Therefore, resilient children bounce back through an instinctive reframing of their environments that restores hope. They conclude that they are bad and have caused their own suffering, that their caregivers truly love them, and that if they can only try harder or be better, everything will change.
> – *Mark Schwartz, Lori Galperin & William Masters*

Essentially, the client's fear and anxiety disorders can be tackled by first seeking to identify the underlying root cause and then exploring, in detail, the ways in which he has been symptomatically affected. The seeding events or situations that have caused the client's distress to manifest will, almost certainly, need to be traced back to childhood relationships that have impinged upon his need for safety in order to survive. Once these factors have been identified, the practitioner may then wish to ensure that the client has expressed his true feelings about the past, has relinquished his fears and anxieties in full and has reached a degree of understanding about the seeding circumstances. The client can now be invited to accept the consequences of what has happened to him and to consign the past to insignificance. The ways in which the client's symptoms have manifested unconsciously can now be given licence to become irrelevant, unnecessary and easily extinguished in terms of his current wellbeing.

The following suggested passage could be used by the practitioner in order to explain to the client the purpose of the fear from which he may be suffering and to provide him with a clue to its origin. When the client can gain this form of insight into his motivations, he may well be able to relinquish any tendencies he may have for fearing rejection, abandonment and failure.

Nature's blueprint for fear …

Fear is what we experience when we perceive threat or danger – particularly when we realise that we do not have adequate resources to cope with the source of such fear.

The caveman lived continually in fear of his life. He dreaded invasion from other cavemen or from the man-eating tiger. His unhappy existence was aggravated by the fact that he alone had to protect his family. He feared having to leave them for long periods of time when he left the cave to search for food. Finding food was also a hazardous adventure in itself because he had to fight in order to kill his prey. And, because we are all the sons and daughters of the caveman, we have inherited his fears.

Fear can also engender other responses as a result of the domino-effect. If we are frightened, then, we may want to run away or we may want to fight the foe or we may simply freeze in a welter of confusion. In nature, animals and birds fight, freeze or flee. As human beings we adopt the same policy. This policy is often termed the fight-or-flight mechanism and its initiation is automatic when a perceived threat or real danger is encountered both in childhood and in adulthood. This primitive mechanism is designed to keep us alive – regardless of cult, creed, class or colour. It is the only one we have and is, by definition, a mechanism that works on the sledge-hammer-to-crack-a-nut basis because we need to be equipped to cope with every possible eventuality.

We instinctively fear physical hazard because it could harm our person. At an early age, we learn how to recognise physical danger when being guided by our parents or carers. We learn that fire can burn us, that knives can cut us and that a passing car could injure, maim or kill us. If we do not learn from our parents or primary carers, we may have to learn this difficult lesson the hard way. In today's world, however, it is much more likely that emotional fear will beset us rather than a fear of physical danger. And, perhaps, the scars of an emotional fear are more abiding and enduring than physical harm. A physical trauma can often be made better with a bandage or some ointment or a cuddle from Mum but an emotional fear can linger menacingly to disturb us or, even, to haunt us. In childhood, we may continually fear that we may do the wrong thing or that we may step out of line or that we are lacking in ability in some respect. We may also learn to worry that we do not have sufficient courage or that we are too small in stature to overcome any perceived threat. But when we do first meet danger in the face, we learn how to re-experience the caveman's instinctive fears. And these fears affect our emotions deeply. Thus, as children, we constantly seek reassurance from our parents or primary carers that we are under an umbrella of safety and protection at all times both emotionally and physically.

Some degree of fear, of course, can be beneficial for mankind in that it keeps us alive by preventing us from taking too many risks. Harmless fear appears as natural caution or wariness. It keeps us alert when we cross a road or when we drive a car or when we change jobs. It stops us from spending all our savings on a new car or dissuades us from selling the house in order to buy a lottery ticket. It helps us to remember to lock up the car or to turn off the central heating or simply to take an umbrella with us on a rainy day. The trouble arises when natural fear spills over into uncontrollable fear that can dominate our life in an unacceptable way. But, like all emotions, fear breeds and proliferates. A victim of panic attacks, for example, will fear the likelihood of having an attack in public just as much as having the attack itself and will, therefore, studiously avoid certain situations. A phobic sufferer may well fear that he will bring on the condition even when the coast is ostensibly clear of the object of his phobia and, in consequence, may unnecessarily go out of his way to avoid potentially hazardous situations.

So what makes us feel fear for our survival in childhood? Fear will be derived from anything that made you feel unwanted or neglected, unimportant or unworthy, uncertain or unsafe or exposed you to personal danger without the necessary resources to cope with the crisis. In adulthood the residue of this childhood legacy of unruly or uncontrollable fear may manifest itself in any number of ways. Ask yourself some questions about the ways in which your fears and anxieties have manifested within you and answer quietly in an honest manner.

Client Profiling

The analytical-hypnotherapy practitioner may wish to ponder the following points when formulating a profile for the client.

- In what ways does the client overtly and covertly display fear and anxiety?
- What lies at the root of the client's fears and anxieties?
- What is the true foundation of the client's fear and anxiety?
- Does the client exhibit a fear of rejection or a fear of being abandoned?
- Does the client believe that he must do exceptionally well in therapy?
- Does the client view his anxieties realistically or unrealistically?
- Does the client tend to panic or to worry unnecessarily?
- Does the client in any way suffer from phobic disorders?
- Does the client exhibit a tendency to play it safe?
- Does the client tend to need to have control of events?
- What relationship does the client have with food and alcohol?
- Does the client overindulge in drugs or other harmful substances on a regular basis?
- Does the client habitually tend to avoid people or situations?
- Is the client excessively inactive or overactive?
- Does the client tend to become easily despondent or to despair of his ability to cope with life?
- Does the client exhibit a number of differing ego-state personalities?
- Does the client have a realistic opinion of himself?
- Does the client behave in an over-the-top way in social situations?
- Is the client at all rebellious or nonconformist?
- Does the client indicate a tendency towards mood-swings or erratic behaviour?
- Is the client likely to overdepend on others or would he be normally self-sufficient?
- Does the client ever appear to be overanxious or confused by the actions of others?
- Is the practitioner in any way inclined to overcare for her clients or to take on the role of rescuer?

Chapter 8

Guilt and Shame Disorders

So full of artless jealousy is guilt,
It spills itself in fearing to be spilt.

– William Shakespeare

What is Guilt and Shame?

The common denominator for feelings of guilt appears to be the victim's
sense of responsibility for the abuse or events occurring afterward.
– Jeffrey Haugaard & Dickon Reppucci

Guilt is perhaps the most insidiously destructive of all emotive
expression because it will imply that the client has internalised
self-blame and that she may then seek self-punishment as a form
of retribution for her perceived sins (see Figure 2 –
"Symptomology"). Often the guilt-ridden client will be utterly
intolerant of her own perceived misdeeds and, thus, her opinion of
herself and her capabilities will be pathetically low.

The practitioner can help the client to come to terms with guilt by
allowing her to gain insight into the nature of her unconscious misgivings. Once the client has learned to understand that the past
was not her fault and that she was blameless, then this knowledge
will tend to free her from the stifling chains of a guilt-ridden existence. It may be possible, for example, for the therapist to explain
to the client that she was not the guilty party and to negotiate with
her in order to show her that things were somehow different in the
past. When the client feels disinclined to accept such wisdom, it
may be that she has been protecting another and will steadfastly
desire to carry the blame herself. The therapist may continue to
probe and to persuade but, if this fails, then maybe the client can
simply accept that she is not perfect and never will be.

When the client was a child, of course, she will have been at the mercy of her parents. Parents, teachers and other carers will attempt to instil rules of conduct and to insist on socially-acceptable practices when bringing up the young child. The client will, therefore, from a very young age be told what to do, how to do it and whether her actions are either right or wrong. The child, of course, will feel obliged to strive in order to please significant others with the unconscious desire to attain love, care and protection. The tragedy will occur, inevitably, when the child, in vain, must attempt to comply with someone else's rulebook, to guess innocently what is required of her and to live, perhaps, by an illogical code of conduct in the name of social niceties. In this climate, guilt and shame are almost bound to thrive and to permeate the child's entire existence. It will be as if the baby is spoon-fed with guilt and shame from the moment of her birth and beyond. What can be worse will be that there may be no viable alternative to parental dictates if the infant is to be accepted in the social world where she must learn how to protect herself. In other words, virtually everyone on Planet Earth will be carrying around some form of guilt and self-hatred but the client, in therapy, will be required to address this baggage head on. Once the client has realised, however, that she does not owe an eternal debt of gratitude to her parents, then this too will free her from her perceived obligations to pay guilt-provoking homage and deference to such imagined demigods.

The client may feel guilty when she perceives that she has done something wrong, has failed to act appropriately or has been blameworthy because of inaction. A feeling of shame, furthermore, will often mean that the client has taken personal responsibility for actions, inaction or deeds that will impinge on her self-image. Perhaps the guilt-ridden client will feel that she has taken an active part in some form of misdemeanour. Perhaps the client will feel that she should not have consented to do something when pressured by others. Perhaps the client will feel that she was too easily led by others in her youth in the days of teenage gangs. Perhaps the client will feel that she should not have been so vulnerable and dependent on her parents for affection. Perhaps the client will feel that she has been too gullible when she was taken for a ride by a confidence-trickster. Perhaps the client will feel that she should not have enjoyed playing with her genitals or masturbating as a young person. Perhaps the client will feel contaminated or unclean as a result of sexual interference or erotic experimentation. Perhaps the client will feel that she should have been more respectful of her parents and elders in childhood. Perhaps the client will also blame herself for not disclosing any misdeeds in childhood.

All such notions may contribute to the client's underlying feelings of guilt and shame and can provide her with a valid reason for partial or total self-destruction. For any or all of these reasons, a guilt-complex may be set up in the client and may have been there, well entrenched, for years if not decades (see Chapter 2, Volume 1 – "Analytical Psychology"). Essentially, the guilt-complex will become increasingly more pressing if the client feels that she was a willing participant in doing something inherently wrong as opposed to being subjected by force. When such a profound degree of guilt has been laid down, the client will often not wish to disclose the nature of it and, consequently, not gain any degree of relief from her shame. The sexually-abused child, for example, may not confide in a parent or a carer when she has been violated (see Chapter 14 – "The Nature of Childhood Abuse"). If the child discloses any abuse, however, the news of which is then not heard or the disclosure is met with disbelief, then more profound guilt will be installed in the client's unconscious mind because the guilt-factor will have been compounded (see Chapter 15 – "The Effects of Childhood Abuse"). The victim of childhood abuse, therefore, will then feel helpless and bereft and her guilt-complex may, therefore, surface as resistance during therapeutic intervention (see Chapter 12, Volume 1 – "Resistance").

> Shame is a painful feeling about identity, rather than about a
> particular action.
> – *Joel Covitz*

Guilt and Shame Manifestations

> Many parents consciously or unconsciously deny their guilt toward their
> children – to the detriment of everyone concerned with society at large. I
> believe nearly every child would be willing to freely forgive its parents
> for even grave mistakes if only the parents showed themselves willing to
> co-operate in bringing about a reconciliation.
> – *Konrad Stettbacher*

The client's manifestations of guilt and shame can lead to self-blaming, self-destructive and, perhaps, even suicidal tendencies as well as to depressive and dissociative disorders (see Chapter 9 – "Sorrow and Grief Disorders"). Often the emotive expression that underlies obsessive-compulsive disorders, addictions and substance-abuse disorders, moreover, may be those of the client's unconscious guilt and shame (see Chapter 7 – "Fear and Anxiety Disorders"). Activities such as excessive cleaning or washing, for example, can be the client's primitive way of expunging her perceived wickedness. The client who is an idealist or a perfectionist may also be attempting unconsciously to put matters right.

Self-blame

> Unacceptable emotions experienced at the time of the critical event are repressed by the Parent ego state since their expression would meet with profound parental disapproval and the possibility of abandonment, if not physically then at least emotionally. It is the fear of this rejection and the possible parental abandonment which gives to guilt its intense power to control.
> – *Edgar Barnett*

Often guilt will be engendered because the client may unconsciously feel that she was somehow to blame for any ill-treatment by others. This premise will obtain particularly for the victim of childhood abuse – whether the abuse be emotional, physical or sexual. Perhaps it was something the child said or did that resulted in such punishment. Perhaps it was the way in which the child acted that encouraged the abuser. Perhaps it was the way in which the child sought attention or affection by seeking out her perpetrator or by complying with the abuser's demands. Perhaps it was the way in which the child was vulnerable that attracted the attention of the assailant. Perhaps it was the way in which the client did not protest or prevent any recurrence of the attacks. This sub-surface-level stance will be the client's form of childish logic at work that has put the guilt-factor in place and will endeavour to keep it there. The therapist should attempt to evaluate the client from the viewpoint of the machinations of her childish logic in order to be able to track down and expose the guilt-component within her psyche. In many respects, the main thrust of analytical hypnotherapy may need to deal with exploring the client's guilt about all aspects of her past (see Chapter 2 – "Therapeutic Investigation"). Analytical investigation should, of course, enable the client to discover the root of her guilt but, in addition, some cognitive persuasion may need to be applied in order to ensure that she resolves unsettled scores within her mind (see Chapter 9, Volume 1 – "Cognitive Therapy").

When dealing with an overload of the client's self-blame, the practitioner could encourage her to settle to the idea of not having to perpetuate her negative stance and her unpleasant symptoms. The client's unconscious mind will have to be assured that there is currently no further need to hold on to her symptoms and that she can be freed from any psychological or physiological danger. The client can be invited to mature with her adult knowledge, skills and resources. It will be as if the client's unconscious mind will have to be exposed to a degree of logic in order to be persuaded that symptoms are no longer necessary because they no longer have a purpose to fulfil in the present.

Once guilt-complexes have been dealt with, the practitioner can then explain to the client that her former need to exhibit symptoms can now be renounced. The smoke can, therefore, die down now because there no longer is a fire in the form of repressed cognitive activity, buried emotive expression or encased physical sensation. There is no longer a fire because there is no fuel. There may still be some ashes but these will get swept away by the wind in due course. Because the human organism tends to be a creature of habit, it may be some while before the client will be able to let go of inhibiting guilt and its resultant symptoms. The client may sometimes feel that she needs to go over old ground again and again or that previous progress has been lost or, even, that she has taken a retrograde step. The key factor that will need to be considered here will be that the client's mind will require time to adjust to its new guilt-free software-program (see Chapter 5 – "Therapeutic Resolution").

Guilt and shame are another frequently observed reaction to child sexual abuse, but few studies give clear percentages. De Francis observed that 64% of his sample expressed guilt, although more about the problems created by disclosure than about the molestation itself. Anderson et al reported guilt reactions in 25% of the victims.
– *David Finkelhor & Angela Browne*

The therapist may wish to utilise some questioning techniques when treating the client who suffers from a self-blaming tendency. Perhaps some surreptitious questioning as set out below can, therefore, be employed by the practitioner in order to help the client to identify such tendencies.

• Do you always strive to be a perfectionist?
• Do you frequently become impatient even with yourself?
• Do you feel you are inherently bad or wicked by nature?
• Do you ever feel inclined to misjudge yourself?
• Do you frequently find yourself constantly apologising to others?
• Do you ever suffer from a feeling of continually being watched or judged by others?
• Do you ever feel uncertain or uneasy about any of your actions or motivations?
• Do you ever feel that you are carrying around with you a closely-guarded secret?
• Do you keep yourself very much to yourself?
• Are you normally a very secretive and private person?
• Do you dislike asking for help or advice from others?
• Do you not tend to bother other people with your problems?
• Do you have the feeling that you do not deserve any favours from anyone?
• Do you feel that it is often your fault when things go wrong?
• Do you frequently believe yourself to be the fly in the ointment?
• Do you consider that you are always letting other people down?

The following client narrative can provide the therapist with some insight into the way in which a client can develop a self-blaming tendency.

Client narrative – I was always to blame …

When I was at school we were asked to complete certain tasks. When each of these tasks was completed, the pupil was given a tick by the side of her name on a list pinned up in the classroom. The expression, being "ticked off", was thus adopted by me and my classmates. To be ticked off was, to me, an honour, an achievement and a privilege. One day when I proudly told my mother that I had been ticked off at school, she had a semi-seizure. I desperately tried to explain the situation (not knowing at all of the adult meaning of the phrase) but was not given the benefit of the doubt. The feelings of shame and injustice that I felt as a child were paramount and incomparable. My world fell apart. Here was something that I had, at last, managed to do well and this fact was utterly negated by my mother. And, furthermore, I was actually scolded for it. I kept quiet in future.

On occasions when I did achieve something at school or at work and the fact was undeniable, my mother's demeaning retort would invariably be "Well it is, after all, only what I expect of you" – the phrase delivered with a hideously condescending smile that withered me to dust.

When I had a dispute with some children who came to my house to play, my mother's view, as always, was that I must have started the argument. Whatever befell, it had to be my fault. I also felt that my mother could not be wrong and so I must be at fault. I began to blame myself for everything after that – whether I deserved it or not.

Self-destruction

> To commit violence on oneself is the method preferred by our culture for several reasons. Obviously, it is easier to maintain a social structure that appears to be in control of itself. However, I think there is another, more compelling reason – by internalising our natural propensity to resolve life-threatening events, we are denying that the need even exists – it remains hidden.
> – *Peter Levine*

When the client's unconscious guilt and self-blame begin to throttle her psyche, she may decide on a supposedly-just form of self-punishment. Self-destruction in its mildest form can result in high-risk-taking activities whereby the client will have a need to live dangerously – psychologically, physically or financially, for example. Self-mutilation will also be a common symptom exhibited by the client with a well entrenched guilt-complex. The ultimate form of self-destruction will, of course, be suicide – both its attempt and its contemplation. The guilt-ridden client will often feel unconsciously that the only way of escaping from the sheer pain of guilt will be to exterminate herself utterly.

> Self-mutilation is sometimes used by victims of abuse to control their experience of pain. It can also provide an intense feeling of relief and release that is often craved. It can be an attempt to control something in one's life, a type of self-punishment, a means of expressing anger or a way of having feelings. It can be manifested in both children and adults. Sometimes the physical pain can be a distraction from the more feared emotional pain or it can be an attempt to indicate to others just how strong the emotional pain is.
> *– Penny Parks*

Other symptoms that may have arisen because of a residue of destructive guilt in the client could be heavy smoking, excessive drinking, drug-abuse or any other addictive activity that will appear to comprise a self-punishing nature. The client may, more-over, become a doormat on whom others merely trample. The client may find herself working all hours and even then taking work home. The workaholic may be beavering away endlessly in order to avoid facing the inner truth about her assumed transgressions. The client may also become the bait of a nagging spouse or a violent partner. The excessive carer and the do-gooder, similarly, may be trying to recompense the universe for the past wrongs that she believes she has committed. The eternal people-pleaser will have guilt written in indelible ink on her forehead. The practitioner can often cite numerous examples of the client's self-destructive tendencies.

> A surprising number of survivors engage in behaviour that is painful or disfiguring to themselves. Cuts and burns are perhaps the most frequently reported. Milder forms include compulsively cutting hair, pulling out eyebrows or patches of hair, picking at skin blemishes, biting finger nails or cuticles, piercing other than earlobes and using bizarre makeup styles. Getting a tattoo, especially self tattooing, may in some cases be regarded as self-mutilation.
> *– Ken Graber*

The therapist may wish to utilise any of the following questioning techniques in order to probe the client's self-destructive tendencies.

- Do you feel that you are in some way tainted or contaminated?
- Do you feel that you are unable to wash away your sins?
- Do you feel a sense of having done much wrong in the past?
- Do you always tend to take the blame when things go wrong – even if you know it was not really your fault?
- Do you ever consider that you are a nuisance to other people?

- Do you ever feel that you are a waste of space in this world?
- Do you consider that people should be severely punished when they make mistakes or commit crimes?
- Do you sometimes feel as if you have sinned against humanity?
- Do you often set a standard of performance for yourself that you secretly know you can never actually achieve?
- Do you believe that you are not good enough to mix with certain people?
- Did you do a lot of damage to people or to property when you were a teenager?
- Do you believe in corporal punishment for criminals?
- Do you believe that the authorities should assiduously hunt down and make an example of dangerous criminals?

The following passage can help the client to come to terms with relieving any self-destructive or self-mutilating tendencies that are based on feelings of guilt and shame.

Why destroy yourself with guilt?

In life, we are instructed in the moral code of society that dictates that pleasures such as sex are a naughty-but-nice forbidden fruit. The image-creators pander to our guilt by beseeching us to be slim or fashionable or young or rich or knowledgeable or one step ahead of the crowd. Such attributes may well either reinforce what we have been taught to believe or be at variance with that which we were taught in our formative years. Either way our guilt-strings are being continually tugged quite hard.

There really are no advantages at all to having guilty feelings. All that can be said in its favour is that it is generally necessary for a child to be schooled in the ethics of acceptable human behaviour and good conduct in order to enable her to take her place in society and to succeed in the world. If human beings were not taught the difference between right and wrong, then we might be breeding a society of individuals without any social or moral conscience. Essentially the function of guilt, therefore, will be to make us law-abiding citizens with a healthy respect for others in the community – but it is an extremely hard way of learning this lesson! The trouble arises when we have unfailingly learned to regard ourselves as being inherently guilty by nature because we will then seek to punish ourselves severely.

Guilt often engenders more guilt because the guilt-sufferer will feel guilty about feeling guilty. Guilt-sufferers often carry around a feeling of being inherently evil. The guilt-victim will often feel shame and self-blame for much of her waking and sleeping hours. Guilt often manifests itself in hopelessness,

227

despondency and lack of self-worth. Beliefs about being guilty also bring about a need for self-inflicted punishment or, even, self-destructive tendencies. If we know we are guilty by nature, then how could we possibly be blameless or infallible? And, when we know we are the guilty-type, then we must inevitably be punished. So if we are not or cannot be punished publicly by others, then, of course, we will have a need to punish ourselves. The drinkers and drug-abusers are often the guilt-sufferers in our society. Substance-abuse is used not only as a means of self-punishment but also as an attempt to anaesthetise the sufferer from that relentless anguish felt deep inside. We often perpetuate the very habit of which we wish to rid ourselves in order to feel more guilty. Weight-watchers and smokers are prime examples of guilt-breeders. The ultimate in self-punishment is, of course, utter self-destruction.

The guilt-sufferer, in addition, will often be prone to exploitation, to manipulation or to abuse from others because of her resultant feelings of worthlessness and lack of self-esteem. Guilt often compels us to allow our mind and our body to be manipulated or abused by others and, of course, bitterness and resentment will be the natural result when we are treated in such a manner.

In the following case-study example, the client found the origins of his underlying self-destructive tendencies by identifying the guilt-complex within his psyche.

Case-study example – self-punishment
This client had a self-mutilating tendency for which he sought analytical therapy because he believed that his tendency had its origins in his relationship with his father.

The client described the way in which his life had been shattered when his father had left the family home and had gone to live abroad. The client later went to visit his father and met his new girlfriend. The client's father then asked him not to tell his mother about his new girlfriend. The client, naturally, complied with his father's wishes on his return home. The client reasoned that his mother would get hurt if he told her about his father's girlfriend.

Finally, the client was invited to realise that the responsibility for keeping quiet about his father's secret should not have been his responsibility and he should not have borne the guilt over this conflict between his parents. The client acknowledged that his father was the guilty party and conceded that he had, in the past, been asked to withstand an intolerable burden that should not rightly have been his. By this means, the client was able to let go of his tendency towards self-blame and self-destruction.

Apportioning Blame

Children usually believe the abuse is their fault. Adult survivors must
place the blame where it belongs – directly on the shoulders of
the abusers.
– *Ellen Bass & Laura Davis*

The client may need to apportion blame in the right quarter in
order to be equipped to relieve the guilt aspects associated with
her past. It will be important for the client's unconscious mind to
accept fully that she was a victim at the mercy of thoughtless, preoccupied, negligent, violent or abusive malefactors. The client
should be invited, therefore, to accept the fact that her perpetrators
of injustice were 100 per cent blameworthy and that she was 100
per cent guiltless. There are no exceptions to this rule. Even some
seemingly-innocent acts may appear to the child to constitute
injustice. The child who wants to show a parent her drawing but is
shunned will indulge in self-blame. The child who wants father's
attention just as he is going off to work will feel she is not worth
the effort. The child whose request for sweets from mother is met
with disapproval will naturally justify her mother's reasons for her
refusal to comply with her wishes. Parents may be consoled by
knowing that no parent has ever been able to bring up a child who
can emerge guilt-free into adulthood. In the main, however, when
the client comes to sit in the therapist's consulting-room chair,
every injustice or ill-treatment that her mind has perceived may
need to be ironed out and blame may need to be realistically
apportioned against the violator of the crime as beheld in the
child's eyes.

In apportioning blame, it should be remembered that a reason is
not an excuse. If a parent suffered hardship in his or her own
childhood or was mistreated by his or her own parentage, then this
does not give him or her a licence to wrong the client. If the client
was misused by one parent, then the other parent should not be
blamed as a means of absolving the primary offender of his or her
responsibility for the crime. When the child has been ill-treated by
one parent, for example, there may often be a tendency for her to
transfer the blame to the other parent, who was guilty of neglect or
collusion – thus absolving the offending parent from any responsibility for blame. Both are blameworthy but for different reasons.

When apportioning blame, the client should bear in mind that one party was the perpetrator and the other an accessory. The client will need to get things into proportion and not let one party off the hook because of the actions of the other. Both parties are palpably responsible for the crime perpetrated against the child but these transgressions are different in nature. The client, therefore, will need to be made aware of whom she is blaming and for what. The perpetrator needs to be blamed for his or her actions and the colluder should be blamed for his or her inaction.

When the client has been a victim of childhood abuse or domestic violence, for example, the practitioner may need to allow the child to identify precisely the way in which she was forced into the abusive relationship (see Chapter 14 – "The Nature of Childhood Abuse"). Once this factor has been identified, the practitioner can then work on helping the client to understand the way in which the abuse could not have been her fault. The danger will, of course, arise when the client attempts to rationalise these concepts (see Chapter 11, Volume 1 – "Defensive Strategies"). The client must, in essence, persuade her own unconscious mind to accept these blame-apportioning doctrines in order to relieve the below-surface guilt that may well be at the heart of her distress.

Guilt is a perception of wrongdoing on the part of the client and the birthplace of this guilt-seeding will need to be unearthed during the therapeutic process. All adults who carry out misdeeds against children will have acted in a premeditated manner and would have been responsible for their actions – however, neurotically-driven those actions might have been. The abusive or neglectful perpetrator, for example, will have engineered his or her innocent victim towards an abusive act by whatever means were at his or her disposal. The molester would have misused his or her authority, strength, knowledge and experience to secure his or her victim. The predator was, therefore, to blame for manipulating circumstances in order to ensure that events went his or her way. The abuser exploited the child-victim for his or her own gratification. The abuser, moreover, may have even gone to extraordinary lengths in order to cover up his or her tracks – again, at the client's expense.

In the case of childhood sexual or violent abuse, the client will
need to appreciate the way in which she was jockeyed into keeping the violation a secret. Was the child silenced by being threatened by the abuser? Was the child silenced by the abuser's furtive
or underhand behaviour so that self-blame prevented any disclosure? Was the child silenced by the fearful effects of the attack that
rendered her speechless? Was the child silenced because there was
simply no-one available to tell or no-one around who might understand? Did the child attempt to tell someone but her meagre
attempts fell upon deaf ears? Did the child tell someone and then
not receive any relief? Did the child tell someone but was not
believed or even blamed for the abuse? Did the child tell a parent
but the recipient of the news was powerless to effect any action in
order to prevent further occurrences? Did the child tell someone
who was, in fact, a colluder or a conspirator and, thus, had a vested
interest in perpetuating the abusive violations? The blame for
childhood exploitation, neglect or abuse should, undoubtedly and
without exception, be laid at the door of the perpetrator of the
crimes.

> Victims often believe they are to blame for being sexually abused. Many
> adult survivors continue to hold this belief. Although large numbers of
> children and adolescents are abused, it is never the fault of any of them.
> – *Ellen Bass & Laura Davis*

The client who can make the appropriate realisation when apportioning blame where blame is due should be vociferously encouraged to realise that she is no longer required to feel guilt-ridden
and that it is currently inappropriate for her to do so. Fears will no
longer need to be felt because the client is no longer in danger.
Tears will no longer need to be shed over the loss of innocence or
because of neglect in childhood because the client is no longer a
needy child. Anger will no longer need to be expressed because the
client's enemy has gone and the danger has been averted. It will be
the client's unconscious mind, however, that will need to grasp
these tricky concepts rather than her cognitive mechanisms. No
amount of logic will ever relieve the client of her guilt, shame,
remorse or anxieties until her unconscious mind has crossed this
vitally-important bridge.

An emotion which has been located, identified and accepted, needs, before it can be relinquished, to be recognised as currently irrelevant to the present environment. The present situation must be seen to be different from that responsible for the original emotion. Furthermore, the past protective nature of the emotion must be seen no longer to be necessary since the individual now has for his defence access to his normal emotions.
– *Edgar Barnett*

In the following narrative, the client discusses the fact that she was never able to tell her mother about the fact that her father was sexually abusing her. The client, in this case, took on all the blame because she felt she was personally unable to halt the abuse.

Client narrative – I could never tell my mother ...

My mother was not available for consultation when I was a child. She adopted a closed-door policy and I was shut out. This, in itself, would have been damaging enough but, in my particular circumstances, it had devastating repercussions. The reasons why I considered my mother to be unapproachable were fundamentally that she was a prude as far as sex was concerned, she had a tendency either to blame me or, at least, not to give me the benefit of the doubt when problems occurred, she was a hypochondriac and she herself indulged in aggressive emotional abuse of me.

Sex was a dirty word to my mother. She considered that she had been conceived in sin because she was illegitimate and sin spelled sex. As a child I could not bring up the subject of sexual abuse because sex was a taboo subject. The difficulty was that as a child I took things literally and did not know that there are exceptions to the rule. The concept of "you mustn't talk about it" holds whatever the circumstances. A child does not know that there are these double standards – you mustn't talk about it when it's right but you must talk about it when it's wrong. Does the logic escape you? Well, it certainly escaped me when I was a child.

My mother did discuss sex with me, one or twice. She told me of the so-called facts of life but at an age when I was really too young to comprehend what she was talking about. She was, in fact, proud of the fact that she had done her duty by providing my sex education. Her ploy, however, was to get it off her chest while I was still virtually an infant and, therefore, save herself the embarrassment of speaking to me when I was old enough to appreciate what she was saying. When I was three years old, my mother explained that the woman across the road was going to have a baby and that she was keeping it warm in her tummy. The rest of the story unfolded gradually over the next few years. As a young child, of course, I hadn't a clue what she was on about. Effectively, therefore, I received no sex education of any value from my mother and my father provided a somewhat distorted view of the subject.

At one point in my childhood (at this time I would have been less than ten years old), I did question my mother about sex and her stance was to get cross and embarrassed. She merely brought the conversation to a swift halt by saying, "I have already told you, the man's penis goes in." I immediately detected the fact that this was a subject definitely not to be discussed and I was left trying to puzzle out where or what exactly the man's penis goes into. I developed the notion that this thing called a penis somehow disappeared up inside the man himself! The man? What man?

I was also magnanimously informed by my mother one day that I would not be evicted from the house – as my maternal grandmother had been – if I ever did get pregnant. I was shocked that such a thought could have ever entered my mother's head in the first place. As a teenager in the 1960s we were, after all, in the permissive age well and truly! Here was an example of a woman who could, without conscience, actually contemplate the never-darken-my-door-again principle in the name of sexual prudery. No wonder I never told her of my father's furtive activities.

Self-Forgiveness

> Forgiveness of the abuser is not an essential part of the healing process, although it tends to be the one most recommended. The only essential forgiveness is for yourself.
> – *Ellen Bass & Laura Davis*

The essential form of forgiveness as far as the client is concerned is self-forgiveness. Self-forgiveness can eradicate any remaining traces of guilt and shame once analytical investigation has been conducted and a fair degree of resolution has been achieved (see Chapter 2 – "Therapeutic Investigation"). If the client feels guilty for being compliant, vulnerable or susceptible, then she should forgive herself for her childish dependencies (see Chapter 5 – "Therapeutic Resolution"). All children are entirely dependent on all adults for their survival needs. All children actively seek attention and love – it will be the child's birthright. If the client feels guilty for having wanted attention and having been jealous of siblings as a result, then she should accept that her survival instincts were industriously at work in childhood.

Even when the child has ostensibly committed only trifling misdemeanours, it will be important for the practitioner to realise that the client's residual guilt will, in her own mind, portray such acts as grossly wicked. The client, for example, may have stolen some sweets or pulled another child's hair at school or, even, thrown a stone at a neighbour's window. These may be pranks that every child has committed at some time, but it should be emphasised that, when the client sits in the consulting-room chair and confesses all, she will be unloading her guilt about something that to her was very real and is still extremely painful. The child, furthermore, may well have been severely castigated or punished by adults for her naughtiness and this punishment may have further cemented her feelings of having gravely sinned.

> Once guilt is resolved, much of the self-sabotaging behaviour stops.
> There will be small bouts now and again as forgotten memories surface,
> but, once the initial battle is over, other episodes are more easily handled.
> – *Penny Parks*

When the client has suffered from childhood misuse, neglect or abuse, of course, the burden of self-blame and the resultant disinclination for self-forgiveness may be abundantly apparent. The client who has been subjected to sexual abuse, for example, may feel guilty for having enjoyed participating in sexual activity and shameful for having relished the attention that this activity afforded her. In such a case, the client could be encouraged to forgive her natural inclinations. Sexuality is an undeniable part of the physiological being that will be there from the moment of conception until the client's death. If the client feels guilty for having been unable to prevent or to halt the abuse by any means, then she can be invited to forgive herself for her body's physical reaction to terror. All children and most adults will react to danger in a primitive way that can immobilise and stultify normal reactions and, thus, render any fleeing-action an impossible task even to contemplate, let alone to execute.

> Prevention of abuse and treatment of abusers *can* benefit from understanding what leads to abuse. However, many people use these explanations as rationalisation: it was because he himself was victimised that he "had to" (rather than "chose to" or "allowed himself to") victimise another, isn't it sad? This rationalising feeds the social tendency to see child molesters as "sick men" rather than as "criminals" or "perpetrators", to resist the notion that they should be brought to the same justice as a man who rapes a woman. The application of "understanding" is unwise. Whatever happens in one's childhood, one is responsible for one's adult acts; one's past does not *cause* one to do violence to another. Allowing oneself to hurt another is an active behavioural choice.
> – *Sue Blume*

In the case of childhood abuse in all its ugly forms, forgiveness of the client's abuser will, of course, be an issue that can give rise to much heated debate. Perhaps the wisest course of action will be to let the client decide what to do in terms of forgiving her abuser. Essentially, it is actually impossible to forgive the abuser for committing an atrocity of such magnitude against the child – regardless of whether or not the molester admitted to his or her crimes and then apologised profusely or was simply psychologically deranged. For the client, however, an acceptance or an acknowledgment of an unchangeable past may be the only means by which she can resolve her torment. The practitioner should appreciate, however, that forgiveness of the abuser can be a manifestation of the client's denial and an ideal harbour for guilt, shame and self-denigration (see Chapter 11, Volume 1 – "Defensive Strategies"). There can be no way of excusing or condoning such conduct, whatever the mitigating circumstances. This point cannot be emphasised too strongly when the therapist is dealing with the client who shows a strong tendency to want to excuse the conduct of her abuser. Forgiveness, of course, is a manmade fibre created by a society that is riddled with guilt. This guilt can so easily be passed on to the client, who will then tend to adopt such warped reasoning as if it were her own. The client, thus, can develop a need to forgive because she will have a need to perpetuate guilt, to protect a once-much-loved guardian, to emulate a parent or to conform to society's mores. Incestuous abuse or parental violence will often have a guilt-component that the client may find difficult to relinquish because of the child's need to protect the image of her parents. If the client were molested by a neighbour, a friend or a stranger, the need to excuse the behaviour of that person would not be so pressing. Eliminate the guilt and, possibly, the client will have no desire to forgive her molesters. If, on the other hand, the client has a steadfastly unforgiving nature that is eating away at her and feeding destructive resentment and bitterness, then she could, perhaps, be gently encouraged to accept the fact that the past was just simply the way it was. The client should vent her anger towards her abuser in a therapeutic context and then move on.

> Mobilising anger and outrage may be an initial part of the therapeutic process, but revenge and retribution do not promote healing nor empower an individual. I believe that therapy should ultimately aim for forgiveness of both offender and self. This is diametrically opposed to the mainstream belief of the sexual abuse industry that there is no place for forgiveness in sexual abuse therapy.
> – *Felicity Goodyear-Smith*

Sometimes the therapist may find himself tiptoeing through a delicate set of the client's emotive distresses with regard to forgiveness issues. The practitioner, in this context, may be internally torn between his own beliefs and those of the client. Walking this particular tightrope will frequently be the lot of the practitioner who handles cases of childhood abuse and neglect. The therapist should, of course, consult a supervisor if issues arise in therapy that can cause such personal self-doubts with regard to the role of forgiveness in the therapeutic context (see Chapter 1 – "The Hypnoanalytic Approach").

> The only necessity as far as healing is concerned is forgiving yourself. Developing compassion and forgiveness for your abuser, or for the members of your family who did not protect you, is *not* a required part of the healing process. It is not something to hope for or shoot for. It is not the final goal. Although there is a need for you to come eventually to some resolution – to make peace with your past and move on – whether or not this resolution encompasses forgiveness is a personal matter. You may never reach an attitude of forgiveness, and that's perfectly all right.
> – *Ellen Bass & Laura Davis*

The following suggested passage can be used to empower the client who is ridden with guilt-complexes. The client can be invited to accept herself utterly with all her faults and imperfections.

Accept yourself ...

Begin to accept yourself as a human being with natural failings. Accept that you are not infallible and not perfection personified. Acknowledge who you are and that you have certain imperfections. That's OK. Rejoice in your own imperfections. Love yourself with all your faults. If you love yourself and are proud of yourself, then others will rejoice and love you, too.

You can now begin to be more assertive and refuse to allow others to take advantage of you any longer. Remember that a doormat will attract muddy feet to trample on it. Why comply with someone else's wishes if you do not wish to? Why be motivated by a self-blaming disposition? Why put yourself down by rejecting compliments from others? Why allow yourself to make an unreasonable compromise? An understanding of why others have a need to overstep a boundary will go part way to preventing such behaviour from recurring repeatedly. Be aware that by complying with the bully or the patro- niser you are also perpetuating his or her problems. Maybe the aggressor is like that because he or she also feels afraid or feels guilty?

Once you accept yourself, others will not be so inclined to misuse you or mal- treat you. Look forward to the task ahead of freeing yourself from the ties that have previously bound you to the past!

Exploring the Client's Guilt and Shame Disorders

For years, the Parent/Child conflict has been a way of life for the patient, and thus a means has to be discovered to end the conflict. Once again the Adult is called upon to deliver its wisdom in the task of terminating this conflict. It is at this time that the Parent ego state is further aided to understanding that its role of controller of the Child can now be modified since the Adult has information adequate for the task.
– *Edgar Barnett*

The following passage can be used by the clinician who wishes to explain to the client the reasons why guilt, shame and self-blame can manifest as an integral part of the growing-up process. The client will need to appreciate how guilt-complexes can insidiously affect her life in the form of tormenting symptoms.

Nature's blueprint for guilt ...

Guilt is the product of a belief or a conviction that we have behaved wrongly or irresponsibly or immorally or unethically or in an unprincipled manner by taking a certain course of action or simply by inaction for which we consider that we are partially or entirely to blame. Guilt can also be particularly difficult to endure when we also believe that our action or inaction has caused harm or been detrimental to the lives of others. Guilt can be closely allied to fear and, in essence, may merely be a subset of fear. However, it deserves special consideration, as guilt is probably the most destructive of all negative emotions because it is so unconsciously deep-seated and obstinate. It insidiously festers and underpins most of our behaviour and motivations until it is resolved.

Guilt is often the natural result of our being reared by our parents, teachers and other carers in childhood. The fact that we need to be warned of potential dangers in life in order to survive will certainly mean that the potential for guilt is often inbred within us. Guilt can be easily established in childhood when our primary carers are training us to behave and to obey. We are taught from a young age not to be greedy or spiteful or lazy or noisy or to act unseemingly. We may also be told not to contradict or to question the authority of our tutors. Being schooled in the ethics of good behaviour or imbued with socially-acceptable conduct or being warned of the dangers of dishonesty can all have the effect of instilling guilt and shame in our souls. Furthermore, if our training in childhood is accompanied by a lengthy tirade, a stiff reprimand, a pained expression from Mum or, even, a slap from Dad, these factors will automatically activate the guilt-generating mechanism.

If we are told that we have misbehaved, then we are sure to feel guilty because we cannot possibly be allowed to regard our primary carers as being at fault. After all, if Mum or Dad or Gran were imperfect then this fact alone would present a threat to our survival. So, if we are reprimanded for even a minor misdemeanour or natural transgression, we will believe that it must be our fault because Mother Nature has designed it to appear that way. And, by the time we grow up, this instinctive programming has become part of our belief structure and a way of life for us.

We will, therefore, automatically go out of our way to conform, to obey and to behave according to the rules set by parents, guardians and keepers in our quest for love and affection. And, if anything upsets this fine balance, then we get extremely worried because we naïvely believe that our survival could be in jeopardy because we have sinned and, in some cases, our existence may well be threatened – particularly if we are exposed to physical punishment. To make matters worse, we are sometimes not even told about the set of rules by which we are expected to abide. It is as if someone has an unwritten set of rules and we are supposed to guess what they are in order to conform to them. It is rather like playing with an invisible pack of cards but with a skilled opponent who can see everything, including our own hand. A game we our bound to lose!

Our parents and teachers, furthermore, may well pass on to us any guilt that resides within them when grooming us in the ethics of good behaviour. Our moral code in adulthood will often be an exact replica of our parents' values handed down to us in childhood. If, however, we rebel against the principles dictated by our parents, then our own adult values may be the exact opposite of those imposed upon us in childhood. But it is important to note that the blueprint was still devised by our parents when we were very young.

So what gave us that horrid guilty feeling inside when we were children? What gave us that belief that we are wicked and blameworthy? What gave us that lingering feeling of having committed a heinous crime for which no just punishment could ever be pronounced or exacted? Guilt can be engendered if you were brought up in an overstrict environment or if you were forced to live by a stringent regime of rules or if you were pressured by superiors in childhood or if you were dictated to by a high moral code of ethics. The prime guilt-sufferers in our society will have learned, by some means in childhood, how to feel that they have in some way sinned or transgressed. In adulthood, the residue of the childhood legacy of self-destructive and self-limiting guilt may manifest itself in any number of ways. Perhaps you can now discover the ways in which guilt might have affected you in your life.

The case-study example below, illustrates the way in which the client can manifest insidious guilt despite the fact that she was ostensibly well cared for in childhood.

Case-study example – smoking
This female client had been trying, unsuccessfully, to stop smoking for some years.

When the client was questioned about her childhood upbringing, she reported that she had been reasonably happy but that her working-class parents had been required to struggle in order to make a living. The client explained that her parents were working all hours in order to make ends meet and that her mother was constantly cooking and cleaning the house. The client's parents were also strict and religious and saw their hard life as the normal price they had to pay for their existence.

Despite the fact that the client had felt loved by both parents, she also keenly felt the hardship that had surrounded her upbringing. The client, furthermore, felt that because her parents were constantly working, her mother had not really had time to devote to her children. The client, therefore, had suffered by feeling emotionally-deprived. The client also constantly made excuses for her parents and these excuses covered up her underlying feelings of guilt, shame and resentment.

The client was invited to acknowledge the fact that she had felt somewhat neglected by her parents and that the harsh regime in the household had taken its toll. It was only when the client was able to cease to make excuses for her parents, however, that she became able to relinquish the feelings of guilt that had kept her smoking habit in place.

Client Profiling

The analytical-hypnotherapy practitioner may wish to ponder the following points when formulating a profile for the client.

- In what ways has the client internalised guilt or shame?
- Does the client have a tendency to blame herself for all that occurs?
- Did the client live under a tyranny of oppressive rules when she was a child?
- Were the client's parents overstrict or inflexible in their attitude to life?
- Was the client brought up by parents who were painfully moralistic or prudish?
- Does the client feel that she has sinned against her own children?
- Can the client's guilt-complexes be readily identified?
- Does the client display any tendencies towards self-destruction or self-mutilation?
- Does the client in any way punish herself?
- In what ways does the client show hatred of herself?
- Does the client have any excessively self-punishing traits or habits?
- Is the client overconsiderate of others?
- Is the client grossly subservient to others?
- Does the client appear to be secretive in any way?
- Does the client get easily embarrassed?
- Can the client realistically apportion blame to those people who have betrayed or misused her in the past?
- Does the client vociferously excuse the conduct of others who may have misused or abused her in the past?
- Does the client protest that her parents were beyond reproach in their treatment of her?

- Is the client able to forgive herself for any perceived weaknesses or indiscretions?
- Is the client able to accept herself as the equal of others?
- Does the client feel that she does not deserve to undertake therapy because there are many others who are more in need of the practitioner's help?

Chapter 9

Sorrow and Grief Disorders

The thought of suicide is a great comfort; with it a calm
passage is to be made across many a bad night.

– Friedrich Nietzsche

What is Sorrow and Grief?

A sense of loss is also experienced by many victims: loss of their family if
they are placed in foster care or if the family choose to support the
perpetrator rather than the victim, loss of their innocence, and loss of
their "normalcy".
– Jeffrey Haugaard & Dickon Reppucci

Sorrow and grief will be the client's way of expressing intense
emotional pain. The grief-stricken client may suffer from sorrow
and grief disorders as a result of unhappiness, bereavement and
loss (see Figure 2 – "Symptomology"). The child will grieve, for
example, for the loss of his childhood innocence and any lack of
parental protection. This will be particularly true if he underwent
events in childhood that might have plunged him into the adult
world prematurely. The client may unconsciously feel such loss
manifestations when, for example, a parent was unwell for a
lengthy period or was absent from home for a long period during
childhood. Similarly, the client may have suffered psychologically
if he had to fend for himself and if he was made to look after siblings. Psychological distress in the form of sorrow and sadness,
therefore, can be installed in the client's mind because he was once
hungry for love and affection from the moment of birth and
throughout formative years in childhood. The child will, obviously, have been dependent, vulnerable and needy and could easily be hurt by any form of rejection, abandonment or lack of care.
Intense emotional distress can, of course, lead the client to attempt
suicide or to engage in self-harm (see Chapter 8 – "Guilt and

243

Shame Disorders"). The client may, therefore, feel that the only way out of his distress will be to terminate his intolerable existence. A high incidence of childhood abuse or neglect will often be responsible for the client's intense outpourings of sadness and grief (see Chapter 15 – "The Effects of Childhood Abuse").

The client should, of course, be permitted and, indeed, be encouraged to grieve, to mourn and to wallow in self-pity in order to release himself from the bondage of misery. The grieving process can also encompass feelings of fury, indignation, rage, terror and shame. Tears are probably the most natural form of abreaction to which the client can readily succumb in the therapeutic context and can often provide him with a passport to psychological freedom regardless of the nature of his presenting symptoms.

> In the clinical literature, depression is the symptom most commonly reported among adults molested as children, and empirical findings seem to confirm this.
> – *David Finkelhor & Angela Browne*

Sorrow and Grief Manifestations

> In one sense the cause of suicide is simple: overwhelming pain. This overwhelming pain, however, is the aggregate of thousands of pains.
> – *Joel Covitz*

Sorrow and grief can permeate the client's life in a number of ways. Often the client will be reticent about admitting to his sorrows or will be reluctant to summon the help of those nearest to him. The client may also feel disinclined to talk to his nearest relatives about his sorrows because he may consider that they will not understand his plight. It may, of course, be for this reason that the client will seek therapy. Let us now discuss those lingering forms in which sorrow and grief can manifest within the client.

Grief and mourning

> As a survivor of child sexual abuse, you have a lot to grieve for. You
> must grieve for the loss of your feelings. You must grieve for your
> abandonment. You must grieve for the past and grieve for the present,
> for the damage you now have to heal, for the time it takes, for the money
> it costs, for the relationships ruined, the pleasure missed. You grieve for
> the opportunities lost while you were too busy coping.
> – *Ellen Bass & Laura Davis*

When the client acutely feels a loss of love and affection, he may
find himself submitting to a grieving and mourning process in the
therapeutic setting as a means of expelling past pain. The client
may also give way to much grief both within the consulting room
and away from the therapeutic environment. Grief can be the
expression of the loss of those things that childhood normally
should hold. The client, for example, may grieve for the lack of
parental affection because his lot instead was neglect and a lack of
respect. The client may mourn his loss of innocence because he was
catapulted into the adult world at a tender age. The client may
grieve for the happy times that never were. The client may regret
that happiness was freely available to everyone else and he, therefore, missed the boat. The client may sorrow because he has never
learned how to be happy and contented but may, conversely, have
learned only about loneliness and isolation. The client may grieve
for the loss of a natural and supportive development into maturity
because he may merely have existed in a welter of confusion not
knowing which way to turn for assistance.

The hurt client may, however, elect to take the path of an emotive
shutdown when his sensitive nature becomes too bruised or punc-
tured. Sometimes the grief-stricken client will endeavour to numb
the sorrow that he feels deeply inside. The client who suffers from
sorrow and grief, therefore, may also turn to martyrdom as a
means of obtaining psychological needs from others by manipulative tactics (see Chapter 10 – "Anger and Rage Disorders"). It will
be as if the client cannot ask for love and affection directly in case
he will be mercilessly rejected (see Chapter 7 – "Fear and Anxiety
Disorders"). The client may then resort to devious devices and
emotional blackmail by which to secure attention from others. The
martyr, moreover, may become a noble and altruistic slave to the
needs of others in order to ensure that he can wallow in self-pity.

When all else fails, a self-effacing and self-denigrating stance may be taken by the client who mourns the loss of parental affection.

The practitioner may wish to utilise some subtle questioning as given below that can help the client to explore any feelings that he may have of sadness and regret.

- Do you feel generally unhappy and unloved?
- Do you often feel totally rejected by others?
- Do you feel a great deal of remorse and regret about your life?
- Do you always feel lonely and isolated – even in a crowd?
- Do you consider that there is actually no-one who really understands you?
- Are you at all prone to having a fantasy-life or indulging in daydreams?
- Do you consider that your emotions are on a roller-coaster?
- Do you frequently wallow in emotional escapism?
- Do you sometimes experience a feeling of crying inside?
- Do you wish that you could make a significant contribution to the lives of those less fortunate than yourself?
- Do you consider that the world is a terrible or a miserable place in which to live?
- Do you ever overreact when someone tells you about a misfortunate or an unhappy event?
- Do you feel a profound sense of unhappiness when you hear of a sad event?
- Do you get upset when you see or hear news of tragedy and suffering?
- Do you often give money to charity because you feel sorry for others who are less fortunate than you are?
- Do you consider that the streets are lined with homeless people?
- Do you feel moved to tears when you watch a sad film or read a book with a tragic ending?
- Do you regularly feel the need to cuddle your teddy-bear or to play nursemaid to your pets?
- Do you take refuge in comfort-eating or tasty treats?
- Do you always cry at weddings and funerals?
- Do you think that some days are totally filled with gloom and doom?
- Do you find that autumn or winter are sad times of the year?

The following client narrative clarifies the way in which a client from a dysfunctional childhood can experience feelings of grief and loss.

Client narrative – I cried an ocean of tears …
My earliest recollection of starting to cry followed a visit to a cousin who was getting married and I was to be a bridesmaid. The bride-to-be was getting married because she dearly wanted children more than anything else in the world and I was the embodiment of the angelic child to her. There are some women to whom mother-hood is the ultimate aim in life and they live only to fulfil this all-consuming, burning desire. The bride on whom I was to attend fell into this category and so I received from her during my stay all the love and affection that was patently absent in my own life as a child.

The return home was devastating. I was back to normality. I began to cry and simply could not stop. My mother, mystified as usual, enquired the reason for my distress when I could contain myself no longer. Confusion reigned in my world. What was this? Why did I feel this way? Why was it so overwhelming and uncontrollable? It was, undoubtedly, the birth of the depression that was to haunt me for decades to come. The first thought of explanation to my mother was that ! missed the teddy-bear I had been playing with during my stay with the bride-to-be. Having provided my mother with a satisfactory explanation, the subject was dismissed together with a directive not to be so silly. No further solicitous enquiries were made.

In general, my mother was unsympathetic, if not heedless, in the main, to any ailments I might have had. If I did not like going to the dentist, I was making a fuss. If I did not like having an injection, I was being a baby. If I drenched several handkerchiefs when watching a sentimental film, I was told that I had to toughen myself up. When I bit my nails, my mother promised to buy me a manicure set at Christmas in order to encourage me to take care of my nails. Is there any nail-biter in the world who can be cajoled into giving up a compulsive habit merely by being offered the carrot of having nice nails in the future?

Bereavement

When parents fail to heal from the death of their spouses, they bring
their child up in a bleak, lonely environment, passing on a distorted view
of death, mourning, and love.
– *Joel Covitz*

If the client sufferers unduly after the loss of a loved one or has
been unable to come to terms with the bereavement, he may be
experiencing an overload of the grief-syndrome that may need to
be released in therapy. Following the loss of a loved one, the client
may pass through a number of phases that can include disbelief
about the loss, anger at being deserted by the deceased, remorse
for things that never transpired in the loved one's lifetime and a
survivor-guilt complex at being still alive when the deceased person exists no longer.

The practitioner may wish to utilise some judicious questioning
techniques as set out below that can help the client to identify any
sorrowful feelings that he may have of being abandoned, bereft
and alone following a bereavement.

- Do you feel that no-one is capable of understanding you or
  comforting you in your distress?
- Do you know anyone to whom you can turn in times of distress?
- Do you often cry into your pillow at night?
- Have you suffered for some time from prolonged or excessive
  grief?
- Are you frequently beset by remorse or regret about what
  never was?
- Do you find that when you cry it does not seem to wash away
  your sadness?
- Do you feel as if you have been left all alone?
- Do you feel cheated that your loved one has departed?
- Do you feel guilty at being the one who has survived?
- Do you dread having to go to a funeral for fear of breaking
  down?
- Do you feel as if your support-network has just collapsed?
- Do you feel unhinged by your devastating personal loss?

The following passage could also be used by the practitioner in
order to help the client to come to terms with his intense pain. Such

a passage should, of course, encourage the client to transit the grieving process but without sidestepping any vital issues.

Why feel sad?

Begin to accept yourself as someone who may feel sad and lonely from time to time. Accept that you have a tender and sensitive side and appreciate the value of this quality. This is your way of caring for yourself. This is your way of acknowledging the hurts of the past. This is your way of proving that you are human.

When you need to shed tears, then give vent to your emotions. Wash away the pain of the past by shedding a heartfelt tear. Every tear that you cry washes away an ocean of uncried tears locked up inside. Often we are hurt but cannot bring ourselves to admit to it. Now may be the time to express that natural sorrow and then to move on. Be open about expressing your feelings and opinions. Be considerate of the feelings of others. Confide in those close to you when you feel emotionally ruffled. Why adopt an ain't-it-awful policy when an unfortunate event occurs? Relieve yourself of the pain and then look up into the blue sky yonder. Nurse your wounds and then bandage them up and kiss them better. Heal your hurts by inspiring yourself with joy and enthusiasm. Seek out a happier life and pursue it vigorously. Banish melancholy in favour of pleasures and comfort. Open your heart to the world and rejoice that you are a vital part of it. Feel privileged to be alive and welcome the new day. This day is a very special day as it marks a turning point in your life. It presents an opportunity to express those deep emotions in order to heal yourself. Give yourself permission to cry whenever you need to do so.

Depressive Disorders

> Depression is the symptom most commonly reported among both male and female adults abused as children. An empirical community study is indicative of this. Bagley and Ramsay, in a community mental health study in Calgary, utilised a random sample of 401 women and 278 men. They found that subjects with a history of child abuse scored higher on depression than did the non-abused.
> – *Susan Ray*

A depressive disorder (or an *affective disorder*) will often signify a combination of the despair, hopelessness, remorse and intense unhappiness that will typically be the result of the client's dysfunctional childhood. A depressive disorder will be a profound cyclic mood-disturbance and psychic distress that will beset the client for an abnormally lengthy period of time. Dissociation will often be the basis of a depressive disorder, whereby the emotive pain felt by the client will be so great that he wishes to be somewhere else in both mind and body (see Chapter 11, Volume 1 – "Defensive Strategies"). This state then will engender a psychological conflict that will result in a depression of the client's natural emotive responses. The condition may stem from the client's life-experiences or social factors and may, in extreme cases, lead to suicide, attempted suicide or suicidal ideation. For the victim of any form of childhood abuse or neglect whereby the depressive disorder is entirely related to the original traumatic experience, the client's condition may be ceaseless until the problem has been satisfactorily resolved. Owing to the nature of the dissociative phenomenon, such a depressive condition may not increasingly worsen in intensity over time for the client but it certainly will not diminish as time elapses until assistance has been sought.

Depression has also been regarded, by certain clinicians, as a manifestation of repressed or unexpressed anger (see Chapter 10 – "Anger and Rage Disorders"). This theory inclines towards the view that the client's mind will fight itself in trying to express simmering anger that, instead of being directed externally, will be turned inwards. The client, hence, will blame himself rather than the perpetrators of an alleged injustice and this self-blame will then manifest in the depressive disorder (see Chapter 8 – "Guilt and Shame Disorders").

In essence, a depressive disorder will be one in which the client's sorrow has been bottled up for too long and, hence, it requires an outlet. When an opportunity to take the cork out of the bottle arises, therefore, the client's mind will do so with an uncontrollable degree of force. Let us now give some consideration to the main types of depressive disorder from which the client may suffer and the differing forms that the condition can take. Many depressive disorders have, of course, been linked to the depressive personality disorder (see Chapter 7 – "Fear and Anxiety Disorders").

> When anger is effectively repressed, it can only be experienced as depression, since it is turned in upon the self. It is then accompanied by feelings of dissatisfaction with the self and self-destructive thoughts which are often the prelude to attempts at suicide.
> – *Edgar Barnett*

Minor depression

Sadness is the most salient and widespread emotional symptom in depression. One person's life was so dominated by sadness that she cried during almost all her waking hours. She was unable to carry on a social conversation because of excessive crying.
– *David Rosenhan & Martin Seligman*

Minor depression (or *unipolar depression*) will be a very common form of psychological condition from which the client may suffer perhaps in addition to other symptoms. This disorder will be characterised by the client's overwhelming symptoms of apathy, lethargy, sadness, futility, negativity, hopelessness and impaired concentration. Any form of minor depression can be exacerbated by the client's general inability to change personal circumstances or to rectify ongoing unsatisfactory conditions. The client who may feel generally despondent about life and may have had some unexpected misfortune may be suffering from a minor form of depression.

Frequently, the client's condition can be considered in terms of emotive expression, cognitive framework, motivational inclinations and somatic symptoms. Such symptoms will manifest in the client in varying degrees of intensity. The client's emotive symptoms may include, for example, sadness, self-blame and absence of joy. The client's cognitive manifestations of depression may result in a low self-opinion, a feeling of hopelessness or a pessimistic outlook on the future. The client's motivational symptoms may manifest as a lack of response-initiation, indecision or social withdrawal. The client may also have somatic symptoms that may be detected as a loss of appetite, unexplained weight-loss, sleep disturbance or sexual dysfunction (see Chapter 11 – "Psychosomatic Disorders").

Depressive illness is a dangerous illness because, as we've seen, patients do kill themselves in moments of despair, even when under treatment. This is a tragedy, because the mood of despair is temporary. When the illness lifts, the patient returns to a normal frame of mind.
– *Margaret Reinhold*

Major depression

> In the last thirty years, we have moved out of the dark ages in our understanding of depression. Substantial strides have been made in the understanding and treatment of the disorder. Between 80 and 90 percent of severe depression can now be markedly alleviated with a brief course of therapy.
> – *David Rosenhan & Martin Seligman*

Major depression will seriously interfere with the client's ability to cope with life and to function successfully. Symptoms of a major depressive disorder will be wide-ranging and the client may report any number of telltale signs. Generally, the client may feel an inability to take pleasure in life, a dissatisfaction with his existence, an extreme apathy, a withdrawal from life and an inability to cope with day-to-day occurrences. The client may also suffer from fatigue, lethargy and slow reactions as well as intense feelings of sadness, tearfulness, irritability, hopelessness and worthlessness. The client may also harbour suicidal thoughts and may have made one or more attempts at suicide. A number of other underlying stress-related symptoms exhibited by the client may also be in evidence, such as digestive disorders, insomnia and significant weight-gain or weight-loss.

For the client who has had a traumatic childhood with much of it denied or repressed, the more serious forms of major depression are likely to be the result of his suffering. Severe, chronic depression, however, can usually be treated without relapse by analytical hypnotherapy because it can focus on the client's misdirected anger, on resolving dependencies and on overcoming issues of hopelessness at the root-cause level.

> Considering only evidence from representative community studies, with one exception, all studies investigating depression in adult life as an outcome for CSA [Childhood Sexual Abuse] have demonstrated significant results.
> – *John Morton*

The following narrative provides an illustration of the way in which a depressive client viewed his state of despair at the outset of therapeutic investigation.

Client narrative – interminable depression …

These depressive states gave me a feeling of being beyond help, hopeless, no way out, no remedy and, worst of all, an inner belief that I actually deserved to be unhappy and it was a cross that I would have to bear.

I had the soul-in-torment syndrome. I would frequently awake in the morning or in the middle of the night into an atmosphere of impending doom and wonder what the day would bring, as if every day were Friday the Thirteenth. I was constantly seeking ways to lighten my load. I became impulsive, always looking for kicks and excitement. I even took up gambling in secret and lost a lot of money, depriving my wife and family, whom I dearly loved. I was never content with what ordinary people take pleasure in. I was intolerant of others and, more particularly, impatient with myself.

Very few people were able to be there for me. It was not their fault, simply my dilemma. I needed help but didn't know why or how to obtain it. I wanted help but could find no-one qualified to undertake the role of helper. No-one could empathise with me, though some of my friends tried and did give me genuine and heartfelt support. My wife and family were as mystified and as powerless to understand what was going on inside as I was. No-one could cure me and I felt I did not want anyone to pry into my life. Many times I rejected professional help. Fortunately some unknown force, let's call it survival instinct, came to my aid at the eleventh hour before I really went under.

Bipolar depression

> The onset of a manic episode usually occurs fairly suddenly, and the euphoric mood, racing thoughts, frenetic acts, and resulting insomnia stand in marked contrast to the person's usual functioning.
> – *David Rosenhan & Martin Seligman*

Bipolar depression (or *manic depression*) is characterised by the client's alternating mood swings. The client will typically undergo an episode of deep depression interlaced with a period of mania. The average client may, of course, be susceptible to mood swings that may vary according to his circumstances and the events that he encounters, but the manic depressive will suffer from a highly-exaggerated version of such commonplace mood fluctuations. The manic-depressive client will move on a continuum through various moods from a severe depressive phase, to mild mood disturbances, through to a virtually normal state and then into mild hypermania and, finally, into the severe manic state. Bipolar depression has, of course, been linked to the hypermanic personality disorder (see Chapter 7 – "Fear and Anxiety Disorders").

The client's manic episodes can comprise euphoric moods, grandiosity, delusional thoughts, frenetic activity and exhaustive hyposomnia. The client's manic symptoms, for instance, may include excessive elation, uncontrollable euphoria, excessive energy and hyperactivity, as well as mental and physical efficiency. The client may also have a decreased need for sleep and show an inability to relax. The client may display exaggerated speech-patterns, overstated movements, irritability and impatience. The client may also have disconnected or racing thoughts, may have impaired judgment and may be very impulsive or excitable. At such times, the client may also be prone to overspending or reckless overindulgence, may succumb to substance-abuse and may exhibit inappropriate or antisocial behaviour.

Conversely, the client may report a number of contrasting symptoms during the depressive phase of the disorder. The client may, for example, feel intensely sad and tearful, have a reduced self-confidence, exhibit a low self-esteem and may feel empty, hopeless and pessimistic. The client may, moreover, harbour feelings of guilt, shame and worthlessness (see Chapter 8 – "Guilt and Shame Disorders"). The client may generally feel a dissatisfaction with life, a blanket apathy and a need to withdraw from social interaction. The depressive client may also suffer from fatigue, lethargy and slow reactions. Symptoms of insomnia and restlessness and a loss of appetite, furthermore, may also be the result of the client's depressive condition. It will, of course, be in this phase of the cycle that the client could entertain thoughts of suicide and may engage in self-mutilating or self-destructive practices.

The most common, everyday manifestation of bipolar depression has been cited as the notoriously-common seasonal affective disorder (SAD) from which many people suffer. With SAD, the client will be subject to despondency and withdrawal throughout the winter months when all is bleak and dreary while, on the other hand, the warmer, longer days see him in a flurry of feverish activity. Severe manic depression is sometimes classified as a psychotic disorder for which psychotherapy may not be the answer for the client. In such cases, the practitioner would be advised to refer the client to a general medical practitioner.

> Some people's experience of clinical depression is of a combination of periods of depression with periods of what known as mania – excessive elation, talkativeness, inflated self-esteem and so on. This type of depression is known as bipolar depression, since the person's mood swings between the two poles, or extremes of mood. Another term for this problem is manic depressive psychosis, and it is often classified among the psychotic disorders.
> – Nicky Hayes

Endogenous depression

> The word endogenous (biological – with melancholia) means "coming from within the body" and exogenous (psychological – without melancholia) means "coming from outside the body". The implication of these terms is that an exogenous depression is precipitated by a life stressor, while an endogenous depression arises from a disordered biology. But in practice, endogenous depressions have been found to have no fewer precipitating events than exogenous depressions.
> – David Rosenhan & Martin Seligman

Endogenous depression (or *clinical depression*) will be said to have its roots from within the client. If the client's depressive state, for example, has emanated from within his own psyche whereby no obviously-identifiable external cause can be traced, this form of depression can be regarded as inner depression. With this form of depression, the hypnoanalytical practitioner's job will be mainly to unearth and to deal with the originating cause (see Chapter 2 – "Therapeutic Investigation"). In practice, of course, the practitioner may frequently be treating the client who cannot consciously identify a given cause for his condition but the process of analytical enquiry will allow this factor to establish itself.

Exogenous depression

An exogenous depression is a depression which has an identifiable
external cause, like being depressed after the death of a parent, or after
rape or sexual abuse. For that reason it is sometimes also called reactive
depression. Endogenous depression, on the other hand, is depression
which appears to be coming from within body, rather than from an
external life stressor.
– *Nicky Hayes*

Exogenous depression (or *reactive depression*) will be considered to
derive its cause from an external factor or circumstance that seriously besets the client. When the client's depression stems from an
identifiable external cause, it is traditionally classified as exogenous depression. In this case, the client may, for example, have suffered a bereavement or endured a tragic accident. With exogenous
depression, the practitioner's role will be to assist the client to
come to terms with his life circumstances or external stressors by
allowing him to identify clearly the reasons for his distress and
then to grieve adequately. The analytical practitioner, of course,
will need to be able to distinguish between any internally-gener-
ated and externally-manifested forms of depression from which
the client may be suffering.

Chronic depression

In chronic depression, dysthymic disorder, the individual has been
depressed for at least two solid years without having had a remission to
normality of at least two months in duration.
– *David Rosenhan & Martin Seligman*

Chronic depression (or *dysthymic depression*) will be a condition
that may have had a persistent, long-term effect on the client.
Chronic depression will usually affect him for several years, if not
decades. When the client reports chronic depression, the practitioner can be virtually certain that much work may need to be done
and that the originating cause may often be found in childhood.

Episodic depression

An episodic depression, which is much more common, is of less than two
years' duration and has a clear onset, which distinguishes it from
previous non-depressed functioning.
– *David Rosenhan & Martin Seligman*

Episodic depression occurs at sporadic intervals in the client's life
and may not be as long-lasting as a chronic condition. Usually the
client will be able readily to identify the reasons why episodic
depression will have manifested. When the client reports states of
episodic depression, the practitioner will need to tease out the reasons why he can be prone to such states.

Double depression

Some unfortunate people have double depression, consisting of a
depressive episode on top of an underlying dysthymic disorder. Those
suffering from double depression have more severe symptoms and a low
rate of remission.
– *David Rosenhan & Martin Seligman*

Double depression will be believed to be a combination of chronic
depression and episodic depression. With this form of depression,
the client may develop an episodic condition on top of his chronic
state, that will then initiate a downward spiral. In such cases, the
practitioner will need to deal not only with the root cause of the
client's depression but also with the reasons why he appears to
have a tendency to relapse. It may well transpire that the root cause
of the client's depression will need to be further investigated and
enquiry could be directed at the reasons why the client seems
unable to let go of the past.

Exploring the Client's Grief and Sorrow Disorders

Only the suicide makes a voluntary decision to bring about his own death.
He sees death as a solution; his act has an intention, a goal, a purpose
had by no other. He wants to escape, to reject, to revenge, to seize power
and control. His action is an affirmation that there is a better alternative
in death than he could find in life. He makes a moral statement: he is
unworthy of us, we are unworthy of him, life itself is not worth living.
– *David Conroy*

When the practitioner deals with the client with a depressive disorder, much investigative work may need to be undertaken (see Chapter 2 – "Therapeutic Investigation"). It will be essential that the underlying root cause has been thoroughly excavated before the client will be able to release himself from his despondency. Investigative methodology, therefore, may form the bulk of the work with the depressive client. Depression will invariably indicate an underlying distress in some form and, therefore, the client should be given ample opportunity to explore subsurface issues. For this reason, the client's therapeutic work cannot usually be completed in a short period of time. The client may well be considering a commitment in excess of six therapeutic sessions and, for more severe forms of depression, he may realistically need to commit himself to ten to sixteen sessions in order to achieve therapeutic success.

The following passage could be utilised by the practitioner in order to assist the client to understand the way in which sorrow and grief have afflicted him. This passage will set the scene for the client to embark on the exploration of his underlying issues. It has been claimed that some form of depression will accompany most symptoms or problems with which the client will present.

Nature's blueprint for sadness ...

Sadness is the internalised expression of our need to take flight from the perceived threat or danger or our desire to freeze in the jaws of jeopardy. We register our hurt and pain by turning it inwards on ourselves in the hope that we may escape from the danger or anaesthetise ourselves against the shock. Sadness may be our only way of dealing with fear by taking it within ourselves and, thus, relieving others of their responsibilities. It is our way of putting on a brave face for the world by suffering inwardly in silence.

A baby finds that crying is an effective alarm-signal but, in adulthood, we are often too afraid to express this basic human emotion. We are often crying out for the love that eluded us so cleverly in the past or for the loss of genuine affection that has never come our way. We may feel lonely and sad because we feel unloved and, when we have felt unloved for long enough, we conclude that we are unlovable and despise ourselves accordingly. The shedding of tears is a fundamental way of expressing tenderness and compassion. Such an emotion can often have an uplifting effect on us if we are expressing joy or are touched by what our senses perceive. Sadness makes us a compassionate carer, gives vent to our romantic inclinations, permits us to daydream or simply demonstrates that we are human. It can relieve stress and release pain when we wish to express it.

The trouble will arise, of course, when the sadness that we feel is not acknowledged as a cry from our own soul for help. Sadness can spiral downwards until we feel in the depths of despair from which we cannot extricate ourselves. We feel tearful at the slightest provocation. We lose interest in life and in dragging ourselves out of the trough. Grief remains unresolved and we feel as if we are powerless ever to lead a fruitful life again. Everything is beyond our reach and lethargy sets in. We proclaim that there is no-one out there to help or to understand our distress because we are inherently unlovable and worthless.

So what makes us feel sadness in childhood? Sadness is born out of anything that caused you deep grief, hurt or pain or that makes you feel unloved, neglected, unwanted, betrayed or misused. Often profound or prolonged unhappiness can lead you to the unshakable conclusion that you are inherently unlovable because you are unworthy or undeserving. In adulthood, the residue of our childhood legacy of unresolved hurt and pain may manifest itself in any number of ways. Perhaps you can now ponder on your manifestations of sorrow, sadness, grief and dismay.

The case-study example below ably illustrates the way in which a client was able to resolve her intense depressive states.

Case-study example – severe depression
This female client was troubled by a severe and uncontrollable depressive existence. In many respects, the client was happy and successful yet, from time to time, she was consumed by a need to cry and to withdraw totally from the world. Occasionally, the client would also be prone to bouts of excessive drinking and temper tantrums.

The client reported that she had experienced the condition for as long as she could remember and so the practitioner asked about her childhood. The client stated that she had not been happy as a child but could remember very little about her upbringing. As investigative therapy progressed, the client felt relief from her depression and continued to attend therapy sessions because of this progress. The client, however, reported that she had no idea why she was improving and questioned very little about the therapeutic process itself.

Eventually, the client reported that her symptoms had escalated and she felt devastated when she arrived at the ninth session. By this time, the client had begun to feel that the therapeutic process was, in fact, making her condition worse because she had contemplated suicide since the last session. At this session, the client then dug up the fact that her uncle and her grandfather had both sexually abused her when she was a young child. This was, of course, the turning point for the client, because now her crying fits turned from anguish to relief as she expressed her sadness of this maltreatment in her childhood. As investigation into this area progressed in subsequent sessions, the client also recalled the fact that her uncle and her grandfather had both been members of a local paedophile group. The client, therefore, had also been ill-used by other members of this group.

After about twenty sessions, the client was, finally, able to begin the process of coming to terms with the past – having been given ample opportunity to express her feelings of grief and loss and to unearth her repressed recollections. Furthermore, the client also undertook anger-release work in the form of mattress-bashing in the therapeutic setting. As a result of the therapeutic process, the client has now relinquished her drinking habits and is no longer interminably troubled by her depressive states.

Client Profiling

The analytical-hypnotherapy practitioner may wish to ponder the following points when formulating a profile for the client.

*   In what ways does the client exhibit signs of depressive reactions?
*   Does the client suffer from any prolonged form of bereavement?
*   Does the client appear mysteriously to be in constant mourning?
*   Has the client adequately addressed feelings of grief in the past if he has lost a parent or a close relative in adulthood?
*   Did the client lose a parent or a close relative in childhood?
*   Does the client permit himself to express tears and sadness when necessary?

- Does the client suffer occasionally from despondency or unhappiness?
- Is the client suffering from any form of melancholy as a result of exhibiting other symptoms or problems?
- Does the client engage in unhealthy activities that might be designed to ward off a depressive state?
- Is the client prone to experiencing fluctuating mood swings?
- Does the client blow hot and cold on occasions?
- Does the client alternate between feverish activity followed by extreme lethargy?
- Does the client's depressive condition appear to emanate from within himself or is it ostensibly due to purely external factors?
- In what ways can the client be assisted to come to terms with his sorrows?
- Does the client have the necessary courage to investigate the source of his depressive disturbance?

Chapter 10

Anger and Rage Disorders

When you're in the battlefield, survival is all there is. Death is the only great emotion.

– Sam Fuller

What is Anger and Rage?

Anger is a powerful and liberating force. Whether you need to get in touch with it or have always had plenty to spare, directing your rage squarely at your abuser, and at those who didn't protect you, is pivotal to healing.
– Ellen Bass & Laura Davis

The client will be entitled to feel anger, indignation, frustration, resentment, fury and rage if she has been abused, violated, neglected and mistreated in childhood. Despite the fact that expressing anger will not be considered to be socially acceptable or politically correct, the client should be permitted and, even, encouraged to express anger in the therapeutic context. Restrained anger can lead to further psychological damage if it is, in any way, held back by the client (see Figure 2 – "Symptomology"). A depressive client, for example, may have a tendency to contain anger and the practitioner should be aware of this propensity (see Chapter 9 – "Sorrow and Grief Disorders"). If the client's bridled anger is allowed to remain unexpressed, it will fester and may result in additional unpleasant symptoms. Such symptoms may be of a psychosomatic nature whereby mysterious aches and pains may manifest or serious illness may be the result (see Chapter 11 – "Psychosomatic Disorders"). The client, moreover, may tend to resort to manipulative tactics, become overtly aggressive or, paradoxically, may be unable to assert herself effectively.

Women are frequently encouraged to contain anger while men may be admired for displaying it in competitive and challenging ways. Both stances could, of course, be potentially damaging for the client if the outlet for anger is inappropriate. The female client who continues to deny that she feels angry with someone who has misused her will be suppressing a part of her nature. This client may, for example, defend her violator, apply understanding and minimise the effect that the ill-treatment has had on her rather than acknowledge her true feelings of anger (see Chapter 11, Volume 1 – "Defensive Strategies"). The male client who becomes the tyrannical employer, who is constantly spoiling for a fight or who becomes obsessed with his own machismo image will be allowing his anger to swamp him.

The client who externalises anger will be projecting that anger at others and then remaining in denial about her behavioural tendencies. This may be because the client will be using others as a narcissistic mirror with which to gauge her own self-worth rather than really facing up to her own angry feelings and expressing them appropriately (see Chapter 7 – "Fear and Anxiety Disorders").

If anger spills out into the client's personal life, then the practitioner should take a nonjudgmental stance. If the client's anger erupts and turns to physical violence, then the therapist should not assume the role of judge and jury. This neutral stance will allow the client to understand her own motivations by giving her licence to speak. If the client's anger can be successfully managed within the therapeutic setting, of course, then the need for her to retaliate against work colleagues, remonstrate against her parents or lash out at loved ones in her immediate circle will be diminished. Certainly, the practitioner should give the client the freedom to choose the ways in which the backlash of her anger and rage can defuse naturally in the consulting room. For the client who has endured a severely neglectful or abusive childhood, anger may well be ripe for cascading out in the consulting room (see Chapter 15 – "The Effects of Childhood Abuse"). Anger will undoubtedly be an integral part of the effects of any form of childhood abuse, often because the client will begin to feel the outrage that may result when she realises that she has been misused and betrayed. The client may report that she had previously displayed antisocial behaviour and this might be an indication that she might have some anger-related issues to resolve. The victim of physical abuse may, for example, have displayed delinquent traits, played truant or run away from home. Such rebellious manifestations of behaviour are likely to be a direct result of the trap in which the child or young person found herself and, therefore, the need to escape will have been paramount in the her mind. For the young adult, a period working abroad or an early marriage may well have been her escape route from a dysfunctional family.

Steering a neutral, middle course will be by far the best action for the practitioner to take when handling the client's angry outbursts – particularly when her defences have been uncovered in therapy. The client should not, however, be encouraged to start haranguing her wrongdoers or filing law-suits but, if that is the course of action that she wishes to take, then the therapist should be supportive and nonjudgmental. In practice, of course, the client will often wish to express her anger in the therapeutic setting and should be encouraged to do so in order to lessen the need for her to explode in the outside world. When anger can be properly channelled into a thirst for life, the client will benefit by finding a positive outlet for excess wrath rather than harbouring resentment or feeling generally frustrated. The primitive caveman needed to undertake exercise in order to burn off any excess energy that might normally be used for aggression against his foes and stray wild beasts. If the client's excessive rage manifestations can be discharged in active pursuits, then an evacuation of any surfeit of anger can usually take place. While repressed anger may need to be released in the therapeutic setting, the client's superficial anger can usually be discharged naturally in appropriate and productive ways away from the consulting room.

> Another initial effect in children is reactions of anger and hostility. Tufts researchers found that 45% to 50% of the 7- to 13-year-olds showed hostility levels that were substantially elevated on measures of aggression and antisocial behaviour, as did 35% on the measure of hostility directed outward.
> – *David Finkelhor & Angela Browne*

Anger and Rage Manifestations

> There are countless books detailing the lives of "serial killers", many of
> them best-sellers. The theme of justice and revenge is probably the
> subject of more movies than any other single topic.
> – *Peter Levine*

The client's outward manifestations of anger can result in aggressive or violent behaviour when her anger has been externalised. Often, such manifestations can be considered as a cry for help from the client. Let us now consider some of the ominous ways in which unconsciously-motivated anger and rage may be exhibited by the client as rebellion, jealousy, envy, destructive criticism and gratuitous violence.

Rebellion

> Aggression is often used by people who are determined to 1) get what
> they want and 2) to get it at the expense of other people.
> – *Gael Lindenfield*

The client who, when on the threshold of adulthood, decides to rebel against her parentage, against society and against life in general may be holding on to a caldron of undischarged anger and rage. Rebellion will display the client's overall resentment of other people and the laws that mankind has put in place for the good of all members of society. It may be as if the client will merely give up the ghost and decide to go against the flow of the river. The rebellious client may, for example, challenge her family by acting in a manner that she knows will deliberately displease and annoy them – despite the fact that such actions may cost her dearly. The client may turn to crime or violence as a way of showing contempt for society's rules or law and order. Rebellion can also take a subtle form when the client shows contempt for others by being devious and manipulative. The client may, for instance, be fighting others by securing backhander deals or playing crafty office-politics games. Martyrdom and hypochondria are also devious forms of rebellion that may conceal the client's dormant anger.

The practitioner may wish to utilise some surreptitious questioning techniques – some typical examples of which are given below – in order to bring the client's unexpressed anger to the surface. This form of enquiry can help the client to identify her rebellious manifestations of anger and rage.

- Do you often become restless and bored with life?
- Do you sometimes feel bitter and resentful about the way in which life has treated you?
- Do you rejoice in being a rebel or a trendsetter?
- Do you frequently feel frustrated, impatient and irritable?
- Would you consider that you are the world's biggest cynic?
- Do you often feel a sense of irritation with the way in which your world ticks?
- Do you sometimes feel as if your blood were boiling?
- Do you sometimes feel as if you were smouldering inside?
- Do you often have temper tantrums for little or no apparent reason?
- Do you get ratty when things do not go your way?
- Do you feel a frequent need to break free?
- Do you resent having to conform in any way?
- Do you sometimes catch yourself frowning or scowling?
- Do you hate officialdom, bureaucracy and red tape?
- Would you simply like to drop out of the rat-race?
- Do you have a tendency to take big risks, especially with other people's money?
- Do you think that you have had a very raw deal in life?
- Do you think that all dictators and tyrants should be exterminated from existence?

The client narrative below shows the way in which a client was seriously affected by her mother's withering criticism and, therefore, sought to rebel against the regime.

Client narrative – my mother's stern regime …

A regime was set up by my tyrant of a mother whereby I was required to undertake my fair share of the household chores, especially during the school holidays. My mother would virtually drag me out of bed in the mornings and insist that I write a list of my chores for the day. I then spent the entire day alone (a crime that would, in itself, make today's large-type headlines – "HOME-

ALONE CHILD IS UNPAID CHARLADY") anticipating a row because I might not perform my tasks to my mother's satisfaction. It goes without saying that there would be hell to pay if I should forget even one! This was my mother's ridiculous way of training me for adulthood, she said. Cleanliness was considered a high-priority virtue.

A surfeit of aggression was the hallmark of my mother's character. Effusively kind and obliging to friends, neighbours and colleagues, my mother delivered the full vent of her anger on all those in the family circle. In my teens, she had the habit of getting up each morning at about 7 a.m. and deciding that it was time to clean the front step. This was her main aggression-discharging vehicle. Unfortunately for me and my stepfather, this was the worse time of the day to pick, as we are both night-owls, not dawn-larks. During this morning interlude, my mother would do anything from delivering a mild lecture to shouting at the top of her voice at anyone who got in her way. And guess who got in her way? This provided a great source of amusement to the neighbours, some of whom told me subsequently that they no longer needed an alarm clock!

Whenever I entered the house I was beset by an overwhelming fear that I would be shouted at on arrival. Sometimes this fear was so all-pervading that I carried it around with me all day long. The living nightmare. The living hell. In addition, I came to despise myself for not being brave enough to stand up to her. Consequently, I allowed her to run roughshod over my life.

On one occasion the worm turned and I retaliated by attacking her physically. I think the lid had finally been blown off my anger towards by mother! I was doing some sewing, an activity in which my mother always interfered by offering me uncalled-for advice or telling me how I should have done it. I could stand it no longer and began to hit out at her violently, heedless of the consequences that I knew would be dire. They were. I was confined to barracks for several weeks and, after that, the curfew for being home in the evening was 9.30 p.m. (as opposed to the previous 11 p.m.). Going out with my boyfriend was my only means of escape, but the escape route had now been blocked.

My answer to all this was simply to get up and walk when I was eventually able to do so. I saved up some money and took myself across Europe. Sometimes I lived rough and sometimes I got in with the most dangerous people but, at least, I had attained a semblance of freedom from the tyranny.

Jealousy and envy

> Chaotic transferences take place at the unconscious level, and the resultant outbreaks of rage, anger, distress and fear usually have little or nothing to do with the real situation.
> – *Konrad Stettbacher*

In intimate relationships, the angry client may exhibit signs of extreme jealousy and envy that, in turn, may lead her to become violent towards the person who may be the object of her jealousy (see Chapter 12 – "Dysfunctional Relationships"). Frequently, the jealous spouse or suspicious lover will feel unloved and, thus, will have a deep-seated desire to hurt the person who has caused such unbearable pain. The jealous client may well fear rejection or abandonment and this may, consequently, prompt desperate measures in order to avoid such unpleasant states (see Chapter 7 – "Fear and Anxiety Disorders"). The resentful client may, of course, often actually alienate the person whose love and attention she so arduously covets. The envious client may also feel a sense of not being good enough to attain the true affection of another. Such a feeling of inadequacy may also impinge upon the client's sexual performance in an intimate relationship. Jealousy and envy may also motivate the client to become grasping and acquisitive. The client may, for instance, become money-grabbing or power-hungry or attach too much importance to material possessions. These inclinations can then lead the client to feel that others are more fortunate in having more of the commodities that she earnestly craves. This, too, will expose the client's feelings of insecurity and inadequacy.

> Envy has two aspects. In its primary sense envy is the experience of pain when we see that someone else has something desirable that we lack. We practice a good deal of semi-conscious denial on this type of envy: it often involves the recognition that someone else is better and that we are inferior. Envy is also the experience of pleasure when the person who has that desirable quality suffers misfortune. This experience tends to be privately acknowledged and publicly stifled or disguised.
> – *Joel Covitz*

The therapist may wish to utilise some surreptitious questioning techniques – such as those suggested below – that can help the client to identify her manifestations of jealousy and envy.

- Do you frequently feel envious or jealous of others?
- Do you find yourself continually carping on about the injustice in this world?
- Do you sometimes feel you need to keep your cool in order to avoid a row or a fight?
- Do you sometimes feel overcome by your hatred of someone?
- Do other people sometimes annoy you intensely because they are the way they are?
- Do you sometimes feel that you want to hit out at people or objects?
- Do you frequently feel a keen sense of injustice in terms of your life and the way in which the world ticks?
- Do you frequently feel let down by unreliable people?
- Do you often think that it is all right for the wealthy people in the world because they have everything?
- Do you hate that woman next door because she looks so happy?
- Do you resent the fact that your boss has just bought a brand-new car?

In the following case-study example, the client suffered from uncontrollable states of jealousy and possessiveness that were ruining her relationships with both family and friends.

Case-study example – jealousy and possessiveness
This female client sought therapy in order to resolve relationship issues that included excessive jealousy, possessiveness, a low self-esteem and a diminished self-worth.

The client recalled the fact that there were constant arguments between her father and her mother when she was a child. The client's father frequently had ex-marital affairs and her parents had eventually separated. This led to her being brought up in a foreign country and, hence, not understanding the language.

The client recollected being taken on holiday by her father and seeing him in bed with another woman. The client then saw her father's attention being given to his new partner. The client, subsequently, became outraged that her father had left her and her mother and had acquired a substitute to whom he could give his affection. This incident accounted for the client's propensity to be jealous of anyone who received affection or who did not show affection towards her.

Destructive criticism

> Few women have wholeheartedly embraced anger as a positive healing force. Traditionally women have been taught to be nice, conciliatory, understanding, polite. Angry women are labelled man-haters, castraters, bitches. Even in new-age psychotherapy circles, anger is usually seen as a stage to work through or as something toxic to eliminate. And most religious or spiritual ideologies encourage us to forgive and love. As a result, many survivors have suppressed their anger, turning it inward.
> – *Ellen Bass & Laura Davis*

The client who sneers at the world, who becomes a patroniser or a bully, may well have a surfeit of repressed anger that needs to be unearthed. Here the client will be using her tongue to lash people with destructive criticism. Destructive criticism may take the form of prejudice, sarcasm, bigotry and discrimination. Such stances will involve the client in harbouring destructive feelings based on negative, judgmental attitudes and opinions that will give her the illusion of safety or superiority by oppressing her fellow human beings in an unrelenting and unsympathetic manner. Often the anger in such interactions will be displaced anger, whereby the client will be unconsciously venting her anger at the wrong person (see Chapter 11, Volume 1 – "Defensive Strategies"). Alternatively, the client may be projecting anger at another because she feels annoyed with herself but dare not admit to this fearsome fact.

The practitioner may wish to utilise some surreptitious questioning techniques that can help the client to identify any patronising or bullying tendencies. The questions below are some examples that can invite the client to realise that she may have a disposition towards destructive criticism.

- Do you suffer from bouts of aggressiveness?
- Do you view others with suspicion or regard others as the enemy?

- Do you often seethe with indignation?
- Are you quick to condemn others and often on very little evidence?
- Do you like to play the revenge-tactics game?
- Do you excel at office-politics or power-game warfare?
- Do you ever derive pleasure from manipulating or controlling other people?
- Do you find that you do not suffer fools gladly?
- Do you ever feel affronted or indignant as a result of the way in which others have treated you?
- Are you always quick to point out the mistakes that other people make?
- Do you enjoy gossiping in a bitchy way?
- Do you sometimes feel like sneering or jeering at others?
- Do you like giving orders and being the boss?
- Do you take sly pleasure in kicking the underdog?
- Do you have a need to be a table-thumper, a desktop-banger or a door-slammer?
- Do you enjoy playing mind-games?
- Have you ever indulged in any backstabbing in the office?
- Are you preoccupied with military tactics or political intrigue?
- Do you often lose patience with friends and colleagues?
- Do you tend to want to lash out when you become frustrated with people?

Violence

> Parents who carry their tyranny to extremes are often guilty of physical child abuse – beatings, burnings, severe neglect – that leave the child scarred, physically and emotionally.
> *– Joel Covitz*

Physical violence is the most extreme form of the client's anger and rage symptomology. Violence towards others that can erupt unexpectedly in the client can be severely damaging to both parties and could escalate if it remains untreated. The practitioner should seek to allow the client to understand the basis for her motivations. Sometimes the client's physical violence may stem from the fact that she was herself physically abused in childhood and her violent behaviour will be her own means of coping with her distress (see Chapter 15 – "The Effects of Childhood Abuse"). The role of the practitioner will be to allow the client to explore the originating cause of her anger manifestation, enable her to release her wrath in a safe setting and then assist her to defuse the mechanism that has hitherto been ripe for ignition.

The following passage could be used by the therapist as a means of helping the client to come to terms with the way in which anger may have distorted her relationships with others and permeated her existence.

Why feel angry?

Begin to accept yourself as someone who is allowed to get cross occasionally. You have a right to feel resentment when someone takes advantage of you. You have a right to feel frustrated when things do not go your way or when life gets on top of you. You have a right to express your indignation when you are unfairly treated.

Sometimes, however, we spend our life feeling resentment, frustration and indignation over things that have happened a long time ago. It is called bearing a grudge. If you resent being put upon, then cease being treated unfairly. Take a different course and move on. When life gets hard, find a way out of your dilemma by taking action. Do not allow yourself to be drawn into a heated argument. Listen attentively to both sides of a discussion. State your case calmly and rationally when you believe that you have been unfairly treated. Aim for a sense of fair play in situations of potential conflict.

Now is the time to let go of those past hurts or to stop seeking revenge and retribution. Accept that such feelings can do nothing but fester inside you and really not affect the other person at all. Free yourself in this way by becoming complacent about the past. Consign it to insignificance. Be wise now and stop being a victim. Empower yourself to develop and grow in strength and self-made understanding. Rise above those people who have mistreated you in the past! Spread your wings and fly!

In the following case-study example, the client felt intense remorse over his violence towards his wife. This case also demonstrates the extent of the client's accumulated anger against those who have previously wronged him.

Case-study example – violent behaviour

A young male client sought therapy because he had a problem with being uncontrollably violent towards his wife.

This client had revealed, at the outset of therapy, that he had been forced to endure severe emotional, psychological and sexual abuse for several years at the behest of his stepfather. The client had, however, collated the necessary evidence and presented this case to his mother in the hope that she would intervene on his behalf, but things only got worse for him. The client's first recollection of sexual abuse had been at the age of approximately five when he was, among other things, forced to have intercourse with his sister. The client also unearthed repressed memories of further abuse while in therapy. The client had been sent to foster parents between the ages nine and eleven and, during this period, three other foster children varying in age from fifteen to nineteen years had also sexually abused him. When the client was at home and at school, the client's behaviour had become increasingly disruptive at an early age and the uncovering of these memories explained his behaviour.

At the age of approximately eleven, the client had sought his real father, who was an alcoholic at that time. The client had then managed to persuade his father to allow him to live with him. This then marked the end of the chapter of childhood abuse for this client.

In the therapeutic context, fortunately, the client found a means of giving vent to his anger. When releasing his violent feelings towards both parents and his abusers, however, the client had exhibited such rage that he had burst a blood vessel in his eye and had broken two baseball bats when pummelling a mattress.

The client narrative set out below shows how subtle childhood violence can sometimes be when it is displayed in public. This client subsequently caught herself beating her own child and, when this occurred, she felt it was time to address these issues in therapy.

Client narrative – my mother's violence …

When I was of the age when I needed to have my long hair brushed by my mother, some schoolfriends, on one occasion, happened to be present to witness the process. I was confused by their reaction to an everyday event. Why were these children squirming and backing away from the scene? The confused me questioned these friends, only to learn that they had regarded the inhumane way in which my mother was brushing my hair was beyond endurance. I was even more amazed to hear this news from two children who were, in my opinion, severely ill-treated themselves by their own mother. I learned that day that I had come to regard my mother's treatment of me as the norm.

What my friends did not know, of course, was that my mother had previously thrown me across the room when I neglected to tidy my room and, on one occasion, had pushed me down a flight of stairs because I was late home from school.

Exploring the Client's Anger and Rage Disorders

> Anger is extremely therapeutic for a variety of emotional disturbances.
> But before the ability to be angry can be achieved,
> the patient needs support.
> – *Margaret Reinhold*

One of the primary ways in which the client can be prompted to resolve her anger and rage will be to invite her to acknowledge such natural tendencies. Throughout life, the client may well have been indoctrinated with the feeling that the expression of anger would be inappropriate and, therefore, she may well fear that a tentative expression might lead to a lack of personal control. Often, the client who has been severely beset with rage can vent her anger at a significant other by means of pillow-punching or mattress-bashing with the aid of a baseball bat. This overt expression of anger with the significant other firmly in mind may then effect the necessary discharge for the extravert client. For the more reserved client, an imaginative expression of anger may, of course, be more appropriate.

The following passage could be used by the therapist in order to help the client to understand the way in which anger and rage have afflicted her.

Nature's blueprint for anger ...

Anger is the externalised expression of our need to fight against the perceived threat or danger. We register our fear by turning it towards others in the hope that we may destroy or annihilate the danger by facing up to the foe, standing our ground and displaying aggression. Anger stems from the need to protect ourselves and germinates from our instinctive fight-mechanism. It personifies our need to break away from the shackles of our parents or primary carers who have instilled fear and guilt in us in our upbringing. It may also surface as a means of assuaging our own guilt by punishing others or seeking revenge against past disappointments and betrayals.

Anger can be seen readily in nature. A cornered animal will attack its predator even if that enemy is larger and more powerful than itself. The fledgling in the nest wants to break free in order to experience the world. Anger personifies your strength, bravery and courage. Anger is the emotion that denotes that you are able to put up a fight when the odds are strongly against you. Anger makes you persistently determined to win, to rise to the challenge and to go all out to succeed. Anger gives you the energy and the vitality to tackle new projects with enthusiasm. Anger is nature's prime motivator and it gets things done! David slew Goliath because of the power of his anger and it gave him the strength to do so. A challenging game of tennis or a good workout in the gym is a way of channelling anger in a creative manner. The marathon-runners and the competition-winners in our society are those of us who have learned to capitalise on anger in creative ways.

The trouble will arise, of course, when the mighty power of our anger is such that we lose control of ourselves and we physically or emotionally hurt ourselves or harm others. Uncontrollable anger can be seen today in violent crime, in wars and in road-rage incidents at one extreme. Less dramatic – though still potentially explosive – examples may be escalating family rows, complaining attitudes, temper tantrums and rebellion against authority. A further problem is that in some societies we celebrate inclinations towards anger and aggression. To be brave is often considered manly and heroic. War-heroes are decorated and carried shoulder high. Prizefighters become superstars. We regard authoritarian or dictatorial figures as those from whom protection can be sought. If, however, we feel that the expression of anger is not politically-correct in polite society, we sometimes turn our anger in on ourselves. Thus, we fume silently inside or become depressed or get a headache or a skin rash or an upset stomach. Or we simply sulk or seek to play the office-politics game in the hope that we might triumph secretly over another.

The danger with uncontrollable anger and aggression is that the victim can become intoxicated with her own power and strength. The aggressor may then see that her menacing stance actually gets results. The bully watches people cower and enjoys the feeling. The complainer receives satisfaction or recompense. The gossip feels a sense of control and self-worth in having power over others. The looter or the rebel feels some illusory sense of relief maybe in revenge. Such members of our society are often themselves crying out for help and may be desperately in need of strength from others. But all we do is seek to punish the miscreants for their crimes – thus displaying more aggression in the interests of justice.

So what makes us feel anger in childhood? Anger is derived from anything that demeaned or debased you, invaded your person, your property or your privacy, affronted your integrity, undermined your dignity, betrayed your trust, restrained your self-expression or anything that you regarded as a danger or a threat to be overcome, attacked or rebelled against. In adulthood, the residue of our childhood legacy of unharnessed anger and aggression may manifest itself in any number of ways. Ask yourself whether you have buried any of these feelings because they are considered to be unacceptable and politically incorrect.

In the case-study example below, the client was effectively invited to release anger imaginatively.

Case-study example – anger discharge
This female client was eaten up with hatred for her abusive brother but she feared the expression of such a dangerous emotion.

The client claimed that she felt as if there were a monster within her chest who could do infinite damage. The therapist gently invited the client to make friends with the demon as a friendly dragon. The client now proceeded to allow the monster to breathe fire and brimstone on her family home and all her family – including her brother. The client described how the house was burned to a cinder and turned to ashes. The client watched this scene with glee and satisfaction with due encouragement from the therapist. Finally, the client was prompted to watch as the ashes were blown away by the north wind, that was depicted as her faithful servant on whom she could everlastingly depend.

Client Profiling

The analytical-hypnotherapy practitioner may wish to ponder the following points when formulating a profile for the client.

- In what ways does the client's anger surface into conscious awareness or overt behaviour?
- What lies behind the client's anger and rage reactions?
- In what ways does the client display aggressive tendencies?
- Is the client prone to being rebellious?
- Has the client ever rebelled against her parents or her upbringing?

- Does the client wish to be seen in any way as a trendsetter or a trailblazer?
- Does the client appear to be jealous or envious of others?
- Does the client feel at all deprived or hard done by?
- Is the client at all hypercritical of others?
- Does the client employ a range of manipulative tactics?
- Is the client at all scathing or contemptuous of others?
- Does the client have a history of gratuitous violence?
- In what ways were the client's parents or primary carers aggressive towards her in childhood?
- Has the client in any way been physically abused in her lifetime?

Chapter 11
Psychosomatic Disorders

"The Beast stands for strong mutually antagonistic
governments everywhere," he said. "Self-sufficiency at home,
self-assertion abroad."

– Evelyn Waugh

What is a Psychosomatic Disorder?

The quintessential demonstration of a psychosomatic phenomenon: a
mental state causing the body to react in a way usually thought of as
being purely physical.
– David Rosenhan & Martin Seligman

A psychosomatic symptom will be the human organism's way of
expressing pain, distress and conflict in a manner that impacts
upon the client's physiological being (see Figure 2 –
"Symptomology"). When distress or trauma has overwhelmed the
client, his psychological mechanism may turn the disturbance into
a psychological symptom, but if a psychological outlet cannot be
found or the outlet-path could be better handled by his physiology,
then he may find himself suffering from a psychosomatic disorder.
A psychosomatic disorder is, in fact, what Freud called a conver-
sion symptom and these conditions are far more common that the
person in street may actually realise or, even, the average practitioner may truly acknowledge (see Chapter 11, Volume 1 –
"Defensive Strategies").

Orthodox medicine in fact looks on the body as a machine, and this is
both its success and its failure. The failure of orthodoxy is its apparent
inability to distinguish between the body and the person, and in making
the assumption that they are identical. This is the inevitable consequence
of the convergent, analytical approach based on specialisation, where
increasing technology allows us to focus on ever smaller details of the
"machine" at the expense of the "owner".
– John Ball

A psychosomatic disorder will occur when the sufferer has a physical manifestation of an illness coupled with a psychological disturbance that will account for its presence in the client's body and will contribute to its maintenance. The alternative practitioner will consider the mind and the body to be inextricably interrelated and this notion will give rise to the concept of a psychologically-oriented illness, malfunction and disease in the client. The *diathesis-stress* theory, for example, considers that the client will have a physical weakness that will then be exacerbated by a stress-related factor. When the client is constitutionally weak, therefore, his illness can easily be triggered by stress and even when his constitution is strong it may still be undermined.

> "Diathesis" refers to the constitutional weakness that underlies the physical pathology, and "stress" to the psychological reaction to meaningful events. According to this model, an individual develops a psychosomatic disorder when he both has some physical vulnerability (diathesis) and experiences psychological disturbance (stress).
> – *David Rosenhan & Martin Seligman*

Childhood trauma and deep-seated burial of childhood issues will frequently result in stress-related physical conditions for the client such as asthma, migraines, skin disorders, digestive tract problems, gynaecological troubles and general aches and pains. When such conditions cannot be explained or cured by either surgical or medical procedures, the client's state may often be pointing the finger at a psychological disturbance that will have manifested as a psychosomatic disorder. In this chapter, we shall briefly consider the various manifestations of psychosomatic disorders from which the client may suffer.

Cardiovascular System Disorders

> Coronary heart disease (CHD) kills more people than any other disease in the Western world.
> – *David Rosenhan & Martin Seligman*

Diseases of the cardiovascular system are those that will affect the client's heart and blood circulation. Cardiovascular disorders include coronary heart disease, angina pectoris, pericarditis, hypertension (or *high blood pressure*) and rheumatic fever. Often sudden death from heart attacks will have been the result of arte-riosclerosis (or *hardening of the arteries*), when an excessive build-up of fat deposits has clogged up the arteries that serve the client's heart. Malfunctions of the cardiovascular system, of course, may be exacerbated by risk-factors such as a stressful lifestyle, a hyper-active personality, excessive smoking and physical inactivity (see Chapter 7 – "Fear and Anxiety Disorders").

> Emotions, though interpreted and named by the mind, are integrally an experience of the body.
> – *Babette Rothschild*

The cardiologists Meyer Friedman and Ray Rosenman have iden-tified personality types that are prone to stress-related heart dis-ease and hypertension. The Type A personality, for instance, has been found to have a higher propensity to heart disease than the Type B personality. The Type A personality can be said to have an exaggerated sense of urgency, to be competitive and ambitious and to display aggressiveness and hostility towards others. Type A per-sonality traits are thought to be caused by factors such as insecu-rity, crisis-management tendencies, defensiveness, egoism, suspiciousness, competitiveness, prejudice and impatience. This client may also be a perfectionist who will be highly self-critical. The Type B personality, in contrast, will usually be more calm and relaxed and will not pressurise himself and, for these reasons, he will obviously have less chance of developing a fatal disease.

> Hypertension is well known to be substantially due to chronic heightened emotional arousal, usually involving suppressed and intense anger on the part of the patient (who may be less aware of the aura of rage around him than the people to whom he is close).
> – *Hellmut Karle & Jennifer Boys*

Respiratory System Disorders

> My observations of scores of traumatised people has led me to conclude that post-traumatic symptoms are fundamentally, incomplete physiological responses suspended in fear. Reactions to life-threatening situations remain symptomatic until they are completed.
> – *Peter Levine*

Respiratory system disorders are those that will affect the client's breathing apparatus. Respiratory disorders that can affect the human organism include respiratory tract infections such as laryngitis, bronchitis, emphysema and influenza. Some of the most common psychosomatic manifestations of anxiety-provocation in the client are likely to be bronchial asthma (or *intrinsic asthma*), allergy-related asthma (or *extrinsic asthma*), shortness of breath, excessive catarrh, hyperventilation and lung congestion.

> Memories of traumatic events can be encoded just like other memories, both explicitly and implicitly. Typically, however, individuals with PTS [Post-Trauma Syndrome] and PTSD [Post-Traumatic Stress Disorder] are missing the explicit information necessary to make sense of their distressing somatic symptoms – body sensations – many of which are implicit memories of trauma.
> – Babette Rothschild

Minor complaints frequently clear up during the course of analytical therapy when the reason for the existence of the client's symptoms can be brought to light. Asthma and hay fever, for example, may be due to the client's suppressed emotive response to external events. The analytical therapist should always endeavour to identify the originating cause of the client's symptoms and then take steps to resolve the problem in order to ensure that the symptoms will not be maintained. With the client who may be allergic to a given animal, for example, the practitioner might begin investigation by considering whether he has previously been frightened by the animal in question (see Chapter 2 – "Therapeutic Investigation"). The therapist may then wish to pinpoint any episode in which the animal was present and, therefore, might have traumatised the client. Following the discovery of the originating cause, the therapist could then employ desensitisation techniques in order to complete the task of symptom-elimination.

> General relaxation, discharge of tension and the exploration of underlying anxieties, frustration and anger can all be highly beneficial in reducing the incidence and severity of asthmatic episodes and of more or less chronic bronchospasm. In addition, the use of imagery directly relating to freeing the bronchi and the muscles of the chest can be helpful in giving the patient some degree of direct control over his own body, especially when he feels an attack beginning, when he can use such imagery prophylactically.
> – Hellmut Karle & Jennifer Boys

282

Gastrointestinal System Disorders

A stress reaction can either be a short-term emotional reaction induced by
a specific situation, or it can be a long-term pattern of such emotional
reactions, adding up to an ulcer-prone personality.
– David Rosenhan & Martin Seligman

Digestive system disorders are those that will affect the client's digestive tract and the workings of his digestive system. Digestive disorders are, of course, frequently associated with anxiety and stress in the client. Perhaps the most serious disorder that can arise from stress in the client will be that of ulceration. Peptic ulcers may develop either in the client's stomach or in his duodenum when the delicate mucous lining of these organs has been eroded. Such ulceration can be aggravated by stress, moreover, when the stressor increases the client's gastric secretions during the digestive process. It has been found that both stomach ulcers and duodenal ulcers can be irritated by stress-related factors such as emotional conflict, shock-reactions, unpredictable circumstances and lack of control over events in the client's life. Other conditions that have a known stress-factor are those of colitis, irritable-bowel syndrome (IBS), diarrhoea, constipation, Coeliac's disease, Crohn's disease, candida, diverticulitis, gingivitis and haemorrhoids.

The causes of irritable bowel are uncertain, but emotional factors often
play a part, and some are overtly depressed. The illness is in many ways
the female equivalent of a duodenal ulcer with its occurrence in tense,
overconscientious people, often with exacerbations before a period.
– John Ball

Urogenital System Disorders

Psychosexual difficulties should be brought under this heading, since
they are so frequently physical responses of emotional origin.
– David Waxman

Urogenital system disorders are those that will affect the client's kidneys, bladder and genitalia. The principal disorders that will affect the client's urinary system and can often have a stress-related component are likely to be infections of the urinary tract, overfrequent urination and, in some cases, nephritis (or *kidney inflammation*).

> In childhood trauma, abuse usually involves pain to the body in some
> way. It begets dissociation and the development of ego states. Using
> stress symptomatology to contact ego states, therefore, can be a subtle
> but productive inroad for conducting ego state therapy.
> – *John Watkins & Helen Watkins*

The human reproductive system, similarly, can be afflicted by
infections or diseases that may have a stressful element.
Malfunctions within the client's reproductive system, furthermore,
are commonly associated with an accumulation of clock-stopping
stress. Most forms of sexual dysfunction, however, such as impotence, frigidity and anorgasmia, can usually be tackled via analytical hypnotherapy with the client. Painful menstruation (or
dysmenaria) may also beset the traumatised female client.

> A man who initially complained of impotence discovered that he was
> afraid of the consequences of his aggressive feelings towards women, a
> fear that originated through his relationship with his mother; as he
> resolved this conflict, he discovered that he could also be more
> appropriately assertive in other areas of his life.
> – *Dennis Brown & Jonathan Pedder*

In the following case-study example, the client reported extreme
pain during sexual intercourse for which no medical explanation
was possible.

Case-study example – sexual dysfunction
The client reported extreme pain during sexual intercourse and,
therefore, decided to seek therapeutic assistance. The client had
also been embarrassed to admit that her parents had separated and
that her mother had left her father for another woman and was in
a lesbian relationship.

Therapeutic enquiry revealed that the client had been sexually
abused at about the age of seven or eight years. The client had been
taken to a shed by her uncle (her mother's brother), whereupon she
had been sexually penetrated. This incident had been totally
repressed and, when it was recalled, the client relived the physical
pain of this event. After this abusive incident, the client then sat
waiting for her mother to come home. When the client's mother
arrived home, however, she was too fearful to tell of her experiences – particularly because her mother had been prone to anger
tantrums. In this case, the client's unconscious mind had locked

inside her body the story of the abuse and had repressed her recollections of the horrors of her ordeal.

Nervous System Disorders

> These isolated responses may occur in any system of the body in people
> confronted with some stressful situation. It is when such a symptom
> becomes recurring and incapacitating that treatment is required. In some
> people the symptoms seem to have a predilection for a particular part of
> the body, and there is evidence of a constitutional and emotional factor
> involved in determining this.
> – David Waxman

Nervous system disorders are those that will affect the client's central nervous system and peripheral nervous system. The central
nervous system, that comprises the brain and the spinal column,
will control the body's movement and sensory functions. The
peripheral nervous system, that consists of the cranial nerves, the
spinal nerves and the autonomic nervous system, will principally
control the body's involuntary functions and will direct the unconscious working of the client's internal organs and somatic systems.
The autonomic nervous system consists of the sympathetic nervous system (or the *thoracolumbar outflow*) and the parasympathetic
nervous system (or the *craniosacral outflow*). It will, of course, be
this involuntary nervous system that can cause the client to experience problems of a psychosomatic nature. Conditions that may
be attributed to the malfunctioning of the client's nervous system
are often more wide ranging in their manifestation. In this category, we can include hormonal deficiencies, headaches, chronic-
fatigue syndrome (or *myalgic encephalomyelitis*) and epilepsy, to
name but a few. Such ailments may often be overt manifestations
of the client's psychological distress and the practitioner can
enable him to trace the complaint to its source.

> Traumatic symptoms not only affect our emotional and mental states, but
> our physical health as well. When no other cause for a physical malady
> can be found, stress and trauma are likely candidates. Trauma can make
> a person blind, mute, or deaf: it can cause paralysis in legs, arms, or both;
> it can bring about chronic neck and back pain, chronic fatigue syndrome,
> bronchitis, asthma, gastrointestinal problems, severe PMS, migraines, and
> a whole host of so-called psychosomatic conditions. Any physical system
> capable of binding the undischarged arousal caused by trauma is fair game.
> – Peter Levine

Immune System Disorders

> Our natural ability to withstand outside interference from micro-
> organisms is assisted by several defence mechanisms (defensive from our
> point of view at any rate), and the chief of these is the immune system.
> – *John Ball*

Immune system disorders will affect the client's ability to fend off disease and infection. The role of the immune system will be to attack the body's foreign invaders (or *antigens*). This important work will be undertaken when the immune system recognises an antigen and then the antibodies will set about destroying it and removing it from the human system. The memory within the immune system – known as the *immunologic memory* – will also undergo an educational process whereby, once an invader has struck, the human system will remember how to deal with that same antigen in future. In this way, the client can build up immunity to harmful invaders. When immunity has been built up by the client, his system will then become *immunocompetent* in dealing with unwarranted invasion. Stress factors, however, can not only lower the client's resistance to infection or disease but also can reduce his immunocompetence. Factors such as depression, hopelessness, traumatic distress and psychological conflict have all been cited as elements that can affect the functioning of the human organism's immune system.

Immune system disorders will include autoimmune system diseases such as Addison's disease, alopecia (or sporadic hair loss), Crohn's disease, diabetes mellitus, glomerulonephritis (or kidney disease), myasthenia gravis (or muscle fatigue), pernicious anaemia, rheumatoid arthritis, systemic lupus erythematosus (SLE) and a number of thyroid diseases. With an autoimmune system disease, the body's own defence-mechanism will attack its own body-tissue which it believes to be a foreign invader.

Allergic reactions are also the province of the human immune system. The causes of the client's different allergic reactions may be as varied as the types of allergies that can exist. Often an allergy will manifest when the client has been under stress and will continue until the stress-inducing factors have been resolved or removed.

There is a field of health psychology, called psychoneuroimmunology
(PNI), which studies how psychological factors change the immune
system and ultimately increase the risk for disease. The basic findings in
the field are that personality, behaviour, emotion, and cognition can all
change the body's immune response, and thereby change risk for these
diseases. The hope in this field is that psychotherapy can be used to
prevent, and perhaps to cure, such physical illnesses.
– *David Rosenhan & Martin Seligman*

Cancer is a condition that will, typically, affect the body's cell-regeneration process and will upset the fine balance of the process of cell-division and cell-replacement. A number of psychological theories, however, have been suggested in order to explain the causes of carcinogenic conditions. It has been proposed that traumatic loss in the client's early childhood may be a factor and that his belief in the inevitability of getting cancer will also be a significant factor in its development. Cancer may also be a way of enabling the client's body to attack itself or to close itself down. The knowledge of having contracted cancer will also usually put the client under a great deal of stress and this stress-response will further depress his immune-response. If the cancer sufferer, moreover, has to undergo chemotherapy or radiotherapy, this procedure will also depress his body's immune response. Chemotherapy will, of course, poison the client's entire system but, because the cancerous cells are dividing at a faster rate, more of the these cells will die than the healthy cells.

If the practitioner works with the cancer-sufferer, it will, of course, be wise to assist the client to pinpoint the root cause of the cancerous condition and to identify the reasons why it continues to persist. Investigative analysis and ideomotor questioning can again assist greatly in this quest (see Chapter 2 – "Therapeutic Investigation"). Relaxation and visualisation techniques, furthermore, can often be effectively combined with hypnoanalytic procedures in order to allay the client's fears of the disease. If the client undergoes chemotherapy or radiotherapy, then visualisation can often be judiciously used in order to assist his system to kill off all the cancerous cells but to leave a sufficient number of healthy cells alive. The practitioner, therefore, would be advised to find out what the client believes about his condition and the prognosis for recovery. In some cases, the client may strongly believe that medical assistance will be the answer and, in other cases, alternative therapies are what he may prefer. If the client has a deep conviction that one particular form of therapy is not helping, therefore, the therapist would then be ill-advised to encourage this form of treatment because it may not work for him. If the client does not have a firm conviction of the efficacy of a given treatment, there will be little point in working with it because it may achieve very little, if anything. The therapist should, therefore, suspend his own beliefs and focus only on what the client truly believes will work for him.

> Many other illnesses are thought to be related to mental and emotional upheaval, notably cancer of the breast. Recent researches in this last illness indicate that severe stress may not only cause cancer of the breast in the first place but may be related to recurrence of the cancer after surgery or other treatment has taken place.
> – *Margaret Reinhold*

The following passage can be used by the therapist in order to assist the client who has contracted cancer. The client could, in addition, be asked to draw both his tumour(s) and his white blood cells in order to assist with this important form of healing. The practitioner, of course, should tailor this passage to the client's exact requirements.

Healing your cells ...

Can you imagine yourself standing under a beam of light – just like a golden waterfall? Imagine the light entering your body at your head and at the tops of your shoulders. Watch as it leaves your feet as a muddy brown colour. Remain there until the light coming out of your feet is the same colour as the light entering your head and shoulders. Feel it washing those toxins away, cleansing, healing, balancing and repairing your body.

Perhaps you can visualise those X-rays actively targeting your tumour cells, gently bypassing the healthy cells all around your tumour. Perhaps these X-rays can explode, burn up, vaporise and suffocate some individual cells. Maybe those X-rays can shrink that tumour or remove small pieces from it. I don't know what is best for you but I do know that you will know. Perhaps you can also see those nutrients you have been taking strengthening your immune system, protecting your healthy cells and starving those cancerous cells.

Perhaps you can also see and feel the calmness in your stomach – an easy stomach, feeling good and comfortable and your hair growing normally and healthily. Everything happening easily and effortlessly – guiding and helping your recovery. You can feel calm, comfortable and relaxed. You can enjoy life, you can notice the perfume of the flowers, you can enjoy the feeling of the wind and the sun on your face. You can enjoy brushing a luxuriant head of hair, feeling and seeing your hair as you brush it, secure in the knowledge that it is there for you and will remain there for you for ever. You can feel vitality and energy coursing through your body. This is the unstoppable healing process!

Skeletal Disorders

> Bone is a living tissue and as such is constantly changing, in the sense that its constituents are continually being deposited and removed.
> – *John Ball*

Skeletal disorders and malfunctions will affect the client's bony structure together with his joints, muscles, ligaments and tendons. The body, as the vehicle for the expulsion of psychic pain, will, undoubtedly, be a target for aches and pain within the human skeleton and the joints. Conditions such as osteoarthritis, rheumatoid arthritis, gout, muscular hypertension and any number of strains, aches and pains can often find their roots in the client's stress-related anxiety.

> Every emotion is characterised by a discrete pattern of skeletal muscle contraction visible on the face and in the body posture (somatic nervous system).
> – *Babette Rothschild*

In the case-study example given below, the client suffered from a number of aches and pains but was able to address these issues in therapy and then to find the symbolic representation of her symptoms.

Case-study example – aching limbs
This female client suffered from a number of mysterious aches and pains that included a stiff neck, aching joints, knee and wrist problems. It had been medically confirmed that her condition was not due to any arthritic or viral disorder and so her doctor had concluded that her ailments were stress-related. This diagnosis, therefore, prompted the client to seek therapy.

The client worked through a number of issues during analytical investigation in connection with her relationship with her father, who had shown her little affection. The client had spent most of her life trying to win her father's affection and, of course, felt aggrieved about the fact that she had always miserably failed to do so. The client spoke of the way in which she had yearned for her father's affection yet had been constantly rejected by him throughout her life.

Finally, the client made the realisation that, if she had to strive in order to gain her father's affection, she would, by definition, never be able to attain it. Having expressed her sorrow and anger over this situation, the client was then able to come to terms with the fact that she could now give up trying. The client described her aches and pains as her yearning for her father's love but conceded that she could now let go of her resentment, bitterness and regret over the love of which she had been deprived in the past.

Skin Disorders

> Our skin is much more than just an imperious envelope enclosing the body, it is a complete organ in itself, in fact the largest sense organ in the body. Its other functions include controlling body temperature, screening the sun's rays with the pigment melanin, insulating the body with a layer of fat, manufacturing vitamin D, secreting certain unwanted substances and signalling our emotional states by flushing (whether we like it or not). There are even areas of specialised skin – the hair and nails – for different protective functions, and one or more of these may malfunction in a variety of ways.
> – *John Ball*

A number of skin disorders can be attributed to the client's psychic disturbance and frequently such disorders will be closely allied with nervous system disorders. Examples of the client's stress-related skin conditions may include dermatitis, urticaria and psoriasis, as well as sebaceous disorders such as acne, rosacea, eczema and pruritis. Other ailments such as viral infections, bacterial infections and fungal infections of the skin may also exhibit a stress-component or induce stress in the client. Alopecia (or *sporadic hair loss*) has also been cited as having an anxiety-related function for the client.

> Uncovering techniques to reveal underlying psychological stresses and conflicts is desirable in all skin conditions. While repressed or suppressed affect is improbable in eczema in neonates, it is highly probable that the distressing experiences inevitably associated with severe infantile eczema

do indeed lay the foundations for stresses of this kind. That is to say, the condition of skin, the sometimes extreme physical discomfort and distress resulting from this, the reactions of the significant adults in the child's life and the effects of all these on the child's self-image and relationships may all contribute to the establishment of an underlying reservoir of anger, frustration and distress which may be responsible for maintaining the eczema into later years.
– *Hellmut Karle & Jennifer Boys*

When dealing with skin disorders, the practitioner would be advised first to examine the source of the complaint prior to attempting to resolve the problem or before providing him with a coping-strategy for everyday existence. Irritating skin complaints such as pruritis, psoriasis and eczema can usually be finally resolved by asking the client to visualise, for example, a healing pool full of water or a waterfall that feels like silk on the skin. This nectar-like imagery can then have a soothing effect on the client's irritation once the root cause of the complaint has been excavated. A tube of magic cream, alternatively, can have the effect of sooth-ing, cleansing, healing and protecting the client's skin. The client may also be invited imaginatively to visit a special type of masseur whose lovely warm hands can rub in wonderful oils that can leave his skin calm and restore it to its former state before the trauma struck. If the client's complaint is still persistent, perhaps ideomo-tor techniques can be employed in order to highlight the body's reasons for hanging on to the problem (see Chapter 2 – "Therapeutic Investigation"). When the therapist uses ideomotor techniques, the reasons for the maintenance of the problem can often be elicited by questioning the client's unconscious mind and, then, a negotiation process can ensue either with his mind or with the affected area.

The somatic bridge can be useful to let the physical symptom, such as a pain or an ulcer, speak for itself.
– *John Watkins & Helen Watkins*

In the following case-study example, the client found an effective means of communicating with his penis in order to heal a fungal infection.

Case-study example – fungal infection

A male client had a persistent fungal infection under the foreskin of his penis. After two years of treatment with various steroidal creams, the client's condition had stabilised but had not completely disappeared.

The client was asked to allow his penis to make contact with his unconscious mind so that he could talk to it. By this means, the client discovered that he was ignoring this part of his body and denying his sexuality. Negotiation with the client's penis permitted the infection to reduce, provided that he continued to consider this important facet of his life. When the client's sexuality issues had been resolved and he had begun to pay sufficient attention to his penis and to his sex life, then the fungal condition naturally resolved. The client was a homosexual but had not had a partner for several years. The client was having difficulty with accepting his sexual preference and also felt somewhat guilty that he had been such a disappointment to his parents because of his sexual inclinations.

The client had previously been focused on improving many areas of his life with the exception of his sexuality, that he had pushed into the background. The client, finally, decided to start concentrating on this area of his life in order to resolve the problem and to have a better communication with his own body. The client also came to the realisation that he could not live his life in order to please his parents.

Traumatic Somatisation Disorders

A somatoform disorder is one of the most difficult disorders to diagnose correctly.
– *David Rosenhan & Martin Seligman*

A traumatic somatisation disorder (or *somatoform disorder*) will be a form of psychosomatic disorder in which the psychological component of the condition will not be readily apparent, or only vaguely implied, when the client suffers. It will be as if the emotive trauma has been placed out of reach but will manifest in the client's body, where it cannot readily be accessed consciously. An ostensibly-physiological disorder may, therefore, superficially appear to have no traceable cause. With this form of disorder, the client will have a physical manifestation that cannot be diagnosed according to any clearly-identifiable physiological or neurological criteria. The client's condition may, thus, be attributed to underlying psychological distress about which he will may have no conscious cognisance. An example of a somatoform disorder might include Briquet's syndrome and pain disorders (or *psychalgia*), both of which will have ostensibly obscure causation.

> Somatisation refers to situations when physical pain or physical problems are forms of re-experiencing the trauma.
> – *Aphrodite Matsakis*

One particularly-puzzling feature of a somatoform disorder will be that the client may have no detectable distress as a result of his condition in that the anxiety bound up within it will not be overt or consciously manifested. It will be as if the nature of the client's psychological trauma has been so unbearable for him that he dare not express his emotive feelings and so this expression will have been driven underground, where it will be lost in his physiology (see Chapter 13 – "Post-traumatic Stress Disorder"). The hypnoanalyst, therefore, should be alert to the possibility that the client's ostensibly-physiological condition may be a somatoform disorder with a definite psychological link of which he appears to remain blissfully unaware.

> Many other diseases are often thought to have psychosomatic components: migraine headaches, arthritis, chronic pain, and asthma, among others.
> – *David Rosenhan & Martin Seligman*

The following client narrative gives some insight into the way in which a client may be afflicted by traumatic somatisation.

Client narrative – traumatic somatisation …
Because I had such a good survival-mechanism, my emotional state of mind was not evident to the outside world. Buried memories, however, do take their toll. I, therefore, paid a heavy price physically in consequence.

One evening I came home from an exercise class with a slight pain in my knees. Old age creeping on, I wondered? I ignored it. I couldn't think that its cause was other than overexertion. Life carried on as usual. Maybe I had pulled a muscle and a bit more exercise would do it good. I went to my next class as usual. The next evening I went to a social event in which disco dancing was the order of the night and I partook heartily. I noticed, however, that my knees felt very cold. A strange icy feeling. Never mind, I thought. I will warm them up with a bit more exercise.

The next day I found myself sitting rather than standing. The day after that I declined an invitation to go for a walk in the park. What was this? Was it about time that I started taking these pains seriously? Surely not? Back at work, I was short of breath with the pain and convinced that I should seek medical treatment urgently. My doctor's surgery was now closed for the day and so I rang the casualty department of my local hospital. I was told that I would have to wait several hours to be seen but that actually a knee injury, as it was termed, was not something that could be treated in casualty. I pumped myself full of pills and went to bed. The pills had no effect on the pain whatsoever. That night the pain was so excruciating that I could not, in my wildest imagination, perceive that it was possible for an individual to experience so much pain. I was also totally mystified as to why I should suddenly, out of the blue, for no discernible reason at all, be rendered in such a state. I eventually cried myself to sleep in agony. The next day the pain appeared to have eased somewhat but all that had happened was that I had learned to live with it. My body was obviously turning into a vehicle for the release of pain. This is what my body was doing because it knew of no other way to cleanse itself of my childhood traumas. For the next two weeks I slept practically 24 hours a day. For the next six weeks I was almost totally crippled and bedridden. For over a year I was severely disabled. Walking was an activity that I restricted to an absolute minimum. My whole life was confined to survival level.

As a self-employed person, I lost out financially to the tune of approximately half a year's salary because of my demise. I spent the next year trying to fathom out what the hell was wrong with me. This consumed even more money. I saw a series of medical practitioners, who scratched their heads and relieved me of some more of my now-dwindling financial resources. My only plea to the medical fraternity is please, in future, be aware of the fact that psychosomatic conditions are a concrete fact of human existence. During the period of my disability, I consulted four or five general medical practitioners, four physiotherapists, four osteopaths, two chiropractors and two orthopaedic surgeons. In all cases hope triumphed over experience. After nine months of waiting for an improvement, an orthopaedic surgeon performed an operation on me that cost me an arm and a leg. I put all my savings and hopes into the success of this operation. The relief was negligible. If anything, I got worse because I now had to recover from the operation. But it served a vital purpose – it amplified my troubles and made me look at my mind.

When I finally despaired of ever making a complete recovery and of ever leading even a semi-normal existence, I decided to undertake psychotherapy under hypnosis. Almost a year after the operation, I finally came to the conclusion that my condition was as a direct result of my childhood legacy. I had not only the emotional legacy for which to thank my parents but I also had this utterly crippling condition with which to contend. It had brought my life to a complete standstill.

Exploring the Client's Psychosomatic Disorders

Integrated trauma therapy must consider, consist of, and utilise tools for identifying, understanding and treating trauma's effects on both mind and body. Language is necessary for both. The somatic disturbances of trauma require language to make sense of them, comprehend their meaning, extract their message, and resolve their impact.
– *Babette Rothschild*

When exploring the client's psychosomatic disorders, the practitioner will often need to access psychological distress in order to deal with the physiological manifestation. In unearthing the root cause of a symptom, however, the client will need to be able to express the underlying pain and to ascribe a meaning to it. In order to relieve the client of the dormant and imprisoned trauma held within his body tissue, he will need to excavate deeply his physiological sensations and to extract the psychological component. The case-study example below provides some guidance as to the way in which a client took this monumental step and released a long-standing physical condition.

Case-study example – frozen shoulder

This male client sought therapy because he was experiencing anxiety about the fact that he was not able to recover from a frozen-shoulder injury. The client was otherwise young and healthy and no medical reason could be provided for his condition and lack of recovery.

The client examined that period of his life when he was accepted for adoption by adoptive parents with whom he did not get on. The client's adoptive parents had tried hard to give him affection but had, in fact, been more interested in another child whom they had adopted some years earlier. The client felt that he had been adopted only in order to provide a playmate for this other, female, child. The client believed, therefore, that he was only second best. This fact caused him to seek out his natural parents, only to discover that his father had died and that his mother now lived abroad and did not really want to be pursued by her natural child. Apparently, the client's mother had given birth to him out of wedlock and had put the child up for adoption at birth. Making these discoveries, however, set up anxiety within the client and, shortly afterwards, his physical condition manifested.

When the client was able to relate to the fact that he had been abandoned at birth and even before he was actually born, he was able to come to terms with his anxiety both overt and covert. The client, thus, was able to recover from his day-to-day anxieties by settling his score with his mother and his adoptive parents in therapy. The client, moreover, was also able to release the emotive content of his frozen shoulder by expelling his sense of grief, loss and resentment towards both sets of parents. By this means, the client's frozen shoulder could then be invited to defrost.

Client Profiling

The analytical-hypnotherapy practitioner may wish to ponder the following points when formulating a profile for the client.

- Does the client complain of any form of physiological suffering?

- In what ways might the client's psychological distress have manifested physiologically?
- Does the client experience discomfort when sitting in the consulting-room chair?
- Does the client appear to be in physical pain in any way?
- Does the client suffer from any mysterious or unaccountable physical symptoms?
- Has the client sought medical advice about any ailments that he may have?
- Has the client been told that his physiological ailments have a stress-related component?
- Does the client experience any difficulty with breathing when relaxing?
- Does the client ever suffer from any physiological disorders that may be exacerbated by stress?
- Does the client need to visit the loo overfrequently when he arrives for therapy?
- Does the client exhibit any obvious skin disorders or unsightly skin conditions?
- Does the client often catch the latest virus that has been circulating?
- Does the client frequently complain of physical aches and pains?
- Does the client have any mysterious physical symptoms about which he seems not to want to complain?

Chapter 12

Dysfunctional Relationships

When lovely woman stoops to folly
And finds too late that men betray,
What charm can soothe her melancholy,
What art can wash her guilt away?

– Oliver Goldsmith

The Client in the Social World

The child trapped in an abusive environment is faced with formidable
tasks of adaptation. She must find a way to preserve a sense of trust in
people who are untrustworthy, safety in a situation that is unsafe, control
in a situation that is terrifyingly unpredictable, power in a situation of
helplessness. Unable to care for or protect herself, she must compensate
for the failures of adult care and protection with the only means at her
disposal, an immature system of psychological defences.
– Judith Lewis Herman

The practitioner will undoubtedly need to consider the client in
terms of her social interaction as this will reflect both her own self-
image and her ability to communicate and form satisfactory relationships with others.

The client's relationship with the self

When you were abused, your boundaries, your right to say no, your
sense of control in the world, were violated. You were powerless. The
abuse humiliated you, gave you the message that you were of little
value. Nothing you did could stop it.
– Ellen Bass & Laura Davis

The child will grow up surrounded by others in the social world.
There may be many people about the child – parents, siblings,

grandparents, distant relatives, friends, schoolmates, teachers, neighbours and strangers. The child must meet and interact with others daily throughout her childhood. In going about her daily business, the child, therefore, will be forced to compare herself with others and to note the reactions of others. It will, of course, be those things that the child learns about herself in childhood that will shape her personal self-concept and self-image (see Chapter 6, Volume 1 – "Client-Centred Therapy"). The child will gain an appreciation of her self-worth from the words and the deeds of those dearest to her. The degree of worthiness that the child may feel will, in turn, affect the way in which the client will regard herself. The client's self-concept, moreover, will then affect her actions and her interactions with others. The client whom the therapist will meet in the consulting room will, inevitably, have issues, to a greater or lesser extent, with her self-concept and this element will, in turn, impact upon her relationships with others (see Figure 2 – "Symptomology").

The client's relationship with others

> The genuine lover always perceives the beloved as someone who has a totally separate identity. Moreover, the genuine lover always respects and even encourages this separateness and the unique individuality of the beloved.
> – *Scott Peck*

The victim of dysfunctional parenting will frequently experience difficulties in forming relationships of all kinds. The psychologically-damaged child will, as an adult, attract and enter into friendships and partnerships that may be doomed to failure or that will engender extreme personal dissatisfaction. It will be as if the client has an inner need to perpetuate her original suffering and to copy the ways of her role-models – however bizarre their behaviour may have been. Destructive, demeaning, unfruitful and abusive relationships are typical of the types of relationships that the client with a legacy of childhood neglect, exploitation and abuse will be likely to have encountered (see Chapter 15 – "The Effects of Childhood Abuse").

The client's parents will have been her primary role-models and, if these human examples were inadequate in any way, she will have no satisfactory reference point by which to gauge her subsequent actions and decisions. An abusive relationship, for example, will somehow feel right to the client because that is what she will have learned to accept as the norm. The client may, thus, sincerely believe that life really should be that way because she simply does not know any different. Conversely, if the client has accepted that her treatment at the mercy of another is abnormal and unwelcomed, she may often allow the situation to continue in the hope that she alone can improve it. A dysfunctional childhood will often compel the client to strive constantly in order to rectify an utterly hopeless relationship when the effort will simply not be worth the candle. The client, furthermore, may not be able to muster the psychological strength to rid herself of an unsatisfactory union and so may learn to tolerate a violent or an abusive relationship because of her low self-regard. For the client who has been a victim of childhood abuse, of course, unsatisfactory or abusive relationships may be her unconscious mind's primitive way of attempting to bring such images to the surface. The client from a dysfunctional childhood will, moreover, often sabotage a potentially-viable relationship because a worthwhile union might feel somehow incongruous. The distraught client, for example, may frequently reject the kind-hearted lover and genuine carer. The client may, similarly, not be able to distinguish between a true friend and an obvious foe. The client will have failed to appreciate that friends are those people who can love her and enemies are those who will show hatred or resentment. The client, thus, will have no prior blueprint and insufficient self-worth by which to find a caring relationship acceptable.

Self-Esteem

> Shame-based identity involves a continuous state of self-consciousness about something within that is dishonourable, improper, disgraceful or unworthy. It is a despairing sense of identity based on these inner feelings. It is marked by the feeling of being unworthy at the very core of one's being.
> – *Ken Graber*

The child who grows up in a caring and nurturing environment in which both parents are loving, attentive, encouraging and enthusiastic will usually metamorphose into a reasonably well-balanced and psychologically-healthy adult. Anything less than this standard will, of course, spell some kind of disaster for the client. If the client has been the product of a dysfunctional family environment, then her self-esteem will have been adversely affected because she will have been given the distinct impression that she is substandard in some way as a human being. If the client has been severely maltreated in childhood, for example, she will have been devalued as an individual. If the client has suffered from any form of childhood abuse, her wishes will have been callously disregarded and her physical person will have been mishandled without her consent. Such factors will be likely to generate a severely negative self-image within the client that can lead her to develop a profound lack of confidence and a low self-worth. It will be as if the client will take on board the messages that she has received both overtly and covertly about herself and will then incorporate these childish learnings into her own psyche (see Chapter 11, Volume 1 – "Defensive Strategies").

Often, the ill-treated child will have a poor sense of self and, therefore, will not discover her true identity and will be mystified about the way in which she should fit into society. A further negative factor may be that the client will develop an intense dislike of her appearance or her body-image. This self-view may also be exacerbated if the client, for example, is disabled, becomes obese or suffers from a clearly-visible skin disorder (see Chapter 11 – "Psychosomatic Disorders"). The client may, therefore, wish to avoid any kind of body exposure and may go to great lengths in order to conceal her figure from any public view. The client's stance in this respect may also prompt an avoidance of close or intimate relationships. The client, furthermore, may desire to withdraw from social interaction and, consequently, will feel the accompanying loneliness and isolation that such actions will generate.

For the client with a fragile self-concept, it will be as if everyone in her life were a negative reflection of a part of herself. If the client dislikes someone, that person may be mirroring to her that part of herself that she so vehemently detests. Alternatively, if the client admires a given trait in another, she may have denied its existence within her own psyche in accordance with Jung's concept of the shadow personality coming to the fore (see Chapter 2, Volume 1 – "Analytical Psychology"). A low level of self-worth in the client may also render her oversensitive to the opinions of others. The client may, therefore, become the universal people-pleaser who fears that every step she takes will displease someone else. The compulsive people-pleaser may turn herself into a human doormat and beg to be trampled on while, at the same time, she may secretly resent the role that she has been unconsciously forced to adopt.

> Sexual abuse also is cited as having an effect on self-esteem, but this effect has not yet been established by empirical studies. In the DeFrancis study, 58% of the victims expressed feelings of inferiority or lack of worth as a result of having been victimised.
> *– David Finkelhor & Angela Browne*

The practitioner may be able to utilise questioning techniques according to the examples given below that can help the client to obtain an index of her level of self-worth.

- Do you frequently allow your friends to dump their emotional baggage on you?
- Do you feel that you are a dustbin for all the world's troubles?
- Are you envious of other people's strength or wisdom?
- Would you die of shame if you felt you looked stupid?
- Are you terrified of showing your real self?
- Do you don the garb of your profession by acting out a stereotypical role when at work?
- Do you habitually leave the decision-making to others?
- Do you truly believe everything that you are told by others?
- Do you frequently see yourself in other people?
- Are you constantly the victim of the bully or the patroniser?
- Do you think you are either a top dog or an underdog in life?
- Would you say you are essentially a master or a servant to others?

The passage below might help the client to value herself and to understand the way in which her self-concept may have been inadequately and erroneously formed.

Following the crowd ...

If the follow-the-crowd effect is in operation in your life, you will hate being different from others and may go to any lengths to avoid individuality. But an earnest desire to be one of the crowd or to run with the pack could cost you your identity and bring you a deal of unhappiness and a lack of self-satisfaction as a result. The seeds of self-dissatisfaction, however, will often have been sown long ago.

In childhood, for example, it will be as if we are playing a game of cards. Our opponent is very skilled at playing this game. Our opponent knows the name of the game and has played it many times. Our opponent is very skilled and knows all the tricks and dodges. Our opponent also has many trump cards in her hands and knows how to play them to her advantage. Also, we wonder, whether our opponent has X-ray eyes and can see the fact that we have a very poor hand of cards. We do not know the name of this game, we do not know the rules and certainly we do not know how to play the game with any degree of skill. It will be a game that we are bound to lose. And then we may feel badly about our performance and blame ourselves for losing. This game you had no choice but to play and you may have mercilessly suffered at the hands of this skilled card-player.

We play such games of cards in childhood because we have to appease others in the interests of our survival. Because of our survival instincts, we have a natural tendency – particularly in childhood and early adulthood – to stick together. There is safety in numbers. Other people know better. Others are stronger and wiser and can offer us protection. United we stand! It is very scary to be an individual. You could be rejected, abandoned, isolated, lonely, deserted, ostracised, ridiculed or lost. All your worst fears could be realised. Help! I am not safe when I am alone and different from others!

How much nicer to be yourself, to be an individual in your own right, to be a trendsetter, to be looked up to as an independent being. You could be a free spirit. You could be respected and admired for it! Have you got the courage to take the risk! Maybe you can quietly assess whether you are playing the people-game and what its consequences entail for you?

In the client narrative given below, the client describes the way in which his father's attitude had an adverse effect on his self-esteem.

Client narrative – my father just didn't care ...

As a child and during my formative years, I had no recollection whatsoever of my father treating me as a father would be expected to do. In the whole of my childhood, we played cricket once or twice in the garden but that was the sum total of his involvement with me.

My father took no interest in me at all as a person either as a child or an adult. He knew nothing about me because he never asked and also because he had a fundamental lack of interest in attempting to understand me. If I revealed something about myself in the course of a conversation, he would appear puzzled and confused – the unspoken "Well, really!" or "Fancy that!" hanging on his lips. He also took no interest in my education. He never once attempted to find out what my interests were. I was constantly asked whether I watched cricket or tennis on the television even though my interest in sport of any kind is minimal. I always felt his disappointment and disapproval because I did not have a healthy enthusiasm for sport. He made me feel utterly worthless.

Intimate Relationships

Women who have been victimised as children report a variety of interpersonal problems: difficulty in relating to both women and men, conflicts with their parents, and discomfort in responding to their own children.
– David Finkelhor & Angela Browne

The child who has had a bumpy ride through childhood will have had an inadequate introduction to human relationships. The client's primary carers might have been wholly inadequate role-models who will have taught her everything that she does not need to know about relationships and human interaction. The client, therefore, may be totally incapable of relating to anyone else in a meaningful manner. Unproductive, unfruitful and destructive relationships will often arise as a result of transference between the two parties (see Chapter 13, Volume 1 – "Transference and Countertransference"). The client, for example, may unconsciously be a victim of neglect while her partner will be unconsciously prone to a lack of commitment. It will be important for the practitioner, therefore, to appreciate this concept and to remember that a relationship based on neurotic dysfunction may not stand any chance of success unless both parties can resolve their unconscious negative programming.

Unfruitful relationships

Whether it be shallow or not, commitment is the foundation, the bedrock of any genuinely loving relationship. Deep commitment does not guarantee the success of the relationship but does help more than any other factor to assure it. Initially shallow commitments may grow deep with time; if not, the relationship will likely crumble or else be inevitably sickly or chronically frail.
– Scott Peck

The client who has been the recipient of childhood neglect, exploitation or abuse may feel isolated and, even, dread social interaction. Severe childhood maltreatment, therefore, may mean that the client will develop an inability to form fruitful friendships and loving relationships. Perhaps the client may lack the ability to trust others sufficiently. Perhaps the client may avoid commitment to a rewarding relationship or may withdraw from a successful partnership. Perhaps the client may feel a hostility towards others and, thus, engage in violent or stormy relationships. Perhaps the client may fear sexual encounters. Perhaps the client may continually engage in a repeating pattern of attracting abusive partners. Perhaps the client may be promiscuous and unable to sustain a viable relationship. Perhaps the client may be unwilling to undertake the role of parent and, thus, be unwilling even to consider having children. The childhood product of a dysfunctional upbringing may well find that she can become involved in an imprisoning relationship in adulthood. In an adult relationship, the client may not be able to commit to a relationship or not be able to become emotionally involved in any way. It will be as if the client's emotions have been so damaged and her personal boundaries so infringed that she will feel unwilling to trust another or to show affection to another ever again, even though her need for companionship may, ironically, be paramount.

When love and affection in an intimate relationship is not readily flowing, the client may seek an underhand means in order to secure the illusion of affection. The client may, therefore, become adept at manipulating her partner by employing attention-seeking tactics. Perhaps the client will become a hypochondriac and bask in the glory of the attention that her ailments can attract. Perhaps the client will call for help by her outbursts of violence or expressions of jealousy. Perhaps the client will be prone to sulking and withdrawal. Perhaps the client will be deliberately uncooperative or uncommunicative in her dealings with an intimate partner or a close friend. Perhaps the client will attract into her life people with whom she is in constant conflict, both at work and at play. Perhaps the client will seek sexual gratification by devious or perverted means.

> The motives behind injudicious giving and destructive nurturing are
> many, but such cases invariably have a basic feature in common: the
> "giver", under the guise of love, is responding to and meeting his or her
> own needs without regard to the spiritual needs of the receiver.
> – *Scott Peck*

The following client narrative illustrates the way in which a client
can attract partners without any form of commitment. This client
had a dysfunctional childhood upbringing and so found it difficult, if not impossible, to relate to male partners.

Client narrative – Mr Crab ...

Mr Crab crept into and out of my life for about a decade. When we
had our brief encounters either one of us, or both of us, would also
have a regular partner. We were thus both experts at being unfaithful. It became a sort of game that we played with each other. "I've
found a new boyfriend, darling, so let's go out and celebrate!" We
were both afraid of each other, although I suspect I was less afraid
of him than he was of me because I had really perfected the art of
how not to get involved.

We performed a sort of mirror-image, quadrille-type dance with
each other in our relationship. If he made a move, I followed. If I
made the first move, he dodged out of the way speedily and without fail. The sideways-creeping crab. His excuse for not becoming
involved was that he didn't want to fall in love with me. "That's
OK – that suits me fine" was my reply. But somehow that was not
what he wanted to hear. He said one thing but did another.

He once wrote me the most beautiful love-letter I have ever
received. But that was all it was – a love-letter. He just somehow
never got around to delivering the goods. It was a hopeless situation and eventually we drifted apart. After I had planned and
cooked supper on at least two occasions, only to pick up a message
on my answering machine to tell me that he could not make it that
night, I felt it was time to call a halt. I just never bothered to pick
up the phone again and he stopped writing love-letters.

Co-dependency relationships

> Co-dependency has also been defined many times in recovery literature
> and usually includes a list of core issues such as boundary deficiency,
> detachment, over-control, people-pleasing and caretaking.
> – *Ken Graber*

In a co-dependency relationship, each party attempts to satisfy his or her own emotive needs using the relationship as a vehicle for this endeavour. In this tacit arrangement, each party, therefore, agrees unconsciously to fulfil the needs of the other in some way. The violent aggressor, for example, may be prone to aggressive outbursts but the victim will somehow concede that he or she must accept the battering and can do nothing to assert his or her rights against the injustice. The jealous, overpossessive partner must somehow find someone who wants to or agrees to be possessed or dominated. The excessive carer must find someone who agrees to be nursed or is in need of constant attention. The predator must find his or her prey and the unfortunate victim must be sought out either by the assailant or by the rescuer. The co-dependency relationship, however, will, by its very nature, be doomed to failure. If the client has a pressing unconscious need to gain fulfilment from the actions of another, she will, in effect, be incapable of attaining such satisfaction. Because of the client's own inadequacy and lack of self-sufficiency she will, therefore, be deflecting attention away from herself.

> The second most common misconception about love is the idea that
> dependency is love. This is a misconception with which psychotherapists
> must deal on a daily basis. Its effect is seen most dramatically in an
> individual who makes an attempt or gesture or threat to commit suicide
> or who becomes incapacitatingly depressed in response to a rejection
> from or separation from a spouse or lover.
> – *Scott Peck*

Co-dependency can sometimes take the form of a victim–rescuer psychic partnership. When a victim–rescuer relationship has been set up between two people, it will, of course, be important for the client to remember that no-one wins in this tacit arrangement. The victim cannot move on for fear of not being able to stand on his or her own two feet and the rescuer will feel that he or she would be rendered worthless if he or she were not needed by the underdog. Both parties are, in fact, in a mutually-supportive trap in which neither party can move forward and each takes the line of least resistance. Neither party wishes to grow and to face the reality of existence without a supportive surrogate parent in the background. The victim wants to cling to mother's apron strings and the rescuer wants to impress father with his or her prowess. The victim wants to avoid making an effort while the rescuer wants to try too hard.

The much-neglected client may, of course, develop the classic victimised personality who will perpetually feel sorry for herself. The client may, thus, adopt attention-seeking ploys in order to attract the rescuer into her humdrum life. The client may crave someone to love and to protect her and, in doing so, she may adopt a fatalistic approach to future events and may avoid taking any responsibility for her own welfare. The practitioner should note also that this client may be tempted to blame her childhood upbringing for her intransigence and so she will then become stuck in her own rut of self-pity. It may then be the practitioner's role gently to assist the client to haul herself out of the ditch and, thus, to appreciate the way in which the past has affected her. The client can, of course, be encouraged to break the cycle if she wishes to attain psychological freedom.

> Dependency in a relationship, as you might have experienced in your own life, creates some very unattractive side effects – anger, jealousy, resentment, clinging, nagging – all very unpleasant to live with. These self-defeating qualities are the result of a deep-seated fear of losing that which we see as the basis of our entire identity.
> *– Susan Jeffers*

The client may also become overinvolved with her partner and, thus, psychological boundaries may become blurred or virtually nonexistent. The client, for example, may fear separation from her partner or seek constant and insatiable assurances of love. The client may seek to control her partner totally or to manipulate him or her emotionally in order to fill the emptiness-gap that she feels inside. The client may also become an effusive people-pleaser in the co-dependency relationship. The sycophant may go out of her way to accommodate, serve, oblige, appease or faithfully assist the human race in times of need – usually at great personal cost to herself (see Chapter 11, Volume 1 – "Defensive Strategies"). The subservient people-pleaser will often feel vulnerable because this was what she felt at the hands of her parental guardians. Probably, in childhood, the client gained the impression that she could never do enough in order to solicit the approval of her carers. The client may, thus, spend the rest of her existence trying to make a good impression in the eyes of society and being fearful lest she should fail. This client will, inevitably, court failure because of her lame efforts and her lowly self-estimation. The client may have been the victim of conditional love and may never have received really effective emotional nourishment. Frequently, the child will have suppressed her true opinions of others in the interests of her own survival. The people-pleaser, in other words, will be terrified of rejection and will debase her own self-respect in order to accede to the illusion of security (see Chapter 7 – "Fear and Anxiety Disorders"). The martyr, therefore, will put a low value on her own needs in the interests of being sycophantic to others who may habitually spurn her.

> It is a common myth or misconception that co-dependency is bad for the co-dependent but good for the subject. In fact it is bad for both. Co-dependents cannot become healthy because their energy and attention are directed away from self-recovery and away from taking responsibility for their own lives and issues.
> – *Ken Graber*

Often the co-dependency relationship will be borne out of a state of confusion to which the child has been exposed in childhood. The child may have received conflicting messages from parental figures. Perhaps one moment mother was warm and loving and the next she was cold and uncaring. The child, unceasingly devoted to her guardian, will, thus, become sensitive to these conflicting messages but not able to interpret them accurately. The child, in many respects, will become traumatised by these perceptions and will become fixated at an immature age (see Chapter 16, Volume 1 – "Personality Development"). Being unable to express her feelings, the child will undoubtedly suppress or repress her reactions to this form of childhood conflict. If the conflict occurs during the preverbal period of her life, the client may well develop psychosomatic symptoms as a result of not being able to express her emotive reactions (see Chapter 11 – "Psychosomatic Disorders"). Perhaps, the victim of such childhood conflict will then seek a partner who will be able to undertake the function of emotive expression on her behalf. Alternatively, the client could form an alliance with another who will be equally unable to express normal emotive reactions.

Either way, an unhealthy co-dependency relationship will have been born.

Tactful questioning can become the practitioner's vehicle for helping the client to understand her reluctance to break free from a co-dependency relationship. Perhaps the therapist could consider posing some of the following questions in order to elicit information about the client's ability to form successful relationships.

- Do you think you are looking for a knight in shining armour whom you believe will solve all your problems in life?
- Do you continually hope that someone will arrive in your life who will dissolve all your troubles?
- Do you long for a fairytale, romantic attachment such as you might read about in a novel or see in a film?
- Are you habitually a hero-worshipper?
- Do you thrive on having a pop-idol?
- Do you feel that you can get the degree of attention that you secretly crave only when you are ill or in some kind of difficulty?
- Do you sometimes have a headache in order to get attention?
- Do you sometimes have a headache in order to be left alone?
- Do you have a long list of lovers whom you have left behind?
- Do you have a catalogue of failed relationships?
- Do your partners tend to be the pathologically-faithless type?
- Do your partners end up by spurning your love for them?
- Do you always go out with groups of people rather than on your own?
- Are you overly concerned with what people think of you?
- Do you feel that keeping up appearances is very important?
- Could you not exist without your partner or a close friend?
- Are you sensitive to your partner's every whim?
- Do you often play the helpless female or the dominant male?
- Does your partner or your closest friend remind you of your mother or your father?
- Do people regularly let you down?
- How would you feel about living on a desert island?
- If you are the victim in a relationship, do you feel better when you have been rescued?
- If you are the persecutor in a relationship, do you achieve satisfaction from being known as someone who is aggressive and who is avoided in consequence?

311

- If you are the rescuer in a relationship, what does it feel like to be the hero of the piece?
- If you contrive to get attention from your partner, how do you feel when you get it and for how long does it last?

The following passage could be employed by the practitioner in order to educate the client about the way in which relationships are formed.

Playing the people-game ...

We frequently attract into our lives those people who will fulfil our beliefs about who we are. If you believe you are 100 per cent OK in your relationships and interactions with others, then all is well. Go out and have fun! If, on the other hand, you believe that you are less than somewhat – then your relationships may be affected by this erroneous belief about yourself!

The people-game is a way of life in which you get into a rut because you inwardly believe that you deserve it. You can, thus, become emotionally entwined with another – both of you constantly playing the same no-win game and getting nowhere. Negative beliefs about yourself will attract negative people into your life! The fear-feeler needs to be terrorised. The guilt-victim needs to reinforce her shame. The anger-merchant needs an outlet for her anger. The sadness-monger longs to be loved and goes out of her way to attain that love, but never quite makes it. These factors work on the principle that we need to have people in our lives who will fulfil and confirm the beliefs we have about ourselves. Remember, you are what you think you are.

Furthermore, because we may have been brought up in an environment of conflict or grief, our role-models may have exhibited fears and uncertainly in themselves and all this rubs off on to us. If your parents were continually at war with each other, then you may seek to copy that mode of existence – until you decide to change it. If you find that fear, guilt, anger or sadness is an emotion to which you are frequently susceptible, this negative emotion will influence you and interfere with your ability to form successful and rewarding relationships. Negative emotions can dominate your relationships, your personal interactions with people and your ability to communicate effectively.

We pick our friends, acquaintances, lovers and partners because of the unconscious processes that are at work beneath the surface of our mind in the vain hope that we can relieve all our troubles in this way. But we may soon discover that our negative emotions cannot be taken away by other people. Such feelings may, in fact, get worse because of the people-game factor. No partner can quell your fears or guilt however supportive he or she may be. You may run out of victims on whom to vent your anger or find that there is no human being alive on whom you can really relieve your frustrations. No-one else can really dry your tears or give you the understanding you crave. If you go out of your way to search for love you will, by definition, be unable to attain it. Love cannot be manufactured or conjured up or requested on demand. And maybe you are asking those people who are really unable to return it.

If the you-scratch-my-back-and-I'll-scratch-yours effect is in operation in your life, you will seek partners, friends and acquaintances who will give you what you request on a tit-for-tat basis. They will supply you with your needs in return for what you can do for them. The tennis-player looks for a partner. The orator looks for an audience. The boxer looks for a fight. Do you get the idea now?

There are many examples of emotional partnerships. Mr Universe, the fearless lion, will attract people into his life who will need protection from all the elements of life. Miss Quivering Jelly, on the other hand, will be looking for someone who is undeniably strong, powerful and invincible in order to compensate for her own inadequacies. Consider the Samson and Delilah story, for example. Samson had the strength of which Delilah was secretly jealous. She, therefore, sought to ingratiate herself with Samson until she was in a position ultimately to rob him of his only weapon – his strength. She thought that by doing so she would gain power herself. But did she achieve this aim? And if she did, what was the cost to her? If you feel unsafe or insecure, do you unconsciously seek a partner whose power and strength you can utilise to rescue you from your predicament? And, when you have achieved that, do you seek to destroy or diminish your partner's power? And how do you go about doing that? And does it then make you feel good? And what does it achieve? Can you identify with any of these personality characteristics? And note those emotions that are being most strongly evoked in you.

Are you the tyrant or the oppressor in your relationships? If you like to show your temper, you may seek out a victim on whom you can vent your ruthless anger. Do you feel like a mini-dictator or power-god seeking to put down others and keep them in their place? And do you have a plentiful supply of victims? Does it make you feel really good? Do you feel better as a result of being a dictator and the master of all you survey?

Are you the oppressed slave of duty, perhaps? If you know you are worthless rubbish, then you will need someone to kick you. If you feel timid or inferior, you may pursue people whom you know will spurn you or debase you. Or you may link up with someone whose one desire will be to make you feel small and afraid so that he or she can demonstrate how powerful he or she is. Are you willing to take on all the responsibility you can get and then break under the burden of it? Is the tyrant or the dictator on your emotional shopping list? Maybe you tell yourself that you need a hero to idolise or a guardian of your soul and, therefore, the flak you get is well worth the price? But who are you kidding?

313

Don José wanted to utterly possess Carmen. But Carmen wanted to be as free as a bird. The more Don José pressured Carmen with his jealousy, the more she fought to gain freedom. Carmen's lover and his jealousy finally destroyed her because she ultimately rejected him in her effort to gain her right to freedom. And Don José killed the one thing he wanted more than anything else in the world. The classic no-win situation. If you are the jealous type, you may attract faithless lovers or those who will reject you. And when you are finally abandoned or rejected, do you conclude that you knew all along that your worst fears would be realised?

The hypochondriac cannot take to her bed unless she has a nursery-maid. No-one ever complains unless there is someone to whom that person can complain. Even self-pity has to have an outlet. The grief-stricken person will desire to grieve over a loss. But she knows, of course, that there will always be some-one out there who will never fail to mop up the tears. How do you get your care and attention? By clever means? By trickery? Or by just being plain help-less? And what does it achieve for you?

The following client narrative explains the effect of having an over-possessive mother. This client's mother endeavoured to use her daughter as a means of emotional support and this, then, affected all her subsequent adult relationships.

Client narrative – my over-possessive mother …

As a means of compensating for her own childhood rejection, my mother had one aim in life and that was to insist that I loved her. My role in her life was to compensate for her own childhood rejec-tion and to bridge the gap left by a failed marriage. I was to be the shock-absorber for her own shattered existence. I miserably failed in this duty. I could not fulfil this role as a child and certainly not as an adult. My mother was extremely possessive and highly manipulative – traits well-documented as being characteristic of childhood rejection and instability. She used me in a manipulative fashion in order to fulfil her own deep-seated needs as opposed to making my requirements paramount.

When I returned from a holiday as a teenager, it would be inevitable that I would receive an ear-bashing for my neglect of my mother. On arrival home from a holiday I would be greeted with an angry scowl that denoted deep trouble for me. I would be accused of not buying her a nice enough holiday present. I would be accused of not tidying my room before I left. If I did tidy my room before leaving, she would then find another excuse for reprimanding me.

On one occasion I was given a lengthy tirade because the postcard that I sent her had only just arrived and, therefore, I must have sent it to her as an afterthought at the end of my holiday. "Out of sight, out of mind" was her vicious and wounding accusation. This was, in fact, true, of course, by this time. My holidays were my only relief from the continual torture of an overpossessive and manipulative mother.

Also deep down in my mother's mind was the fear that one day I would get married and that this would mean that I would have to leave her and, for her, the parting would be painful and intolerable. For my part, I could not wait to get away from the tyrant and so took the first opportunity I could to marry the first man that came my way.

All boyfriends were, without a fair hearing, deemed to be the enemy and, therefore, to be taken on in battle. Every boyfriend she met was assessed for his degree of suitability, eligibility and likelihood as a marriage partner for me. My mother doggedly insisted that every boyfriend I ever entertained was to be brought home so that the assessment could take place. The phrase "we must meet him" was often repeated in the household. This was what all respectable families did, she claimed. The embarrassment factor for me as a young person was horrendous to say very the least. Consequently, I could rendezvous with a boy but, if I wanted to see him regularly, I had to decide whether he would have the stamina and whether his regard for me was worth exposing him to the torture. In this way, the sweet-natured boys were automatically weeded out and the aggressive ones survived the fire and brimstone. Little did I know at the time that, in this climate, the chances of my making a successful marriage would have been severely limited, if not, utterly impaired.

In my late teens, I contracted a virulent dose of flu. This presented an ideal opportunity for my mother to confine me to barracks for over a week and to prevent me from going out with my husband-to-be. When I had virtually recovered from this illness, he was allowed to visit for a short while one evening but I was forbidden to leave the house due to my condition. He called in the hope that I would be able to go out but no pass-card was issued by my mother. I was heartbroken that I could not go out with him. I knew that my mother was using my condition as an excuse for preventing me from going out with my fiancé and, simultaneously, exerting her authority and establishing herself as the person in overall charge of our lives.

A close girlfriend (a dear friend of us both) lived across the road and my boyfriend decided that he would spend the rest of the evening with her as our meeting had been curtailed due to my indisposition. Once I was asleep my mother burst into my bedroom like a bullet from a gun and apprised me of the fact that my fiancé was with my best friend. I explained to deaf ears that I was aware of this situation, that it had my full consent and that there was no question of infidelity on his part. My mother may have reluctantly conceded this but her paramount preoccupation was, as always, that my reputation was being soiled and that the neighbours could observe this. I was ordered out of bed and then instructed to go across the road in my nightclothes and break up the party. My mother's concern for the neighbours was far greater, at this point, than her solicitude for my health. Somehow, in her eyes, I was not well enough to go out fully clothed for enjoyment but I was well enough to go out in my nightclothes for the sake of appearances.

Destructive relationships

> Did you ever ask yourself *why* people reach out to connect with one another? Of course, there are the apparent reasons – to find a mate, to gain new clients, to make new friends and so on. But if we looked a little deeper, we would see a complex web of human emotions that makes us reach out for other reasons. Some form the basis of healthy connection and others of unhealthy connection.
> – *Susan Jeffers*

If the client has had a seriously-dysfunctional family-upbringing, she may engage in a series of destructive relationships or abusive partnerships. The practitioner may observe, therefore, that such relationships will be part of the client's psychic mechanism whereby she will hold on to a dysfunctional past. As a result of undergoing therapy, therefore, the client may choose to terminate a current-day troublesome relationship that she has been maintaining for this purpose. In order to gain psychological freedom, the client should be empowered to accept love in an appropriate form and to relinquish any neurotic ties to a relationship that might be abusive or place her in physical danger. A relationship in which the client has been exploited, furthermore, may, of course, need to be redefined so that she will no longer be subjected to such mistreatment.

> One's limits are one's ego boundaries. When we extend our limits
> through love, we do so by reaching out, so to speak, toward the beloved,
> whose growth we wish to nurture.
> – *Scott Peck*

The practitioner may wish to examine the way in which the client has engaged in a destructive relationship with another by judicious questioning. Often this form of enquiry will reveal that the client has accepted abuse or ill-treatment as an inevitable factor within a relationship. Some examples of questions that could be put to the client in this respect are given below.

- Do you continually seek reassurance from your partner of his or her love for you?
- Do you feel that no-one in your life really understands you?
- Do you feel that you are desperately searching for someone to really love you?
- Do you believe that you constantly put more effort into your relationships than your partner does?
- Do you feel desperately lonely most of the time?
- Do you believe that there is simply not enough love in the world?
- Do you feel convinced that you are unlovable?
- Do you often feel rejected or abandoned by your partner?
- Do you find difficulty in fitting into groups of people?
- Do you frequently find a substitute mother-figure or father-figure coming into your life?
- Do you sometimes feel jealous of others who appear to live happy lives?
- Do you feel constantly at the mercy of your own emotions in terms of your relationships with others?
- Do you secretly believe that you should be punished by your partner?
- Do you feel that your partner cannot help being violent or abusive towards you?

The following passage may be used by the practitioner in order to explain to the client the role of love in her life and the way in which relationships should be formed. It may also introduce the client to the idea that an abusive relationship should not be tolerated.

Why do we need love?

As love is the most basic requirement for our survival, we crave it from the moment of birth and for the rest of our lives. In order to survive childhood and to gain the unconditional love that is our birthright, we contrive ways of pleasing our primary carers and of securing a continued reassurance of love and affection. If that love is not abundantly forthcoming, we sometimes attempt to acquire it in perhaps unacceptable ways or even hideous forms. Searching for love drives us to steal from others, to become money-grabbing, to be promiscuous and to seek comfort in unhealthy or self-destructive ways.

Sometimes we spend our lives desperately seeking to please others in a hopeless attempt to recapture that love that was elusive in our childhood. Sometimes this desperation drives us to become victims of injustice or abuse by accepting the pretence of love as a substitute for the real thing. Sometimes this desperation sets us on a mission to seek out numerous bedfellows, each of whom disappoints us in turn. Often these very practices lead us to the erroneous conclusion that we are unlovable and the pain of this realisation can be intolerable.

In the following case-study example, the client sought therapy in order to cope with an abusive relationship in which she was severely beaten.

Case-study example – a violent relationship

This client came into therapy because of feelings of resentment, frustration and anger at her partner's conduct and violent behaviour towards her.

During therapy, the client recollected a partial memory of her father entering her bedroom lying on top of her and having penetrative sex. It transpired that the client's father had had a history of mental disorder and was taking psychiatric treatment and medication that resulted in his being constantly disoriented, incoherent and incapable of making any rational decisions. The client, however, felt responsible for this event because she believed that she could have prevented it from happening but, at the same time, she felt sorry for her father. The client, in time, however, came to realise that, because she carried the guilt for this form of incestuous abuse, she had attracted into her life a series of abusive partners.

The client narrative given below gives insight into the way in which a female client allowed herself to form numerous relationships in which she was the recipient of violent abuse.

Client narrative – the misery in my life …

Most relationships I have had have caused me a lot of pain and misery. This is because I attracted into my life men who have also had abusive childhoods. These men were reliving their own childhood traumas and re-enacting the patterns given to them by their parents. My relationships have always been with men who were suffering themselves from confusion, feelings of worthlessness and aggression. I was also a prisoner of hope, in many cases, in that I felt that I alone could rectify any malfunctions in my relationships and could offer comfort to the men with whom I was involved by giving of myself, my body and my unstinting affection.

I often felt as if I were playing Russian roulette with my own emotions. I took risks that engendered severe feelings of guilt and that were a sort of self-inflicted cruelty, all based on the mistaken premise that I could cope with it! I prostrated myself for men while all the time knowing that I was powerlessly indulging in the sadistic pleasure of torturing myself. These rituals were instinctively carried out because I was somehow engaged in an endless search for the right man. The right man being the one who would take me away from myself, relieve me of my stressful condition and restore order to my existence. Needless to say, no man ever fulfilled that role. Mr Right was always really Mr Wrong in disguise. Mr Right was destined not to exist, of course.

The sad fact, however, remains that I have, for the major part of my life, been unable to sustain a normal, healthy, emotional relationship with any member of the opposite sex. I have been beaten, thrown down the stairs, exploited financially, emotionally blackmailed and neglected. I am, of course, struck by the similarity between these relationships and my childhood when I was physically misused by my parents.

Sexual Dysfunction

> Fears, attractions or avoidances are a powerful warning signal if they are
> about objects or situations that are logically or frequently associated with
> child sexual abuse. Sex is one such situation, and many survivors have
> problems with their sex lives as a result of this "reminder factor". Some
> avoid sex, others become sexually compulsive or overly fascinated with
> it, and still others feel lots of distress during sex as feelings, flashbacks,
> or physical reactions intrude on their sexual pleasure.
> – *Renee Fredrickson*

The analytical hypnotherapist can assist the client to examine the
source of her unconscious disharmony with particular reference to
dysfunctional relationships and relationship-dependencies that
may result in sexual problems. Sexual dysfunction may affect the
client at the deepest psychological levels because sexual activity is
an instinctive human quality that underpins the whole of
mankind's existence. Impotence, frigidity, premature ejaculation or
orgasm, anorgasmia and fear of sexual relations are some of the
most common ways in which the client may display an inability to
undertake healthy sexual activity. Sexual dysfunction can also
include total avoidance of sexual encounters or an overly excessive
interest in the subject. Sexual dysfunction may also stem from the
client's unconsciously-expressed desire to be freed from an
unhappy sexual union. This may be the body's way of protesting
even though the client may not feel consciously able to release herself from the intimate tie. Severe sexual dysfunction that occurs
because of a deeply-rooted psychological disorder may well affect
the victim of childhood sexual abuse (see Chapter 15 – "The Effects
of Childhood Abuse"). In such cases, the client's lack of sexual ability or expression will not stem merely from a loveless relationship
but from an underlying disorder that will have traumatised her
sexuality. It will be virtually certain that, if a child has endured
some form of early sexual encounter, the client will, in adult life,
suffer, in some way, from a sexual malfunction or a sexual dysfunction.

> One of the areas of long-term effect receiving the most attention in the
> empirical literature concerns the impact of early sexual abuse on later
> sexual functioning. Almost all clinically based studies show later sexual
> problems among child sexual abuse victims, particularly among the
> victims of incest.
> – *David Finkelhor & Angela Browne*

Sexual performance

> Feelings are a source of great confusion to the male incest survivor. He is
> afraid to have them because they would lead to loss of control or reveal
> his weakness and he is afraid to not have them because that would be
> evidence that he is a numb, barren, incomplete person.
> – *Mike Lew*

Sexual performance can often be bound up in the client's self-concept in that she may become overly sensitive to what is expected of her in other people's eyes. Often the client who cannot successfully engage in sexual activity with another may report, however, that she is able to masturbate successfully. The practitioner should remember, of course, that the client's sexual apparatus will be operated by an extremely delicate mechanism that, when the slightest hitch occurs, can be adversely affected at the most profound unconscious levels. Poor sexual performance can mean that the client will have an impaired sexual arousal mechanism, unresponsiveness, erectile dysfunction and orgasmic dysfunction, all of which are regular, anxiety-based complaints encountered in the hypnoanalyst's consulting room. If the client has been a victim of childhood sexual abuse, for example, she may lack confidence in her ability to be a successful sexual partner. Often this condition will stem from the time when the child was asked to comply with the adult's wishes but gained little or no true appreciation of what was actually being expected of her at that time. Frequently, the victim of childhood sexual abuse will consider that sex is an obligation or is a privilege that others have the right to demand. This will originate from the time when the client, as a child, had no rights and no choice in the matter but was merely required to deliver the goods at the will of the child-molester. For this reason, the abused child may also have become a rape-victim in adulthood because of this all-pervasive feeling of powerlessness.

For the client with a fear of sex, it may well be that she is able to participate but that her involvement will be in a passive way and without any sense of enjoyment. A fear of sex may result in an avoidance of sexual encounters in adult life. The client may totally abstain from having any sexual relationships or may do so but totally fear the consequences. The male client may be rendered impotent, may suffer from erectile dysfunction or premature ejaculation. The female client may detach herself from any sexual encounter to such an extent that she derives little or no enjoyment from the encounter or she may find the experience terrifying and painful. Any victim of rape in adulthood may also feel inclined to abstain from further sexual practice following the attack. The client who has been traumatised by a rape-attacker may also find that an existing intimate relationship will degenerate as a direct result of her experiences (see Chapter 13 – "Post-traumatic Stress Disorder"). The victim of childhood sexual molestation, moreover, may well find herself unable to indulge in normal sexual relationships because of her intense fear of intimacy in a sexual context.

Sexual orientation

> When children are sexually abused, their natural sexual capacity is stolen. You were introduced to sex on an adult's timetable, according to an adult's needs. You never had a chance to explore naturally, to experience your own desires from the inside. Sexual arousal became linked to feelings of shame, disgust, pain and humiliation. And desire (the abuser's desire) was dangerous, an out-of-control force used to hurt you.
> – *Ellen Bass & Laura Davis*

The client may seek therapy because of a problem with sexual orientation or sexual identity. Perhaps the homosexual or the bisexual client cannot come to terms with her sexuality. The client may also question her sexual identity in terms of whether she is, in fact, homosexual, bisexual or heterosexual. When the client feels an inclination towards homosexuality, there may, of course, be an additional reluctance on her part to accept any unconscious messages. Such evidence, for instance, may not be greeted with acclaim by the client because of the taboos surrounding homosexuality. The client may, for example, fear the disapproval of her family, friends, colleagues or, even, an existing heterosexual partner. Such a discovery may also lead to a relationship-breakdown with a homosexual partner or potential partner because the client may feel that she cannot yet entertain such a union. Frequently, the victim of childhood sexual molestation will question her sexual identity and this misgiving may be a strong cause for concern. Similarly, an abhorrence of sexually-deviant practices or a tendency towards homophobia will not be unusual for a victim of sexual abuse who may have suffered at the hands of a homosexual abuser.

Sexual deviation

If the negative and erroneous messages about caring, affection and sex
are not powerfully contradicted, the incestuously abused child carries
them into adolescence and adulthood. Studies of sexually promiscuous
teenagers, prostitutes and sexually compulsive adults have turned up
large number of individuals who report childhood incest. Many
survivors describe themselves as not liking to be touched while, at the
same time, engaging in compulsive sexual activity.
– Mike Lew

Sexual deviation and promiscuity will often be rife among sexual-
abuse sufferers. In many respects such practices are often an
attempt to overcome the client's underlying fears and an endeavour to discharge simmering anger. The client's unhealthy sexual
interest may take the form of fetishes, transvestism, sadomasochism, exhibitionism, voyeurism, paedophilia and sexual
molestation. The therapist may wish to focus on resolving immature cathectic fixations if the client's deviation can be considered to
be attributable to erroneous conditioning (see Chapter 1, Volume 1
– "Psychoanalysis"). It has been well documented, of course, that
promiscuity and prostitution are indicators of a sexually-abusive
childhood trauma, in which case sex can become a compulsive
need for the client. When the client reports sexual deviance, however, the practitioner should note any accompanying emotive
responses to such revelations. Is the client riddled with guilt at
such a confession or does she merely state the facts with a degree
of unemotional equanimity? From the client's responses, the practitioner will be able to appreciate the level of underlying guilt and
fear that may need to be addressed.

When dealing with cases of sexual deviance, the client may also
report that in childhood she became sexually active at an inappropriate age. The client may, therefore, have exhibited behaviours
that denoted knowledge of adult sexual practices by unashamedly
masturbating, indulging in voyeurism, exhibiting excessive sexual
curiosity or by exposing her genitals. In this sense, the client will
have been acting out her unconscious sexual trauma and this will,
in itself, have been a cry for help – especially if the child-victim was
unaware of the social unacceptability of her behaviour (see
Chapter 11, Volume 1 – "Defensive Strategies"). The child who
exhibits this form of behaviour will usually have been subjected to

some form of sexual abuse. Additional examples of this type of behaviour may be those in which the child spontaneously regressed to a former age via activities such as bedwetting, thumb-sucking and employing baby-talk. In adulthood, the client may also have indulged in a range of sexual activities that could be described as being sexually-deviant such as group-sex or ritualistic sexual practices.

> Several studies of special populations do suggest a connection between child sexual abuse and later prostitution. James and Meyerding interviewed 136 prostitutes and found that 55% had been sexually abused as children by someone 10 or more years older prior to their first intercourse.
> – *David Finkelhor & Angela Browne*

In the case-study example given below, the client reported a life of prostitution that led to much unhappiness.

Case-study example – sexual deviation
This male client reported that he had indulged in prostitution and transvestism for most of his life. The client sought therapy, therefore, in order to resolve issues of sexual identity.

The client was questioned about his current life and his childhood in order to assist him to compare the two scenarios. The client spoke openly of the anguish that he had suffered in terms of being maltreated and ill-used by unseemly people. The client also discussed the way in which he had been compelled to indulge in cross-dressing and yet had felt intensely guilty about such activities. Investigative therapy also focused on the guilt feelings that the client had about exploiting others. These feelings of guilt led the client to explore some childhood issues that had engendered feelings of shame and self-blame. The client revisited his childhood, in which he had been incestuously abused and been used as a prostitute in order to enable his uncle to earn money. The realisation came when the client could look, in retrospect, at his abusive uncle as the instigator of his distress and his career as a prostitute. The client finally came to terms with his confusion, anger, resentment and guilt over his misdeeds that he had been forced into in childhood and had reluctantly continued because he had known no better.

Exploring the Client's Dysfunctional Relationships

> Struck by the way in which people's entire lives seem to play out the
> mess from their childhood, Freud coined the term "repetition
> compulsion" to describe the behaviours, relationships, emotions, and
> dreams that seemed to be replays of early trauma. Central to Freud's
> concept of repetition compulsion was his observation that people
> continue to put themselves in situations strangely reminiscent of an
> original trauma in order to learn new solutions.
> – *Peter Levine*

The practitioner may be able to make some general enquiries, in many cases, in order to establish whether the client possesses a tendency to avoid social interaction and not make the best use of her options in life. Some typical questions of this nature are given below for the practitioner as a guide to this form of therapeutic enquiry with the client. More searching questions can then be posed by the practitioner if he considers that the client has some more pressing issues that may concern destructive relationships or sexual dysfunction.

- Do you tend to avoid crowds and social gatherings?
- Do you attempt to withdraw from relationships with work colleagues?
- Would you dearly like to apply for promotion but feel that you could not possibly endure the scrutiny of an interview?
- Do you steer clear of total commitment or involvement with others generally?
- Do you feel that all your relationships are superficial?
- Do you tend to want to avoid responsibility?
- Would you really like to opt out of the rat-race completely?

The following case-study example illustrates the way in which a client was encouraged to divest himself of a feeling of imprisonment within his relationship with his partner.

Case-study example – fear of violent outbursts
This male client sought therapy because of his history of violence towards a number of his intimate partners. The client had been encouraged to seek therapy by his current partner.

The client was questioned initially about the fact that his partner had been instrumental in urging him to seek therapy. The client confessed that he had a history of violence towards women but now felt able to address this issue because of the strength of feeling he had towards his new partner. The client feared very much that his temper would get the better of him and that he would one day strike his new partner. The client, therefore, greatly feared that the woman whom he loved more than anything else in the world would leave him and, thus, he was ready to face the prospect of therapeutic investigation.

The client spoke at length about his relationship with his mother, who had physically abused him in childhood and had caused him much mental torment throughout his life. The client's mother had recently died and, therefore, he felt guilty about expressing adverse feelings towards her. The client, however, soon came to realise that his feelings of guilt were, in fact, amplified by his mother's death. In working through these issues, the client was able to realise the impact of his mother's treatment of him. The client confessed that in losing his temper with previous partners he was, in fact, unconsciously seeking revenge on his mother.

The client was invited to express his opinion of his mother as if she were still alive and sitting in the consulting room. This led the client to a free expression of his feelings towards his mother. The client also realised that his previous partners had tended to blame him and to indulge in the same mental torment that his mother had taken such delight in perpetrating. The client was, however, then able to assuage the guilt that had been attached to his aggressive tendencies by acknowledging the fact that his former wife had used his violence as a means of provoking guilt and using the ongoing situation as a vehicle for tormenting him. The client was also invited to question whether he was merely defending himself from an abusive partner during his marriage as a means of resolving his feelings of self-blame.

Client Profiling

The analytical-hypnotherapy practitioner may wish to ponder the following points when formulating a profile for the client.

- What is the client's attitude to the social world?
- Did the client's parents or primary carers ever devalue her self-esteem or self-worth?
- Does the client have an abnormally-low opinion of herself?
- Does the client have a history of unsuccessful or destructive relationships?
- Has the client been seriously misused or exploited by others?
- Has the client been subjected to any form of domestic violence or abuse?
- Has the client indulged in any form of domestic violence or abuse?
- Does the client have a tendency to cling to others?
- Does the client toe the line when it comes to conforming to petty rules that may dictate her behaviour in society?
- Does the client avoid being an individualist?
- Is the client a victim of emotional blackmail?
- Is the client unable to act without the approval of others?
- Does the client appear to be controlled in any way by an intimate partner?
- Is the client in some way unhealthily attached to another?
- Is the client easily pushed around by others?
- In what ways might the client's sexual performance or sexual practice seem to be unsatisfactory?
- Has the client ever confessed to any form of deviant sexual practice?

Chapter 13

Post-Traumatic Stress Disorder

Our greatest glory is not in never falling, but in rising every
time we fall.

– Confucius

What is Post-Traumatic Stress Disorder?

Combat veterans, sexual assault survivors, and other victims of trauma
are vulnerable to a condition called Post-traumatic Stress Disorder
(PTSD). People with PTSD suffer from a range of symptoms that interfere
with their capacities to enjoy normal life. People who suffered suicidal
conditions, particularly conditions that were chronic recurrent, or
included one or more attempts, may also be victims of PTSD. According
to its definition, PTSD may result when a person suffers an event or
situation that is outside the range of normal experience, exceeds the
individual's perceived ability to meets its demands, and poses a serious
threat to loss of life.
– David Conroy

Post-traumatic stress disorder (PTSD) is a group of symptoms
that the client will exhibit following exposure to or participation
in an experience that has resulted in a physiological and psychological traumatic response. A traumatic experience is one that
will have been a profound departure from the client's everyday
life-experience and one that will overstretch his capacity to meet
its demands. Usually such an experience will be life-threatening
or will be perceived as life-threatening by the client. Certainly
the trauma-victim will have been faced with terrifying danger
while undergoing the traumatic experience. The traumatic stressor may be encountered by the client in a number of ways. The
client may have been directly involved in actual or threatened

personal danger, for example, or he may have witnessed or learned about the traumatic suffering of another. Being personally attacked or being a witness to a robbery, therefore, could be sufficient to bring on symptoms of PTSD in the client. When the client has been exposed to a traumatic stressor, his response will then be one of fear, helplessness and horror. The result of this trauma-induced response will usually be, on the one hand, that the client will persistently relive his experiences while, on the other hand, he may attempt to numb his response to it.

PTSD has only relatively recently been defined by the *Diagnostic and Statistical Manual of Mental Disorders* (DSM) as an anxiety disorder according to a collective five-axis diagnostic criterion. According to this definition, the client who has been exposed to a traumatic experience will develop persistent and pervasive symptoms of reliving the trauma, avoidant behaviour and autonomic hyperarousal that are characteristic of PTSD. There has been some debate, however, about whether PTSD should be more appropriately classified as a dissociative disorder (see Chapter 11, Volume 1 – "Defensive Strategies"). In addition, the *International Statistical Classification of Diseases and Related Health Problems* (ISD) defines PTSD as a delayed or protracted response to a stressful event or a situation of an exceptionally threatening or catastrophic nature that is likely to cause the client to experience pervasive distress and manifest an enduring personality change. The practitioner, of course, should bear in mind that the official definitions of PTSD can be somewhat limiting with regard to certain clients and not necessarily embrace factors such as traumatic somatisation and other conditions in which shock can manifest within the human system. For this reason, the concept of a post-trauma syndrome or a traumatic stress-reaction could more realistically be regarded by the practitioner as having a wider implication than that which has been officially documented for the purposes of trauma-diagnosis in the official arena.

> Studies that have specifically assessed subjects for PTSD symptoms have varied widely in both their methods and their disorder prevalence rates. Estimates of the prevalence of PTSD in survivors of CSA [Childhood Sexual Abuse] range from 21% to 100%.
> – *Julie Lipovsky*

When Can PTSD Develop?

Studies assessing PTSD in children who have been recently sexually abused show positive diagnostic rates of approximately 50%. In a recent study of a clinical sample of adult survivors of childhood sexual assault, a PTSD rate of 65% was obtained.
– David Foy

PTSD syndrome can develop when the client experiences an overwhelming traumatic stressor. The most commonly cited traumatic stressors are serious accident, manmade disasters, natural disasters, sexual molestation, criminal assault, physical violence, torture, military combat, kidnap and imprisonment. The PTSD client, therefore, will have personally experienced, witnessed, heard about, read about or otherwise been confronted with a traumatic experience or a catastrophic event. The traumatic incident would have involved actual or threatened death, serious injury or threat to the client's physical integrity or to that of others. The client's response will have been one of intense fear, helplessness, horror, shock and confusion, although children, whose comprehension of events will have been distorted, may display disorganised or agitated behaviour.

Recent clinical experience and supporting research has meant that many clinicians are of the opinion that PTSD is a condition from which the victim of childhood abuse will frequently suffer (see Chapter 15 – "The Effects of Childhood Abuse"). The child will naturally be shell-shocked by the catastrophe and this will lead him to experience serious aftereffects. If the client has been subjected to sexual assault, rape, incestuous abuse and physical abuse, therefore, these incidents will be high contenders for the emergence of PTSD symptoms (see Chapter 14 – "The Nature of Childhood Abuse"). The incest-survivor and the childhood sexual-abuse victim, in particular, may suffer most noticeably from symptoms consistent with the PTSD syndrome. Such symptoms may include nightmares, sleep disturbance, generalised anxiety, depression and dissociative disorders (See Chapter 9 – "Sorrow and Grief Disorders"). Researchers have found that prolonged and repeated traumatic experiences in childhood will increase the risk for the client of developing PTSD symptoms. Severe neglect, beating, burning, physical restraint or starvation of the child, for example, will constitute cases of extreme traumatic stress from which PTSD symptoms will almost certainly develop. It is also felt that because personal human cruelty has a far more devastating effect on the human organism than, say, natural disaster or accident, it will be likely that this form of maltreatment will, undoubtedly, be subjectively registered as traumatic by virtually any child.

> PTSD disrupts the functioning of those afflicted by it, interfering with their abilities to meet daily needs and perform the most basic tasks. In PTSD a traumatic event is not remembered and relegated to one's past in the same way as other life events. Trauma continues to intrude with visual, auditory, and/or other somatic reality on the lives of its victims. Again and again they relive the life-threatening experiences they have suffered, reacting in mind and body as though such events were still occurring.
> – *Babette Rothschild*

When trauma strikes, the client may progress through a series of stages as the full realisation of the horror rains down upon the human organism (see Figure 3 – "Traumatic reactions of the human organism"). The trauma-victim may transgress stages of coping with the threat, opposing the stressor and, finally, becoming totally overwhelmed.

The coping state

First, the client's unconscious mind may feel threatened by the traumatic stressor but will be able to cope with the situation of which he has become aware. The client, in this case, may be alert, aroused and wary but will not be overwhelmed by the situation or the circumstances. This will be the level of trauma from which the average person could recover equilibrium in normal circumstances with a degree of support.

The oppositional state

In the oppositional state, the client can remain in relationship to the traumatic stressor yet detached and apart from it. The client may, however, teeter on the brink of activating an overwhelm-state but will remain in juxtaposition to the oncoming threat. At this stage, the human organism may feel unsure whether to give up the ghost and to enter the state of emergency.

Figure 3 – Traumatic reactions of the human organism

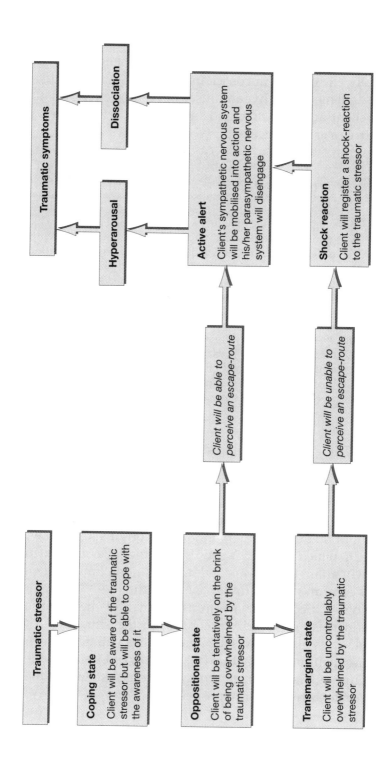

The transmarginal state

In the transmarginal state, the client's barriers will fall irrevocably. Finally, the client's unconscious mind will pull the ultimate level. This will mean that hyperarousal and dissociation will manifest for the client automatically and instinctively without any conscious control over the process.

PTSD Syndrome

> The symptom profile of adults who were abused as children includes post-traumatic and dissociative disorders combined with depression, anxiety syndromes, and addictions. These symptoms include (1) recurrent depression; (2) anxiety, panic, and phobias; (3) anger and rage; (4) low self-esteem, and feeling damaged and/or worthless; (5) shame; (6) somatic pain syndromes; (7) self-destructive thoughts and/or behaviour; (8) substance abuse; (9) eating disorders: bulimia, anorexia, and compulsive over-eating; (10) relationship and intimacy difficulties; (11) sexual dysfunction, including addictions and avoidance; (12) time loss, memory gaps, and a sense of unreality; (13) flashbacks, intrusive thoughts and images of trauma; (14) hyper-vigilance; (15) sleep disturbance: nightmares, insomnia, and sleepwalking; and (16) alternative states of consciousness or personalities.
> – *Joan Turkus*

The PTSD syndrome will result when a terrifying experience punctures the client's psychological existence and functioning so devastatingly that the aftermath will lead to profound impairment of the ways in which he expresses personal emotions and deals with his normal environment – rendering recovery virtually impossible without therapeutic intervention. The original trauma will evoke a state in which the client's senses are either overstimulated whereby he will attain the *hyperarousal state* or understimulated whereby he will enter the *dissociative state* (see Figure 4 – "Traumatic symptomology"). Both the hyperarousal state and the dissociative state can increase in severity according to the situation in which the client finds himself. As such, these states will have an endless and ever-expansive quality that can be observed in the client on a continuum moving between the hyperarousal state and the dissociative state as two polar opposites.

Figure 4 – Traumatic symptomology

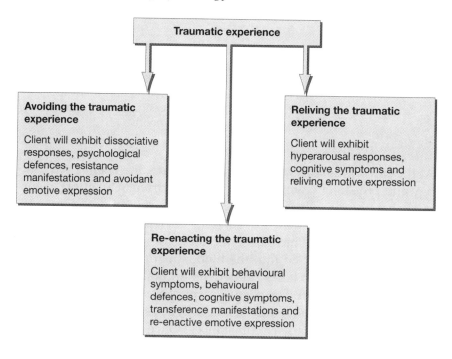

Classic symptom patterns in PTSD consist of intrusive thoughts about the traumatic experience(s) and psychological efforts to avoid reminders or cues related to the trauma.
– *David Foy*

The hyperarousal state

Autonomic arousal upon presentation of trauma-related cues is consistently found among approximately two-thirds of PTSD-positive combat. Although other trauma populations have not yet been assessed for physiological reactivity in laboratory analogue situations, hypervigilance, exaggerated startle responses, and panic symptoms are frequently reported by these survivors.
– *David Foy*

With the hyperarousal state, the client will experience the defensive alarm-reaction in response to the acute terror that he has experienced. This reaction will be a form of the fight-or-flight stress-response in which the client will be rendered in an extreme state of readiness either to fight off the impending danger or to flee from it.

> After a traumatic experience, the human system of self-preservation
> seems to go onto permanent alert, as if the danger might return at any
> moment. Physiological arousal continues unabated. In this state of
> hyperarousal, which is the first cardinal symptom of post-traumatic
> stress disorder, the traumatised person startles easily, reacts irritably to
> small provocations, and sleeps poorly.
> – *Judith Lewis Herman*

At the time of the original traumatic reaction, the client's psychology and physiology will be flung into overdrive in an effort to survive the trauma. The client's sympathetic nervous system will, thus, have been stimulated to its fullest extent. All the organism's sensory systems will have been alerted, stress-response hormones will have been secreted into the bloodstream and certain somatic systems may either have been overstimulated or, alternatively, have been shut down. The client's respiratory system, for instance, may be overstimulated while his digestive system may be forced to shut down in traumatic circumstances. Once the danger has been averted, however, the client's parasympathetic nervous system may not be able to return to the homeostatic state because of the profound nature of the traumatic shock. The client may then be liable to reactivate the alarm-response by any reminder of the original trauma (see Chapter 7 – "Fear and Anxiety Disorders"). The alarm-response may, for example, be triggered in the client by a repeat or a continuation of the initial traumatic experience. After a secondary alarm-response has been triggered, the client will then be likely to suffer from the sensitised-hyperarousal response. The client will, therefore, not only suffer as a result of the original trauma but also may react to a secondary trigger-mechanism. The traumatic response, in this way, will be kept constant and will continually be subject to reactivation in the client.

> Long after the danger is past, traumatised people relive the event as
> though it were continually recurring in the present. They cannot resume
> the normal course of their lives, for the trauma repeatedly interrupts. It is
> as if time stops at the moment of trauma. The traumatic moment
> becomes encoded in an abnormal form of memory, which breaks
> spontaneously into consciousness, both as flashbacks during waking
> states and as traumatic nightmares during sleep.
> – *Judith Lewis Herman*

The dissociative state

Avoidance of trauma-related cues may come to characterise the lifestyles
of survivors who are unable to overcome their immediate trauma crisis
reactions. Feared stimuli eliciting escape or avoidance responses may not
be limited to the physical environment. Strong negative emotions, such
as rage, grief, and intense anxiety or panic, may elicit patterns of
responding very similar to the individual's original trauma reactions (re-
enactment); they may thereby establish escape or avoidant behaviours in
a much wider range of situations.
– *David Foy*

With the dissociative state, the client will experience the freeze-
response or the surrender-response. This reaction will be a form of
the freeze stress-response in which the client will be rendered in an
extreme state of immobilisation (or *tonic immobility*) in an effort to
withdraw from the danger. The human organism will, thus, be
retracting or disengaging as a means of attempting to avoid or to
avert the impending danger. The client, thus, will abandon the task
of saving himself, will not ask for help and will simply hope that
by being passive he can avert the danger by not attracting attention
to himself. Frequently, such a response will immobilise the client
and will result in his surrender or compliance in the belief that he
will come to less harm by this means. The freeze-response, moreover, can often result in a state of confusion for the trauma-victim.
Once the original trauma has abated, the client's parasympathetic
nervous system may not then be able to take hold of the reigns
because of the unstable halting reaction that has taken place within
the human system. The human organism will then adopt a dissociative stance by disengaging from the stimuli of the external
world – particularly when any subsequent form of danger has
been encountered (see Chapter 9 – "Sorrow and Grief Disorders").
This dissociative mechanism will, thus, become a sort of survival-
strategy that the client will adopt as a means of coping with any
stresses and strains in life. After a secondary surrender-response
has been triggered, the client will, subsequently, be likely to learn
ways of dissociating from his emotions, withdrawing his reactions
and generally avoiding people and situations when he considers
that he might be put under pressure.

> When a person is completely powerless, and any form of resistance is
> futile, she may go into a state of surrender. The system of self-defence
> shuts down entirely. The helpless person escapes from her situation not
> by action in the real world but rather by altering her state of
> consciousness.
> – *Judith Lewis Herman*

In the following example, the client describes his feelings of deso-
lation as a result of having been ill-treated in childhood. The client
was in trance while relating this narrative and was partially
regressed. This account, in fact, shows clearly the way in which a
traumatised client can exhibit symptoms of both hyperactivity and
dissociation virtually cheek by jowl.

Client narrative – my stunted growth …
I am looking out of the bedroom window upon the world. The
world consists of the wall of the house on one side and a fence
dividing the neighbouring property on the other. In front of me is
a shelter that protects the back of the house and obscures the back
garden from my view. This is my childhood view of the world.
Barriers on either side and an obscured, distorted view of the
world.

The full horror of my abusive childhood is beginning to dawn on
me. I had expected that living was a happy experience but I am
beginning to doubt this doctrine. Is this really what the world is
about? I am so unhappy. I hadn't realised that this is what life was
meant to be like. The confusion is overwhelming. Have I really got
to endure this? Is this ethically right? Is this the measuring rod I
have in future to use? How could this be? To whom can I turn to
change things? No-one. I am about six years old right now. I am the
product of a sexually and emotionally abusive existence. This
episode has given me a view of life that will colour my thoughts
and tincture my beliefs for the next four decades.

Life stopped for me emotionally because of my childhood crises. I
spent the whole of my childhood in a state of trauma and this took
its toll on my schooling. There was hell to pay, of course, if I got a
bad report from school. I invariably received the "could do better"
phrase on all school reports and once was cited as "the laziest pupil
in the class". The dressing down I received from my father went on
for days but no-one questioned why I behaved in such a way. It

was superficially accepted that laziness was an inherent part of my nature. The result of coping with my childhood traumas was absorbing so much energy that something had to go and I much regret that it was my education.

When I wasn't being lazy, I was hyperactive. No-one questioned that, either. No parent, no teacher, no nobody. What an indictment of our education system to say the very least. The only thing that got me through school examinations was my innate intelligence and the threat of an ear-bashing from my father. No doubt he considered that he was doing me a favour.

My early adulthood, when I was desperately seeking to make my way in the world, was a whirlpool of torture. If I went to an interview for a job, the experience was nightmarish. I visibly shook on several occasions when asked to do, say, a written test at a job interview. The accompanying embarrassment factor was even more unbearable. The only jobs I ever got were the ones where I did not have to submit to a test. I also became an overachiever when I ran my own business and more than once I made myself ill from overwork in order to get recognition from others or to secure a new contract. I learned how to do everything in a hurry, often at breakneck speed. This feverish activity also helped me to try to forget the anguish inside. I have lived by the seat of my pants for years. What am I going to do now?

PTSD Symptoms

Classic symptom patterns in PTSD consist of intrusive thoughts about the traumatic experience(s) and psychological efforts to avoid reminders or cues related to the trauma.
– *David Foy*

PTSD symptoms will develop in the client when his subjective perception of the impact of the traumatic stressor has been exceptionally forceful because the event will have been beyond the normal range of human experience. Such an experience, therefore, will engender a powerful response of objective, realistically-founded anxiety that will debilitate the client's ability to cope with normal life. PTSD, therefore, differs from commonplace stress in that, while certain predisposing factors are capable of lowering the client's resilience-threshold or aggravating the condition, in the main, such factors will be insufficient to justify the materialisation of his symptoms. PTSD syndrome will, therefore, be unique in that it is the only stress-inducing disorder in which the client's symptoms can be exclusively attributed to the occurrence of a known event. The syndrome, therefore, does not manifest from within the client because of an intrinsic personality defect or a debased self-esteem. Even the most resilient client, that is, will succumb to the effects of trauma in appropriate circumstances. The client's symptoms, furthermore, will persist if he does not receive treatment long after the originating stressor has been removed. Magnitude of exposure, previous experience of trauma and lack of social support for the client are cited as the most significant predictors of the development for PTSD symptomology.

Frequently, the manifestation of PTSD symptoms will touch all areas of the client's functioning. The PTSD sufferer will experience symptoms that can cause significant distress and impairment in interpersonal, social and vocational functioning. Symptoms, moreover, can result when the client's trauma has been unconsciously buried in his mind because of the powerful emotive content associated with the traumatic experience (see Chapter 11, Volume 1 – "Defensive Strategies"). The client may then adopt uncharacteristic behaviours when a generalised degree of fear has been embedded within his psyche. Similarly, cognitive irrationality may beset the client, who may feel that his mind has been permanently affected by the traumatic episode (see Chapter 9, Volume 1 – "Cognitive Therapy"). The client's cognitive irrationality may relate to his mistaken perception of an uncontrollable and unpredictable threat that cannot be conquered. Sometimes the occurrence of a traumatic incident in the client's life will leave him with a feeling that life can never be the same again. The client, thus, may have to grapple with issues of personal vulnerability, negative self-image and the perception of a disorderly world. The client may also adopt a victim-mentality as a result of this concept and will be inclined to powerlessness, dependency and, of course, further victimisation (see Chapter 12 – "Dysfunctional Relationships"). Another factor that has been recognised by both clinicians and researchers alike is that, if the client has been a witness to the suffering or destruction of others, he may suffer from survivor-guilt and self-blame as a result. From a physiological and neurological standpoint, moreover, research has proved that long-term neurological change – brought about by increased autonomic reactivity and increased noradrenaline levels in the brain – will contribute to the client's distress. The client's PTSD symptoms, hence, can be exacerbated by a neurochemical responses to stress.

> Hypervigilance occurs when the hyperarousal that accompanies the initial response to danger activates an amplified, compulsive version of the orienting response.
> – *Peter Levine*

A variety of traumatic symptoms are likely to be exhibited by the PTSD sufferer, either as a result of his having to relive the trauma in the hyperarousal state or, conversely, as a result of his trying to disconnect from it in the dissociative state. It will be as if the client's nervous system will kick in so as to reinstate the status quo while, at the same time, the parasympathetic will still be working overtime in order to cope with the original trauma and any subsequent reactivation. The human system, therefore, will be rendered unable to return to the homeostatic state after traumatic excitation and activation because the client's sympathetic nervous system and the parasympathetic nervous system will remain out of balance. In this climate, the client, therefore, will not be able to achieve a psychological or a physiological balance following his past experiences.

> In the aftermath of an experience of overwhelming danger, the two contradictory responses of intrusion and constriction establish an oscillating rhythm. The dialectic of opposing psychological states is perhaps the most characteristic feature of the post-traumatic syndromes. Since neither the intrusive nor the numbing symptoms allow for integration of the traumatic event, the alternation between these two extreme states might be understood as an attempt to find a satisfactory balance between the two.
> – *Judith Lewis Herman*

Reliving the traumatic experience

> Flashbacks can be in the form of quick visual pictures, like watching a
> film, or in the form of feelings (emotional or physical). These often take
> place during lovemaking, but can also accompany everyday activities
> (triggered by some connection with the abuse) or perhaps reading or
> hearing about other victims' abuse experience. Flashbacks are
> fragmented views of the abuse and can offer a "way in" to a more
> complete memory.
> *– Penny Parks*

The client will often, in some way, attempt to relive the original
trauma as a result of the effects of the hyperarousal continuum.
This will usually be achieved by some form of re-enactment of his
past and may also take the form of intrusive thought-patterns or
physiological manifestations.

Psychological responses to hyperarousal

> As in the case of traumatic memories reported by clients with post-
> traumatic stress disorder, fear and distress were the most common
> accompanying emotions. Most memories, but not all, were detailed and
> involved what appeared to be a degree of reliving of the original
> experience. The majority of memories also appeared to be recovered at
> least initially in the form of fragments.
> *– Chris Brewin & Bernice Andrews*

When the client enters the hyperarousal state, he may typically
experience vivid flashbacks to the original trauma, recurrent and
persistent recollections, troubled dreams, nightmares and disturbed sleep (see Chapter 14, Volume 1 – "Dreams and Symbolic
Imagery"). The client will often get the impression that the past is
catching up with him and recurring intrusively and uncontrollably
in the present moment, and this, of course, will give him a general
sense of unreality. The client may also have a feeling of being alienated from or ostracised by others and, therefore, may harbour a
pervasive feeling of detachment or estrangement from the world at
large.

> Trauma symptoms are the organism's way of defending itself against the
> arousal generated by an ever-present perception of threat.
> *– Peter Levine*

The trauma-victim may also be subject to an exaggerated startle-response, whereby he will be continually acting as if danger were nigh (see Chapter 7 – "Fear and Anxiety Disorders"). The client may, for example, appear to be hypervigilant, hyperactive, impulsive and restless. The client may be subject to intense and uncontrollable emotive outbursts. The client may show intense distress, be tearfulness for long periods, suffer from major anxiety reactions and shake uncontrollably. Such a state may also impair the client's ability to concentrate and may result in amnesia for certain aspects of the traumatic episode (see Chapter 10, Volume 1 – "Memory").

> The trauma-inducing event can be experienced again hours, days, months or even years later. The feelings and emotions which were generated at the time can be felt as if they were happening now, in the present. They can vary from being mildly disturbing and upsetting to intense and overwhelming.
> *– Frank Parkinson*

The manifestations of psychological hyperarousal can be recognised when the client experiences recurrent, intrusive and distressing recollections of the original event in the form of images, thoughts and perceptions, distressing dreams and nightmares. The client may, for instance, suddenly act or feel as if the trauma were recurring by experiencing illusions, hallucinations or dissociative flashback episodes – particularly on waking or when intoxicated – that may result from an accumulation of traumatic episodes. The client may also experience intensely-exaggerated psychological distress or trauma-reactivation in response to internal or external cues that may symbolise or resemble any aspect of the original traumatic experience. Distress and anxiety reminiscent of the original trauma may be triggered in the sexual-molestation survivor, for example, when having sexual intercourse, by an unwarranted or unsolicited sexual approach or by sexual innuendo directed personally at the sufferer. Rape-victims, in particular, have been known to react as if the approach of an innocent stranger were hastening a repeated attack. The client may also re-experience his traumatic past in a somatic manner in the guise of physical pain or somatoform disorders such as genital pain, irritation, infection and sexual malfunction (see Chapter 11 – "Psychosomatic Disorders"). The element that often distinguishes PTSD from other distress-reactions will be the fact that the client can often become fixated by the intrusive reliving and re-enactment of thoughts and feelings (see Chapter 16, Volume 1 – "Personality Development"). PTSD symptomology of this nature will become the client's dominating psychological experience – epitomised by emotive flooding that can evoke panic, terror, grief and despair.

It has also been suggested that the reliving process can be experienced, to a greater or lesser extent, in the client's conscious awareness. At one end of the spectrum, the client may have no conscious recollection of his traumatic experience, in which case his mind will have utterly repressed the incident. The client, in some cases, however, may have a vague recollection of the experience but its unconscious suppression will still mean that it has a dominating effect on his life. The client can, hence, be said to be in a *fugue state*, whereby he might live out the traumatic experience in an altered state of consciousness. The client may, for example, enter an abusive relationship after he has been raped or may continue to walk the streets late at night after having been violently accosted. The client may also find himself reliving the trauma in an alternate ego-state (see Chapter 4, Volume 1 – "Ego-State Therapy"). The client will, thus, retain undigested fragments of perception that can haphazardly break into conscious awareness and, in some cases, this dominant ego-state may not be accessible to his conscious mind. Unpredictable and uncharacteristic behaviour can, therefore, take hold of the client who may have only minimal awareness, if any, of his activities and his reactions. The client, furthermore, may fatalistically live out his traumatic legacy by transferring and projecting his distress on to others (see Chapter 13, Volume 1 – "Transference and Countertransference"). The client, for instance, may become violent when he displaces emotive reactions on to others or may become submissive by way of reliving the original seeding experience.

The client should be persuaded to talk about his experiences and the practitioner should attempt to tease out any hidden memories associated with the trauma. Initially, the client may express his thoughts hesitantly but with a compelling sense of purpose. The client, in this way, can then be led towards arranging his thoughts, discharging the accompanying emotive responses and, finally, reorganising his memories into a coherent and reaction-free pattern that will serve to resolve the traumatic psychic imprint.

Physiological responses to hyperarousal

> Like the rest of the body, your central nervous system is vulnerable. Given enough physical or emotional stress it too can bend or even break. When you experience your trauma, your central nervous system received a series of shocks. The greater the intensity and the longer the duration of the trauma, the greater the possibility that the delicate biochemical balances of your body might have been disrupted.
> – *Aphrodite Matsakis*

When threat or danger has been perceived by the client, the limbic system in the brain will control his physiological and psychological responses. The limbic system regulates the human organism's survivalist behaviour and emotive expression by controlling hormonal activity and balancing the action of the hypothalamus, the pituitary gland and the adrenal glands. The hormonal activity initiated by the perception of extreme stress will cause the organism's autonomic nervous system to activate the instinctive fight–flight–freeze response that, under normal circumstances, should abate once the excitement has passed. In cases of traumatic experience, however, the normal functioning of the hypothalamic–pituitary–adrenal axis (*HPA axis*) system will be severely disrupted in the sufferer because the human system will be prevented from returning to the homeostatic state. It will be this key factor that will distinguish PTSD from any normal level of stress-response in the client. When the human organism has been chronically aroused and continues to respond to such arousal, PTSD symptoms will appear in the client as a result of the swamping effect on the amygdala and the hippocampus within the limbic system. The amygdala stores and prioritises highly-charged emotive memories and the hippocampus stores time-related and spatial memories according to the significance assigned to them by the amygdala.

PTSD symptoms are believed to occur because the emotive record of the client's traumatic experiences cannot be properly processed and stored in his long-term memory. The client's traumatic memories, therefore, can only be stored in associative networks in the brain and, because of this, will merely float in time in a fragmented form. Dissociated and fragmented memories will invade the client's present consciousness and this, in turn, can exacerbate his unhealthy physiological responses. The client, therefore, will suffer from continuing physiological hyperarousal and dissociation that will elicit an ongoing psychological and somatic response from the limbic system. These somatosensory elements will then become ripe for reactivation in the client because of his failure to integrate the experience into autobiographical memory (see Chapter 10, Volume 1 – "Memory").

> Part of the function of the orienting response is to identify new information as we become aware of it. If this function is impaired, any amount of new information leads to confusion and overload. Instead of being assimilated and available for future use, new information tends to stack up. It becomes disorganised and unusable. Important pieces of data are misplaced or forgotten. The mind then becomes unable to organise details in a way that makes sense. Rather than retain information that does not make sense, the mind "forgets" it. In the midst of this confusion, any other problem compounds the situation and ordinary circumstances can mushroom into a not-so-comic nightmare of frustration, anger, and anxiety.
> – *Peter Levine*

The following client narrative gives an account of the way in which a male client manifested traumatic symptoms in childhood after being molested by his stepmother.

Client narrative – those nightmares in childhood …

My guardian certainly turned a blind eye when I had the inevitable trauma-reliving nightmares. I saw in my dreams fearsome witches chasing and hounding me. I woke screaming on several occasions. I gave several babysitters a hard time. I would rush out of my room in the middle of the night in order to escape from my dreams, often feeling guilty because I would get into a row for doing so.

When my guardian actually questioned me about such incidents, I told her that I was frightened by a stern female teacher at school. I was enshrouded in confusion myself about these nocturnal traumas. These witches chasing me (as well as the female teacher) represented the female authority-figure in my life in the guise of my abusive stepmother. The stern teacher received a severe reprimand from my guardian but the problem, from my point of view, remain unsolved.

Avoiding the traumatic experience

> When a pattern of numbing of feelings is undertaken by a survivor as a strategy for surviving abuse he may feel better for a while. Ultimately the

behavior gets out of control and causes more pain than it alleviates. At that point the survivor must add one more difficult part to his program – overcoming addiction. He must learn to live without numbing and experience the range of feelings necessary to recovery to a healthy life. The way out of the pain is through it.
– Mike Lew

The client may endeavour to distance himself from his emotive responses by way of manifesting the effects of the dissociative state. This emotive stultification will often be the client's unconscious way of constrictive escape from his perception of the traumatic episode that he has undergone.

When the client enters the dissociative state, he may typically experience psychological shutdown, a lack of interest in life, work, relationships and recreational activities. The client's dissociation may even extend to feeling little or no physical pain. The client may also engage in escapism in order to divorce himself from reality. The client may, for instance, become prone to fantasy and daydreaming, may seek isolation and may tend to withdraw from society. The client may also appear to be unable to accept the seriousness of his condition. The client may also go to great lengths in order to avoid any situations that might act as a reminder of his ordeal. The client may, in desperation, turn to substance-abuse and may become obsessive or compulsive in his attempt to blot out the past (see Chapter 7 – "Fear and Anxiety Disorders"). Such behaviour will attempt to deal with the client's emotive distress by supposedly numbing the pain and by distracting his thoughts from the traumatic incident. It will appear as if the client has been unconsciously endeavouring to regain control of the chaotic situation.

The PTSD client will usually employ a number of unconsciously-motivated behavioural, cognitive and emotive strategies in an attempt to reduce exposure to trauma-mimetic stimuli and to minimise the intensity of his psychological response should such stimuli be unavoidable. The client's avoidant behaviour can be recognised when he avoids thoughts, feelings and conversations associated with or reminiscent of the original trauma. The client may, for instance, shun people, activities and places that can arouse recollections of the original trauma. The client may spontaneously forget an important aspect of the original trauma that will result from dissociative or psychogenic amnesia, possibly as a consequence of emotive suppression or repression. As a result of his traumatic responses, the client may well display a markedly-diminished interest in life and cease to participate in significant activities. The client may seem to be unresponsive to his surroundings and uninterested in himself. The client may also experience a restricted range of emotive expression and may elect to become detached or, even, estranged from those about him. The victim of sexual molestation, for example, may wish to avoid sexual intimacy and, indeed, any human contact in order to escape from reports of sexual brutality or to sidestep a medical examination of an intimate nature. Sometimes the client will experience a sense of foreshortened future because of the devastating nature of his experiences. The client may not, for example, expect to find a partner, to have children, to pursue a career or to have a normal life-expectancy. When the client has such a loose hold on life, this, in itself, can eventually lead to suicidal notions.

> The biggest problem of avoidance is this denial of feelings. If I have been
> through a traumatic experience and someone asks me, "Are you
> suffering from stress?", my likely reaction is to say very firmly, "No".
> I do not want other people to know how I am feeling. If I am frightened
> or ashamed or want to be sick I might wish to keep this secret.
> *– Frank Parkinson*

PTSD Manifestations

> As a rule, don't be too concerned with taking all of these different
> classifications, types and diagnostic criteria on board in order to work
> within a rigid framework. There is a danger of pigeonholing and
> labelling a client. At the end of the day, although an awareness of the
> different manifestations of PTSD is very important, in the end it all boils
> down to being able to work with the individual that you find facing you.
> He is less interested in academic knowledge than you are. All he wants
> to know is "can you help him?" The textbook is useful in its place but
> can't replace empathy, understanding and a willingness to give it
> your best.
> *– Michael O'Sullivan*

PTSD manifestations may take a number of forms as classified by official publications and according to the work of researchers in this field. Let us now consider some of these classifications as a means of clarifying the ways in which traumatic stress and its accompanying symptomology can rear its ugly head.

A supportive family or community environment or crisis intervention
work by a trained professional or layperson can be critical in preventing
the crisis reaction from becoming a more long-term problem.
– *Aphrodite Matsakis*

Acute PTSD

The client's symptoms are said to constitute acute PTSD if his psychic disturbance occurs within three to six months after the traumatic experience but can abate within that time-frame. It may be,
for example, that the client has undergone a single one-off traumatic incident and, because symptoms have manifested early, it
will usually be possible, with appropriate assistance and support,
for him to make an early recovery.

Chronic PTSD

The client's symptoms are said to represent chronic PTSD if his distress manifests almost immediately after the traumatic event but
then continues for several months or years without remission.
Perhaps the client has lacked the appropriate support after the
traumatic event or maybe he was simply not able to resolve the
trauma naturally.

Delayed PTSD

We know that reactions to sexual abuse can lie quiet for many years. The
sexual abuse appears to have left the survivor undamaged until a
triggering life event unleashes dormant feelings and memories. Delayed-
onset PTSD describes those survivors who suddenly begin to experience
PTSD long after the abuse is over.
– *Renee Fredrickson*

One of the most harmful and insidious characteristics of PTSD will
be that symptoms may lay dormant for several years or even
decades after the client has suffered from a traumatic incident. It
may be that the client does not suffer unduly at the time because
his reaction to the event became sealed in his unconscious mind
and was, thus, debarred from conscious awareness. The dormant
PTSD condition can then, of course, subsequently erupt in the

client's later life by alarming personal experiences such as rape, mugging, natural disasters, car accidents, military combat or the loss of a close relative. The delayed traumatic-stress response could also be triggered in the client by any reminder or symbolic representation of the initial trauma.

For the client who has experienced any form of childhood abuse, the effect of the trauma will almost certainly be delayed until it is triggered in adulthood – especially if the memory of the abuse has been vague or repressed (see Chapter 10, Volume 1 – "Memory"). Obviously, no child, at the time of the original abuse, will be able to comprehend fully the implications of the situation and, therefore, his reaction may, of necessity, be deferred until his maturity. In cases of childhood sexual abuse, for instance, some typical ways in which the client's delayed PTSD symptomology can be triggered are that a situation or incident will occur that closely mirrors the original abuse – such as rape or violence assault. If the client, who has been maltreated in childhood, later becomes a victim of violence, is sexually assaulted, encounters a dictatorial authority-figure or reacts significantly to being in an enclosed space, it may well be that he has triggered those long-forgotten symptoms of childhood abuse or neglect. Similarly, symptoms may be triggered if the client's abuser dies and he learns of his or her death. Perhaps the client will meet his former abuser or will be otherwise confronted by the fact that violation has occurred in childhood. Sometimes symptoms may manifest if the client himself becomes a parent or a grandparent or his own child reaches the age at which he was himself abused. The client may also learn of other cases of childhood abuse or the topic will receive some form of publicity and these factors alone can activate the trigger-mechanism. PTSD symptoms may, similarly, be reactivated when the client enters a critical life-phase such as adolescence or midlife, when he may undergo a major psychological upheaval (see Chapter 16, Volume 1 – "Personality Development"). The client's symptoms may, for instance, surface if he overcomes an addiction or substance-abuse problem because this will effectively mean that he no longer has this mode of support on which to rely. Alternatively, symptoms may arise when the client becomes settled in life and feels sufficiently safe, strong and relaxed to begin dealing with his problems (see Chapter 1 – "The Hypnoanalytic Approach").

> After working for more than twenty-five years with people suffering
> from trauma, I can say that at least half of my clients have had traumatic
> symptoms that remained dormant for a significant period of time before
> surfacing. For many people, the interval between the event and the onset
> of symptoms is between six weeks and eighteen months. However, the
> latency period can last for years or even decades. In both instances, the
> reactions are often triggered by seemingly insignificant events.
> *– Peter Levine*

Obviously, the childhood-abuse victim will be vulnerable to becoming a delayed PTSD sufferer at any time in adulthood. The client, in this case, may well be unable to comprehend the meaning of his mysterious symptoms and may endeavour unsuccessfully to explain his reactions in terms of current events in his life. The client's suffering may come seemingly out of the blue and a stubborn and debilitating disorder may manifest. The client, naturally, may not immediately be able to recognise the connection between the original seeding incident and his present state of mind, and this factor, in itself, may cause further unnecessary distress. Because of this element, the client's symptoms may be both delayed and chronic as a result.

> In delayed-onset PTSD, the symptoms occur anytime later than six
> months after the traumatic event. This can be 1 year, 20 years, or even 40
> years after the traumatic event. For example, previously asymptomatic
> 60-year-old people can develop PTSD in response to having been
> sexually or physically abused as children.
> *– Aphrodite Matsakis*

Simple PTSD

> The extent of PTSD is also influenced by whether the client has been
> exposed to one or to more than one traumatic incident. For instance,
> although rape is traumatic, incest, which typically involves multiple
> rapes or molestation over an extended period is more traumatic. Similarly,
> seeing people die in a car accident, although traumatic, is generally not
> as traumatic as being in combat or being a policeman in a deteriorating
> neighborhood and seeing death and violence day in and day out.
> *– Aphrodite Matsakis*

With simple PTSD, the client's life will have been fairly uncomplicated and, therefore, the traumatic incident will have been an isolated event in an otherwise stressless life. The client, in this case, will have to deal with only a single incident and not much else of a disturbing nature. Simple PTSD will arise, for example, if the client were attacked by a stranger on one occasion during an unfortunate chance encounter but, apart from this, he had experienced no significant distress either in childhood or in adulthood. The practitioner, therefore, can focus on the client's specific distress as a direct result of the traumatic incident and will not need to deal with an accumulated backlog of previously-disturbing matter.

Complicated PTSD

> Chronic helplessness occurs as the freezing, orienting, and defending responses become so fixated and weakened that they move primarily along predetermined and dysfunctional pathways. Chronic helplessness joins hypervigilance and the inability to learn new behaviours as yet another common feature of the traumatised person's reality.
> *– Peter Levine*

With complicated PTSD, the client will be beset by a complex syndrome whereby he will have been the subject of much trauma, perhaps throughout the whole of his life. Complicated PTSD, therefore, will manifest when the client undergoes a traumatic incident that has set up a catalogue of trauma-induced symptoms, but these effects must then be considered against a backdrop of his traumatic childhood and its consequent effects. The client, in this case, may well have had a history of psychological disturbance and stress-related conditions. The practitioner, therefore, may need to probe the client's background initially in order to identify the form of PTSD from which the client has been suffering. The therapist may then be able to give the client some indication of the requirements of therapeutic intervention.

Complex PTSD syndrome

> Although the complex traumatic syndrome has never before been outlined systematically, the concept of a spectrum of post-traumatic disorders has been noted, almost in passing, by many experts.
> *– Judith Lewis Herman*

Some researchers take the view that the official diagnosis of PTSD is inadequate to account for the symptoms experienced by victims of sexual molestation and gratuitous violence and have called for new diagnostic labelling in order to describe the aftereffects of severe traumatisation. Terms such as *Complex PTSD*, *Victimisation Sequelae Disorder* (VSD), *Disorders of Extreme Stress Not Otherwise Specified* (DESNOS) and *Syndrome of Chronic Trauma* (SCT) have, therefore, been put forward by a collection of writers who acknowledge the limitations of existing diagnostic criteria and feel that these are more comprehensive titles in certain cases.

> The syndrome that follows upon prolonged, repeated trauma needs its own name. I propose to call it "complex post-traumatic stress disorder". The responses to trauma are best understood as a spectrum of conditions rather than as a single disorder. They range from a brief stress reaction that gets better by itself and never qualifies for a diagnosis, to classic or simple post-traumatic stress disorder, to the complex syndrome of prolonged, repeated trauma.
> – *Judith Lewis Herman*

The practitioner would be advised not to pigeonhole the client by simply regarding PTSD symptomology as an isolated set of factors. The practitioner should, moreover, bear in mind the fact that PTSD symptoms can often lead to comorbid disorders such as anxiety attacks, social phobias, obsessive-compulsive disorders, depression, suicidal ideation, self-mutilation, substance-abuse, drug-dependence, manic-activity bouts, chronic-fatigue syndrome and personality disorders. Additional symptoms that may be exhibited by the trauma-sufferer have been cited as survivor-guilt, self-blame, secondary wounding, low self-esteem and victim-thinking as well as dramatic psychological disturbance, cognitive irrationality and somatisation problems. It will be the role of the clinical practitioner, therefore, to regard the client as a holistic entity and endeavour to treat whatever he presents rather than to adhere to the symptomology rulebook.

> A general acknowledgement that the official PTSD diagnosis continues to describe inadequately the range and tenacity of aftershocks suffered by survivors of prolonged, systemic trauma, has led researchers to propose a new diagnostic category called at various times, "Victimisation Disorder", "Victimisation Sequelae Disorder," and "complex Post-traumatic Stress Disorder"; it is now most commonly referred to as "Disorder of Extreme Stress Not Otherwise Specified (DESNOS)."
> – *Rebecca Coffey*

Disorders of extreme stress

> There is also a vast literature reviewed by van der Kolk that suggests that
> the physiologic concomitants of chronic, inescapable stress are different
> from those for acute stress. For many children who experience PTSD,
> there is a backdrop of stress in the day-to-day atmosphere of abuse,
> neglect, and danger to which some children are subjected both in and out
> of their homes. Whenever children are afraid to walk inside their homes
> because of chaotic, unprovoked, and inconsistent rage and hostility
> randomly projected on to family members, the environment can be
> considered similar to inescapable stress.
> – *Mark Schwartz, Lori Galperin & William Masters*

Disorders of extreme stress (DES) will occur if the client has been consistently and habitually subjected to trauma over a long period of time and particularly when the ill-treatment has occurred at the hands of an intimate associate or close family-member. The client who has been a victim of childhood abuse or neglect, therefore, may fall into this category. The child, in such cases, may have continually lived in dread of an abusive attack. For the victim of an incestuous relationship with a resident parental figure, for instance, the child may have existed for years in an atmosphere of never knowing when the predator was going to pounce. It may well be that this continual uncertainty can, in itself, set up a stress disorder in the client and, hence, exaggerate the traumatic effects of the actual abusive attacks. The stress, thus, can become chronic rather than acute for the client because of its ongoing nature.

> Children who are chronically traumatised by caretakers in an
> environment of endemic family stress may have experiences similar to
> those of torture victims, which include the creation of dependency,
> intimidation, disorientation, and isolation. Children are by definition
> dependent on caretakers. Abusive parents further engender torturous
> dependency by withholding basic care and opportunity. When children
> are forced to submit and obey as the price for being allowed cleanliness,
> food, clothing, access to friends, or just momentary respite from abuse,
> they are made into slaves. Their fates become entirely contingent on the
> whims of the captors/parents, and their realities reshape to fit the rules
> of the game. The name of the game is the subjugation of vulnerable,
> trusting, and ultimately desperate children by adults who are often
> powerless everywhere else in the world.
> – *Mark Schwartz, Lori Galperin & William Masters*

Reactivated PTSD

> In any re-enactment there will always be underlying and unconscious
> patterns of events and beliefs that seemingly have their own power to
> create our experiences according to their dictates. The compulsive
> repetition is not "deliberate" in the usual sense. Deliberate actions
> usually require some consciousness, an ingredient that plays little role in
> the re-enactment. In re-enactments, the human organism is not fully
> aware of the drives and motivations of its behaviour, and consequently, it
> operates in a mode that is like that of the reptilian brain. It simply does
> what it does.
> – *Peter Levine*

A recent traumatic experience that the client has undergone can lead to reactivated PTSD (or *secondary traumatisation*). With this form of PTSD, the client's recollection of an earlier trauma, from which he has ostensibly recovered, can, subsequently, evoke accumulated or secondary traumatic symptoms. Secondary traumatisation can, for instance, occur if the client experiences additional trauma, has been unsympathetically received by others, has been unfairly blamed or stigmatised, has been subjected to enforced disclosure or submits to brutal or overly-inquisitive questioning. For these reasons, the practitioner will need to tread extremely carefully when handling such delicate cases.

PTSD reactivation may, in essence, be either uncomplicated or complicated by other factors to which the client may be subject. Uncomplicated PTSD reactivation will occur when the client's current trauma has become reminiscent of his previous traumatic experience and, consequently, his previous symptoms have become reactivated after a symptom-free period. The client, in this case, may feel unable to assimilate his experiences and may be unable to tolerate any personal reactions associated with trauma. Complicated PTSD reactivation will occur when the client's residual traumatic symptoms have been exacerbated. The client, in this case, may experience an increased sensitivity and susceptibility to external stressors and traumatic stimuli that are, in fact, unrelated to the original traumatic experience. Here, the client will, hence, need to deal with the multiplicity of difficulties that such a condition can create.

Rape-trauma syndrome

> The essential element of rape is the physical, psychological, and moral
> violation of the person. Violation is, in fact, a synonym for rape. The
> purpose of the rapist is to terrorise, dominate, and humiliate his victim,
> to render her utterly helpless. Thus rape, by its nature, is intentionally
> designed to produce psychological trauma.
> — *Judith Lewis Herman*

A degree of research has been carried out with regard to victims of rape and the incidence of PTSD symptoms in such cases. It seems clear from significant research in this field that most victims of sexual molestation, abuse, violation or defilement will suffer from symptoms of PTSD in one form or another. Most of the research undertaken in this arena has focused on rape-victims who have displayed symptoms unique to their distress that falls short of the official diagnostic criteria and, therefore, has led to the formulation of certain rape-specific syndromes based on PTSD symptomology. Additionally, research has established the fact that rape-victims who were victims of sexual abuse in childhood will have an even greater risk of developing chronic or complex forms of PTSD.

Rape-trauma syndrome (RTS) has been recognised as a two-stage reactionary process to the incidence of rape. The initial *acute disorganisation phase* will be characterised either by the client's expressive reactions, such as fear, anger, anxiety, sobbing and tenseness akin to hyperarousal responses, or by controlled reactions whereby he displays a calm exterior akin to dissociative responses. The secondary *reorganisation phase* will be depicted by lifestyle rebuilding and readjustment, when the client undertakes action in order to ensure his safety. For the rape-victim, this can take the form of moving house, rearranging furniture, changing telephone numbers, reading about the syndrome and joining a self-help group. The client, of course, may seek therapeutic assistance at any point along this road to recovery.

Rape-related post-traumatic stress disorder (RR-PTSD) highlights the fact that the client may experience symptoms that are unique to his rape-experience but related in many ways to PSTD symptomology. With RR-PTSD, the client typically will relive his experiences of the rape-incident, will withdraw from social interaction, will adopt avoidant behaviours and will, simultaneously, suffer from the effects of increased autonomic hyperarousal. Often the client will turn to substance-abuse as a coping-strategy for his distress.

Vicarious traumatisation

> Trauma is contagious. In the role of witness to disaster or atrocity, the therapist at times is emotionally overwhelmed. She experiences, to a lesser degree, the same terror, rage, and despair as the patient. This phenomenon is known as "traumatic counter-transference" or "vicarious traumatization". The therapist may begin to experience symptoms of post-traumatic stress disorder.
> – *Judith Lewis Herman*

The therapist who treats the PTSD client can personally suffer from a form of reflective, secondary traumatic reaction known as vicarious victimisation (or *compassion-fatigue*). The symptoms principally associated with this form of PTSD syndrome are those of intrusive cognitions, nightmares and survivor-guilt complexes. These symptoms can interfere with therapeutic neutrality and client–therapist boundaries due to a combination of inexperience with trauma-victims and countertransference manifestations (see Chapter 13, Volume 1 – "Transference and Countertransference"). The analytical hypnotherapist, therefore, should be particularly circumspect when dealing with clients who have undergone tragic and heart-rending experiences. Whereas working with traumatised individuals can be extremely rewarding work for the practitioner, she must also be aware that it can take its personal toll. The practitioner will need to be caring but impartial when assisting the traumatised client and, therefore, she will need to be personally responsible for maintaining an exemplary standard of practice. If the practitioner begins to suffer, then so will the client's welfare because of the precarious and delicate nature of the therapeutic encounter. The practitioner, of course, should be reminded at this juncture to seek therapeutic or supervisory assistance, if she has been in any way affected by working with the traumatised client.

> Kluft points out that therapists working with trauma survivors tend to adopt one of the following roles: detective, savior, advocate, or balanced therapist. You might want to consider which of these stances you might be assuming toward a given client.
> – *Aphrodite Matsakis*

Exploring the Client's PTSD

> To complete its biological and meaningful course of action, the organism
> requires the spontaneous shaking and trembling that we see throughout
> the animal world.
> – *Peter Levine*

When treating the client who exhibits PTSD symptomology, the practitioner will need to adopt a multilayered role in order to assist him. The therapist should allow the client sufficient time and space to tell his story, to uncover repressed or suppressed memories, to pacify any feelings of abnormality and to cognitively restructure his dismal outlook on life. Not only should therapeutic intervention address the client's psychological conflict but also it should investigate the impact that the past trauma has had on his ability to form productive relationships (see Chapter 12 – "Dysfunctional Relationships"). The client, in this way, can then come to terms with the horrors of his past experience and so move forward from the vantage-point of strength rather than despair. The client, of course, will need to marshal the necessary resources in order to be able to cope with the rigours of therapeutic investigation prior to dislodging the trauma of the past. Final resolution can occur for the traumatised client, of course, only when he can remain symptom-free and feel soundly able to interact in society and daily life without any abnormal responses. Frequently, the unravelling process will involve the client in going through the tunnel rather than skating around it. Therapeutic intervention for traumatic stress can be extraordinarily complex in that, on the one hand, the client will be dealing with devastating emotive experiences that will require him to plummet the depths of unconscious probing and to dredge up the most heart-rending of abreactive expression while, simultaneously, he will be required to reshape cognition, outlook, self-image and social interaction in order to achieve psychic homeostasis.

Because of its complexity, therefore, the emphasis in trauma-related therapy should, in general, be on global treatment regimes rather than merely focusing on one specific cluster of symptoms using a single methodology. This factor will particularly hold true when treating victims of childhood abuse who may suffer from a range of PTSD symptomology together with comorbid disorders. Regardless of the methodology employed, an unsympathetic or unskilled practitioner could, of course, inadvertently reactivate trauma in an already-traumatised subject – a situation that must be avoided at all costs. For the client with PTSD symptoms, therefore, the most important therapeutic components will be those of establishing trust, ensuring a safe environment for disclosure and providing psychoeducation. The clinician should pursue a regime that encompasses these elements while, simultaneously, addressing the range of issues likely to be exhibited by victims of traumatisation within an integrative framework. Analytic methodology can examine the client's personal values and the ways in which experiences have affected him. The client can be encouraged to develop effective approaches to resolving and managing unconscious emotive reactions and beliefs that have stemmed collectively from both formative relationships and from more recent trauma. In addition to utilising hypnoanalytic processes, the practitioner should also be aware of the possibility of utilising other approaches that can assist the traumatised client and can neatly dovetail in with her unique therapeutic approach. Let us now examine some important adjuncts to hypnoanalytic methodology that the practitioner could employ with the PTSD client.

Critical-incident stress debriefing

> Critical Incident Debriefing is structured to reduce the level of possible psychological, emotional and physical reactions to a traumatic event. It can be used with groups or individuals after any traumatic incidents in which acute distress, shock, horror of violence are present.
> – *Frank Parkinson*

Critical-incident stress debriefing (CISD) has been established as the obvious group-treatment choice for on-the-scene crisis-intervention because it can assist the trauma-survivor to make sense of his symptoms and can help to avert the development of the PTSD syndrome. CISD is a structured crisis-management process that can help the client to understand and manage intense emotions, to identify personal coping-strategies and to receive peer-support with the emphasis on education, self-regulation and lifestyle rebuilding. CISD can provide the client with a narrative understanding of crisis-experiences by dealing with the immediate impact and the initial effects of the traumatic occurrence. CISD can assist the client with readjustment and life-reconstruction but cannot be regarded as a substitute for longer-term methods of psychotherapy. CISD, therefore, may form part of an overall critical incident stress management (CISM) programme in which hypnoanalytic techniques can, additionally, be employed.

The CISD procedure adheres to an initial debriefing protocol (IDP) that will enable the client to verbalise cathartically and to reflect on his experiences, and will then be concluded by a follow-up debriefing protocol (FDP) that will allow him to integrate fully a coherent understanding of his experiences.

Eye-movement desensitisation and reprocessing

> Because EMDR focuses on personal experience, it downplays what the
> therapist thinks of the event and, instead, deals directly with how the
> experience has affected the client.
> – *Francine Shapiro & Margot Silk Forrest*

Eye-movement desensitisation and reprocessing (EMDR) is a controversial, yet clinically well-supported, treatment based on the premise that traumatic experience causes psychological dissociation of hemispheric processing and implicit memory impairment that can lead to the development of the client's erroneous self-beliefs (see Chapter 10, Volume 1 – "Memory"). With EMDR therapy, the client will be instructed to recall a painful traumatic episode while, simultaneously, focusing on a means of mapping rapid saccadic movement that will mimic rapid eye-movement (REM). At the same time, the client will be asked to replace a self-referent negative cognition associated with the traumatic memory with a positive one – thus combining direct exposure techniques with cognitive elements (see Chapter 9, Volume 1 – "Cognitive Therapy"). EMDR exponents claim that the client's saccadic eye-movements can reprogram his brain-functioning by transferring traumatic data from the cortical right-brain hemisphere to the left-brain hemisphere in order to allow memories to be properly processed, stored and reintegrated within his mind. The client's sensory inputs can be analysed and integrated with left-hemisphere cognitive functions during the *desensitisation* part of the process so that traumatic events can be recontextualised and affective arousal can be neutralised or modulated during the *reprocessing* phase. This technique can be effectively combined with hypnosis in order to greatly assist the client to revisit traumatic memories and, simultaneously, to instigate the organisation of a self-narrative reconstruction that will juxtapose his hyperarousal states with his personal perception of events.

The controversy over the way in which the therapeutic intervention of EMDR functions waivers between, on the one hand, whether its purpose will be to link the client's logical functioning to his emotive, sensual and physical memory, and, on the other hand, whether it can enable him to face the trauma and to seek a positive outcome. Some researchers argue that EMDR is really exposure therapy in disguise and that eye-movement may be superfluous to the process. The EMDR controversy has also fuelled the debate about false-memory syndrome, in which proponents vehemently dispute the fact that the client is, in fact, capable of retrieving repressed traumatic memories, particularly from childhood, that, subsequently, cannot be authenticated and that can lead disastrously to false allegations (see Chapter 10, Volume 1 – "Memory").

> EMDR is a complex, integrated form of psychotherapy. There are many theories about different components of EMDR, but it is not known precisely how eye movement achieves therapeutic effects. In theory traumas leave unprocessed memories, feelings, and thoughts that can be reprocessed or "metabolised" with these eye movements. Similar to the way rapid eye movement (REM) or dream sleep works, the eye movements help to process this blocked information, allowing the body-mind to release it.
> – *Laurel Parnell*

In the following case-study example, the client was able to come to terms with the fact that she had been gang-raped in adulthood.

Case-study example – traumatic rape
This female client sought therapy because she had recently been gang-raped by a number of youths on her way home from a late-night party.

The client had only a vague memory of the incident but reported that most of her recollections of the rape manifested in the form of nightmares and intrusive flashbacks. In consequence, the client was very short of sleep and generally highly anxiety-prone. The client had ceased to function effectively in her work as a sales assistance and found any form of interaction with customers quite an ordeal. In this climate, the client feared that she might lose her job but, at the same time, she felt unable to explain to her employer the reason why she was "not really there" when she was at work.

After several sessions, the client, however, was able to regurgitate a complete picture of her hitherto fragmented memories of the incident once a significant degree of trust had been established in the therapeutic context. Most of the therapeutic exploration focused on the way in which the client had experienced terror in the hands of her rapists. The client relived her feelings of fear by physically shaking as a means of releasing the pent-up terror that had resulted from her horrific ordeal because it had lasted for several hours. Once the client had thoroughly worked through her feelings of guilt, shame and self-disgust, moreover, she was also able to deal with related issues of rejection during her childhood. When the client came to deal with issues of anger and rage, she found that she was generally on a very short fuse. This hitherto unresolved anger then began to pour out with regard to her rapists and her father, who had constantly rejected her in childhood.

The client was eventually able to lay to rest the effects of her ordeals both in adulthood and in childhood and was able to understand why she had reacted so profoundly to the rape incident and why she had put herself in a vulnerable position prior to the rape. This insight, together with her emotive expression during therapy, was the key to releasing her anguish and distress and the traumatic aftereffects of her experiences.

Client Profiling

The analytical-hypnotherapy practitioner may wish to ponder the following points when formulating a profile for the client.

- In what respect might the client have been exposed to trauma in his life?
- In what ways can the practitioner identify or recognise PSTD symptoms in the client?
- In what ways has the client coped with past trauma?

- Has the client's trauma manifested solely in childhood?
- Can the client make a connection between his symptoms and the cause of such symptoms?
- Does the client report that he experiences recurring and disturbing dreams or nightmares?
- Does the client experience any intrusive thoughts or flashbacks?
- Can the client recollect most of the experiences in his life?
- Is the client easily startled?
- Does the client appear to be hyperactive?
- Does the client believe that the past has not affected him?
- Does the client make light of his past traumatic experiences?
- Does the client tend to suppress or to hold back his emotive expression?
- Does the client have a high physical pain-threshold?
- Does the client avoid any recollection of his past traumatic experiences?
- Has the client's reaction to any traumatic experiences been delayed for some time?
- Does the client suffer from any symptoms that might go hand in hand with PTSD symptomology?
- Has the client's life been complicated by a series of traumatic experiences that have left him highly confused and anxiety-prone?
- Is the client's past traumatic experience ripe for reactivation in the present?
- Does the practitioner find it an ordeal to listen to the client's heart-rending experiences?
- Does the practitioner feel that there is any aspect at all of the client's traumatic experience that he would personally wish to bypass?

Chapter 14

The Nature of Childhood Abuse

Until thought is linked with purpose there is no intelligent
accomplishment. With the majority the bark of thought is
allowed to "drift" upon the ocean of life.

– James Allen

What is Childhood Abuse?

Abuse is a particular form of trauma done by one human being to
another. Abuse, simply defined, is a trauma inflicted deliberately,
wrongly and unjustly to harm another human being.
– Renee Fredrickson

Childhood abuse would usually encompass emotional abuse,
physical abuse and sexual abuse and there can be no question that
any form of abuse will have a profound psychological effect on the
child-victim (see Chapter 15 – "The Effects of Childhood Abuse").
Whereas this chapter will focus, in the main, on childhood sexual
abuse, the practitioner will still be able to consider the principles
behind all forms of childhood abuse by investigating the theories
that have been presented here in umbrella terms.

Emotional abuse will manifest when the child has been physically
neglected, emotionally starved of affection or the recipient of emotional cruelty, blackmail or similar ill-treatment. Physical abuse
will occur if the child has been excessively punished, excessively
bullied, physically attacked or harmed with malicious intent.
Psychological maltreatment can also occur if the child's parents or
carers were dictatorial or overstrict. The child, in this instance,
would suffer from experiencing a lack of freedom or a limitation to

her freedom of expression. The client may also become disturbed if her carers frequently argued or fought and if they were divorced or separated during her childhood. If the child's guardians were absent for a prolonged period of time during her upbringing, this, too, will manifest psychological distress. The client's unconscious mind might also consider that her carers were absent if they were physically or emotionally ill, if they died or committed suicide. The child, moreover, can suffer if her family had to endure financial instability or undue hardship and if she was, consequently, forced to assume some form of responsibility for the family, the home or her own welfare. The client, therefore, will, inevitably, be affected by any form of cruelty or instability that had caused a degree of anxiety or confusion because she could not have been able to rely on a harmonious and nurturing environment during her critical developmental years.

Sexual abuse will occur when the child has been sexually exploited for another's benefit. Childhood sexual abuse will take place, by definition, because the adult has greater knowledge, status and resources. The abuser will, therefore, have the menacing power to force, exploit, coerce and persuade the child in order to ensure her cooperation. Often the abuser will need minimal justification, owing to his or her privileged status or the nature of his or her relationship with the child. The violator, moreover, may also project his or her own weakness on to the child-victim by way of identifying with his or her prey. The child, in a sexually-abusive situation, therefore, will lack the ability to consent, the ability to make a choice, and may, furthermore, feel obliged to comply with the abuser's wishes in an endeavour to preserve an established bond with the adult.

Childhood Sexual Abuse Manifestation

A widely used definition of child sexual abuse is the involvement of dependent, developmentally immature children and adolescents in sexual activities which they do not truly comprehend, are unable to give informed consent to, and that violate the social taboos of family roles.
– *Kim Oates*

The manifestations of childhood sexual abuse can be considered in a number of ways according to the way in which the client has been involved in the abuse and the form that the abuse would have taken.

> There are two basic ways in which the offender gains sexual access to the child. One is by pressuring the child into sexual activity through enticement, encouragement, or instruction, and the other is by forcing the child into the sexual activity through threat, intimidation, or physical duress.
> – *Nicholas Groth & Jean Birnhaum*

Contact and noncontact sexual abuse

> Sexual abuse is a term seldom defined legally. Different countries have a variety of sexual crimes against children on their statutes. These include child molestation, indecent assault, sexual violation, sexual victimisation, unlawful sexual connection, sexual misuse, carnal knowledge, child rape and incest.
> – *Felicity Goodyear-Smith*

Abusive acts can be graded in terms of whether the child received physical contact from the perpetrator or not. Forms of abuse that do not involve any physical contact may include exhibitionism, enforced witness of sexual activity, obscene talk and innuendo and, indeed, any set of circumstances in which the child felt discomfort in a sexualised context. Forms of abuse that involve physical contact between the perpetrator and the victim will be by far the most damaging for the client. Abuse in which physical contact has been made with the client, therefore, will normally be more devastating psychologically for her. Psychological trauma will usually manifest because of the greater involvement of the child in the sexual activity. Contact abuse may include vaginal, oral or anal penetration or attempted penetration of the child as well as all permutations of masturbation of either the victim or the perpetrator. This category would also include sexual violence such as spanking the naked child or any other form of sexually-motivated touch or interference.

Coercive sexual abuse

> Unlike rape, sexual abuse does not nearly so often involve physical force
> or attempts to achieve sexual intercourse. Many sexual abusers entice
> children into sexual activity through the authority they hold over the
> children, through rewards or enticements they offer the child, or through
> misrepresenting the nature of moral standards. The sexual acts they
> initiate often involve touching and manipulating the genitals,
> not actual penetration.
> – *David Finkelhor*

The practitioner should also bear in mind the way in which the
client might have been inveigled into becoming a target for sexual
practice and whether the child-molester was someone either from
within the family or a stranger. Coercive sexual abuse will take
place when the child has been enticed into a sexual encounter. This
may be achieved by persuasion on the part of the violator, who will
be in full command of his or her actions and will comprehend the
intended outcome. The abuser, therefore, may appear to be behav-
ing by chance when, in reality, he or she will be acting by design.
Coercive sexual abuse can be either an impulsive or a premeditated course of action taken by the adult. The molester will, thus,
be the original instigator of the sexually-inappropriate relationship
and the child's illusionary consent to the encounter will have been
either minimal or nonexistent.

> Force is not necessary in incest, and is rarely used. The child's natural
> dependence and powerlessness are used against her. The closer the
> relationship, the less necessary force is and the less likely the perpetrator
> is to use violence. Fathers are least likely to resort to violence: the child's
> need, as well as the power of his guardianship role, virtually guarantee
> access. More distant relationships may necessitate some threat of force,
> or, more rarely, some actual violence.
> – *Sue Blume*

Essentially, coercive sexual abuse will take place when the child
appears to have consented to sexual activity as a result of having
been persuaded or tricked into the encounter. The child's consent
may be gained by threats, trickery or bribery. The most emotion-
ally-crippling scenario of all will, of course, be to bargain for the
child's sexual favours using the weapon of affection for which she
naturally craves. The abuser may, for example, make promises of
love or threats of the withdrawal of affection in such instances. In

cases of coercive sexual abuse, the client will usually have been molested repeatedly – perhaps over a long period of time.

The practitioner should remember that, in all cases, it will be the child-molester who will have been the initiator of the crime and not the client as an innocent child. This premise will obtain even in extreme cases of child-prostitution, whereby the client may appear to be the instigator of the sexual encounter with an adult. The child-prostitute will, almost certainly, have previously been a victim of abuse and, therefore, will have been conditioned to act in a certain way. The child, therefore, will have received her original indoctrination from a previous perpetrator. The adult who is sexually accosted in this way should, of course, invariably act in a responsible manner, even if the sexual encounter was earnestly solicited by the child herself.

> The most commonly used technique of luring the child into this pressured sexual activity is by capitalising on the child's need for attention, approval, and human contact. In such situations, the offender spends considerable time with the child, gives the child a lot of attention, and makes the child out to be special or a favourite. Children respond to attention and are taught to be obedient, so the intended victim co-operates and goes along with sexual demands of the offender in order to secure the promised rewards, or because the child is somewhat confused and does not fully appreciate the ramifications of the situation or does it for approval and recognition.
> – *Nicholas Groth & Jean Birnhaum*

Enforced sexual abuse

> Rape is traumatic because adults consider it so. Adults can speak eloquently about their experience and communicate its pain. Child sexual abuse should be similarly viewed, especially because children cannot speak for themselves.
> – *David Finkelhor*

Enforced sexual abuse will occur when the child has not been given the benefit of any supposed choice at all. Such abuse may befall the child as a chance encounter with a stranger or when a known person simply applies his or her might and strength in order to overpower the victim. Enforced abuse or child-rape, therefore, may or may not occur as a one-off incident. If the child has been repeatedly raped, it will be likely to happen when the perpetrator has uninterrupted access to the victim. The child-victim, for example, could be in community care or otherwise isolated from her family, in which case the perpetrator may or may not be known to the family in question. Where force or duress has been inflicted on the child, of course, the abuser will be able to carry out whatever practices he or she wishes. There may, therefore, be no limit to the extent of the abuse in terms of what actually happened to the client. The violent or sadistic aspects of such experiences do, of course, mean that the client will also have to deal with the emotive issues associated with physical violence. In cases of child rape, moreover, there may be more than one abuser involved in the acts perpetrated against the client. Let us now consider some of the forms that enforced childhood sexual abuse can take.

> In these assaults, sexuality becomes an expression of power and anger. Such offenders describe the victim as small, weak, helpless, unable to resist, easily controlled, and vulnerable. They feel stronger and more dominant in regard to a child. Any resistance on the part of a child may result in increased aggression on the part of the offender; he does not take no for an answer and will enforce his sexual demands.
> – *Nicholas Groth & Jean Birnhaum*

Anger assault

> Sex may become a weapon and a means of discharging anger and frustration when it plays a part in the battering of a child. The intent is to hurt the victim, and the rage of the offender is expressed through both a physical and a sexual assault. Sometimes, the sexual components of such attacks are overshadowed by the general physical brutality directed against the victim.
> – *Nicholas Groth & Jean Birnhaum*

One of the main components in enforced sexual abuse will be the abuser's anger that he or she wishes to discharge directly at the child. The abuser's anger will have been displaced in that it should really be directed at another and will, perhaps, be an expression of frustration at an ongoing or past situation (see Chapter 11, Volume 1 – "Defensive Strategies"). An anger assault, for instance, will be similar to a road-rage incident in that the perpetrator will become angry with an unknown motorist – when, in fact, he or she will actually be inflamed by the pressures and frustrations of life in general and may be looking for an outlet for such pent-up emotive expression.

Power assault

> Sex may come to serve as an expression of power when the offender uses threat, intimidation, and force to capture, command, and control the victim. Such offenders capitalise on the relative helplessness of a child to coerce her or him into sexual activity. A child is targeted as the victim because the child is physically small, unable to resist, weak, and vulnerable. Although it is not the specific intent of such offenders to hurt their victims, resistance on the child's part may release hostility or increased aggression on the part of the offender.
> *– Nicholas Groth & Jean Birnhaum*

Sexual abuse can often be regarded as an abuse of power. The victim will be selected simply because she is defenceless and can, consequently, be forced to submit to the demands of the abuser. The perpetrator will again be looking for a means of expressing his or her strength in human interaction usually as a result of not being able to achieve this state with other adults in normal life. It may also be that the adult's attempts to exercise controlling power have been disastrously thwarted in the past and this factor will have, hence, undermined his or her self-confidence. The abuser may then turn to someone who is obviously helpless and without protection so that he or she can endeavour to prove that he or she has the requisite personal power. The perpetrator, of course, may rarely succeed in such a quest and his or her self-esteem may remain at its low level. For this reason, the molester may wish to continue his or her abusive regime in the hope of succeeding next time.

Sadistic assault

> There is a small group of sexual offenders who derive pleasure in actually hurting the child. Sexuality and aggression become components of a single psychological experience: sadism. Such offenders may torture, mutilate, and, in some cases, murder their victims in the context of the sexual assault.
> *– Nicholas Groth & Jean Birnhaum*

Sadistic sexual abuse will be a means of combining aggression and sexuality in order to cater for the abuser's psychological needs. Sadistic acts can often be compulsive and ritualistic. The offender may plan an attack in advance and may fantasise over its execution until he or she is able to identify an accessible and defenceless target.

Intrafamilial sexual abuse

> The new definition took into consideration that incest – unlike abuse by a
> stranger or acquaintance – violates an ongoing bond of trust between a
> child and a caretaker. Because the perpetrator of incest derives authority
> through a dependency relationship, incest has more serious emotional
> consequences than does abuse by a stranger. Not only is the body
> violated, but the child's trust and love as well.
> – *Sue Blume*

Intrafamilial sexual abuse is usually referred to as incest because it
will occur within the family circle or within the child's immediate
social group. The abuser may, for instance, be a parent, a step-
parent, a grandparent, a sibling, an uncle, an aunt, a cousin or
other more distant relative. Intrafamilial abuse, however, can also
occur when a member of the child's extended family becomes the
perpetrator. A close friend of the family, a neighbour or a babysitter, for example, can become a child-molester virtually as a consequence of having ready access to the victim. The abuser will have
the supposed passport of being in the family circle through which
to enact his or her crime and will have already established a relationship-bond with the child. The practitioner should also remember, however, that older children and teenagers are quite capable of
committing acts of abuse. A child of twelve, for instance, who
abuses a child of five can, of course, do as much psychological
damaged to the client as an adult abuser.

> Incest differs from other forms of sexual abuse in that the perpetrator is
> assumed to stand in a protective parental role to the victim. The very person
> that the child should be able to turn to for care, comfort and understand-
> ing violates that trust by sexualising the relationship. For this to be a
> traumatic experience, it is not necessary that the "parenting" figure be a
> family member. Children naturally trust those adults who are closest to
> them – until there is reason not to. Sexual exploitation by any older care-
> taker is by my definition incestuous because it destroys that natural trust.
> – *Mike Lew*

The closer the relationship-bond to the child, the more the client
will suffer psychologically. This suffering will usually result
because the child will have been confused by the abusive relationship. The client may be disinclined to question the ethics of the
abuser and, thus, will be more likely to comply with his or her
wishes. It will be as if the close relationship-bond will rubber-
stamp the abuser's conduct and this fact will often set up guilt

within the client, who may believe that she has consented. In the case of a more distant relative or a surrogate parent, the abuser will still be known to the child's parents and, therefore, the violation will similarly be given some justification in the child's eyes. Incest is considered to have the greatest psychological consequence for the client because there will have been a betrayal of trust and her childhood security will have been undermined. Because such circumstances often emanate from a greater complexity of family dynamics, moreover, the client will usually have been affected by a number of issues in this situation. Incestuous abuse will also be likely to render the client guilt-ridden because of the taboo nature of incestuous activities in the social and cultural context. Often the client may suffer more from the emotive and mental torment than from the actual form that the abuse might have taken.

> In terms of manifest symptoms, the effects of incestuous abuse can be similar to the effects of paedophilia or child rape. There are, however, some fundamental differences which stem from the fact that incest involves a complex array of variables, which are related both to family dynamics and to the fact that incest victims usually are female. These differences are important and determine therapeutic goals, treatment strategies, and prognosis.
> – *Adele Mayer*

Extrafamilial sexual abuse

> Authorities believe that approximately 80% of paedophiles were themselves molested as children. Paedophilic acts appear to provide these men with reassurance of their masculinity and give them a sense of power over helpless victims. Some paedophiles are compulsively and repetitively re-enacting the trauma of early molestation. Many of these men appear to be fixated at the age when they were molested, ie, if they were molested at eight or nine, their emotional and psychological growth remains stunted and they tend to have sexual preferences for boys or girls of the same age.
> – *Adele Mayer*

Extrafamilial sexual abuse will transpire when the abuser is not a member of the child's immediate family circle but may, officially, be known to the family. A neighbour, a teacher, a care-worker or a similar unknown party may, for example, become the perpetrator of this form of abuse. If the offender is known to or, in some way, recognised by the client's family, however, the abusive acts may gain acceptance in the child's eyes. In adulthood, the client may still hold her family responsible for the abuse even if the offender was a complete stranger to the family and the abuse took place as a result of a chance encounter. The client, in such cases, may justifiably consider that she was insufficiently well protected by her own family.

Extrafamilial paedophilic acts may occur because the child was enticed into becoming a chance victim or lured into forming a temporary relationship the child-molester. It may transpire, moreover, that the abuse took place because the child was forcibly attacked or raped. The child who is solicited with a view to becoming a child-prostitute or is exploited for pornographic purposes, therefore, will also be a victim of extrafamilial abuse. The child may often be exploited for several reasons in connection with the sexual gratification of the adult for both prostitution and pornography and, indeed, violent attacks may also enter into this equation. While intrafamilial abuse may affect the client more profoundly in psychological terms because of her close family connection with the violator of the abuse, extrafamilial abuse, on the other hand, may be more terrifying in view of its grossly horrific nature.

> Some of the most widely cited theories about paedophilia explain that sexual abusers choose children for sexual partners because children have some especially compelling emotional meaning for them.
> – *David Finkelhor & Sharon Araji*

Theories of Intrafamilial Sexual Abuse

> The incest taboo is universal in human culture. Though no single definition of the taboo applies among all peoples, no known culture permits unrestricted sexual union among kin. Almost all cultures prohibit intercourse and marriage within what is known as the nuclear family, that is, between parents and children, brothers and sisters.
> – *Judith Lewis Herman & Lisa Hirschman*

Childhood sexual abuse will be likely to occur when the client's family has been mildly or severely dysfunctional and it will often be useful for the practitioner to identify which system or collection of systems may have been in operation when dealing with the abused victim. Let us now consider some theories of intrafamilial childhood sexual abuse with a view to understanding the psychological logic behind the motivation for incestuous relationships.

The functional theory

> The functional explanation suggests that the act of incest serves some
> purpose. The function usually occurs within the family, although the
> incest can also serve a more general function in larger societal units or in
> a family's interactions with society.
> *– Jeffrey Haugaard & Dickon Reppucci*

The functional theory of incestuous abuse states that the abuse
holds a function in maintaining the behavioural patterns of the
family-unit in which it occurs. Sometimes the function that the
incestuous abuse will serve may be to provide a form of sexual
indulgence that will be overtly or covertly sanctioned by the unit.
Sexual licence might be seen as the only way of keeping the unit
intact or keeping it running smoothly. A delinquent boy, for example, might be pacified by having sex with his sister rather as an
infant can be quietened by being given sweets. In a closely-knit
society, moreover, sex among siblings might be considered a better
alternative than taking partners from nonmembers of the enclave.

> This family too teaches all the wrong lessons about power and
> powerlessness, control and loss of control. This father also acts on a sense
> of entitlement at the expense of others. He does not ask for what he
> wants; he simply takes. If assertiveness can be seen as a respectful,
> healthy pursuit of one's needs, he is no more *assertive* than the dominant,
> abusing father. He simply focuses his domination only on his children,
> for he does not have the capacity to face his adult partner with his
> complaints or emotional needs. In the outside world, where he must
> compete for his rights with other men, he is often seen as a wimp.
> *– Sue Blume*

The family-systems theory

> The family systems theory on incest has its roots in the functional
> explanation and is currently the most widely accepted theory in the
> mental health field. Rather than viewing the incest as the cause of the
> problems that are almost always associated with incestuous families, this
> theory sees incest as a symptom of an already dysfunctional family
> system. By their nature as a set of interacting individuals, families
> develop rules of behaviour that govern the functioning of each
> individual and the family as a whole.
> *– Jeffrey Haugaard & Dickon Reppucci*

The family-systems theory of childhood sexual abuse is the most widely acknowledged systemic model used to account for father–daughter incest. This theory, therefore, will be of particular relevance to the client who has been a victim of this form of molestation. The family-systems theory ascribes the abuser's motivation to a product of a dysfunctional element that already exists within the family. The family will, thus, live by a set of rules that govern the behaviour and interactions of each of its members. Whatever behaviour gains acceptance within the family-unit will obtain even if such conduct is totally unacceptable outside the family-unit in society as a whole.

The most commonly-noted behavioural pattern documented by family therapists with regard to incest, attributes the reason for its occurrence to the deterioration in the incestuous father's relationship with his wife or partner – usually the victim's mother. The incestuous father will then view his daughter as a better alternative to his wife or partner. The daughter-victim will be regarded by her father as being able to fulfil all his psychological needs by giving unstinting love and affection and will be someone over whom he can have absolute control. Often the incestuous father will have himself been a childhood victim of sexual abuse and his incestuous acts will, therefore, be committed as a coping-strategy for his own psychological trauma. The incestuous father will, of course, be in a supreme position of trust and his daughter will be naturally predisposed to need affection even when it may only be forthcoming in a particularly perverted form. In families with many children, the daughter-victim may occasionally feel that her status has been elevated as a result of being an abuse-victim (see Chapter 3, Volume 1 – "Individual Psychology"). Statistically, it seems that the eldest daughter will usually be the most favoured target but such a victim may suffer tenfold if the incestuous father later turns his attentions to another sibling.

> Denial has always been the incestuous father's first line of defence. For a long time it has served him well. The belief that incest is extremely uncommon, and the tendency to discredit children's reports of sexual encounters with adults, have until recently remained entrenched in the public consciousness. With the collusion of the larger society, the incestuous father has thus been largely successful in preserving his secret.
> – *Judith Lewis Herman & Lisa Hirschman*

Abusive acts are often rationalised by the incestuous father when he convinces himself that he is showing love to his daughter, teaching her about sex or avoiding an extramarital affair (see Chapter 11, Volume 1 – "Defensive Strategies"). Such rationalisation, of course, will disguise the fact that the father-perpetrator will have a total disregard for the true feelings of his daughter in the interests of satisfying his own salacious needs.

With father–daughter incest, the role of the victim's mother will also be called into question. Mother may be, in some circumstances, colluding with the abuser in an endeavour to resolve the conflict within her own relationship with her partner. Mother, alternatively, may merely be absent or not overly protective of the child. In dealing with the client who had been the victim of father–daughter incest, it may well be necessary for the practitioner to decipher which family dynamics have been at work in any given case.

> If it must be conceded, first, that father–daughter incest occurs commonly, and second, that it is not a harmless pastime, then apologists for the incestuous father are thrown back upon their third an final excuse: he is not responsible for his actions. Most commonly, they blame his daughter, his wife, or both. Thus we make the acquaintance of the two major culprits in the incest romance, the Seductive Daughter and the Collusive Mother. Ensnared by the charms of a small temptress, or driven to her arms by a frigid, unloving wife, Poor Father can hardly help himself, or so his defenders would have us believe. Often he believes it himself.
> – *Judith Lewis Herman & Lisa Hirschman*

The feminist theory

> Rather than conceptualising incest as serving a function, the feminist explanation sees incest as another example of the basic inequality between the sexes that has been perpetrated throughout history by the patriarchal social system. Most men are taught openly or subtly that they have the right to have their sexual urges satisfied. The social system reinforces both this belief and the obligation of other family members to keep the father content. Incest occurs because the father feels justified in turning to his daughter for sex if it is unavailable from his wife.
> – *Jeffrey Haugaard & Dickon Reppucci*

The feminist theory of childhood sexual abuse has been based on patriarchal principles in which the male is the dominant member of any family-unit, society or social group. Women and children in such a system will be dependent on the male, whose demands and wishes must be satisfied. Any unfair or deviant behaviour on the part of the male will be impossible to change because of the absolute dependence of others on him and the need for utter compliance with his demands. The abusive male will, therefore, be absolved of any responsibility for his actions because he will be king of his own realm. All blame will, thus, be automatically attributed to the females in the family-unit or the close-knit society. If a female, for example, is totally dependent on her male partner for financial survival, he may elect to misuse this position of power and give himself carte blanche to act as he pleases. If the dominant male in this situation desires to abuse both mother and children, then the explanation will be that the women and the children are to blame for attracting the abuse or otherwise upsetting the dominant male. The females, consequently, will become submissive and obedient by consent, even though they may be harming themselves and deceiving themselves in the process.

> The incest experience represents abuses of power and loss of control. Families where paternal incest occurs are generally characterised by a power imbalance wherein a father wields absolute authority over a relatively powerless wife and children. He asks no one's permission or approval for anything he does. He takes what he wants, expecting others to accommodate him. Often, he exercises his power in abusive, violent ways. What passes for order is really frozen chaos.
> – *Sue Blume*

The chaotic theory

> A few historical studies have found an apparently high incidence of incest in communities that are undergoing tremendous change and that as a consequence do not have a solid sense of community standards.
> – *Jeffrey Haugaard & Dickon Reppucci*

The chaotic theory of childhood sexual abuse will assume that the family-unit will be undergoing some form of serious change or disruption that will affect all members. The stress associated with such fundamental life-disruption will then invite the abuser to lift his or her inhibitions about incest. The abuser will, thus, home in on the chaotic situation as an excuse for relieving the stress of the situation. A family rendered homeless or in financial crisis, for example, might be regarded as a situation of chaos that could engender extraordinary behavioural patterns. The chaos, hence, will become a fertile breeding-ground for incestuous activity that will then appear to be condoned by all members of the unit.

The individual-pathology theory

> Much of the early theorising about those who broke the incest taboo postulated that they were mentally or emotionally disturbed. One belief was that most of the perpetrators of incest were schizophrenic or were suffering from some other sort of psychosis that put them out of touch with normal societal expectations.
> – *Jeffrey Haugaard & Dickon Reppucci*

The individual-pathology theory of childhood sexual abuse tends to label the child-molester as being in some way mentally deranged. Subsequent research, however, has proved that only a small minority of abusive cases are perpetrated by abusers who are seriously psychotic. The abuser, in most cases, will manage to function reasonably well in society and may display only a few signs of psychological turmoil to the onlooker in the outside world. Often the molester will know precisely what he or she is doing and has been known to plan repeatedly premeditated acts that will then remain undetected.

The cycle-of-abuse theory

> But there do seem to be occasions when a family may show such a cycle of abuse. One suggestion is that abusing parents provide role models, which mean that their children learn to see distressed behaviour as a signal for aggressive reactions. It has also been suggested that abusing parents inhibit the natural empathetic tendencies of their children, which in turn could produce these effects. This means that the child does not really come to see events from the other person's point of view, and this links with some of the recent research into children's understanding of people's minds.
> – *Nicky Hayes*

The cycle-of-childhood-sexual-abuse theory states that the abused child can become an abusive molester in adulthood and will continue to perpetuate the wrongs that were originally inflicted on him or her. The child will learn an inappropriate form of behaviour from a role-model because he or she has not been properly shown how to behave towards others and, therefore, did not develop appropriate and empathetic responses to others. The child, in these circumstances, can become conditioned to associating distress with an aggressive response and so will be able to commit abuse in a nonchalant and cold-hearted manner. It will be as if the child-molester renders himself or herself devoid of emotive concern for the child and, therefore, remains in heavy and unshakable denial (see Chapter 11, Volume 1 – "Defensive Strategies").

Why Does Childhood Sexual Abuse Occur?

This tendency to blame the victim has strongly influenced the direction of psychological inquiry. It has led researchers and clinicians to seek an explanation for the perpetrator's crimes in the character of the victim.
– *Judith Lewis Herman*

Before studying the effect of childhood abuse on the client, we need to look at the source of the problem – the perpetrator. The fact is that it will be the state of mind and the psychology of the abuser that will lead to childhood abuse and not the vulnerability of the victim. The perpetrator must plan, initiate and carry out the acts of abuse. Without an abuser there would be no abuse and the potential victim would not, hence, become a victim. From an eclectic perspective, we can make the assumption that the abuser will have freedom of choice – albeit limited – although unconscious mechanisms often seem uncontrollably to dictate the options available to him or her. The exception to this might possibly be the psychotic who has lost total control of his or her reasoning abilities, but even this individual will still be susceptible to the psychological mechanisms that generate abusive tendencies. The practitioner should, therefore, regard the client who has been a victim of childhood abuse as being entirely blameless – even if she did later in life tread the same intrepid path as her perpetrator. If this stance if adopted by the practitioner, the client will then be free to release her innermost psychological turmoil in a neutral climate.

We are indebted to David Finkelhor and his colleagues who were instrumental in pioneering some research in the 1970s and 1980s on the question of childhood sexual abuse. Finkelhor unearthed and questioned much of the existing published literature about the characteristics and the role of the child sexual abuser. Finkelhor has developed what he describes as the *multifactor analysis of sexual abusers*, that identifies the possible reasons why an individual may become a child-molester. This four-level model distils the variety of research theories proposed by integrating a number of different ideas and not relying on any one set of doctrines. The first three factors of *emotional congruence, sexual arousal* and *sexual blockage* illustrate the way in which a potential child-molester can be motivated to become an abuser and the final factor of *disinhibition* relates to the way in which this interest can be translated into the abusive behaviours (see Figure 5 – "The child-abuser's psychology and motivation"). A child-abuser would need to fulfil all these requirements prior to committing an act of violation against a child. The potential abuser, however, does not necessarily become a child-molester if certain inhibiting factors can keep that individual within the bounds of the law and within the compass of social ethics.

> I cannot imagine that any murderers or criminals do not act out of an inner compulsion. Nevertheless they are guilty when they destroy or mutilate human life. Although the law acknowledges "mitigating circumstances" when it can be proved that the criminal is not responsible for his actions, his motivation and personal plight do not alter the fact that one or more human lives had to be sacrificed for his situation.
> – Alice Miller

Emotional congruence

> We have called this "emotional congruence" because it conveys the idea of a "fit" between the adult's emotional needs and the child's characteristics, a fit for which the theories are trying to account.
> – David Finkelhor

The emotional-congruence factor was formulated in an attempt to answer the question, "Why would a person find relating sexually to a child to be emotionally gratifying and congruent?" Emotional congruence means that the offender will relate sexually to the child because the relationship will satisfy some emotive need within him

Figure 5 – The child-abuser's psychology and motivation

The abuser's psychology	Personal motivation	Social and cultural motivation
Emotional congruence The abuser's psychological needs will be fulfilled by the child-victim	**Emotional congruence factors** The abuser may have an arrested development, may have a need to feel powerful and may have a need to re-enact his or her own traumatic past	**Emotional congruence factors** There may be an acceptance of masculine sexual dominance
Sexual arousal The abuser will have a sexual interest in the child-victim	**Sexual arousal factors** The abuser may have had previous sexual conditioning to child-molestation	**Sexual arousal factors** There may be an acceptance of the child-sex culture and the masculine tendency to sexualise psychological needs
Sexual blockage The abuser will have a developmental restraint or a situational impediment to sexual expression	**Sexual blockage factors** The abuser may have an unresolved oedipus/electra complex and may have relationship difficulties with other adults	**Sexual blockage factors** There may be repressive norms about masturbation and extramarital sex
Disinhibition The abuser will overcome the child-victim's resistance	**Overcoming internal inhibitors** The abuser may indulge in substance-abuse, may suffer from psychosis and may suffer from senile dementia	**Internal inhibition factors** There may be an acceptance of the child-sex culture, patriarchal prerogatives and weak criminal sanctions against offenders
	Overcoming external inhibitors The child-victim may lack protection, may be inadequately supervised and may be readily accessible to the abuser	**External inhibition factors** There may be a lack of social support for the mother, barriers to women's equality, an erosion of social networks and an ideology of family-sanctity
	Overcoming the child's resistance The child-victim may be emotionally insecure, may be emotionally deprived, may lack appropriate knowledge and may trust the abuser implicitly	**Childhood factors** There may be a lack of sex education for the child-victim and the child-victim may be rendered socially powerless

or her. The child-molester may be an individual with an arrested psychological and psychosexual development – usually exhibiting a narcissistic overidentification with the self (see Chapter 7 – "Fear and Anxiety Disorders"). The abuser, therefore, may be locked into his or her own childhood and fixated on his or her own traumatic past experience (see Chapter 16, Volume 1 – "Personality Development"). Because the abuser will have immature psychological needs he or she may, thus, relate to the child as an extension of himself or herself. The sexual relationship with the child may ostensibly be the means by which the molester can validate himself or herself in terms of personal relationships and social interaction. If the offender has a narcissistic personality disorder, moreover, then the child may be a same-gender victim. In the abusive relationship, the abuser will be given a feeling of power and dominance that can appear to compensate for his or her personal sense of inadequacy and shame (see Chapter 8 – "Guilt and Shame Disorders"). This emotional congruence may be generated because the child will appear to be powerless and, therefore, can be easily controlled and dominated by the abuser. The offender will possibly possess a low self-esteem that may need that extra boost that dominance over another would provide (see Chapter 12 – "Dysfunctional Relationships"). The child-molester may also be attempting to reverse the power roles in order to overcome his or her own previous traumatic abuse. The former victim may then become the victimiser in the mistaken belief that this will relieve her own feelings of powerlessness that were experienced at the hands of another violator.

Sexual arousal

> "Sexually arousing" would mean a physiological response (such things as penile tumescence) to the presence of children or to fantasies of children in sexual activities. There are good experimental data, using physiological measurements, that child molesters, including incest offenders, do show unusual levels of sexual arousal to children.
> – *David Finkelhor*

The sexual arousal factor was formulated in an attempt to answer the question, "Why would a person be capable of being sexually aroused by a child?" Sexual arousal will occur when the child becomes a potential source of sexual gratification for the abuser (see Chapter 12 – "Dysfunctional Relationships"). The issue here will centre on the fact that the molester will be intrinsically sexually attracted to a child-subject. It seems clear that the attraction will be undeniably strong and virtually uncontrollable and it is considered that such attraction will be ever-present because of the molester's previous experiences or prior learning. The abuser will have, therefore, been conditioned to evoke a sexual response to the child. This reaction may be employed as a coping-strategy for past trauma, as a means of recapturing past fantasies of pleasure or as a way of escaping from reality. A sexual response may be evoked because of the abuser's early conditioning to sexual arousal in a childhood environment – perhaps when he or she was himself or herself violated as a child. Such conditioning may, in addition, dictate the abuser's choice of gender of the child-victim. It may be that the abuser, in some way, will confuse affectionate contact with the child with acts of sexual involvement. It has also been postulated that the reasons for this will be that society has become accustomed to the idea that child-pornography is a relatively freely accessible part of our culture.

Sexual blockage

> The man who finds himself to be impotent in his first sexual attempts, or abandoned by his first lover, may come to associate adult sexuality with pain and frustration. This avenue having been filled with trauma, he chooses children as a substitute gratification.
> – *David Finkelhor*

The sexual-blockage factor was formulated in an attempt to answer the question, "Why would a person be frustrated or blocked in efforts to obtain sexual and emotional gratification from more normatively approved sources?" The blockage factor implies that alternative sources of sexual and emotive gratification were not available to the offender or were, in some way, less satisfying. Blockage to sexual and emotive expression will often result from the abuser's inability to form sustaining and fruitful relationships with other adults (see Chapter 12 – "Dysfunctional Relationships"). The abuser may feel sexually inadequate in the presence of prospective adult sexual partners, for instance, and this sense of inadequacy will then serve as a blockage to normal adult sexual relationships. The child-molester has been described as timid, unassertive, inadequate and awkward in social situations with particular reference to sexual relationships.

The developmental blockage
A developmental blockage to sexual expression will occur if the offender has his or her own in-built inhibitive factors that will block any outlet for normal and satisfactory sexual expression. The offender, for example, may be someone who does not have a sexual partner or who has been unable to secure one of a satisfactory nature. Some theorists ascribe the reason for the offender's inhibited social interaction to the oedipus complex or the electra complex (see Chapter 16, Volume 1 – "Personality Development"). If the abuser has been suffering from an unresolved oedipus complex or electra complex, then the choice of gender of the child-victim may depend on the past relationship with the molester's parent. An overdependency on a parent, moreover, may induce an attraction towards a victim of the same sex as the parent. Conversely, if a dictatorial parent has instilled terror in the abuser, then this may mean that he or she will be inclined to turn his or her attentions towards a child of the opposite sex from that of the authoritative parent.

The situational blockage
A situational blockage to sexual expression will refer to an ongoing crisis in which, perhaps, an existing sexual partnership was continually problematic for the offender. When one considers the plethora of sexual taboos in society, of course, the options available to a potential sexual violator may well mean that child-abuse, for example, may, ironically, be considered to be preferable to having an extramarital affair or to raping another adult. The choice of gender of the child-subject may well, consequently, be dictated by the gender of the partner with whom the abuser has been in conflict.

Disinhibition

> A final factor that needs to be explained about child molesters is why conventional inhibitions against having sex with children are overcome or are not present. Among sex abusers, apparently, ordinary controls are circumvented or there is a higher level of acceptability for such behaviour.
> – *David Finkelhor*

The disinhibition factor was formulated in an attempt to answer the question, "Why would a person not be deterred by the conventional social restraints and inhibitions against having sexual relations with a child?" The potential child-molester, who will have a lack of inhibition to the sexual abuse of children or minors, will often be an individual with certain personality characteristics that render him or her incapable of making appropriate decisions about his or her actions (see Chapter 15, Volume 1 – "Personality Structure"). The offender, for instance, may suffer from having a poor impulse-control tendency, may have a substance-abuse problem, may be psychotic or may be potentially senile. Any means by which a potential offender's inhibitions are lowered, furthermore, can give rise to a debased impulse-control factor and, thus, could lead him or her to sexually-deviant behavioural tendencies (see Chapter 12 – "Dysfunctional Relationships").

In some societies, of course, there may be an implied sanctioning of the abuse of minors. In cultures, for example, that subscribe to patriarchal philosophies by unquestionably condoning parental authority, credence may then be given to the belief that the male is all-powerful and should be dominant towards all females and minors. Here the environment will be ripe for child-abuse should the potential perpetrator care to take advantage of the situation and, in any case, he or she may be suffering from some form of psychological disturbance that will have already broken down restrictive social and cultural conditioning. An intensely stressful situation – such as homelessness, destitution or bereavement – may also act as the straw that breaks the camel's back in the case of a potential abuser who, for most of his or her life, will have managed to exercise restraint as a result of social conditioning. Cultural and social taboos, in some cases, may well act as an inhibitor when the abuser selects a victim in terms of gender. The girl-victim, for example, may be selected by the male who fears being a homosexual. The boy-victim, similarly, may be chosen because the idea of raping a helpless girl will not be in the offender's personal code of conduct.

We shall now analyse an uncannily-typical hypothetical case of incestuous abuse that can serve to illustrate the way in which the practitioner can identify the multifactor analysis of sexual abusers. In this example, Robert enters into a relationship with his daughter that attempts to solve a number of his psychological problems.

The relationship serves not only to settle the score with his wife but also becomes an attempt to relieve some of Robert's own childhood trauma.

Case-study example – incestuous abuse

A shy, introverted man called Robert married an aggressive and dominant woman called Angela, who had a high-powered job and earned most of the family income.

Robert had not had any sexual experience prior to his marriage, although his wife had had a number of previous encounters. Because of Robert's lack of experience, his low sexual self-esteem was further dented after his marriage because his wife was attractive and flirtatious. When conflict arose in the marriage, Angela turned her attentions to others. Robert then felt even more sexually inadequate and eventually became impotent towards his wife as a result. Robert was not only jealous of his wife's admirers but also was envious of her sexual prowess. Robert was, thus, hurt by the loss of his wife's affection but was powerless to recapture it. Robert also felt angry with Angela for hurting him and for robbing him of his manhood. Moreover, Robert also felt angry with himself for being unable to challenge Angela about her infidelity because of his impotence and personal inadequacies and because of her aggressive nature. Any attempts to regain his wife were met by ridicule and only served to reinforce Robert's inadequacies. Robert was, therefore, in a sexual dilemma of being unable to satisfy his wife and yet unable to seek relief from his sexual frustrations outside the marriage.

Robert's young daughter, Mary, doted on him, although his son, Daniel, the first born, tended to favour Angela. Mary was shy and retiring but became "Daddy's favourite" and gloried in this exalted position. Robert relished Mary's unfailing and unequivocal devotion. Because of Angela's high-profile job, Robert frequently found himself responsible for looking after the children. When tragedy struck and Robert lost his job, his marriage was thrown into jeopardy because his wife felt disinclined to support him financially. Robert agreed, however, to take on the full-time role of caring for the children until he could find alternative work. Robert then had plenty of time to be alone with his devoted daughter.

By this time, Robert now felt personally and sexually inadequate and yet could see no way of bettering himself and could find no outlet for his desires. This personal *sexual blockage* made Robert feel frustrated and hurt. Because of his low self-esteem, Robert also felt an *emotional congruence* with his daughter because of her dependence on him.

Because Robert had, as a child, been sexually abused by a female babysitter, he found that he had a tendency towards *sexual arousal* with regard to young children. In fact, Robert had also been secretly reading some child-pornography magazines that a drinking-acquaintance had lent him recently. One day, during a game with Mary, he found that he had achieved an erection. Robert was delighted because he had not been able to be aroused by a female for some time. Robert then decided that he could encourage Mary to fondle his erect penis in the mistaken belief that she was too young to realise what was actually happening. Robert also believed that he could persuade her not to tell Angela and so took the opportunity to indulge in this form of supposedly-innocent pleasure. Robert felt that his own encounter with the babysitter had not had any effect on him and so he seized this longed-for opportunity and thus *disinhibition* occurred. Robert was then able to masturbate himself and to achieve orgasmic relief. Mary now merely became an onlooker with a rather confused expression on her face.

When Does Childhood Sexual Abuse Occur?

The factors and preconditions that will be in evidence prior to the point at which the abuser will descend upon his or her prey have also been documented. Finkelhor has formulated the *four-preconditions model of sexual abuse*, that draws together research into the reasons why the ground may be fertile for the child to be abused. These preconditions follow a logical progression starting from the initial motivation to molest, followed by the unveiling of inhibitions through to overcoming the child's resistance. With this model, again, all preconditions must be fulfilled prior to the occurrence of the sexually-abusive act.

Motivation

> A model of sexual abuse needs to account for how a person (an adult or adolescent) becomes motivated for or interested in having sexual contact with a child.
> – *David Finkelhor*

The precondition of motivation to abuse the child sexually has been formulated because it became apparent in research that the potential offender would need to have some motivation to do so. When considering sexual motivation, the first three factors in the multifactor analysis of sexual abusers have been taken into account as being components of the motivational precondition. Thus, emotional congruence, sexual arousal and sexual blockage factors are motivational components. These three components will need to exist – although not all in equal proportions – in the molester's mind in order to account for the source of the motivation. The proportions of these components will influence whether the offender's interest in the child will be strong and persistent or, conversely, will be weak and episodic. The abuser's choice of victim by gender would also be similarly influenced.

Personal factors

The main personal factors that will motivate the potential abuser to perform sexually-abusive acts in terms of emotional congruence have been cited as being that he or she may have an arrested psychological development. The abuser may have a need to feel powerful and controlling because of a low self-esteem that will usually be the result of a narcissistic identification with the self as a young child (see Chapter 7 – "Fear and Anxiety Disorders"). Additionally, the abuser may also have a need to re-enact his or her own childhood trauma in order to attempt to relieve the accompanying psychological distress (see Chapter 11, Volume 1 – "Defensive Strategies").

The main personal factors that will motivate the potential abuser to perform sexually-abusive acts in terms of sexual arousal have been cited as being that he or she may have had a childhood sexual experience that was traumatic and, consequently, strongly conditioning. The perpetrator may, therefore, have a model to follow of sexual interest in children that was created by someone else. The abuser may also suffer from an abnormality that can result in a misattribution of arousal cues so that the child will become the target of sexual arousal rather than another adult.

The main personal factors that will motivate the potential abuser to perform sexually-abusive acts in terms of blockage to sexual and emotive expression have been cited as being that he or she may have an unresolved Oedipus complex or Electra complex (see Chapter 16, Volume 1 – "Personality Development"). The child-molester may, for instance, have a fear of the opposite sex, owing to inadequate social skills, may have a marital or partnership problem and may have had a traumatic sexual experience with another adult (see Chapter 12 – "Dysfunctional Relationships").

Social and cultural factors
The main social and cultural factors that will motivate the potential abuser to perform sexually-abusive acts in terms of emotional congruence have been cited as being that in many societies and cultures there may be a male need for dominance and power in any sexual encounter.

The main social and cultural factors that will motivate the potential abuser to perform sexually-abusive acts in terms of sexual arousal have been cited as being that in many societies and cultures there may be an acceptance of child-pornography, an erotic portrayal of children in advertising and the masculine tendency to sexualise all emotional needs.

The main social and cultural factors that will motivate the potential abuser to perform sexually-abusive acts in terms of blockage to sexual expression have been cited as being that in many societies and cultures there may be repressive norms about masturbation and extramarital sex. There may, thus, often be an urgent need for the potential abuser to find an alternative and fulfilling outlet for sexual gratification when there has been strife in his or her immediate environment.

Overcoming internal inhibitors

> In order for sexual abuse to occur, a potential offender not only needs to
> be motivated to commit abuse, but the offender must overcome internal
> inhibitions against acting on those motives. We presume that most
> members of society have such inhibitions. If there are those who do not,
> then the absence of inhibitions needs to be explained.
> *– David Finkelhor*

The precondition to overcome internal inhibitors has been formulated because it became apparent in research that the potential
offender had to overcome internal inhibitions against acting on his
or her motivation. Lack of inhibition will be the main reason why
the abuser's motivation will be unleashed. It seems clear that this
prerequisite will need to be indisputable because the potential
abuser might desire to abuse the child but may be strongly inhibited from doing so and, therefore, would remain only a potential
threat to the victim.

Personal factors
The main personal factors that will predispose the potential abuser
to overcome internal inhibitors have been cited as being that he or
she may suffer from an alcohol-abuse problem, psychosis or senile
dementia. The potential abuser may, moreover, exhibit an inappropriate impulse-disorder and a failure of the inhibition-mechanism,
particularly in family-dynamics.

Social and cultural factors
The main social and cultural factors that will predispose the potential abuser to overcome internal inhibitors have been cited as being
that in many societies and cultures there may be a social tolerance
of sexual interest in children and an acceptance of child-pornography. Similarly, there may be an ideology of patriarchal prerogatives
for fathers as well as the masculine inability to identify with the
needs of children. From a legal point of view, there may also be
weak criminal sanctions against offenders and a social tolerance of
deviance committed while a criminal is drugged or intoxicated.

Overcoming external inhibitors

> The first two preconditions try to account for the behaviour of
> perpetrators. But it is quite clear that such accounts do not fully explain
> to whom or why abuse occurs. A man fully motivated to abuse sexually
> who is also disinhibited may not do so, and he certainly may not do so
> with a particular child. There are factors outside himself that control
> whether he abuses and who he abuses.
> *– David Finkelhor*

The precondition to overcome external inhibitors has been formulated because it became apparent in research that the potential
offender would need to overcome external impediments to committing childhood sexual abuse.

Personal factors
The main personal factors that will predispose the potential abuser
to overcome external inhibitors have been cited as being that the
child's mother may be absent or ill, she may not be close to the
child, she may not adequately protect the child and she may be
dominated by her male partner. Perhaps there may also be a general lack of supervision of the child and there may be unusual
opportunities for the potential abuser to be alone with the child.
The child may also have been socially isolated from her family –
for example, when she has been placed at a boarding school or in
community care. Similarly, there may be unusual sleeping or
rooming conditions that render the child readily accessible to the
abuser.

Social and cultural factors
The main social and cultural factors that will predispose the potential abuser to overcome external inhibitors have been cited as being
that in many societies and cultures there may be a lack of social
support for mothers and there are barriers to women's equality.
There may also be an erosion of social networks that can leave the
child stranded. There may, moreover, be an ideology of family-
sanctity that would give the potential abuser an unimpeded
licence to abuse the child incestuously.

Overcoming resistance

> Children themselves play an important role in whether or not they are
> abused, and any full explanation of why abuse occurs needs to take into
> account factors related to the child. Children have a capacity to avoid or
> resist abuse. Unfortunately, since professionals are mostly in contact
> with children who were abused, the importance of this capacity is not
> often realised.
> – *David Finkelhor*

The precondition to overcome the victim's resistance has been formulated because it became apparent in research that the potential
offender would have to undermine or to overcome the child's possible resistance to the sexually-abusive activity initiated by the
child-molester.

Personal factors
The main personal factors that will predispose the potential abuser
to overcome the child's resistance have been cited as being that the
victim may be emotionally insecure or deprived. The child, for
instance, may lack knowledge about what constitutes sexual abuse
– usually, of course, due to her innocence and naïveté. A position
of unusual trust, furthermore, may exist between the child and the
abuser and, so, the crime-perpetrator should be able to easily
coerce the child into indulging in inappropriate behaviour.

Social and cultural factors
The main social and cultural factors that will predispose the potential abuser to overcome the child's resistance have been cited as
being that in many societies and cultures there may be a lack of
sex-education for children about the dangers of sexual abuse and
children may often have a strong degree of social powerlessness.

Let us now return to our hypothetical example of incestuous abuse
in which the four-preconditions model of childhood sexual abuse
can be illustrated.

Case-study example – incestuous sexual abuse

In our example of Robert's abuse of his daughter Mary, we can see that he was *sexually motivated* because of his affinity and rapport with his daughter, his failed marriage and his personal sexual inadequacies. Because of Robert's own abusive childhood, he also had a low sexual self-esteem and a need to re-enact his own childhood sexual trauma.

Robert would also have been able to *overcome internal inhibitions* to the abuse of his daughter because he believed that his own trauma had not affected him and that Mary was too young to understand anyway. The existence and accessibility of the pornographic literature did, in Robert's mind, moreover, convey an acceptance of this activity with his daughter. Because Robert had been rather sexually desperate, he also felt that he could not miss an opportunity to gain sexual gratification and so he acted on impulse. Robert also observed that Angela had taken little interest in the upbringing of her children and that he had, therefore, been in a unique position to gain access to the child as her primary carer. Robert knew that no-one would be around to witness or to question his actions and, so, he was easily able to *overcome external inhibitors*, owing to his privileged position and the easy availability of his victim.

As Mary had been such a doting daughter with whom Robert played often, he would have been easily able to *overcome resistance* to any approach he might make towards her. The abuse, in fact, had occurred almost naturally – as if by accident. Because Robert had enjoyed a special relationship with his daughter and because Angela was not a particularly attentive mother, silencing Mary had been successfully achieved. Robert was able to convince Mary that they shared a special secret because she was his favourite child. Naturally, Robert knew all about domination, because he himself had been dominated by his mother and was now being dominated by his wife. Robert could, therefore, slip easily and effortlessly into the role of powerful parent when the victim was an adoring and trusting child.

What is the Psychology of the Abuser?

In examining the developmental histories of repetitive sexual aggressors
(rapists and child molesters), about one-third of these men appear to
have experienced some type of sexual trauma during their formative years.
– Nicholas Groth & Jean Birnhaum

The practitioner may benefit from an understanding of the psychology of the abuser when treating the client who has been the
victim of sexual abuse. The therapist may then be able to help the
client to appreciate the abuser's standpoint when it comes to
apportioning blame (see Chapter 8 – "Guilt and Shame Disorders").
The practitioner may also find it necessary to understand the
abuser's psychological disposition in case he finds himself actually
faced – whether by choice or by chance – with the client who has
previously abused a child in a sexual context.

Myths about the sexual abuser

Female children are regularly subjected to sexual assaults by adult males
who are part of their intimate social world. The aggressors are not
outcasts and strangers; they are neighbours, family friends, uncles,
cousins, stepfathers, and fathers. To be sexually exploited by a known
and trusted adult is a central and formative experience in the lives of
countless women. This disturbing fact, embarrassing to men in general
and to fathers in particular, has been repeatedly unearthed in the past
hundred years, and just as repeatedly buried. Any serious investigation
of the emotional and sexual lives of women leads eventually to the
discovery of the incest secret. But until recently, each investigator who
has made this discovery has ended by suppressing it. The information
was simply too threatening to be maintained in public consciousness.
– Judith Lewis Herman & Lisa Hirschman

Initially, we can dispel the commonly-held myths about the characteristics of the child-molester. All such myths can often be traced
back to a convenient explanation that the layman would wish to
adopt in order to avoid having to face up to the more unpleasant
side of human nature. Obviously, when looking for an explanation
of abnormal behaviour, the public can be inclined to blame external factors for the occurrence of childhood sexual abuse. The myths
that abound about the abusive characteristics of mankind will
often be the public's uncomplicated way of evading personal
responsibility and not touching personal unpleasantness. It will be

important for the practitioner, however, to be knowledgeable about the facts and statistics relating to childhood sexual abuse and to be clear in his own mind about what may be fact and what may be fiction in readiness for those occasions when he will need to dispel any prevailing myths in the client's mind.

> In this theory sexual abusers of children were seen as psychopathic, feeble-minded, physical and moral degenerates, but such preconceptions did not long withstand the light of evidence.
> – *David Finkelhor*

Perhaps the abuser was a dirty old man

> The sexual attraction to children is sometimes attributed to senility. In fact, we found that the offenders range in age from 14 to 73, with the majority (105, or 71%) of the subjects referred to us under the age of 35.
> – *Nicholas Groth & Jean Birnhaum*

The child offender can sometimes be erroneously regarded as simply a "dirty old man" who has lost control of all mental faculties. Often the abuser will be far from senile or unaware of his or her actions, owing to advancing years. Most attacks on children are premeditated and preplanned and the abuser, therefore, will certainly be in full control of his or her actions.

Perhaps the abuser was a stranger

> Often parents caution their children not to talk to strangers in the hope of protecting them from sexual victimisation. The irony is that only 43 (29%) of the offenders who were studied selected victims who were complete strangers. In the majority (105, or 71%) of cases, the offender and the victim knew each other at least casually, and in 20 (14%) of the cases, the offender was a member of the child's immediate family (father, brother, or grand-father). Further, it is reasonable to assume that when the offender is a family member or a close friend, there may be less willingness on the part of the family to prosecute him, and our data on the familiarity between the offender and his victim may, therefore, be a conservative estimate.
> – *Nicholas Groth & Jean Birnhaum*

Another myth perpetrates the misconception that the abuser will invariably be a complete stranger to the child. Childhood sexual abuse often occurs when the child has been readily accessible to the child-molester and intrafamilial abuse has been a more frequent statistic by far than the chance encounter with a stranger. Most people, however, would like to think that evil is something that happens on someone else's doorstep and this tendency may, consequently, explain the existence of this comfort-seeking myth.

Perhaps the abuser was mentally retarded

It is sometimes thought that the child offender is of low or defective intelligence and therefore doesn't know any better. On the basis of their performance on a standard intelligence test, the Wechsler Adult Intelligence Scale, there was no significant difference between the convicted child offenders and the general population in regard to intellectual ability: 111 (80%) of the subjects fell within the normal range of intelligence.

– Nicholas Groth & Jean Birnhaum

The abuser has also been viewed as someone who would be mentally retarded. There has been no evidence, however, to assume that the abuser would be mentally subnormal or of lower intelligence than the average person. In order to perpetrate an act of sexual violation, the abuser will need to be very cunning and astute. The abuser will, of course, need to be able to calculate the implications of isolating, enticing and silencing the child and, consequently, avoiding discovery.

Perhaps the abuser was insane

One of the most frightening stereotypes of the child offender is that of the demented "sex fiend". Fortunately, it appears that such cases are rare exceptions: only 7 (5%) subjects showed clinical evidence of some psychotic process operating at the time of their offence.

– Nicholas Groth & Jean Birnhaum

The child-molester has also been labelled as being insane. Often the abuser will be severely neurotic rather than psychotic. Again, some degree of intellectual prowess will be required for the offender to determine the ways in which he or she can execute the crime.

Perhaps the abuser was drunk or drugged

Some offenders themselves allege that the offence happened only
because they were in a state of intoxication, and people commonly
believe that alcohol and/or drugs play a part in the commission of sexual
offences against children. Drug use was essentially non-existent among
our subjects, and less than one-third (45, or 30%) of them would be
described as alcohol-dependent.
– *Nicholas Groth & Jean Birnhaum*

It has sometimes been claimed that the child-abuser tends to be an
alcoholic or a drug-addict who will really have no notion of his or
her actions. It appears that, while substance-abuse may be a symptom of psychological disturbance, it does not seem to follow that
the child-molester will necessarily be an alcoholic or a drug-addict.
The reasoning may be that drink or drugs took hold of the abuser
and, thus, he or she was not responsible for his or her actions.
Again, this is a comfort-zone explanation that tends easily to
relieve the public of any unpleasant truths. The law prosecutes
people for driving under the influence of drink or drugs on the
basis that offenders had control of their senses when they elected
to administer the substance. Why should the child-molester be any
different or above the law in this respect?

Perhaps the abuser was sexually frustrated

It is sometimes thought that children are turned to because the offender
has no other outlets for his sexual needs or no other opportunities for
sexual gratification. We found that approximately as many child
offenders were married (70, or 47%) as not (78, or 53%). In fact, the sexual
encounters with children coexisted with sexual contacts with adults.
– *Nicholas Groth & Jean Birnhaum*

Another myth that has been broadcast purports that the child-
offender is a severely sexually-frustrated person and desperately
requires sexual gratification. While it may be true that, in certain
circumstances, the abuser will have a sexual-blockage factor in that
there may not be an easy outlet for his or her sexual energies, it
does not necessarily follow that he or she will not have a regular
sexual partner in addition to the child-victim. This myth, moreover, will also give credence to the bizarre belief that every individual is entitled to his or her quota of sexual gratification and that
if this bounty has not been continually forthcoming then that

individual may be licensed, permitted or forced into using savage means in order to gratify salacious desires.

Perhaps the abuser will become gradually worse

The assumption that the child offender will repeat is a legitimate one. Although about one-fourth (38, or 26%) of the subjects referred for evaluation were "first offenders" according to the law, it was a rare exception where the first conviction constituted the first such incident in the offender's life. Child offenders do not spontaneously abandon their sexual involvements with children. However, there does not appear to be any reason to assume that an offender will necessarily become more dangerous over time; this was not evident in the majority of cases.
– *Nicholas Groth & Jean Birnhaum*

Another common myth states that the child-offender will commit increasingly-violent acts as time progresses. Often, the public will believe that child-molesters will commit certain low-key offences and then, in time, their acts of abuse will increasingly worsen. It seems, however, that abusers will be of a particular psychological type and, therefore, that they will act according to prescribed personal characteristics. Normally, an offender will tend to stick to a regular pattern of securing his or her conquests. The abuser, for example, who may be opportunistic will entice victims only when they are readily accessible and are willing to comply with his or her wishes. The violent or sadistic abuser, similarly, will commit acts of violence in order to satisfy neurotic needs, but, once these have been satiated, he or she may then decide to desist from further violence.

Perhaps the abuser was a homosexual

It has been alleged that homosexual males are especially prone to actively recruit and indoctrinate young boys into their lifestyles. In fact, 75 (51%) of the men in our sample selected only female children as their victims, 42 (28%) selected only male children; and 31 (21%) selected both boys and girls as their victims. Female children were victimised almost twice as often as male children.
– *Nicholas Groth & Jean Birnhaum*

The fact that the child could be at greater risk of sexual victimisation from a homosexual adult than from a heterosexual adult is another myth keenly voiced abroad. It is obvious from the evidence collated that both boys and girls have become victims and both men and women have been perpetrators. The abuser, moreover, can be heterosexual, bisexual or homosexual. Psychological disorders affects us all – whatever our sexual orientation – and in different and uniquely individual ways. The sexual orientation of the offender does not, in any way, constitute a significant part of the sexual-abuse equation.

Classifications of the sexual abuser

> Child-molesters were once pictured as sexually frustrated old men who loitered in public parks or outside of schoolyards in hopes of luring naïve youngsters into their clutches with offers of candy or money. Study after study has punctured this stereotype, so that if any vestige of it remains – as it certainly does – it is because the truth is more unpalatable than the myth.
> – David Finkelhor

When considering the tendencies of child-molesters, research seems to indicate that they will fall into one of three distinct categories according to the ways in which they will react to their victims (see Figure 6 – "Classifications of the child-abuser").

The regressive abuser

> The regressed paedophile tends to revert to an early mode of (fantasised) behaviour, satisfaction and/or gratification when he is under stress. Because his behaviour is neither habitual nor compulsive, he tends to be more amenable to therapeutic intervention.
> – Adele Mayer

The regressive abuser will have a tendency to react opportunistically to situations that can lead to an abusive incident. This classification of child-molester will describe the type who indulges in spontaneously-regressive behaviour in order to recreate the past (see Chapter 11, Volume 1 – "Defensive Strategies"). The regressive offender will tend to turn to the child in times of crisis as a substitute for an adult. When a sexual relationship with another adult engenders conflict or does not provide emotional fulfilment, for example, the regressive abuser may then turn to the child as a consolation. Through regression, offenders will be attempting to recapture what they perceive as a former pleasure-state in order to

Figure 6 – Classifications of the child-abuser

The abuser's classification	The abuser's characteristics	The function of the abusive act for the abuser	The abuser's relationship with the child-victim	The abuser's therapeutic potential
The regressive abuser	The abuser will regress spontaneously, will react opportunistically and will re-enact his or her own traumatic past	The abuser may adopt a coping-strategy for current stress, may resolve psychological blockage, may resolve sexual blockage, may obtain self-value and may engage in fantasy-oriented pleasure	The abuser will have a weak sexual preference for the child-victim	The abuser-client will need to be highly cooperative and compliant with the therapeutic process
The fixated abuser	The abuser will be fixated on past trauma and will identify with the child-victim	The abuser may obtain relief from a traumatic past and may find a primary object of sexual gratification in the child-victim	The abuser will have a strong sexual preference for the child-victim	The abuser-client will be unlikely want to resolve his or her sexual inclinations
The mysopedic abuser	The abuser will be a child-hater and will have a need to perform sadistic or ritualistic torture	The abuser may discharge displaced anger and may find a role-reversal vehicle in the child-victim	The abuser will have a strong need to combine sexual gratification with cruelty towards the child-victim	The abuser-client will be virtually incurable

relieve their current-day stresses. With regressive offenders, the adult may have an emotional blockage that will need to be resolved or satisfied. The regressive type will often exhibit only a weak sexual preference for children and will not necessarily be exclusively interested in children as sexual partners. The incestuous offender will be more likely to be the regressive abuser because he or she will regress in fantasy to an earlier time as a means of attaining pleasure, acquiring self-value and employing a coping-strategy.

Some clinicians believe that this type of abuser can be helped if conditions are right and when he or she is wholeheartedly cooperative and compliant with the therapeutic process. The regressive abuser may be the type of client that the average practitioner will encounter in his consulting room. It has to be said, of course, that the child-molester does not normally have the wherewithal to undergo investigative therapy. Here, the abuser-client will not only have to face his or her own childhood trauma but also will have to deal with the psychologically-devastating consequences of his or her subsequent actions.

The fixated abuser

> Unlike the regressed paedophile, the fixated paedophile is emotionally
> and psychologically "stuck" at an early age, often at an age when
> he was molested.
> *– Adele Mayer*

The fixated abuser will have a detectable sexual preference for children. This classification of sexual offender will describe the type who exhibits fixated behaviours as a result of being locked into a traumatic past (see Chapter 16, Volume 1 – "Personality Development"). The fixated child-molester will psychologically identify with the child and may have himself or herself been fixated at the victim's age. The fixated offender will usually have a high emotional congruence with the child-victim. The fixated abuser will often exhibit a high degree of sexual preference for children and may be solely interested in children as sexual partners. The opportunistic paedophile may be the fixated type who will display a tendency to being attracted to children as sexual objects. The fixated offender can be regarded as the most common type of abuser, although therapeutic intervention does not have a very good track record of success in curing such cases.

The mysopedic abuser

> There is a third type of paedophile, uncommon but still meriting attention because of the sadistic and lethal nature of his activities. He is the vicious child rapist, sometimes involved in sado-masochistic cults, who often mutilates and murders his victims, sometimes in ritualistic fashion.
> – *Adele Mayer*

The mysopedic abuser will be the child-hater (or *mysoped*). This offender's aim in life will be to perpetrate sadistic forms of cruelty on his or her victims. Often this type of victimisation will be the result of the offender's misplaced anger or a role-reversal coping-strategy that will be reactionary against his or her own abusive childhood. The mysopedic abuser – who may be either an incestuous abuser or an opportunistic paedophile – may regard children as objects on whom he or she can unleash aggression in an erotic manner. Because of the extreme nature of this form of maladaptive behaviour, it may be fair to assume that such perpetrators are virtually untreatable in therapeutic terms.

Why Does Childhood Abuse Occur in Society?

> In the last decade, as increasing evidence of the wide prevalence of father–daughter incest has been amassed, and as the victims themselves have become emboldened to speak out, it has grown more difficult to suppress the truth about incest. But the exposure of such large-scale an abuse of power on the part of fathers represents a serious challenge to the ideology of male dominance, and inevitably provokes a defensive reaction.
> – *Judith Lewis Herman & Lisa Hirschman*

A number of cultural, psychological and stress-related explanations have been cited as the causes of sexual offences against children in today's society and some possible explanations for its occurrence have been advanced. Let us now, therefore, summarise the factors that contribute to the existence of childhood sexual abuse in modern society.

The argument that incest is harmless has been promoted aggressively in recent years by the publishers of men's sex magazines.
– *Judith Lewis Herman & Lisa Hirschman*

Sociological and cultural factors

Paedophilia appears to be more equally distributed across all socio-economic, educational, and professional levels, and it does not appear to diminish in time.
– *Nicholas Groth & Jean Birnhaum*

The media and society at large are preoccupied with sexuality and sexual prowess. Sex-power has become a topic that cannot be avoided in our daily perambulations through life. Politicians are brought down by indiscretions, royalty are pursued relentlessly for any whiff of dishonour and pop stars are idolised for leading profligate lives. The public is hungry for scandal at any price. Both men and women are judged by their sexual conquests and by the sexual company that they attract. We are all constantly brainwashed into an awareness of sex and made to believe how important it is to our self-image. The dilemma lies in the fact that we are expected to be more sexually active but, in practice, the outlet for such expression will not necessarily be forthcoming. There are, however, repressive norms lingering in society that mean that activities such as masturbation and extramarital relationships are still taboo, and this factor tends to aggravate any sexual problems that the individual may have. Society, therefore, will create a sexual thirst that then cannot be easily be quenched.

The need for power and notoriety have become similar commodities that many people will ruthlessly pursue merely for the pleasure of doing so. Anyone with a worldwide profile in today's society is regarded as having made the grade. We admire powerful figures such as world-leaders or superstars. Famous men and women are respected for the accumulation of their wealth and their reputation for influence. Both in the family setting and within relationships, individuals vie for power and demand attention in order to satisfy their psychological needs. If abusing a child is on a megalomaniac's agenda, then he or she will see no reason at all why this whim should not be readily gratified.

Greater communications and technological advancement have meant that people are more mobile, may be alienated from their origins and may be left to fend for themselves. Examples of this phenomenon are seen in the unemployed, the homeless and the single mother. The financially-dependent mother may feel forced to remain with a partner who mistreats or abuses her child because she may feel trapped in the relationship and cannot call on members of the wider family structure for assistance. The single mother may need to go out to work in order to provide for her offspring, but she may also feel obliged to leave her child in the care of relatively unknown persons. In this climate, the child, of necessity, will be less well protected and less closely guarded by parental figures.

The demise of the family circle as the ultimate entity has meant that the child today will be given greater scope to express herself without the presence of oppressive parental control. The child may have a greater personal choice concerning living conditions, schooling, friends and leisure-time activities. The child may need to be personally responsible for her own entertainment, transportation and meal-preparation and this independence may arise for some children at an early age. Such freedom, however, may not be accompanied by teachings about how to avoid the overtures of the potential child-molester. The Internet is readily accessible in most homes and sexual chat-lines and child-pornography are not unknown features of this so-called technological advancement. Freedom of expression is, of course, a magnificent commodity for the individual and, perhaps, has now become inevitable in the name of progress but, unfortunately, it may carry a sore price.

Despite greater freedom in society, the child will often be regarded by the adult population as a citizen without rights. The child can sometimes be viewed by her parents and other adults alike as an object or a possession rather than as an individual personality in her own right. Such warped thinking could, inevitably, lead the potential molester to consider that the child has no rights, no feelings and no choice. With the wider availability of drugs or alcohol, moreover, society tends to consider that those under its influence cannot be held responsible for their actions. The motorist can kill or maim and yet somehow remain blameless and, even, escape prosecution. Similarly, the abuser can violate the child and then hide behind the drug-induced mask of irresponsibility for his or her personal wilfulness and premeditated actions.

It may also be beyond the scope of the legal system and the social welfare system in many countries to be able to bring the perpetrator of abusive crime to justice effectively. There may often be a great deal of injustice because of numerous loopholes within the legal system and the social-care system that will ensure that the offender cannot be effectively apprehended, convicted and detained. Even the knowledge of this will render the climate ripe for the potential child-molester and will give him or her a supposed licence to perform acts of child-violation at his or her own discretion.

When considering all these factors, we are, in today's society, in a no-win situation with no light at the end of the tunnel. Man's self-image and the media that pander to it, the family setting and the political machinery are not really geared up to cope with the endemic and underground problem of maltreatment, neglect, exploitation and abuse of children. The only saving grace may be that the practitioner can be prepared to help the client who has suffered from a stormy crossing in childhood.

Psychological factors

> The offender's adult crimes may be in part a repetition and an acting out of a sexual offence he was subjected to as a child, a maladaptive effort to solve an unresolved early sexual trauma. It can be observed, especially with reference to the child molester, that his later offences often appear to duplicate the aspects of his own victimisation, that is, age of victim, type of acts performed, and the like.
> – *Nicholas Groth & Jean Birnhaum*

There is ample evidence to justify the claim that frequently an abusive perpetrator will have personally been a childhood-victim of violation and that the abuse of another will merely be a coping-strategy on his or her part. The abuser may be suffering from repressed or suppressed trauma usually emanating from his or her own childhood that will then be inappropriately directed at the child-victim. This theory has been supported by the fact that sexual abuse of another person will be, by its very nature, a harmful activity that disregards the feelings of the victim. The violator will often have had an unsatisfactory childhood not only in terms of abuse but also in terms of neglect and lack of adequate nurturing. In saying this, of course, the practitioner should not make the mistake of assuming that the client who comes for therapeutic assistance because she has been abused in childhood is automatically a potential child-molester herself or, conversely, that the child-abuser has previously been a victim of childhood abuse.

The perpetrator of sexually-abusive acts may have suffered a degree of psychological damage that may manifest as a number of maladaptive behaviours or psychological disorders. The abusive perpetrator may suffer from disturbances such as addictive or dependency disorders (see Chapter 7 – "Fear and Anxiety Disorders"), depressive disorders (see Chapter 9 – "Sorrow and Grief Disorders") and low self-esteem (see Chapter 12 – "Dysfunctional Relationships"). The molester may also have a low frustration-tolerance, a poor impulse-control mechanism and a requirement for instant gratification of needs (see Chapter 10 – "Anger and Rage Disorders"). Offenders will usually have an impaired ability to comprehend the notion of guilt, will show a pathetically low degree of empathy with others and may not, in consequence, be capable of feeling regret or remorse over their actions (see Chapter 8 – "Guilt and Shame Disorders").

Gender factors

> Incest often manifests itself in a manner consistent with gender socialisation: for a man, the abuse is generally overtly and directly sexual; for a women, it may be more emotional, more focused on relationship and bonding, or perhaps manifested through care of the child's body, her primary domain.
> – *Sue Blume*

Let us now compare the male abuser and the female abuser – again dispelling some of the commonly-held myths that only men are capable of perpetrating crimes of child-molestation.

> Children are more likely to be targets of sexual assaults by female offenders than are adults, since children are more vulnerable. Again, for a variety of reasons, such victimisation is not highly visible, but the

dynamics in the female offender appear to be identical to those operating
in the male offender.
– Nicholas Groth & Jean Birnhaum

The male abuser

Another very important difference between sexual abuse and physical
abuse also explains the more cautious response to the problem: sexual
abuse is committed primarily by men. Virtually all data collected show
this male preponderance.
– David Finkelhor

Research has conclusively proven that men are overwhelmingly
cited as the principal perpetrators of childhood sexual abuse and
the theories behind this indulgence in sexually-abusive practices
have been similarly examined. The motivation behind the activities
of the male abuser may revolve around issues of his inability to
show appropriate affection to the child, his self-image, his inability
to express emotion and his lack of ability to secure an adequate
sexual mate.

Women learn earlier and much more completely to distinguish between
sexual and non-sexual forms of affection.
– David Finkelhor

It has been claimed that the masculine psyche may be more readily fitted to adopting an abusive role in given circumstances than
that of the female. The male may seek a caring relationship in order
to fulfil his psychological needs but, for example, he may only be
able to relate to others by sexualising the relationship. The male,
furthermore, may well be more able to detach himself from any
emotional involvement when engaged in an intimate relationship.
The male may often be conditioned to place emphasis on erotic
media of which child-pornography may be a component. The male
can normally be sexually aroused by an erotic picture, an object or
an idea, whereas the female will usually learn to view a romantic
attachment as a whole entity in which sex is but a part.

Men are socialised to be able to focus their sexual interest around sexual
acts isolated from the context of a relationship.
– David Finkelhor

The little boy will not usually be expected to play with dolls or care lovingly for pets. Instead, the boy-child's stereotypical role may be to compete on the football field and to excel academically at school. The teenage boy will not normally be selected to be an ideal babysitter when the time comes for the young man to earn some spare cash. The girl-child, on the other hand, will more frequently be taught to distinguish between sexual and nonsexual forms of affection. Usually social conditioning and child-rearing, therefore, will prepare the girl for motherhood and its nurturing role. The boy-child, however, may not be so fortunate in this respect. The female's psychological needs, therefore, will usually be met in caring for others and, in many cases, this will mean caring for her own children.

> Men grow up seeing heterosexual success as much more important to
> their gender identities than women do.
> *– David Finkelhor*

The male, perhaps more so than the female, may have a need to seek confirmation of his sexual prowess and his gender-identity in order to confirm that he is a satisfactory personality. Any fractures to the male's ego may appear to be counteracted by better sexual performance and, therefore, the easiest path to this fulfilment may be taken. The little boy will be required to show that he is a man by achievement and success in the eyes of his parents and his schoolmates. The male child's parents may sometimes feel that it is more necessary to encourage his high performance because he will eventually become a primary breadwinner. The little boy may not normally be taught commitment to a relationship but may merely be encouraged to become a provider and a protector. The girl in the same family may not, however, be subject to such pressures. The male, therefore, will generally be conditioned to view a sexual partner as someone younger and more helpless than himself and, unfortunately, in times of need, the child might fit the bill for the potential child-molester. The little boy will soon learn that he is different from the little girl because he is evidently stronger and more robust and, indeed, may often be encouraged to prove this point. The boy-child will, thus, often learn to regard the opposite sex as unequal in a variety of ways by generalising this initial learning.

Finally, men are socialised to see as their appropriate sexual partners
persons who are younger and smaller than themselves, while women are
socialised to see as their appropriate sexual partners persons older
and larger.
– *David Finkelhor*

The female abuser

Incest between mother and son is so extraordinary that a single case is
considered worthy of publication, and we have been able to find a grand
total of only twenty-two documented cases in the entire literature.
Another eight cases reported as mother–son incest might more accurately
be described as rape, since they involve situations in which an adolescent
or adult son subjected his mother to forced intercourse. In most of these
cases, the son was psychotic, mentally retarded, or otherwise
severely disturbed.
– *Judith Lewis Herman & Lisa Hirschman*

The practitioner will, of course, need to appreciate that statistics are
available to verify that it is perfectly possible for the female perpetrator to abuse the child. There has been a tendency in the past,
however, either to ignore or to discount the fact that the female can
be quite capable of becoming a sexual-abuse perpetrator.

Although women sometimes abuse in overtly sexual or violent ways,
their abuse is typically more subtle and less forceful. Women's abuse is
often masked in cuddling and daily care-taking. The violation is often
fuzzier, less clear-cut than a penis in a vagina. But it is no
less devastating.
– *Ellen Bass and Laura Davis*

In refuting the documented research in this area, Finkelhor posed
a number of questions as a means of explaining why there have,
hitherto, been unrealistically-low estimates of female perpetrators
of childhood sexual abuse. In questioning documented research
that tended to ignore the role of the female abuser, a number of
questions have been posed by researchers. Is sexual abuse by the
adult female perpetrator less often perceived as abusive? Can
women mask sexually inappropriate behaviour more easily than
men? Do women commit special kinds of abuse that go unnoticed
and unmeasured? Are sexual offences by females less likely to be
reported because they are primarily intrafamilial? Is sexual abuse
by females obscured because female abusers more often abuse
boys who, compared with girls, are more reluctant to report? Often

enough, it will be difficult for researchers to obtain statistics but, in the case of the female abuser, the task may be even more onerous. Let us turn our attention now to discussing and evaluating these issues with regarded to the female child-molester.

> An important question raised by some observers is whether there is a great amount of contact between children and older or adult women that goes unnoticed in surveys because the younger partners do not consider it abuse or victimisation or even upsetting, in fact, may consider it positive and pleasurable.
> – *David Finkelhor*

The female can, of course, initiate and carry through an improper act with the child that may not, on first inspection, be regarded as abusive. It will, of course, be perfectly possible for the female to carry out a sexually-abusive act and for the child initially not to be aware that the encounter was in any way abusive. This would be particularly true in the case of the young child who will require physical contact as a basic survival need. If such contact is, in standard terms, inappropriate, then the child will be unlikely to complain – especially if it is the only contact that has been forthcoming. It may often be the case that the client will report an incident to the practitioner but may not realise that such behaviour could be regarded as sexually-abusive. It will only be when this realisation surfaces in the client's mind that the issue may need to be dealt with promptly. It would, of course, be inappropriate for the practitioner to make interpretations of the client's narrative that could cloud his own evaluation of the situation (see Chapter 10, Volume 1 – "Memory"). The client may discover that abuse has taken place only when reflecting on the past and taking into account the whole picture from an adult perspective. The client may look back on a given incident and, with the benefit of hindsight, may realise then that the activity engaged in could have been of a sexually-abusive nature and, therefore, could be psychologically damaging.

> A possibility raised by both Groth and Plummer is that since women have more socially prescribed and accepted physical intimacy with children, they might carry on sexual contacts with children that would go unnoticed. For example, a woman could presumably have an inappropriately old child suck on her breast as a way of gaining sexual gratification, but the behaviour might not be noticed as abuse.
> – *David Finkelhor*

The female can often neatly disguise sexually-inappropriate behaviour that might involve the child. It may be possible for the female to disguise a certain amount of sexually-abusive behaviour because she may be in a special nurturing position or in a unique relationship with the child. Mothers, babysitters, aunts and friends of the family, for example, are all in privileged positions with ready access to the child. The female abuser, therefore, could commit certain forms of abuse that may go unnoticed by the child or anyone else. There could, of course, be ample opportunity for the female to abuse the child in the normal course of his or her upbringing. Particularly with mother–son incest, the child's mother will be in an omnipotent position in deciding on such matters as sleeping arrangements and privacy requirements. Again, the client may fail to realise that abuse has actually taken place and, when such realisations are ready to surface, may, then, be in a position to deal with the trauma resulting from it. Intrafamilial offences, in particular, may proceed unreported perhaps for a lengthy period of time and may, in fact, be met by disbelief from others, even if the child were able to disclose the violation. It has been ascertained that abuse by women can occur both within and outside the family. When cases occur incestuously, however, there may be a reluctance or an inability on the part of the child to disclose it and to prevent its recurrence. When incestuous abuse by the female perpetrator occurs, the client may not only experience the guilt and shame associated with the encounters but also may suffer from a sense of disloyalty when disclosing the abuse even in the therapeutic context. The male client, for example, may be so psychologically entwined with his mother that he will resist divulging information or suspicions about any such molestation as a means of protecting her reputation and upholding the family honour.

> In discussion of abuse by women, certain activities are mentioned that are not otherwise often considered in discussions of abuse. Justice and Justice, for example, talk about "sleeping with a son, caressing in a sexual way, exposing her body to him, and keeping him tied to her emotionally with implied promises of sexual payoff" as forms of sexual abuse by women that go unrecorded.
> – *David Finkelhor*

The boy-victim can sometimes feel less inclined to disclose abuse by the female than the girl-victim. It has been established that both boys and girls can be abused by the female perpetrator but that there may be a tendency for the boy not to report incidents of abuse. The boy, for example, may not wish to disclose abuse by the female because he may feel that there will be less stigma attached to such encounters and, therefore, his need to report the abusive encounters may not be so pressing. The male client, in such cases, may wish to keep the secret to himself and may wish to negate its psychological effect (see Chapter 11, Volume 1 – "Defensive Strategies"). For the adult male client, the issues surrounding the need to disclose and the resultant stigmatisation will need to be addressed in the course of therapeutic assistance. For the male client who has been reluctant to tell tales about his abuser, a guilt-factor will undoubtedly be in operation that will need to be unearthed in the therapeutic context.

> Some have speculated that sexual abuse by females does not appear very frequently because it occurs predominantly to boys, and boys are less likely to report. While it does appear to be true from prior research that boys are less likely to report abuse either to parents or to public agencies, it is not necessarily true that most abuse by females occurs to boys.
> – *David Finkelhor*

Collusion factors

> The literature presents a stereotypic picture of the incestuous triad, which typically is composed of mother, daughter and father/stepfather. In some literature, the mother is described as an unconscious participant in the "conspiracy of silence". This means that on some level mother knows that incest is occurring and uses the defence mechanism of denial to block the reality of the family's situation.
> – *Adele Mayer*

When considering the role of the child-abuser, it must also be borne in mind that other persons may be cognisant – even at an unconscious level – of what had been taking place when the child was being molested. A close relative, for example, may suspect that the child has been violated but may simply turn a blind eye. The child may, moreover, be neglected, in some way, and, therefore, her primary carer will be so unconcerned with her welfare or her whereabouts that the abusive incidents may remain unnoticed. The child's mother, for example, who had a series of lovers, who had a problem with either drink or drugs, who had been a hypochondriac or who had been frequently absent from the childhood home, would not be in a position either to notice or to care if her child were being regularly violated. In principle, the client may come to realise that either her parents knew of the abuse and, by some means, condoned it or, alternatively, genuinely did not know of the abuse and yet were unable or unwilling to detect it. The adult-victim whom the therapist sees in the course of his therapeutic practice will, of course, need to deal with any additional issues of collusion that have resulted from her own violation.

Sometimes the client's parents may discover that she has been abused but, then, may not act in her interests by preventing further occurrences and adequately assisting her to recover. The client, in this instance, will be likely to suffer additional psychological distress as a result of this form of betrayal. The client will also suffer greater distress if the attitude taken by her guardians – who may discover that abuse has taken place – has been wholly inappropriate in terms of nurturing the child. If, for example, the parent takes a prudish attitude to the disclosure or attempts to blame the child, then the guilt-factor will be added to the client's pain resulting from the abusive event.

> If a mother could feel how she is injuring her child, she would be able to discover how she was once injured herself and so could rid herself of her compulsion to repeat the past.
> – *Alice Miller*

When considering the motivations of the male abuser and the female colluder, a number of theories have been proffered that are generally related to social conditioning. The main theory focuses on the notion that the male may become the abuser while the female will become the colluder. The female, for example, may tend to prefer a partner who is older, larger and more dominant than herself. The female may not generally initiate a sexual encounter but, once one has been initiated, she can become a willing participant. The female may be less inclined to be promiscuous or to sexualise her relationships. The female may be less likely to be aroused by external sexual stimuli such as pornography but may instead seek totality in an intimate relationship. The female can usually distinguish between expressions of affection and sexual expression and may be less motivated to seek sexual gratification as a means of maintaining her self-image and self-esteem. The female may be more likely to bond with the child and to comply with maternal instincts. The female may also be better able to have sympathy with the victim of sexual exploitation since women have traditionally been exploited sexually themselves in the past and sexual contact with the child has not readily been condoned by the female subculture.

When considering the dynamics entailed in the family-systems model of father–daughter incest, the mother's role as the colluder may occur for a variety of reasons. Mother may, for example, have herself been an abuse-victim and so, unconsciously, she may condone the same fate for her daughter. Mother may, therefore, unconsciously engineer the abusive situation in order to avoid addressing her own traumatic past by claiming to see no injustice in such a situation. The collusive mother may, moreover, wish to avoid sexual contact with her partner at any price. Collusion, furthermore, may be the mother's way of attempting to keep the family together. Frequently, the colluding mother will usually have issues of dependency to address herself with regard to her own mother. Displaced anger may lead the colluder to punish her daughter or a fear of rejection may mean that she will sacrifice her daughter in order to ensure that the family does not disintegrate if the molestation is uncovered.

Parental responsibilities should, in essence, be to educate the child in the ways of the world and to allow her to express herself freely. The child's parents should be open to approach by the child, who may wish to seek advice or to enlist protection. The parent will be doing a great disservice to the child by, in any way, giving the impression that she may not speak freely or may not broach the delicate subject of sex in the parental presence. The prudish parent, for example, may often set up the child as a potential victim because the abuser will calculate that his or her prey will not be believed even if she does disclose an abusive incident. In any dispute, however, if the parent gives the benefit of the doubt to the abusive assailant once the child has disclosed the offence, then the damage to the client will be even greater. The client's feelings of guilt and shame, in this case, will be monstrously exacerbated. In instances whereby the client has been blamed for the occurrence of the abuse, she will also need to deal with her anger at the negligence and irresponsibility of the carer in question. Often disclosure will be an ordeal, in its own right, for the client – especially if she has been bribed or threatened into remaining silent. If such divulgence has been met with an inappropriate response, the consequences for the client can be psychologically devastating. These are the kinds of factor that the practitioner who may deal with any form of childhood abuse will need to address wholeheartedly in his therapeutic practice. It is very worthwhile work that can bring inestimable job-satisfaction for the practitioner but it will be an area that can be a dangerous path to tread if he is, in any way, psychologically ill-equipped or lacking in knowledge.

> On the subject of the mother's responsibility or complicity, there is a similar concordance of opinion among authors who might ordinarily shun each other's company. The doctor, the man of letters, and the pornographer, each in his accustomed language, render similar judgements of the incestuous father's mate. By and large, they suggest, she drove him to it. The indictment of the mother includes three counts: first, she failed to perform her marital duties; second, she, not the father, forced the daughter to take her rightful place; and third, she knew about, tolerated or in some cases actively enjoyed the incest.
> *– Judith Lewis Herman & Lisa Hirschman*

Client Profiling

The analytical-hypnotherapy practitioner may wish to ponder the following points when formulating a profile for the client.

- Has the client suffered from any form of mistreatment, neglect or abuse in her childhood?
- What are the client's beliefs concerning any abuse that she has experienced?
- What are the practitioner's beliefs with regard to childhood abuse?
- In what ways might the client have been forced or coerced into becoming involved in an abusive relationship?
- Has the client ever been raped or forced to submit to an aggressive assault?
- Has the client been subjected to one-off or occasional abuse or did she have to endure an ongoing situation of abuse or neglect?
- Has the client been the subject of severe maltreatment by her parental carers?

- In what ways were the client's family dysfunctional?
- Did the client's parents or carers have a history of abuse in their own childhood?
- What were the relationship-dynamics between the client's parents?
- Was the client in any way at risk from neglect or abuse during her childhood?
- In what ways was the client vulnerable to any maltreatment or misuse in childhood?
- What kind of social or cultural factors might have led the client to become an abuse-victim?
- Does the client understand the factors that contributed to her becoming a victim of childhood abuse?
- Does the practitioner understand the factors that motivated the abuser to violate the client?
- Can the practitioner understand the psychology of the client's abuser and the climate in which it occurred?
- Has the practitioner dispelled all prevailing myths about abusive perpetrators?
- Does the client realise that she was utterly blameless with regard to her participation in any abusive acts?
- Did one or more of the client's parents in any way collude with her abusive perpetrator?

Chapter 15

The Effects of Childhood Abuse

In the little world in which children have their existence,
whosoever brings them up, there is nothing so finely
perceived and so finely felt as injustice.

– Charles Dickens

What is the Effect of Childhood Abuse?

The debate over the effects of childhood sexual victimisation spans
almost a century. It was a question of some lengthy consideration for
Freud and has been taken up again in several of the landmark studies of
sexuality since then.
– David Finkelhor

We shall now consider the ways in which a victim of childhood
abuse may be affected in adult life. The practitioner will need to
have an appreciation of the devastating psychological effect that
such violation in childhood can have on the client. The extent to
which the client will be affected by childhood abuse will depend
on the nature and repercussions of his case (see Chapter 14 – "The
Nature of Childhood Abuse"). The adult who has been subjected to
any form of abuse in childhood will, undoubtedly, suffer the consequences but, of course, one client may be affected more than
another or in an entirely different way. The client, of course, may
react in any of a number of ways but, in general, the effects of
childhood trauma may be worsened in certain circumstances.
Abuse, neglect, exploitation and violation in any form will mean
that the child will have missed out on those things that other children would have taken for granted. The child, moreover, will naturally have incorporated his learning about the world into his

419

developmental process. The client, for example, will not have had the security of knowing that he was loved but, instead, will have experienced only an instability underpinning the belief that he may have been unlovable and deserved nothing. This vacuum can then become the client's predisposition for self-doubt and self-blame because the attention that he needed from caring parents in order to assist with his development was fundamentally absent. There may have been, for instance, no bedtime reading, no playing in the park, no fun outings and no special treats – all normal childhood experiences that the average child would expect to enjoy. These important facets of childhood upbringing are all evidence of the nurturing process that the child will require in order to teach him the ways of adapting to life. The unfortunate client, however, will have acquired only inadequate resources and lacked the warmth that would have been essential in order for him to foster feelings of self-security when interacting with others in demanding situations.

> Greater long-term harm is associated with more severe abuse, particularly abuse involving a father or stepfather, penetration, use of force or violence.
> – *John Morton*

The child will suffer if the abuse – whether emotional, physical or sexual – occurred frequently and continued for a long period of time. The client will usually suffer most profoundly if he has been misused by more than one person and, particularly, if he has been maltreated by a close relative. The victim of childhood neglect or abuse, generally, will suffer because he will have been too young to cope adequately with any degree of traumatic experience – particularly one in which devastating and highly-charged emotive reactions are evoked (see Chapter 13 – "Post-Traumatic Stress Disorder").

> Many women who were molested as children claim that they were robbed of their childhood and they feel that their early needs for appropriate nurturance were not met.
> – *Adele Mayer*

In the case of childhood sexual abuse, the client will have received an enduring psychological legacy if there was physical contact with the abuser, if the abuse involved some form of penetration or attempted penetration of vagina, anus or mouth and if the abusive incident was accompanied by some form of aggressive force (see Chapter 14 – "The Nature of Childhood Abuse"). If a sexually-abused client were to have participated, in some way, in the abusive act or if he felt that he had cooperated to some extent with the child-molester, then his psychological damage may have become amplified. If the client's parents or primary carers were unsupportive when the violation was disclosed, he may then be likely to suffer tenfold. Further psychological damage will be sustained if the client was old enough to appreciate that cultural taboos had been violated and, therefore, he may not have been inclined to tell anyone of the abusive occurrence. If the client's disclosure of abuse, moreover, was met with an unfavourable reaction such as nonchalance, disbelief or blame, this will also have had a serious psychological impact on him. Alternatively, if the client at the pre-verbal stage of development was molested, in any way, then a different set of factors will obtain and can bring both psychological distress and physiological distortion or deformation as a result (see Chapter 11 – "Psychosomatic Disorders").

> Given these realities about the true consequences of sexual violation of the dependency bond, incest can be seen as the imposition of sexually inappropriate acts, or acts with sexual overtones, by – or any use of a minor child to meet the sexual or sexual/emotional needs of – one or more persons who derive authority through ongoing emotional bonding with that child.
> – *Sue Blume*

Essentially, the effect of intrafamilial abuse on the client will be complex and convoluted. The client, for example, may keenly feel the loss of childhood care and affection. The client may feel as if he had been forced into an unusual sexual role at an inappropriate age and may exhibit a degree of false maturity that will mask his need for real affection. The client may also exhibit an overdeveloped sense of familial responsibility because he may suffer greatly from guilt, shame and self-blame, may feel responsible for encouraging the abuse, for not preventing its occurrence and for not halting its recurrence. Similarly, the abuse-survivor may feel that he must, in some way, have been personally responsible for being singled out for victimisation and, as such, will tend to fear, mistrust or be suspicious of all authority-figures. The client-victim, in most cases, will, as a matter of course, tend to develop unsatisfactory intimate relationships with others in adulthood (see Chapter 12 – "Dysfunctional Relationships").

> What incest is really is nowhere acknowledged in the traditional application of the word. Actually, it is the most serious and most common form of child sexual abuse. Arguably, it is also the most serious of all types of child abuse.
> – *Sue Blume*

The effect of childhood abuse that takes place outside the family circle will differ in its intensity according to the client's relationship to the perpetrator. The more trauma-inflicting an assault has been – particularly one involving violence – the more the adult survivor may suffer. Essentially, the effect of extrafamilial abuse on the client will be that he may exhibit symptoms of shock, traumatic stress and high degrees of fear and anxiety. The client may also become restless or depressed. Often the client will experience sleep disturbances that can include having nightmares and flashbacks. Sometimes the practitioner will discover that the client has turned to prostitution or crime as a direct result of his experiences. Obviously, the client may also feel a number of the additional effects with regard to his relationship with his family – particularly if his carers were palpably negligent in not caring for or protecting him from the abusive occurrence.

> Long-term effects on victims can be equally devastating. Many of these children become runaways who prostitute themselves for a place to live and food to eat. Later, they may become child molesters, pimps or criminals.
> – *Adele Mayer*

Why is Childhood Sexual Abuse Intrinsically Wrong?

> Legally and morally there is no such thing as consensual sex between a child and an adult. Such abuse often has a distorting effect on personal development and later relationships.
> – *Sydney Brandon*

Few people reading this book would dispute the fact that the sexual exploitation of the child is intrinsically wrong and the very thought of child-molestation would normally engender horror and revulsion in the mind of the public at large. Sexual exploitation of the child is essentially deemed to be wrong because it is biologically unnatural for an adult and a child to enter into a sexual relationship. Worse still will be the fact that sexual abuse is undoubtedly psychologically damaging for the victim, who may suffer from a significant degree of trauma because of the nature of such an experience (see Chapter 13 – "Post-Traumatic Stress Disorder"). The child, for example, may be traumatised by the fearful nature of the encounter, may suffer from a crippling degree of guilt and shame because such a relationship will be socially unacceptable and may, subsequently, be forced to suffer in silence because he may be disinclined to disclose his distress.

Childhood sexual abuse prematurely introduces the child to a form of relationship for which he has little or no resources with which to cope. The child's body has not fully matured physiologically and he will, therefore, be ill-prepared for the emotive involvement that sexual contact necessitates. The pertinent point at issue here will be that the minor will not really be in a position to give informed consent to such an encounter. The child will unfailingly trust and be naïvely gullible and it is this disposition that will make him totally incapable of making a clear-headed and impartial decision about such activities. The child, thus, will become a vulnerable sitting target ripe for exploitation by the scheming predator. The child – by virtue of his innocence and immaturity – cannot be truly and fully aware of what he will be undertaking, even if he may have ostensibly paid lip-service to consent. The child has not, in fact, learned about the reproductive process and cannot appreciate its emotive and social implications fully. The adult will have the benefit of both knowledge and experience that the child patently lacks. The average adult, in fact, might normally find an intimate relationship a taxing ordeal in itself even when he or she supposedly has a full understanding of the subject, has full control of his or her faculties and is long past the age of consent!

The child-victim does not, in reality, have true freedom of choice because of his subordinate position in terms of adult-child relationships. The child will be totally dependent on the adult carer for his basic survival needs and, of course, the perpetrator will be keenly aware of this fact. The child will have been taught to obey his parents, carers and guardians – usually for his own benefit and safety – and this learning will then be applied to all situations and to all adults both within and outside the family. To the child-victim, the adult will be the wisest sage, the most powerful giant and the keeper of the purse-strings that can provide comfort, nourishment and shelter. The child will depend on the adult for social and developmental guidance during his important transition through childhood into the adult world. The child, furthermore, will rely wholeheartedly on the caring adult for the satisfaction of those vital psychological needs. The child's basic instinct will be for attention and affection because this will be part of the human organism's inherent survival mechanism. Adequate love and affection will need, however, to come to the child from an appropriate quarter. If not, the child may be obliged unknowingly to accept it in a hideous form from elsewhere. The drowning man will grasp at straws. The starving man will eat a rat in order to stay alive. The dying woman will sell her grandmother for a painkiller. The child starved of love and appropriate nurturing may seek a parental substitute and may naturally gravitate towards anyone who appears to fit the bill. The child, therefore, will be forced to accept any stop-gap measure in order to satisfy his appetite for affection or, even, the illusion of affection.

> Although the youngster may be sexually mature, she or he is not psychologically equipped to deal with sexual situations on an equal basis with an adult and can therefore be easily taken advantage of by an adult without regard for the impact of such victimisation on the child's psychological development. By definition, children are immature; thus, adults can capitalise in self-serving ways on this immaturity and can exploit the child in a variety of ways: physical, social, psychological, and emotional.
> – *Nicholas Groth & Jean Birnhaum*

In the following client narrative, the client explains the way in which she was physically abused by her father in a number of ways both in childhood and in adulthood. This illustration provides an overall picture of the way in which a client was treated in adult life by an abusive perpetrator from childhood.

Client narrative – physical abuse ...

My father would think nothing of strapping me when I was a child. He could see nothing wrong in his actions. My father thought that this was perfectly OK. And, of course, I began to think it was perfectly OK too. This fact led me to marry a man who was also violent.

When this marriage collapsed, I met my father for lunch. He asked me two questions in ironic juxtaposition in the middle of a crowded restaurant. "I understand that your husband hit you?" and, when I refused to answer such an intimate question in a public place, he added "Is there any chance of a reconciliation?" I flipped. I repeated the two questions aloud and replied to both questions so that the majority of the people nearby would have heard the answer. "Yes, he did hit me, and, no, there is no chance whatsoever of a reconciliation!" I had the satisfaction, at least, of causing him some embarrassment in this crowded place. Appearances were far more important to my father than the fact that I might be exposed to further attack. If a reconciliation were remotely possible to avoid any undue embarrassment on his part, then my being physically beaten would have been a small price to pay, obviously. He was obviously judging me by his own standards!

When is the Child at Risk from Childhood Abuse?

It should be possible for the practitioner to look in general terms at the client's background in order to consider the circumstances that would have made him liable to sexual victimisation. The therapist should, of course, bear in mind that she will be looking in retrospect at the client's background. Any information gleaned from the client should not, of course, be used as a checklist in order to prove that he has been sexually abused in childhood. The practitioner's role will not be to pronounce a diagnosis of the client's condition but merely to deal with his psychological distress in whatever form it may be presented.

Family background and childhood environment

> Although abuse is certainly not limited to the lower classes, as the
> stereotype might suggest, to most researchers it makes sense that the
> frustrations of poverty, joblessness, lack of education, and inadequate
> housing contribute to the conditions that increase violence toward
> children. Child sexual abuse, however, may be an entirely different story.
> The most representative surveys of child sexual abuse in the community
> have been unable to find any relationship between sexual abuse and the
> social class of the family in which the victims grew up.
> *– David Finkelhor & Larry Baron*

The child-abuser can and does emanate from all echelons of society, regardless of education, class, creed or colour, but the client
from a financially-overburdened or low-income family may
appear to be at a slightly greater risk, according to the limited
research undertaken in this area. Where there is hardship in the
family, extra strain can be put on the parent or the carer when performing duties of child-protection, and the child may, therefore, be
neglected as a result of the family's misfortunes. Financial hardship will also bring with it overcrowding in the family residence
and a lack of privacy for family members. If the family resides in a
rural or an isolated area or is, in some way, socially or culturally
solitary, then these factors may, similarly, contribute to the way in
which the child will be treated. If the family is not the subject of
public scrutiny, for instance, the family-dynamics will be devoid of
significant influence from social and cultural norms.

Parental characteristics

> There is hardly a social problem that has not been attributed to marital
> conflict and family disruption, and sexual victimisation is certainly no
> exception. The literature is full of suggestions that children are more
> sexually vulnerable when parents fight or parents leave.
> *– David Finkelhor*

The child whose parents were unhappily united or whose carers
showed little mutual affection will often be vulnerable to attack. If
parental figures are in conflict as a result of an unsuccessful union,
then the child may suffer adversely in consequence. Incestuous
abuse, for example, may occur because the offending parent may
feel starved of affection and, possibly, may feel deprived of sexual

gratification. If the child has been living in a loveless environment, moreover, he may be vulnerable to accepting alternative forms of affection. The child whose parents or carers have a great deal of their own emotional baggage will certainly be at risk from some form of childhood abuse. The parent whose own childhood has been one of neglect may, subsequently, tend to neglect his or her own children. The child will not, of course, be in any gross danger of falling victim to the child-molester if he is well enough protected by his guardians. If mother has been neglectful, abusive or willing to turn a blind eye to any hint of indiscretion, then the child can become a prime target. The child of a neglectful single mother – perhaps with a succession of casual male lovers or acquaintances – may be particularly at risk from neglect or exploitation in this inclement climate.

Typical victims of abuse

From the point of view of the sexual abuser, the child is an ideal victim. The child knows that responsible adults should be obeyed. The child believes that the threats of the abusing adult may be carried out if the child tells of the abuse, so he or she does not reveal it and then feels confused and guilty. Successful child molesters are often attractive to children and parents and they cultivate these characteristics so that parents are happy for them to mind their children or take them on outings. However, many sexual abusers do not have to cultivate these skills, as the victim is in their own family.
– *Kim Oates*

The child may be susceptible to attack or to approach from an abusive perpetrator if it is clear that he has been physically or emotionally neglected. If the child has been in community care or, in any other way, separated from his parents, he may lack the protection necessary to ward off any harmful approach. An absentee parent will mean that the child may well become the responsibility of a step-parent or a foster-parent whose dedication to nurturing him may be unsatisfactory and inadequate. If the child is readily accessible to an offender or a potential abuser, then the ground will be fertile and he can become a principal target. If the child has been unguarded or inadequately supervised, moreover, then he may be devoid of someone to whom he can turn. An abusive incident could then occur because the child will not be in a position to disclose the occurrence of any violation to an attentive listener. If the child does not have a good relationship with his mother, he may also be likely to be a candidate for victimisation. A lack of rapport with mother will inevitably mean that she will be unapproachable should the need arise. The person to whom the child would be most likely to disclose events, therefore, will be the very person whom he will be least likely to approach. The child-victim will, therefore, be rendered in a powerless Catch-22 position.

> Psychological trauma is an affliction of the powerless. At the moment of trauma, the victim is rendered helpless by overwhelming force. When the force is that of nature, we speak of disasters. When the force is that of other human beings, we speak of atrocities. Traumatic events overwhelm the ordinary systems of care that give people a sense of control, connection and meaning.
> – *Judith Lewis Herman*

The girl as a victim of sexual abuse

> As we now know from many reports, victims include both girls and boys, although girls predominate. The most common ages are between 8 and 12, although younger children are also well represented.
> – *David Finkelhor*

There has been little dispute about the fact that by far the majority of cases of childhood sexual abuse involve the girl-child as the victim. The family-systems model that deals with father–daughter incest, for instance, has drawn particular attention to this form of childhood sexual abuse. As tragic as this evidence may be, it tends to overshadow the fact that the boy can also be the victim and the psychological consequences of such molestation can be just as devastating.

> Women who have been sexually abused often have problems with trust and intimacy in later life. Some of these victims have multiple marriages, some become lesbians and others suffer from various forms of sexual dysfunction.
> – *Adele Mayer*

The boy as a victim of sexual abuse

> Some uneasiness appears in simply defining the sexual abuse of boys in
> the same way as the sexual abuse of girls. This uneasiness when
> articulated, usually stems from two presumptions. One is that sexual
> activities between boys and older persons is more often initiated by the
> boys themselves. The second is that boys are less negatively affected by
> what sexual contacts they may have with older persons. Not a great deal
> of evidence exists concerning either of these presumptions.
> – *David Finkelhor*

If the sexual abuse of children has been ignored in the past as a
matter of concern, then the sexual abuse of the boy-victim as
opposed to the girl-victim has been ignored to an even greater
extent. There has been a general assumption, for example, that the
boy can look after himself and that, in any case, he would be flat-
tered by having a sexual relationship with an older person. This, of
course, is blatantly not the case. Any child when placed in a vulnerable and potentially harmful situation will react adversely.
Feelings of guilt due to the sexual encounter will still persist – perhaps more so if the encounter was, in some way, encouraged by the
boy. The point at issue here, however, will be that no adult should
consent to any kind of sexual activity even if the encounter has
been requested by the child. If such overtures are made from the
child then a degree of encouragement may have been forthcoming
from the adult or the victim will have been conditioned by another
person to expect sexual activity with others.

The boy-child may have been indoctrinated with the grin-and-
bare-it adage in today's societal ethics. It is not, for example, considered manly to show emotions or to tell tales. The boy-victim,
therefore, may be desirous of disguising his psychological turmoil
by keeping his deadly secrets to himself. In doing this, he will be
unaware of the fact that this kind of conditioning will be stacking
up dire psychological problems for him in the future. Sexual abuse
of the boy by a male violator, moreover, will leave the child with
unanswered questions in his mind about his sexual identity and
his masculinity (see Chapter 12 – "Dysfunctional Relationships").
For the male client to discuss such matters will inevitably be a
painful process when he is grappling with some fundamental
issues that may be bringing into question the very essence of his
manhood. The male client, thus, will suffer guilt about possibly

being homosexual or fearing that he may potentially be inclined towards homosexuality. If the abuse has been reported and the boy's parents take a hush-hush stance over the fact that he has been violated by a man, then the consequences for the male client will be profound. Because normally the boy-child will tend to be less closely supervised in childhood than the girl, he may be disinclined to report any sexual encounters for fear that his freedom will be curtailed in the future. The boy, therefore, may feel that the price of secrecy may be worth paying for the sake of his independence. A lack of freedom and independence for the boy-victim could mean that he would be further punished by being isolated, say, from his friends. Indeed, because the boy may enjoy a greater freedom of movement than the girl, it may well be that he will, ironically, be more susceptible to extrafamilial abuse and also more likely to be violated as a young child.

> Follow-up studies on sexually abused boys indicate that they tend to internalise the trauma and to react through self-destructive activities resulting in such characteristics as obesity, anorexia, self-mutilation, suicide, self-medication, or depression. Some boys completely externalise the trauma through acts of child abuse, spousal abuse or murder. Girls generally tend to internalise trauma and often react self-destructively.
> – *Adele Mayer*

The Traumagenic-Dynamics Model

> These dynamics, when present, alter the child's cognitive and emotional orientation to the world, and create trauma by distorting a child's self-concept, worldview, and affective capacities.
> – *David Finkelhor & Angela Browne*

David Finkelhor and Angela Browne have devised a model that analyses the sexually-abusive experience in terms of those factors that will have a traumatic effect on the victim. There are four components of the *traumagenic-dynamics model of childhood sexual abuse* that will summarise the long-term effects of sexual abuse and can, therefore, provide a basis for treatment. The four traumagenic dynamics of sexual abuse comprise elements of *traumatic sexualisation, betrayal, powerlessness* and *stigmatisation*. A number of these components will be evident in the client whose upbringing has taken its toll but, in cases of childhood sexual abuse, the four dynamics will concurrently interplay.

The practitioner will usually be able to help the client to trace pre-senting symptoms back to the originating abusive incidents in order to deal with the subsequent effects. The traumagenic dynam-ics will come into play regardless of the type of abuse to which the client has been exposed, regardless of the abuser's psychology and whether or not the offender was related to the child (see Chapter 14 – "The Nature of Childhood Abuse"). It is commonly consid-ered that extreme effects on the victim will be exhibited if the client has been violated by a close relative who employed violent force over a long period of time and secured the active participation of the child. The practitioner may wish to view the client's case both in terms of the traumatic effects of these four dynamics and the psychological environment that existed in his family prior to the original initiation of the abusive event. The practitioner will, in this way, be able to construct a lucid picture of the effects that sexual abuse has had on the client.

Traumatic sexualisation

> Traumatic sexualisation refers to a process in which a child's sexuality (including both sexual feelings and sexual attitudes) is shaped in a developmentally inappropriate and interpersonally dysfunctional fashion as a result of sexual abuse.
> – David Finkelhor & Angela Browne

Traumatic sexualisation will transpire because the child has been introduced to a sexual experience at an inappropriate age and in unfitting circumstances. The sexual encounter is, of course, a sur-vivalist activity that stirs up the most profound and earth-shatter-ing of emotive expression within the human organism. The result of this early, age-inappropriate experience for the child will be that all future sexual encounters and behaviours will be distorted by this initial sexual introduction. Sexual traumatisation will be most likely to occur in circumstances in which the client has been actively involved in the abusive acts and when physical contact with the molester has taken place. The client may, for example, learn that sexual activity is something of which to be fearful – par-ticularly if any violence has been employed during the abusive incident. The result, in this case, may mean that the client will avoid sexual intimacy and may develop an abhorrence of sexual practice.

> We are inextricably drawn into situations that replicate the original trauma in both obvious and unobvious ways. The prostitute or "stripper" with a history of childhood sexual abuse is a common example.
> – *Peter Levine*

The child may also learn that sexual favours are a matter for barter – particularly if the offender had enticed the child by gifts, rewards or bribes and if the molester had traded affection for sexual compliance. The child, thus, will have learned to be a sexual manipulator and this learning may affect all the client's subsequent intimate relationships. The client could, for instance, become an exhibitionist or someone to whom group sexual activity would appeal. The client may become aggressively preoccupied by sex, may become obsessed with the idea of sex and may become promiscuous. The client may also become a prostitute and develop a dependency on sex as a means of fulfilling his psychological needs either in childhood or in adulthood. The client may, furthermore, suffer from dysfunctional sexual problems, be totally averse to any form of sexual encounter and may masturbate excessively.

The child will, undoubtedly, be confused by the adult perpetrator's actions because sexual relations will have been a new experience for which he was not yet developmentally prepared. The client, therefore, could develop misconceptions about sexual behaviour and sexual morality. This would account for the reasons why the child-victim could grow up to be an abuser himself, could have loose morals and, in some way, might condone the abuse of others. Often the question of true sexual identity will be raised in the client's mind. The male client, for example, may wonder whether he is a homosexual and the female client may question her ability to be sexually desirable. The main psychological impact of traumatic sexualisation, in this case, will be that the client may question his sexual identity, may become confused about sexual norms and may be utterly baffled about the role of sex in caring relationships. If certain parts of the client's body are given undue importance or a distorted meaning during abusive activity, the client may acquire a similar fetish and grow up with a distorted sense of self in terms of his genitalia. In reviewing the client's case, it may be necessary for the practitioner to evaluate the ways in which the client was sexually traumatised and the degree of traumatisation that he has endured. The therapist might also wish to assess the length of time during which the molestation continued and to what extent the client was a supposedly-willing participant over this period.

> Studies of sexually promiscuous teenagers, prostitutes (male and female, teenager and adult), and sexually compulsive adults have turned up large numbers of individuals who report childhood incest. Many survivors describe themselves as not liking to be touched while, at the same time, engaging in compulsive sexual activity. This appears contradictory only to someone who is unaware of the way that sexual abuse leads to the sexualisation of any expression of caring.
> *– Mike Lew*

The client narrative below illustrates the way in which sexual abuse in childhood subsequently prevented the client from ever having children of her own and this caused her considerable remorse.

Client narrative – I simply couldn't have children …
Here was another avoidance syndrome. In my early teens I announced to one and all that I was a liberated woman and so did not intend to have children. Perhaps I was quietly punishing my mother by not delivering her the expected grandchild. Perhaps I felt myself to be too emotionally unstable to be able to cope with children. A more likely reason was that my mind was telling me that the world was not fit to receive children. I could not bring children into the world if there was the slightest risk of their receiving what I had endured as a child.

Although I do not beat my bosom over the fact that I was deprived of my natural instinct to give birth to a child, I do sincerely regret that I do not have any children of my own. This fact alone has been a source of much grief.

Betrayal

> Betrayal refers to the dynamic in which children discover that someone on whom they are vitally dependent has caused them harm.
> *– David Finkelhor & Angela Browne*

Betrayal will be experienced when the child inevitably discovers that a trusted person has utterly let him down. The child will wholeheartedly rely on the adult to love and to protect him from harm in childhood and, therefore, he will, of necessity, place his absolute trust in the adult perpetrator of any form of crime against him. Even if the client was, by any chance, tended and nurtured during or following an abusive incident, he will still suffer from a sense of keen betrayal. When abuse occurs, of course, the client's feelings will have been ill-considered and, therefore, the feeling of betrayal will manifest. If the client, moreover, was not given an opportunity to tell of his plight, disbelieved or blamed, the betrayal factor will have been amplified and may emanate from many quarters. The issue of betrayal will have severe psychological repercussions in cases of intrafamilial abuse because of the depth of the client's dependency on the abusive carer for his survival needs. The incestuously-abused client, therefore, will need to confront intense issues of deception during therapeutic intervention. The victim of extrafamilial abuse may also have difficulty trusting even relative strangers. The client, in this case, may feel keenly that other family-members have failed in their duty of care and protection. This disappointment may then manifest because the client may blame his immediate family for allowing the abuse to occur in the first place, for not preventing its recurrence or for taking a laissez-faire attitude if any abusive incidents were disclosed by him.

The main psychological impact of betrayal will be that the client may feel grief, remorse and despair, may develop an overdependence on others, may experience relationship problems and may develop parenting problems. The client may also be unable or unwilling to trust others generally, be obsessively suspicious of others and may harbour feelings of vulnerability (see Chapter 7 – "Fear and Anxiety Disorders"). The client, moreover, may well suffer from depressive disorders and may have a need for revenge against his violators (see Chapter 9 – "Sorrow and Grief Disorders"). The effects that may develop as a result of betrayal may also be that the client will often enter into a series of destructive co-dependency relationships and will be vulnerable to further abuse, victimisation and exploitation (see Chapter 12 – "Dysfunctional Relationships"). Similarly, the sufferer may allow his own children to be abused and become antisocial, delinquent, violent or overaggressive (see Chapter 10 – "Anger and Rage

Disorders"). In reviewing the client's case, it may be necessary for the practitioner to evaluate the ways in which the child was betrayed, by whom he was let down and to what extent he was dependent on the child-molester.

> It is accurate when clients feel the abuser or colluding parent has betrayed the role of protector, nurturer or rescuer, but clients will usually feel very guilty for feeling betrayed.
> – *Penny Parks*

Let us now consider a client narrative in which the abused child was betrayed by her paternal grandmother.

Client narrative – my horrid grandmother …
My paternal grandmother was a woman of Victorian principles, a martinet of a women who ruled her household with a rod of iron. She tyrannised my grandfather as well as her son, on whom she doted. She desperately wanted my father to have been a girl, even to the point of dressing him up as a girl when he was a baby. My grandmother actively encouraged my father not to think for himself and discouraged any degree of independence or maturity to adulthood that he might assume. My father, therefore, was a Mummy's boy and he had no control over his life.

My grandmother, in fact, knew that my father was having sex with me when I was a child and young teenager. Indeed, on at least one occasion, she caught my father in the act. Before I realised that my grandmother knew of the abuse, I had contemplated going to her for help. However, her Victorian values prevented my raising such a delicate subject. I made some half-hearted attempts to tell her but quickly realised that the door was not open and not even ajar. For a long time she elected to turn a blind eye. It was easier that way. Furthermore, I believe, both she and my father would have justified themselves with the belief that I didn't much mind anyway.

On one occasion when I thought she was having difficulty seeing the truth, I was determined that she should face the consequences of my abuse and ran to her soiled with the evidence, in shock and uncontrollably in tears. She comforted me, cleaned me up and made me an apple sandwich. She gave a reprimand to my father who replied, "I didn't mean to do it; I don't know what came over me." Actually he was right, in a way. After the clean-up operation, my grandmother's reaction was merely, "Well, you're all right now, aren't you?" The classic rhetorical question to which I realised it was futile to even attempt a reply. The clean-up procedure, I realised, extended to a cover-up operation also.

So did this incident end my torture? Not on your life! My grandmother had given my father a stiff talking to but there was no question of ringing the police or telling my mother. This, of course, was his licence to continue. He only learned to be slightly more discreet about his activities in the future. Of course, he would know unconsciously that his doting mother would do no more than reprimand him. So, in essence, I was abused by my grandmother as well. And so the pattern continued: abuse, reprimand, clean-up and cover-up routine. This pattern was, in a strange way, the way that each inflicted punishment on the other. My father got a buzz out of shocking his puritanical mother and my grandmother had the satisfaction of being able to voice righteous indignation at her son's conduct. I was, in fact, the weapon by which both abuser and accomplice hit out at each other and gained a payoff.

My mother used to go shopping on Saturday mornings. I was left with my father and grandparents. My father, of course, had unlimited access to me at this time. On one occasion when I was abused on a Saturday morning and the household learned of my demise, I was told by my grandmother that "You should have gone shopping with your mother." I see! So I was to blame for my own abuse because I had made myself available to my father. This degree of logic from my grandmother was the law by which I had to develop my understanding of the world.

Powerlessness

> Powerlessness – or what might also be called "disempowerment," the dynamic of rendering the victim powerless – refers to the process in which the child's will, desires, and sense of efficacy are continually contravened.
> – *David Finkelhor & Angela Browne*

Powerlessness will be manifested when the adult takes control of circumstances and elects to violate the helpless child. The child may be overpowered by force, trickery or coercion when his body-space has been invaded against his will and the perpetrator has imposed his wishes on him. The client, thus, will have had his freedom restricted and will then be, to a greater or lesser extent, at the mercy of the abusive violator. When the client has been sexually abused by force, this will, of course, carry with it a greater degree of powerlessness, helplessness and despair. Powerlessness may also be felt if the client has been unable to curtail the abuse. The client, for example, may also have felt inescapably trapped by circumstances and by persons who may have become colluders and conspirators. This can occur if the client had disclosed the abusive incident and was then not believed or if those adults to whom he imparted the news failed to prevent further occurrences of the abusive attack. For the child, who keenly felt a sense of powerlessness, the client may then make repeated attempts to regain power and to overcompensate for loss of power. The client may, for instance, develop control-freak tendencies, may become power-hungry or may become inordinately self-sufficient.

> What distinguishes abuse is a power imbalance. Such an imbalance may exist even between two children of the same age if one (usually male) is physically larger or has more status or more power in the eyes of the victim and/or her family or society.
> – *Sue Blume*

The main psychological impact of powerlessness may be that the client will feel intense fear and anxiety, may become helpless, may feel ineffectual, may lack personal autonomy and may then regard himself as a perpetual victim. The client may also develop a keen desire to control events or to dominate others, and may even sympathise with the abusive perpetrator. The client may, for instance, experience uncontrollable anxiety, become an excessive worrier, develop dramatic phobias and may suffer from depressive conditions. The client may also desire to be a nonconformist, may become overly aggressive and, indeed, may himself become an abuser or submit to further sexual violence. In reviewing the client's case, it may be necessary for the practitioner to evaluate the ways in which the child was rendered powerless, whether coercion and/or force were employed, the duration of the abusive period and the ways in which the abusive relationship may have been terminated.

> As a child, the incest survivor realised that he had little or no control
> over whether or not the abuse would take place. Smaller, weaker, and
> less experienced than the adult perpetrator, he was forced to submit to
> his or her greater power. At best he learned to manipulate the situation to
> shorten the duration or lessen the intensity of the abuse.
> – Mike Lew

In the following case-study example, the client suffered from travel sickness that had its roots in a traumatic incident from her past.

Case-study example – travel-sickness and snake-phobia

This client came into therapy because she had a problem with car-sickness and an obsessive fear of snakes. The client had sought therapy because she was not capable of travelling by any means of transport whatsoever due to her intense anxiety. The client also reported that throughout her life she had suffered from depression and thoughts of suicide.

A preliminary case-history investigation had been conducted by the therapist over two sessions because of the amount of detail that the client had to disclose about her life and her illnesses. The client, for example, had a number of gynaecological problems including a displaced uterus, had undergone five abortions, owing to her condition, and had experienced seven miscarriages.

During analytical investigation, progress was quite slow because the client had very little conscious memory of her childhood days. Most of the preliminary investigative sessions with this client, therefore, tended to focus on her emotional experiences when travelling. The client did, however, recall being physically and psychologically abused by a man when she was eighteen years old. On several occasions, the client spoke of a scene in which she was travelling in a car with her husband and her in-laws along a dual carriageway. The client's father-in-law had been driving erratically on a particularly hot day. The client had felt nausea and had eventually fainted on this journey. The client believed that the hot weather and the fact that she was menstruating were the cause of her condition. The practitioner employed desensitisation methodology in order to assist the client with her dread of travel with particular reference to this journey.

When this journey was examined in detail, however, the client came to realise the significance of the image, to which she frequently felt compelled to return. The client's attention had been arrested by the fact that she had seen a child sitting on a man's lap on a swing. The client eventually revealed that, while she was visiting her aunt's house, her uncle had enticed her to sit on his lap when he was sitting on a swing. The child's uncle placed the client on his lap so that she was facing him with her legs spread across his hips. The client's uncle then began to touch her vagina and to masturbate himself. Later that afternoon, when playing in the local forest with her two cousins (a boy aged fourteen and a girl of nine), the client had witnessed her uncle meeting a blonde-haired woman. An argument ensued and the woman struck the client's uncle. The client's uncle then retaliated by grabbing the woman's neck, forcing her to the ground and strangling her. The boy-cousin had instructed both his sister and the client not to speak of this incident.

On the client's return that evening, while sharing a room with her cousins, she had been told by her boy-cousin not to make any sound and to pretend to be asleep if anybody walked into the room. The client's uncle later walked into the bedroom, lifted her out of bed and took her to the attic. The client's uncle then tied a ribbon across her mouth and he sexually abused her in various ways, including penetration. Having ejaculated, her uncle lay down beside the client and fell asleep. Throughout the incident, the client had been fixated on an old cabinet that had a Chinese dragon carved on the front. Later, while the client was lying steeped in blood beside her uncle, her boy-cousin had walked into the room, quietly lifted her up, carried her into the bathroom and washed her. The client's cousin then put her back into her bed, but she did not speak for the next three days. The client's abusive uncle had died some two years after the incident, as he had worked in the army clearing mines left over from the war. During investigative therapy, the client was, at all times, completely associated in the incidents even though when, out of trance, she had no recollection of the session-contents for about three days, whereupon she would write to let the therapist know what had come into her mind about the session.

The client, in later years, had married a man who had a full-length snake tattooed on his back. This man had been particularly violent to the point where, on one occasion, he had broken the client's arm. On another occasion, the client's husband had broken a rib and, on another, he had attempted to strangle her. The client's husband had been aware of her fear of snakes and had once placed a live grass-snake in her bed while she was asleep. The client's husband had, however, been institutionalised and she had not seen or spoken to him for many years. The client also disclosed that, between the ages of approximately 22 and 28, she had bleached her hair blonde and had taken up prostitution. The client had, however, remarried and her present husband was a man whose life mission seems to have been to protect her.

The client was due for a hospital appointment because she had been advised to have a hysterectomy because her womb had been displaced. The displacement of the client's womb was probably brought about by the violence of the original abusive incident in childhood.

Stigmatisation

> Stigmatisation, the final dynamic, refers to the negative connotations –
> for example, badness, shame and guilt – that are communicated to the
> child about the experiences and that then become incorporated into the
> child's self-image.
> – *David Finkelhor & Angela Browne*

Stigmatisation can develop in the client when he realises that the sexual activity in which he had been asked to participate was furtive or underhand. The client may, for instance, develop a feeling of being unclean or contaminated by his interaction with the molester. The abuser may also blame the client for the abusive occurrence by suggesting that he acted in a provocative manner. The client may, thus, feel denigrated by what he has perceived to be his own shameful actions and behaviour. The abused child will then inevitably develop a poor opinion of himself, owing to feelings of guilt and shame (see Chapter 8 – "Guilt and Shame Disorders"). Perhaps the client had been treated in such a way as to confirm his own feelings about himself. If the abuse had been discovered or disclosed, the client may have been negatively labelled for his part in the activities. The client may, for example, have been ostracised by family-members or may have had a sense of shame instilled by the parent who instructed him not to tell any-one else. Shame may also be borne in adolescence when the client discovers the nature of prevailing social opinions and cultural mores with regard to adult sexual relationships. This premise will also obtain when two children elect to undertake some sexual experimentation at an early age.

The main psychological impact of stigmatisation will be that the client will feel intense guilt, shame and self-blame that may engen-der a low self-esteem and may generate a feeling of being some-how different from others. The client may, consequently, feel isolated or ostracised by society and may tend to withdraw from human interaction. The client may also exhibit a dependency on drugs or alcohol, may turn to crime and may indulge in self-pun-ishment or self-mutilation. In reviewing the client's case, it may be necessary for the practitioner to evaluate the ways in which the client was stigmatised, the age of the child at the time of the molestation, who might have known of the abuse and whether he was in any way blamed for its occurrence.

> It is impossible to understand the effects of incest without considering shame. Adult survivors of sexual abuse live their lives in the face of massive shame. As was previously stated, "men are not supposed to be victims" in our culture. If they have been victimised (even if it happened to them as infants), they conclude that they are failures as men. Survivors face shame that they "allowed themselves" to be demeaned, demasculinized, and weakened.
> – *Mike Lew*

The case-study example below shows the effect of the client's rev-elation of a sexually-abusive incident and how often such violation can be met with indifference by a parent.

Case-study example – revealing abuse
This female client had suffered from the aftereffects of incestuous abuse when her father molested her as a young child.

It subsequently transpired that the client's father had also abused her sister. Both children had suffered from intense psychological distress and disruptive behaviour patterns. The two children had then been sent to a psychiatrist, who had uncovered the abuse. In this case, the client's mother had detected her children's distraught state of mind and had taken the appropriate action. But the story did not end there. No action had been taken against the client's father. The client's father had been given drugs to suppress his sexual desires and was ridiculed by a number of members of the family. The client's father, however, was not reported to the authorities, he was not sent to prison, and he had not even been banned from the house. The client's mother had, moreover, remained married to the abuser of her own children.

The client's mother had felt that her action was perfectly justifiable because informing the police would have meant that her daughters would have had to live with the stigma of having the outside world know that they had been incestuously violated. The client's mother was at pains to explain that, because they lived in a small, narrow-minded community, the stigma would have meant that her daughters would not have made "good marriages". The client simply felt that this was taking the what-will-the-neighbours-think syndrome a bit too far! The client realised that her mother was, in fact, playing the same don't-tell game as her father, and this was the main issue that she elected to address in therapy.

The Aftermath of Childhood Abuse

Mental-health professionals and the public are aware that sexual abuse causes lifelong damage. The after-effects are varied and pervasive. A deep sense of sexual shame, depression, anxiety, worthlessness, guilt and difficulties with careers and relationships are some of the well-documented consequences of childhood sexual abuse.
– *Renee Fredrickson*

The child of an abusive background and a dysfunctional family will have a weighty burden to carry. The psychological effects of childhood abuse in any form will render untold damage, will manifest insidiously and may often result in the suppression or the repression of the client's emotive expression. The abused child may also suffer from a variety of unfounded and irrational beliefs that will unconsciously motivate him, will dictate the course of his life and will control his behavioural patterns.

Future life is sacrificed to secure a forced respect for people who, having grossly misused their power when their children were small and trusting, do not deserve this respect.
– *Alice Miller*

The effect of burying the truth

It seems reasonably clear, however, that one of the crucial factors associated with the rise of the recovered memory movement is the extensive denial of the reality of child sexual abuse which has reigned both among lawyers and among mental health professionals throughout most of the twentieth century.
– *Richard Webster*

A history of childhood abuse may mean that the client will suffer from a range of psychological disorders that will stem from unexpressed, suppressed or repressed emotive expression that may be linked to the original traumatic incidents. Psychological torment, physical misuse and sexual violation will generally stir up within the client a whole plethora of symptoms, conditions and aftereffects. Poor or inadequate parenting may render the client in an almost permanent state of trepidation and wariness. When is the cat next going to spring? This feeling will be carried into adulthood and projected on to all the client's new acquaintances and fresh experiences. Fear and an inability to trust others may also be in evidence in the lives of victims of any form of childhood abuse. Concealed fear will uncover itself in the form of irrational fears, phobias, panic attacks, nightmares and sleep disturbances (see Chapter 7 – "Fear and Anxiety Disorders"). Depressive states may, similarly, be warning-signals that there may be some underlying fear, anger and guilt below the surface of the client's mind that may stem from his dysfunctional upbringing (see Chapter 9 – "Sorrow and Grief Disorders"). The client who has undergone physical abuse as a child may, for example, harbour fears of being alone, pursued, threatened or trapped. Sometimes the client will have an aversion to noise and become hypervigilant as a direct result of traumatic ill-treatment. Guilt-complexes and self-blame will be common disorders because the client may have an underlying belief that the abuse was somehow his own fault or that his behaviour, in some way, caused the mistreatment (see Chapter 8 – "Guilt and Shame Disorders"). The fault, however, will never lie with the victim. There can be no exceptions to this rule. The client's guilt may also engender his need to remain invisible or to seek security. The client may, for example, harbour a fear of being watched. The client may, similarly, have a need to be a perfectionist or a workaholic for similar reasons. The client may, moreover, appear secretive and have an unconscious fear of carrying a precious secret. Self-abuse may be common among the casualty of childhood misuse. This may take the form of the client's overindulgence in drink, drugs, cigarettes and food. The client's self-mutilation, self-disfigurement and suicidal tendencies can also be a major legacy left over from an abusive or a dysfunctional childhood. The ultimate destruction of the self in the form of suicide can often result if the sufferer's demons are not exorcised before it is too late.

> A growing number of prospective and retrospective studies have found that somewhere between 20 per cent and 60 per cent of clients in therapy for the effects of child sexual abuse report having periods in their lives (often lasting for several years) when they could not remember that the abuse had taken place.
> – *Chris Brewin & Bernice Andrews*

In the following case-study example, the client reported surfacing memories that related to the fact that he had been sexually abused by a close neighbour.

Case-study example – sexual frigidity

This young male client had been experiencing surfacing memories that he found confusing and that led him to wonder whether he had been sexually abused in childhood. The client also reported suffering from depression, anxiety attacks, overconcern about what others think, sexual frigidity and feelings of being ugly and dirty.

The client reported generally having difficulty with sexual intimacy. In a previous relationship, he had experienced difficulties with sex and this had led his partner to be unfaithful to him with a close friend. The client had suffered greatly, at this time, from the psychological upheaval of this infidelity and believed that other distressing symptoms had developed as a result of this stress. The client had felt both jealous and betrayed over the demise of this relationship. The client felt, in general, that relationships with women would become difficult the more emotionally involved he became with a partner. The client would then usually become frightened of having sexual intercourse and sought to remove himself both physically and psychologically from any type of sexual experience if one could not be avoided.

The client believed that his mother must have known about the fact that this so-called friend of the family had sexually abused him, although he had never spoken openly to her about this fact. The client had, however, confided in his aunt, who had given him a sympathetic ear. The client believed that the abusive neighbour may have had some form of intimate relationship with his mother because the abuser had, in fact, treated him as special at a time when both his natural parents had been ignoring him. Later on, of course, the client began to hate his abuser for taking this stance and considered that he had made him feel personally responsible for the abuse.

The client also spoke of being numbed by his experiences with his violator. The client was unable to provide any fine detail about the abusive incidents because he, at quite a young age, had not really been sure what had been going on. Confusion soon developed in the client's mind as he realised that he had become numbed and deadened by the assault. From this image, the client concluded that he had taken the blame for the attack. The client felt that his feelings of deadness had been a way of protecting himself from feeling guilty and he could recognise that he had previously had a reluctance to part with this numbed feeling because of the gap it might leave behind.

The client will, undoubtedly, feel that he has been tricked into participating in sexual acts either because he was taken by force or because he was coerced. A number of questions may, of course, arise for the client in connection with the betrayal factor. Perhaps the abuser lied to the client or to his parents. Perhaps the abuser failed in his or her duty of care or misused his or her position of trust with the client. Perhaps the abuser misrepresented the truth about sexual mores. Perhaps the abuser heartlessly disregarded the client's feelings. Perhaps the colluders did not believe the client or did not do all that could have been done to prevent further incidents. From the client's point of view, there will almost certainly be issues of bitterness and resentment about the actions of others that will need to be addressed in the therapeutic context.

445

In the following case-study example, the client was prone to excessive worrying because she could not divorce herself from her parent's clutches and could not keep any boyfriends.

Case-study example – parental dependency
This client was a female in her late twenties who was still living with her parents. The client's presenting symptom was an inability to maintain an intimate relationship because she was unable to have sex. The client also mentioned that her brother had recently declared that he was a homosexual.

This client had totally forgotten a period in her life at the age of eight or nine that was uncovered during analytical investigation. While the client was being taken care of by a male servant of the household, he would enter her bedroom at night and sexually assault her. Although there had been no penetrative sex involved, the molester would touch the client and manipulate her body in order to suit his sexual needs.

During therapeutic intervention, the client also recalled not having told her mother because she felt that she would never believe her. The client soon realised, however, that she could not move away from the parental fold because of the guilty secret she harboured in her breast. The client also unconsciously felt that this deadly secret might be exposed if she were to have a sexual relationship with a member of the opposite sex. Armed with this knowledge, however, the client was able to move on and to appreciate the role her parents had taken in her distress.

The client who has been a victim of abuse will, undoubtedly, wear a secure social mask in order to conceal his suffering (see Chapter 2, Volume 1 – "Analytical Psychology"). Sometimes, however, the client may be able to keep the persona securely in place for some while until his unconscious mind gives up the ghost. The outside world, often, may be totally unaware of the client's suffering. The client with a poor survival-mechanism may appear fragile, vulnerable and often out of control. The effects, however, are the same, whether the client has been a survivor or a nonsurvivor in the social world. Often the victim of childhood abuse will have only a vague notion, if any, of what once occurred. Not only will the client exhibit a poor memory-capability but also may have difficulty in concentrating on anything because his mind has already been overloaded with psychic trauma. Perhaps the client will report having failed examinations or not having taken up further education because his mind has been clouded with distress.

> Most adult survivors kept the abuse a secret in childhood. Telling another human being about what happened to you is a powerful healing force that can dispel the shame of being a victim.
> *– Ellen Bass & Laura Davis*

The survivor of childhood sexual abuse may, in general, have a poor body-image or may have been neglectful of his personal hygiene. Frequently, the female client may suffer from gynaecological disorders or a fear childbirth. The client may also have weak personal boundaries when entering into relationships with others and may have a tendency towards victimisation and a loss of personal power. The client, moreover, may be terrified by the prospect of any form of rejection or abandonment. Sometimes the client will have a perception of being insane, different or unreal and may have the desire to change his name or identity. A victim of oral sexual abuse may have trouble swallowing or may have a gagging sensitivity. Similarly, the client may also suffer from gastrointestinal disorders – particularly when he has suffered any form of oral or anal abuse. Infections and other disorders, of course, that relate to genitalia have been known to be commonplace among the victim of childhood sexual molestation.

> As children being abused, and later as adults struggling to survive, most survivors haven't yet felt their losses. Grieving is a way to honour your pain, let go, and move into the present.
> *– Ellen Bass & Laura Davis*

A lack of self-confidence and a low self-image will be another blueprint that can be instilled in the victim of childhood abuse and neglect (see Chapter 12 – "Dysfunctional Relationships"). These disorders will often result from the client's deep-rooted belief that he must have deserved his fate or that violation occurred because he was intrinsically wicked in the first place. A belief about being dirty and contaminated may also be imbued in the mishandled child. The client may, for example, have been made to feel that he had done something wrong or was a typical problem-child whose parents had been highly displeased by his conduct. Frequently, this belief will be encouraged by the offender, whose interest will be in keeping the client silent in order to avoid detection and in order to allow the abuse to continue.

In the following case-study example, the client, who had previously uncovered some unfortunate experiences, was then able to deal tentatively with his abusive childhood because the period of therapeutic assistance had extended over several months.

Case-study example – lack of self-confidence
This male client's presenting problem was a profound lack of confidence and a nonexistent sex-life.

Therapeutic investigation under hypnosis revealed that, when the client was approximately five or six, his father had attempted anal penetration of the boy several times while he was taking an afternoon nap in his parents' bedroom. Having failed, the client's father left the room and the client had resumed his sleep. This incident had been completely repressed by the client, although he had been left with total confusion and with no explanation consciously of his feelings of low self-esteem and an inability to bond emotionally with the opposite sex.

The client had made several other attempts at therapy prior to arriving for analytical hypnotherapy. The client, having uncovered this repression, then spoke openly of the fact that his mother and father had separated and that his father had declared himself to be a homosexual and was in a relationship with another man.

The effect of uncovering the truth

> An essential part of healing from child sexual abuse is telling the truth about your life. The sexual molestation of children, and the shame that results, thrive in an atmosphere of silence. Breaking that silence is a powerful healing tool. Yet it is something many survivors find difficult.
> – *Ellen Bass & Laura Davis*

When the client who has been the subject of childhood abuse comes into therapy, one of the practitioner's main functions will be to allow him to understand the full truth about his past. The child within the client will need to understand that he was in no way to blame for events and that the blame should be squarely laid at the door of the abuser (see Chapter 5 – "Therapeutic Resolution"). The client should be encouraged, therefore, to see it like it is!

Once the truth has been revealed, the client can then apportion blame where it is deserved, can relieve himself of self-guilt, can relinquish feelings of self-doubt or uncertainty and, generally, can gain more inner strength in the process. If the abuse happened many years ago, however, the client may not be able to verify that, in fact, it had occurred. Corroboration may simply not be possible, owing to the passage of time, the abuser's absence or his death and the overall lack of an eyewitness who might conceivably be willing to testify. The client may, of course, often enter a period of disbelief merely because he simply does not wish to face the consequences of the truth and often a guilt-complex will facilitate any adherence to this nonacceptance. Unconsciously, this may also be the same reason why the client may have deferred seeking help previously. The client, in some cases, may have an awareness of having been abused but may want to blame an innocent person as a means of protecting the guilty party who may be a close relative. The power of the client's avoidance and resistance should not ever be under-estimated by the practitioner (see Chapter 12, Volume 1 – "Resistance"). The practitioner, of course, should not in any way encourage the client to believe what he might have recalled. The client must be allowed to come to realisations in his own time and, even if that this would mean that he wishes to reject the validity of some recollections, then this should be his personal prerogative. The client's secrets should break the surface of silence naturally so that he will be able to divulge the truth about his traumatic past and gain therapeutic relief from doing so. It will, of course, be very therapeutic for the client to unburden his soul and he should be given limitless opportunities to do so with full abreactive expression (see Chapter 1 – "The Hypnoanalytic Approach"). The primary reason for inviting the client to divulge all will be to relieve his guilt so that he can have his story sympathetically received in a supportive environment. The importance of this part of the process for the client cannot be overemphasised. The client may, in the past, have had little or no opportunity for such a release of thoughts and emotive expression. The client may, for example, have been prevented from telling his tale, may have feared divulging the truth or may have suffered many years of repression and denial. The relief of being able to outpour the truth will, almost certainly, be of inestimable value to the client. The practitioner, of course, may be the only person to whom the client can divulge his misery. It should be the practitioner's empathetic support and inner strength that will reassure the client that it can be safe to tell all in the therapeutic climate.

> If physicians have been slow to mobilise against sexual abuse, an important reason is that so few victims of sexual abuse show any medically significant physical trauma. Physicians are trained to minister to physical ailments, and conditions that do not pose major medical challenges – like sexual abuse – fall outside their interest. Second the group of physicians who might be most appropriately concerned about sexual abuse – psychiatrists – have been slow to react to the problem.
> *– David Finkelhor*

The whole therapeutic and healthcare profession have, at some time, been upbraided for incompetence with regard to the handling of childhood-abuse cases. There has, moreover, been a lobby of people who feel that the therapeutic community can attach too much importance to the phenomenon of childhood sexual abuse and its aftermath on the client. In upholding this belief, the practitioner would be doing a monstrous disservice to the client by minimising and negating his suffering (see Chapter 11, Volume 1 – "Defensive Strategies").

> Oscillating and dialectical in nature, the traumatic syndromes defy any attempt to impose such single-minded order. In fact, patients and therapists alike frequently become discouraged when issues that have supposedly been put to rest stubbornly reappear. One therapist describes the progression through the stages of recovery as a spiral, in which earlier issues are continually revisited on a higher level of integration. However, in the course of a successful recovery, it should be possible to recognise a gradual shift from unpredictable danger to reliable safety, from dissociated trauma to acknowledged memory, and from stigmatised isolation to restored social connection.
> *– Judith Lewis Herman*

The effects of childhood sexual abuse should be put in context in terms of what the client presents. The client's pain may be unbearable and intolerable to behold because he may well have reached the point of no return. Alternatively, the client may react hardly at all because he may be unaware of the past and unready to face the consequences of disclosure. Between these two extremes, the practitioner can expect anything in terms of the client's effects, symptoms and abreactive expression. The therapist should simply deal with what the client can handle at any given point in time without either overemphasising the magnitude of the problem or, conversely, belittling its impacts. The practitioner should, of course, remember that every client will be continually firing at a moving target when excavating his unconscious mind.

> Directly confronting your abuser and/or your family is not for every
> survivor, but it can be a dramatic, cleansing tool.
> – *Ellen Bass & Laura Davis*

When the client takes a decision to disclose abuse to his family or to confront his abuser, it should, of course, be his decision and his decision alone. When taking such a decision, however, the client should be aware of the consequences. In general terms, the client should understand what his motivations are in coming out of the closet. Will the client be seeking revenge? Will the client be trying to humiliate the abuser? Will the client be seeking the comfort and support that eluded him in the past? Will the client be trying to recapture the lost love of his childhood? Will the client be expecting an apology or a confession from the abuser? Will the client be seeking corroboration or exoneration for his own part in the abusive acts? Will the client be expecting a given reaction of any kind from the perpetrators of past crimes? Will the client be making a stand on behalf of all victims of abuse? Once the client has identified the nature of his motives, he will then be in a position to evaluate whether or not confrontation and disclosure are viable options. The practitioner's role may be to question the client subtly in order to make him aware of such motivations. If the client has unrealistic expectations of the outcome of such endeavours, subtle probing by the therapist may allow him to come to such realisations virtually unaided. If possible, the client should leave some time between a decision to confront the abuser and his own family in order to ensure that the decision will be the correct one for him. At this stage, the client may be progressing so speedily that a few days' reflection could mean that he turns to a completely different frame of mind. A hasty decision on the client's part, therefore, would not be advisable. Acting in the heat of the moment may be unwise for the client unless time has been allotted for reflection and consideration.

> Many survivors have a compelling desire to speak out. Yet whenever you consider breaking the taboo of secrecy, you are apt to feel fear and confusion. You may question your right to tell or criticize your motives. In order to understand the strength of these feelings, you must remember that you are emerging from a context of severe cultural and personal repression. You are challenging the secrecy that is the foundation of abusive family structures. You are taking revolutionary steps toward self-respect and respect for all children. You are exercising your power.
> – *Ellen Bass & Laura Davis*

If a decision to confront the abuser has been made and the possible consequences of the outcome have been deliberated by the client, the tactics and logistics of the way in which this can be achieved will also need to be considered. A face-to-face confrontation may be effective, but will it disempower the client? A letter may seem a cowardly option for the client, but will it have the intended impact on the recipient, who will be able to reflect at length on the contents of the message? A lawsuit may seem dramatic action for the client, but will it be the only possible way of ensuring that the abuser does not continue to violate others? Will a lawsuit and, eventually, imprisonment be considered by the client to be just punishment for the abuser? Will the client's accusations be upheld by the court? Can conclusive evidence be mustered by the client? Will a court hearing mean that the client will need to undergo the humiliating ordeal of having to face his dreaded abuser and to endure embarrassing questioning in court? If the abuser, furthermore, is exonerated, will that result in further distress for the client, who may now fear retaliation from the offender himself? These and many other questions will need to be carefully considered and evaluated at length before any action might be taken by the client.

> There may be a difference in the direction of anger for boys and girls: Dixon, Arnold, and Calestro found that boys abused by their fathers were angry at their fathers but did not experience the same amount of anger toward their mothers as did girls who were abused by their fathers.
> – *Jeffrey Haugaard & Dickon Reppucci*

In the following case-study example, the client was sexually abused but was encouraged to forgive his abuser and thus serious consequences manifested for him. This case-study example illustrates the delicate position in which the client may be placed and ably highlights the imperative need for the practitioner to take an utterly neutral stance.

Case-study example – fear of rejection

This male client was brought up in the Jewish tradition whereby forgiveness was an integral part of his culture. As a child, this client had been regularly sexually abused by his uncle and was suffering psychologically as a result. The client's main presenting symptom was jealousy and insecurity in his relationship with his partner.

The client's uncle eventually ceased to abuse the child and stated that he would seek assistance from his rabbi because of his abusive behaviour. The rabbi's instructions to the abusive uncle were simply to go to the child and to repeat three times in his presence the words, "Will you forgive me?" The client, at the age of approximately ten, was, thus, required to forgive his uncle. The client complied with his uncle's wishes and said that he had forgiven him.

After therapeutic investigation, the client realised that he had no option but to comply with his uncle's wish to be forgiven. The client, however, also made the realisation that, as a child, he wished to avoid rejection and feared losing the affection of his family. This motivation had stayed with the client for most of his life in that he was constantly seeking reassurance from his partner in order to avoid being rejected.

Exploring the Client's Childhood Abuse

Among women, incest is so common as to be epidemic. Incest is easily the greatest single underlying reason why women seek therapy or other treatment. At any given time more than three quarters of my clients are women who were molested in childhood by someone they knew. Yet virtually none of these women has identified child sexual abuse as the reason for her problems.
– *Sue Blume*

In exploring the client's abusive past, the practitioner would be advised to utilise any means of encouraging the client to release his buried memories and openly express his pent-up abreactive expression. Simultaneously, of course, the practitioner should remain supportive and neutral in the therapeutic environment. A good deal of investigative therapy may need to be carried out with the client for this purpose. It will, of course, be unlikely that any quick-fix techniques can be employed with the client who may have suffered in this way. The practitioner, therefore, will need to exercise patience and simply to play the waiting game until the time arrives when the client is truly ready and able to divulge the horrors of his past traumatic experience. Client-led therapeutic intervention in this instance will be imperative because therapeutic intervention that may be essentially technique-based and practitioner-driven may divert the client from his natural course during psychic unfoldment.

The client narrative given below illustrates the way in which an abuse-survivor can be affected in a variety of ways by incestuous childhood abuse. This example serves to illustrate the complex nature of the client's innermost distress.

Client narrative – cycle of incestuous abuse …

One has to pose the question as to whether it is possible for a woman to be married to a man who is abusing their daughter and not know of the state of affairs. And, more importantly, if not, why not?

My parents' sex life was virtually nonexistent. I was conceived on their honeymoon but, for the most part, my father was impotent as far as my mother was concerned. By her own admission, my mother was herself incredulous that any conception was able to take place because of my father's impotence. She told me that he expressed a desire for anal intercourse with her in order to resolve the problem. This news, in itself, blew my mind. My mother, however, did not wish to participate in this particular form of sexual expression and so their sexual life diminished. My mother's inability to attract my father as a lover was, of course, a blow of her self-confidence and, when she did manage to attract him, he made unpleasant demands on her. At this point, I suspect that my father, humiliated and degraded, turned his sexual perversions and desires towards me. I was, therefore, caught in the trap of servicing my father's needs in order to assist both parents. I was able to help "poor Daddy", who could not maintain normal sexual relations with his wife, and also to relieve my mother of her ordeals. How convenient that I was available to supply that need and relieve the pressure on both my parents!

My legacy was that I thought I was helping out and making things better in the household. The classic keeping-the-family-together role of the abused child, I suspect. When I realised that the formula was not working, I felt bad. There must have been something I was doing wrong. When my parents separated, my anguish was over-whelming. I had utterly failed in my duty as a child. I had not kept the family together and, in addition, had actually intervened between my mother and father. The self-blame and guilt were mortifying.

Even if I accept that my mother did not consciously have knowl-edge of any of the abusive incidents that continued for a period of over twelve years (and she vociferously maintains that she did not), this still leaves a number of questions unanswered to this day. Did she know unconsciously? Should she have discovered the truth? Should she have noticed that I was a highly distraught child? Should she have made it her business to investigate my state of mind? Should she have been the type of person to whom I could have spoken? How did she assume that my father was obtaining any sexual gratification? In essence, I feel that, even if she didn't know, she should have fucking well discovered the truth for her-self! In searching my soul, I regret to say that I cannot, in any way, absolve my mother of, at least, some of the blame in this matter.

My mother was illegitimate and, as an infant, was given over to foster parents, who were responsible for her upbringing. The iden-tity of my maternal grandfather is unknown. My mother was aban-doned to foster parents shortly after her birth. My mother's problem was, almost certainly, that of rejection by her own mother. She has admitted as much to me many times. She desperately wanted affection from her mother but this was in no way ever forthcoming. Her foster father was noted for his temper tantrums, certainly towards his wife and possibly towards my mother. She may well have been the victim of abuse of some kind herself from her foster father. A physically abusive father may well have also been abusive in others ways – it all amounts to the same thing.

Later on in my life the rejection pattern was repeated. My mother rejected me when I attempted to tell her of my childhood traumas. In childhood, my vain attempts to apprise her of my plight fell on deaf ears and blind eyes. I drew some pictures of naked people but I was simply reprimanded for such obscenity. No enquiries were made as to why I might have done something like that.

My mother never did come to my rescue, not even in later life when I actually told her about my childhood horrors. When she learned from me, as an adult, about my father's abuse, her concern was solely that of clearing her own name and trying to convince me that she was blameless. I remain unconvinced. Her reaction to the news of my childhood dilemma was to say that she had made it a policy not to criticise my father in my presence after they had separated. A wise doctrine but instead I was sent back to him during the school holidays in order to discover for myself what his faults and inadequacies were without the need for words.

It was hell coming to these realisations in therapy and it took some time before I could, in any way, come to terms with my parents' action. I certainly wish to be estranged from my parents now for the rest of my life.

Client Profiling

The analytical-hypnotherapy practitioner may wish to ponder the following points when formulating a profile for the client.

- In what ways has the client been affected by an abusive childhood?
- In what ways has the client been sexually traumatised?
- In what ways has the client suffered in terms of his friendships and relationships with others?
- In what ways has the client's self-confidence or self-esteem been affected by an abusive childhood?
- In what ways does the client view himself in terms of body-image?

- Does the client understand why childhood abuse is intrinsically wrong?
- In what ways might the client have been vulnerable to abuse in childhood?
- What evidence is there that the client has been in any way betrayed by his childhood carers?
- In what ways does the client appear to be helpless or powerless as a result of past abusive experiences?
- In what ways does the client appear to have been stigmatised by an abusive past?
- Can the practitioner trace the ways in which the client's life has been shaped as a result of any past traumatic experience?
- What has been the effect on the client of burying his past experience?
- In what ways can the client cope with the fact that he may be uncovering an abusive experience?
- Can the practitioner take a patient and neutral stance when assisting the client to uncover and to deal with his abusive ordeals?

Appendix

Professional Training and Development Resources

For the therapist who may wish to develop more fully in the practice of analytical hypnotherapy, some additional training and development resources are listed below.

Further Training Resources

The International College of Eclectic Therapies (ICET) runs a number of courses that may be of interest to the analytical hypnotherapist as given below.

Diploma in Clinical and Analytical Hypnotherapy with Psychotherapy
This course will equip the delegate with the skills to set up in practice as a qualified hypnotherapist and psychotherapist who can specialise in permanently resolving psychological trauma and liberating the client from psychic or neurotic disorders.

Certification and Diploma in Stress Management Counselling
This two-part course has been designed to enable the practitioner to become fully conversant with and skilled in dealing with the client suffering from the effects of both chronic and acute stress.

Diploma in Gold® Psychotherapeutic Counselling and Master-Level Gold® Creative Psychotherapy
This series of courses will offer comprehensive training in the restructuring and management of beliefs and will provide the practitioner with a unique philosophy and the necessary skills to bring about rapid change.

Diploma in Post-Traumatic Stress Disorder Therapy
This course will provide a vehicle for the practising therapist to gain an appreciation and an essential understanding of the mechanism of PTSD and its treatment.

Diploma in Victims of Childhood Abuse Therapy
This course will be for the professional therapist who seeks neither to paper over the cracks of childhood abuse nor to teach the client to forgive and forget, but rather to look at the consequences of childhood abuse and to examine really practical ways in which the client can live life after such ordeals.

Supervisory Skills Training
This course – which has been approved by the National Council of Psychotherapy – will examine the key role of the supervisor in assisting the practitioner to become more productive and effective within a supportive, professional and caring framework.

Details of these and other courses may be obtained from:

ICET, 808a High Road, Finchley, London N12 9QU, UK
Tel: 44 (0)20 8446 2210
Fax: 44 (0)20 8343 9474
Email: training@icet.net
Website: www.icet.net

Professional supervision may be sought either from Jacquelyne Morison in the Kent and Sussex area, whose email address is:

jacquelyne.morison@btinternet.com

or from Georges Philips in the London area, whose email address is

gp@georgesphilips.com

A copy of a comprehensive client questionnaire that could be used by the analytical hypnotherapist can also be obtained from ICET, contact details for which are given above.

Further Reading Resources

Other publications by the contributor Georges Philips that deal specifically with aspects of analytical hypnotherapy are given below.

Gold Counselling: A Structured Psychotherapeutic Approach to the Mapping and Re-Aligning of Belief Systems, by Georges Philips and Lyn Buncher, Crown House Publishing Ltd (2000)

Rapid Cognitive Therapy: The Professional Therapist's Guide To Rapid Change Work, by Georges Philips and Terence Watts, Crown House Publishing Ltd (1999)

Bibliography

Adams KM. *Silently Seduced: When Parents Make Their Children Partners: Understanding Covert Incest.* Health Communications Inc, 1991.

Ainscough C, Toon K. *Breaking Free: Help for Survivors of Child Sexual Abuse.* Sheldon Press, 1993.

Amendolia R. *A Narrative Constructivist Perspective of Treatment of Post-Traumatic Stress Disorders with Ericksonian Hypnosis and Eye-Movement Desensitisation and Reprocessing.* American Academy of Experts in Traumatic Stress Inc, 1998.

Andersen SM, Miranda R. Transference: How Past Relationships Emerge in the Present. *The Psychologist*, British Psychological Society, 2000.

Andrews B, Brewin CR. Psychological Defence Mechanisms: The Example of Repression. *The Psychologist*, British Psychological Society, 2000.

Andrews B, Brewin CR. What Did Freud Get Right? *The Psychologist*, British Psychological Society, 2000.

Appignanesi R, Zarate O. *Freud for Beginners.* Pantheon Books, 1979.

Baldwin DV. 'Consequences of Early Traumatic Experiences.' Article on Trauma Information website: www.trauma-pages.com, 1997.

Ball J. *Understanding Disease: A Health Practitioner's Handbook.* CW Daniel Company Ltd, 1990.

Barnett E. *Analytical Hypnotherapy: Principles and Practice.* Westwood Publishing Co., 1989.

Bass E, Davis L. *The Courage To Heal: A Guide For Women Survivors of Child Sexual Abuse.* Vermillion, 1997.

Ben-Shahar AR. Patterns of Abuse: Application of Integrative-Massage-Therapy (IMT) to Physical, Emotional and Sexual Abuse Victims. *The Journal*, National Council of Psychotherapists & National Council for Hypnotherapy, 2000.

Bifulco A, Brown GW, Adler Z. Early Sexual Abuse and Clinical Depression in Adult Life. *British Journal of Psychiatry*, Royal College of Psychiatrists, 1991.

Blume ES. *Secret Survivors: Uncovering Incest and Its After-Effects in Women.* John Wiley & Sons Inc, 1990.

Bowlby J. *Attachment.* Pimlico, 1997.

Bowlby J. *Attachment and Loss.* Pimlico, 1998.

Bradshaw J. *Healing the Shame That Binds You.* Health Communications, 1991.

Bradshaw J. *Homecoming.* Judy Piatkus (Publishers) Ltd, 1991.

Brandon S, Boakes J, Glaser D, Green D. Recovered Memories of Childhood Sexual Abuse: Implications for Clinical Practice. *British Journal of Psychiatry*, Royal College of Psychiatrists, 1998.

Brandon S, Boakes J, Glaser S, Green R, MacKeith J, Whewell P. Reported Recovered Memories of Child Sexual Abuse. *Psychiatric Bulletin*, Royal College of Psychiatrists, 1997.

Brown D, Pedder J. *Introduction To Psychotherapy: An Outline of Psychodynamic Principles and Practice.* Routledge, 1996.

Bull T. Eating Disorders and Related Problems. *The Journal*, National Council of Psychotherapists & National Council for Hypnotherapy, 1996.

Burgess AW, Holmstrom LL. Rape Trauma Syndrome. *American Journal of Psychiatry*, American Psychiatric Press, 1974.

Burgess AW, Holmstrom LL. Coping Behaviour of the Rape Victim. *American Journal of Psychiatry*, American Psychiatric Press, 1976.

Burgess AW, Holmstrom LL. Adaptive Strategies and Recovery from Rape. *American Journal of Psychiatry*, American Psychiatric Press, 1979.

Byrne J. The Use of EMDR in Therapy. *The Journal*, National Council of Psychotherapists & National Council for Hypnotherapy, 1998.

Byrne J, Pelser SKS, Poggenpoel M, Myburgh CPH. The Underlying Subconscious Dynamics of Two Women Who Were Sexually Abused as Children. *European Journal of Clinical Hypnosis*, British Society of Medical & Clinical Hypnosis, 1998.

Chopra D. *The Seven Spiritual Laws of Success: A Practical Guide to the Fulfilment of Your Dreams*. Amber-Allen Publishing, 1993.

Chu JA. *Rebuilding Shattered Lives: The Responsible Treatment of Complex Post-Traumatic and Dissociative Disorders*. John Wiley & Sons Inc, 1998.

Clarkson P. *Gestalt Counselling in Action*. Sage Publications, 1989.

Coffey R. *Unspeakable Truths and Happy Endings: Human Cruelty and the New Trauma Therapy*. Sidran Press, 1998.

Coles R. *The Erik Erikson Reader*. WW Norton & Co. Inc, 2001.

Conroy DL. *Out of the Nightmare: Recovery From Depression and Suicidal Pain*. New Liberty Press, 1991.

Conte JR, Shore D. *Social Work and Child Sexual Abuse*. Haworth, 1982.

Corey G. *Theory and Practice of Counselling and Psychotherapy*. Brooks/Cole Publishing Company, 1997.

Cottle TJ. *Children's Secrets*. Addison-Wesley Publishing Co. Inc, 1980.

Covitz J. *The Family Curse: Emotional Child Abuse*. Sigo Press, 1986.

Crook G. False Memory Syndrome. *The Journal*, National Council of Psychotherapists & Hypnotherapy Register, 1995.

Davies JM, Frawley MG. *Treating the Adult Survivor of Childhood Sexual Abuse: A Psychoanalytic Perspective*. Basic Books, 1994.

Dryden W(ed.). *Handbook of Individual Therapy*. Sage Publications, 1997.

DSM-IV-R: Diagnostic and Statistical Manual of Mental Disorders. American Psychiatric Press, 1994.

Durbin PG. My Tribute to Viktor Frankl. *The Journal*, National Council of Psychotherapists & National Council for Hypnotherapy, 1999.

Elman D. *Hypnotherapy*. Westwood Publishing Co., 1964.

Erikson EH. *Childhood and Society*. Vintage, 1995.

Espinosa R. Understanding the Mind Body Connection in Chronic Illness. *The Hypnotherapy Journal*, National Council for Hypnotherapy, 2001.

Farmer S. *Adult Children of Abusive Parents: A Healing Program for Those Who Have Been Physically, Sexually or Emotionally Abused.* RGA Publishing Group Inc, 1989.

Finkelhor D. *Sexually Victimised Children.* The Free Press, 1979.

Finkelhor D. *Child Sexual Abuse: New Theory and Research.* The Free Press, 1984.

Finkelhor D. *A Sourcebook on Child Sexual Abuse.* Sage Publications, 1986.

Foa EB, Davidson JRT, Frances A. Treatment of Posttraumatic Stress Disorder. *Journal of Clinical Psychiatry*, Physicians Postgraduate Press Inc, 1999.

Foa EB, Keane TM, Friedman MJ. *Effective Treatments for PTSD: Practice Guidelines from the International Society for Traumatic Stress Studies.* Guilford Press, 2000.

Fonagy P. The Outcome of Psychoanalysis: The Hope of the Future. *The Psychologist*, British Psychological Society, 2000.

Fordham F. *An Introduction to Jung's Psychology.* Penguin Books, 1966.

Foy DW. *Treating PTSD: Cognitive-Behavioural Strategies.* The Guilford Press, 1992.

Fredrickson R. *Repressed Memories.* Simon & Schuster, 1992.

Freud S. *Introductory Lectures on Psychoanalysis.* Penguin Books, 1991.

Freyd JJ. *Betrayal Trauma: The Logic of Forgetting Childhood Abuse.* Harvard University Press, 1997.

Friedman MJ. *Post-Traumatic Stress Disorder: An Overview.* National Center for Post-Traumatic Stress Disorder, 1997.

Friedman MJ. *PTSD Diagnosis and Treatment for Mental Health Clinicians.* National Center for Post-Traumatic Stress Disorder, 1998.

Fromm E. *The Art of Listening.* Constable & Co. Ltd, 1994.

Gawain S. *Creative Visualisation.* Bantam New Age Books, 1982.

Gay P. *The Freud Reader.* WW Norton & Co. Inc, 1995.

Gilvarry CM. Repressed Memories or Unleashed Fantasy. *European Journal of Clinical Hypnosis*, British Society of Medical & Clinical Hypnosis, 1997.

Goodyear-Smith F. *First Do No Harm: The Sexual Abuse Industry*. Benton-Guy Publishing, 1993.

Gorman AG. Unconscious Memory: False or Fact. *European Journal of Clinical Hypnosis*, British Society of Medical & Clinical Hypnosis, 1997.

Graber K. *Ghosts in the Bedroom*. Health Communications Inc, 1991.

Gross R. *Psychology: The Science of Mind and Behaviour*. Hodder & Stoughton, 1996.

Gross R. & McIlveen R. *Psychology: A New Introduction*. Hodder & Stoughton, 1998.

Groth NA, Birnbaum J. *Men Who Rape: The Psychology of the Offender*. Plenum Press, 1990.

Gucciardi I. Hypnotherapy and Post Traumatic Stress Disorder. *Fidelity*, National Council of Psychotherapists, 2000.

Hammond DC. *Handbook of Hypnotic Suggestions and Metaphors*. American Society of Clinical Hypnosis, 1990.

Harner M. *The Way of the Shaman*. HarperCollins Publishers, 1980.

Harris TA. *I'm OK – You're OK*. Pan Books, 1969.

Harvey MR, Herman JL. The Trauma of Sexual Victimisation: Feminist Contributions to Theory, Research and Practice. *PTSD Research Quarterly*, National Center for Post-Traumatic Stress Disorder, 1992.

Haugaard JJ, Reppucci ND. *The Sexual Abuse of Children: A Comprehensive Guide to Current Knowledge and Intervention Strategies*. Jossey-Bass Publishers, 1988.

Hawkings PH, Almeida A, Hemmings M, Ranz R. Sexuality: Narrative and Hypnosis. *European Journal of Clinical Hypnosis*, British Society of Medical & Clinical Hypnosis, 1998.

Hawkins PJ. Hypnosis in Sex Therapy. *European Journal of Clinical Hypnosis*, British Society of Medical & Clinical Hypnosis, 1996.

Hayes N. *Foundations of Psychology: An Introductory Text*. Thomas Nelson & Sons Ltd, 1998.

Henri D. Eating Disorders. *The Journal*, National Council of Psychotherapists & National Council for Hypnotherapy, 1997.

Herman JL. *Trauma and Recovery: From Domestic Violence to Political Terror*. Basic Books, 1997.

Herman JL, Hirschman L. *Father–Daughter Incest*. Harvard University Press, 1981.

Hofmann A, Fischer G, Galley N, Shapiro F. EMDR Memory Reprocessing. *European Journal of Clinical Hypnosis*, British Society of Medical & Clinical Hypnosis, 1998.

Holmes J. *John Bowlby and Attachment Theory*. Routledge, 1993.

Hotchkiss B. *Your Owner's Manual*. International College of Eclectic Therapies, 1997.

Hudson J. The Epigenetic Theory of Erik Erikson. *The Journal*, National Council of Psychotherapists & National Council for Hypnotherapy, 1996.

Hunter CR. *The Art of Hypnotherapy: Diversified Client-Centered Hypnosis*. Kendall/Hunt Publishing Company, 1995.

Hunter M. *Adult Survivors of Sexual Abuse: Treatment Innovations*. Sage Publications Inc, 1995.

Hyde M, McGuinness M. *Jung for Beginners*. Icon Books Ltd, 1992.

Hyer L, McCranie EW, Peralme L. Psychotherapeutic Treatment of Chronic PTSD. *PTSD Research Quarterly*, National Center for Post-Traumatic Stress Disorder, 1993.

ICD-10: International Statistical Classification of Diseases and Related Health Problems. World Health Organisation, 1992.

Jacoby M. *The Analytic Encounter: Transference and Human Relationship*. Inner City Books, 1984.

Jampolsky GG. *Loving is Letting Go of Fear*. Celestial Arts, 1988.

Jeffers S. *Feel the Fear and Do It Anyway: How To Turn Your Fear and Indecision into Confidence and Action*. Arrow Books, 1991.

Jeffers S. *Dare to Connect: How to Create Confidence, Trust and Loving Relationships.* Judy Piatkus (Publishers) Ltd, 1992.

Jenkins DG, Newman D, Sawyer A. Hypnotherapy and Depression. *European Journal of Clinical Hypnosis*, British Society of Medical & Clinical Hypnosis, 1997.

Johannes CK. EMDR: An Overview of Procedure and Research. *The Hypnotherapy Journal*, National Council for Hypnotherapy, 2001.

Jung C. *The Development of Personality*, Princeton University Press, 1981.

Karle H, Boys J. *Hypnotherapy: A Practical Handbook.* Free Association Books, 1987.

Kern M. *Wisdom in the Body: The Craniosacral Approach to Essential Health.* HarperCollins Publishers, 2001.

Kirschenbaum H, Henderson VL. *The Carl Rogers Reader.* Constable & Co. Ltd, 1990.

Lake F. *Clinical Theology.* Longman & Todd, 1986.

Levine PA, Frederick A. *Waking the Tiger: Healing Trauma.* North Atlantic Books, 1997.

Lew M. *Victims No Longer: A Guide for Men Recovering from Sexual Child Abuse.* Cedar, 1990.

Lindenfield F. *Self Esteem.* Thorsons, 1995.

Lindsay DS, Read JD. Memory, Remembering and Misremembering. *PTSD Research Quarterly*, National Center for Post-Traumatic Stress Disorder, 1995.

Living Without Fear: An Integrated Approach to Tackling Violence Against Women. Women's Unit, Cabinet Office, 1999.

Loftus E, Ketcham K. *The Myth of Repressed Memory: False Memory and Allegations of Sexual Abuse.* St Martin's Press, 1994.

Lüscher M. *The Lüscher Color Test.* Washington Square Press, 1971.

Mackinnon C. Working with Adult Survivors of Child Sexual Abuse: Theoretical Approaches, Long Term Effects and the Therapeutic Process.

European Journal of Clinical Hypnosis, British Society of Medical & Clinical Hypnosis, 1995.

Mackinnon C. Legacy of Abuse: Long Term Effects and Symptoms. *European Journal of Clinical Hypnosis*, British Society of Medical & Clinical Hypnosis, 1996.

Mackinnon C. Beyond Sexual Abuse. *European Journal of Clinical Hypnosis*, British Society of Medical & Clinical Hypnosis, 1997.

Mackinnon C. Working with Adult Survivors of Child Sexual Abuse. *European Journal of Clinical Hypnosis*, British Society of Medical & Clinical Hypnosis, 1998.

McNally RJ. Research on Eye Movement Desensitisation and Reprocessing (EMDR) as a Treatment for PTSD. *PTSD Research Quarterly*, National Center for Post-Traumatic Stress Disorder, 1999.

Mahler MS, Pine F, Bergmann A. *The Psychological Birth of the Human Infant: Symbiosis and Individuation*. Basic Books, 2000.

Maslow A. *Toward a Psychology of Being*. John Wiley & Sons Inc, 1968.

Masson J. *The Assault on Truth: Freud and Child Sexual Abuse*. Fontana Press, 1992.

Masson J. *Against Therapy*. HarperCollins, 1993.

Matsakis A. *Post-Traumatic Stress Disorder: A Complete Treatment Guide*. New Harbinger Publications Inc, 1994.

Matsakis A. *I Can't Get Over It: A Handbook For Trauma Survivors*. New Harbinger Publications Inc, 1996.

Matthews A. *Being Happy*. Media Masters Pte Ltd, 1988.

Mearns D, Thorne B. *Person-Centred Counselling in Action*. Sage Publications, 1986.

Mayer A. *Sexual Abuse: Causes, Consequences and Treatment of Incestuous and Pedophilic Acts*. Learning Publications Inc, 1985.

Miller A. *Banished Knowledge: Facing Childhood Injuries*. Virago Press, 1997.

Miller GA. *Psychology: The Science of Mental Life*. Penguin Books, 1991.

Mitchell J. *The Selected Melanie Klein*. Penguin Books, 1991.

Morgan D. Memory. *The Journal*, National Council of Psychotherapists & National Council for Hypnotherapy, 1996.

Morgan D. The Defensive Persona. *The Journal*, National Council of Psychotherapists & National Council for Hypnotherapy, 1996.

Morgan D. *The Principles of Hypnotherapy*. Eildon Press, 1996.

Morison JA. Reported Recovered Memories of Child Sexual Abuse. *The Journal*, National Council of Psychotherapists & National Council for Hypnotherapy, Spring, 1998.

Morison JA. Reported Recovered Memories of Child Sexual Abuse: Implications for Clinical Practice. *The Journal*, National Council of Psychotherapists & National Council for Hypnotherapy, Summer/Autumn, 1998.

Morison JA. PTSD in Victims of Sexual Molestation: Its Incidence, Characteristics and Treatment Strategies. *Empathy*, Hypnotherapy Society, 2000.

Morton J, Andrews B, Bekerian D, Brewin C, Davies G, Mollon P. *Recovered Memories*. British Psychological Society, 1995.

Naish PLN. *What is Hypnosis? Current Theories and Research*. Open University Press, 1986.

Nelson-Jones R. *The Theory and Practice of Counselling*. Cassell, 1995.

Northcott I. Is Humanistic Psychology Too Simplistic to be a True "Third Force"? *Empathy*, Hypnotherapy Society, 2001.

Oates RK. *The Spectrum of Child Abuse: Assessment, Treatment and its After-Effects in Women*. Brunner/Mazel, 1996.

Ochberg FM, Wilson JP, Raphael B. *Posttraumatic Therapy*. International Handbook of Traumatic Stress Syndromes, Plenum Press, 1993.

O'Sullivan M. Post Traumatic Stress. *The Journal*, National Council of Psychotherapists & Hypnotherapy Register, 1995.

O'Sullivan M. Introducing PTSD. *Empathy*, Hypnotherapy Society, 2000.

O'Sullivan M. Categories of PTSD Sufferers. *Fidelity*, National Council of Psychotherapists, 2001.

Parkinson F. *Critical Incident Debriefing: Understanding and Dealing with Trauma*. Souvenir Press, 1997.

Parkinson F. *Post-Trauma Stress*. Sheldon Press, 1998.

Parks P. *Rescuing the Inner Child: Therapy for Adults Sexually Abused as Children*. Souvenir Press, 1990.

Parnell L. *Transforming Trauma: EMDR*. WW Norton & Co. Inc, 1997.

Parnell L. *EMDR in the Treatment of Adults Abused as Children*. WW Norton & Co. Inc, 1999.

Peck MS. *Further Along the Road Less Travelled: The Unending Journey Towards Spiritual Growth*. Simon & Schuster, 1997.

Peck MS. *The Road Less Travelled: The New Psychology of Love, Traditional Values and Spiritual Growth*. Simon & Schuster, 1997.

Peck MS. *The Road Less Travelled and Beyond: Spiritual Growth in an Age of Anxiety*. Simon & Schuster, 1999.

Peiffer V. *Positive Thinking*. Element Books, 1989.

Pendergast M. *Victims of Memory: Incest Accusations and Shattered Lives*. HarperCollins Publishers, 1996.

Philips G, Buncher L. *Gold Counselling: A Structured Psychotherapeutic Approach to the Mapping and Re-Aligning of Belief Systems*. Crown House Publishing Ltd, 2000.

Philips G, Watts T. *Rapid Cognitive Therapy: The Professional Therapist's Guide to Rapid Change Work*. Crown House Publishing Ltd, 1999.

Plowman J. Mind, Body and Regression: Using "Past Life Memories" to Solve Real Life Problems. *European Journal of Clinical Hypnosis*, British Society of Medical & Clinical Hypnosis, 1996.

Power M. Freud and the Unconscious. *The Psychologist*, British Psychological Society, 2000.

Reason J. The Freudian Slip Revised. *The Psychologist*, British Psychological Society, 2000.

Reber AS. *The Penguin Dictionary of Psychology*. Viking, 1985.

Reinhold M. *How to Survive in Spite of Your Parents: Coping with Hurtful Childhood Legacies*. Cedar, 1996.

Rogers M. False Memory Syndrome: Is There Such a Phenomenon? *The Journal*, National Council of Psychotherapists & National Council for Hypnotherapy, 1998.

Rosenhan DL, Seligman ME. *Abnormal Psychology*. WW Norton & Co. Ltd, 1995.

Roth S, Friedman MJ. *Childhood Trauma Remembered: A Report on the Current Scientific Knowledge Base and its Applications*. International Society for Traumatic Stress Studies, 1997.

Rothschild B. *Post-Traumatic Stress Disorder: Identification and Diagnosis*. Soziale Arbeit Schweiz, 1998.

Rothschild B. *The Body Remembers: The Psychophysiology of Trauma and Trauma Treatment*. WW Norton & Co. Inc, 2000.

Rothschild B. A Trauma Case History. *The Fulcrum*, Craniosacral Therapy Association of the United Kingdom, 2001.

Rowe R. *Beyond Fear*. HarperCollins Publishers, 1987.

Sayers J. *Mothers of Psychoanalysis: Helen Deutsch, Karen Horney, Anna Freud, and Melanie Klein*. WW Norton & Co. Inc, 1993.

Sayers J. *Kleinians: Psychoanalysis Inside Out*. Polarity Press, 2000.

Shapiro F, Forrest MS. *EMDR: The Breakthrough Therapy for Overcoming Anxiety, Stress and Trauma*. Basic Books, 1997.

Sills F, Degranges D. *Craniosacral Biodynamics: The Breath of Life, Biodynamics and Fundamental Skills Volume 1*. North Atlantic Books, 2001.

Silva J. *The Silva Mind Control Method*. HarperCollins Publishers, 1993.

Solms M. Freudian Dream Theory Today. *The Psychologist*, British Psychological Society, 2000.

Stettbacher JK. *Making Sense of Suffering: The Healing Confrontation with your Own Past*. Meridian, 1991.

Stewart I, Joines V. *TA Today: A New Introduction to Transactional Analysis.* Lifespace Publishing, 1987.

Stewart J. Notes on the Inferiority Complex, Anxiety/Panic Disorders and Depression. *The Journal*, National Council of Psychotherapists & Hypnotherapy Register, 1995.

Stewart J. ME (Myalgic Encephalomyelitis), PVFS (Post Viral Fatigue Syndrome), CFS (Chronic Fatigue Syndrome), Yuppie Flu, Malingerers Disease & English Sweat. *The Journal*, National Council of Psychotherapists & National Council for Hypnotherapy, 1996.

Stewart J. Memory. *The Journal*, National Council of Psychotherapists & National Council for Hypnotherapy, 1996.

Storr A. *Freud.* Oxford University Press, 1989.

Storr A. *Jung.* Fontana Press, 1995.

Storr A. *The Essential Jung.* Fontana Press, 1998.

Szasz T. *The Ethics of Psychoanalysis Psychotherapy: The Theory and Method of Autonomous Psychotherapy.* Syracuse University Press, 1988.

Van der Kolk BA. *The Body Keeps the Score: Memory and the Evolving Psychobiology of Post Traumatic Stress.* Harvard Medical School, 1994.

Van der Kolk BA, Van der Hart O, Burbridge H. *Approaches to the Treatment of PTSD.* Harvard Medical School, 1995.

Watkins JG. *The Practice of Clinical Hypnotherapy: Volume 1, Hypnotherapeutic Techniques.* Evington Publishing, 1987.

Watkins JG. *The Practice of Clinical Hypnotherapy: Volume 2, Hypnoanalytic Techniques.* Evington Publishing, 1987.

Watkins JG, Watkins HH. *Ego States: Theory and Therapy.* WW Norton & Co. Inc, 1997.

Webster R. *Freud's False Memories: Psychoanalysis and the Recovered Memory Movement.* The Orwell Press, 1996.

Whitfield CL. *Memory and Abuse: Remembering and Healing the Effects of Trauma.* Health Communications Inc, 1995.

Wickes FG. *The Inner World of Childhood: A Study in Analytical Psychology.* Appleton-Century-Crofts Inc, 1927.

Woolger R. Past Life Regression. *The Journal,* National Council of Psychotherapists & National Council for Hypnotherapy, 1996.

Yapko MD. *Suggestions of Abuse: True and False Memories of Childhood Sexual Trauma.* Simon & Schuster, 1994.

Yapko MD. *Essentials of Hypnosis.* Brunner/Mazel Inc, 1995.

Young BH, Ford JD, Ruzek JI, Friedman MJ, Gusman FD. *A Guidebook for Clinicians and Administrators.* The National Center for Post-Traumatic Stress Disorder, 1998.

Index